KT-487-452

China's Imperial Past

China's Imperial Past

An Introduction to Chinese History and Culture

CHARLES O. HUCKER

DUCKWORTH

First published in U.K. in 1975 by
Gerald Duckworth & Company Limited
The Old Piano Factory
43 Gloucester Crescent, London NW1
© 1975 by the Board of Trustees of the
Leland Stanford Junior University

All rights reserved.
No part of this publication may be reproduced,
stored in a retrieval system, or transmitted,
in any form or by any means, electronic,
mechanical, photocopying, recording or otherwise,
without the prior permission of the copyright owner
ISBN 0 7156 0958 0

For
H. G. Creel, E. A. Kracke,
and all my many other teachers
through the years

Nothing benefits learning more than being associated
with the right people. HSÜN-TZU

Preface

THIS BOOK is of course not the only way in which the history of traditional Chinese civilization can be presented. But its approach is
the most satisfactory way I have found, in a quarter century of teaching
and writing, to do justice to the myriad complexities of Chinese history—by giving balanced attention to all the major elements that constituted Chinese civilization in any period, to their interrelationships,
and to their changes over time.

My emphasis is on patterns and themes rather than factual data.
Unfortunately for the nonspecialist reader, however, no treatment of
China can avoid distractingly strange names and terms. I have tried to
keep them to an irreducible minimum. As a further convenience, I have
generally referred to Chinese places only by their modern names, ignoring their historic mutations.

It would be impossible for me to give proper credit to all my professional peers and all my students whose analyses, interpretations, and
insights have shaped and reshaped my understanding of Chinese civilization and who have thus contributed to this book. I hope the ded-
ication page will acknowledge, even if it cannot discharge, my heavy
obligation to all those from whom I have learned, and especially my
obligation to the two distinguished University of Chicago scholars, now
retired, under whose guidance I am proud to have begun my study of
China.

My preparation of this book in particular has been facilitated by the
encouragement and helpfulness of many colleagues at the University
of Michigan, notably Robert H. Brower, Douglas D. Crary, James I.
Crump, Kenneth J. DeWoskin, Richard Edwards, Albert Feuerwerker,
Virginia C. Kane, Shuen-fu Lin, Wei-yi Ma, Rhoads Murphey, Edward

Seidensticker, and Wei-ying Wan; and by the kindness of James Cahill, W. T. Chase, Laurence Sickman, Alexander Soper, and Michael Sullivan among professional colleagues elsewhere. Although none of these is in any way responsible for the substance of the book, I greatly appreciate their courtesies and their ready assumption that the cause was worthwhile.

I am more specifically indebted to the Center for Chinese Studies of the University of Michigan, from which I received partial financial support at a crucial stage of writing; to my colleague Jing-heng S. Ma for the standard modern calligraphy on page 8; to Fischer Peng and Mrs. Nora Ling-yün Shih Liu, both of Ann Arbor, for the examples of "cursive" and "grass" script on pages 240 and 248, respectively; and to J. G. Bell, Barbara E. Mnookin, Albert Burkhardt, and others of the Stanford University Press staff for the interest and care with which they have labored to bring the book to publication.

For tolerating, helping, and caring for me throughout the prolonged writing and production of the book, my wife deserves more gratitude than I can ever express. I hope she can continue to believe that her sacrifices are not in vain.

C.O.H.

Ann Arbor
May 1975

Contents

The Later Empire, 960-1850

Illustrations

Maps

CHINA
in the Nineteenth Century

0   100   200   300   400   500
MILES

SINKIANG

KANSU

TIBET

SZECHWAN

Yangtze R.

INDIA

KWEICHOW

YUNNAN

BURMA

BAY OF
BENGAL

VIETNAM

MONGOLIA

MANCHURIA

KOREA

Yellow R.

WALL

GREAT

Peking

CHIHLI
(HOPEI)

GULF OF CHIHLI

SHANSI

SHANTUNG

Yellow R.

YELLOW SEA

Sian

Loyang   Kaifeng

GRAND

CANAL

SHENSI

HONAN

ANHWEI

KIANGSU

Soochow

HUPEI

Nanking

Shanghai

Yangtze R.

Hangchow

CHEKIANG

*EAST CHINA
SEA*

HUNAN

KIANGSI

FUKIEN

KWANGSI

KWANGTUNG

Canton

TAIWAN
(PART OF FUKIEN)

*SOUTH CHINA
SEA*

HAINAN
(PART OF KWANGTUNG)

China's Imperial Past

Introduction

As PRESENTED in the following chapters, the history of China is divided into three major epochs, during each of which the patterns and problems of Chinese civilization changed significantly. They are (1) a formative age, from high antiquity into the third century B.C.; (2) an early imperial age, from the third century B.C. into the tenth century A.D.; and (3) a later imperial age, from the tenth century to the mid-nineteenth century. For practical purposes, 1850 marks the end of traditional or premodern Chinese civilization; the main currents of China's history since then are discussed very briefly in a final chapter, as an epilogue. Each major epoch of the premodern era is considered analytically in several chapters—on general or political history, modes of governmental and socioeconomic organization, developments in religion and thought, and achievements in letters and arts. Chapters are arranged in sequence so that all aspects of one age are considered before the following age is introduced, but readers can easily go through the chapters in topical sequence if they choose. The general history chapters, together with the epilogue, provide a unified overview of China's political history, which is also outlined in a simple chronological chart in Appendix A (pp. 434-35).

The remaining pages of this introductory section are devoted to some basic considerations that underlie, or weave in and out of, everything that follows. These consist of brief descriptions of the Chinese land, people, language, and writing system, and analytical suggestions about some of the main themes that pervade Chinese life and history.

THE LAND AND THE PEOPLE

The geographic setting. China today stretches some 2,500 miles from the Pamirs in the west to the Pacific Ocean in the east and more than

2,000 miles from the Amur River in the farthest north to the South China Sea and the mainland tier of Southeast Asian countries—Vietnam, Thailand, and Burma—in the south. The territories it incorporates are logically separable into two categories. In one category are large outlying, peripheral territories that traditionally have not been occupied by the Chinese people in substantial numbers: Tibet, Sinkiang (Chinese Turkestan), Inner Mongolia, and the northeastern realm that Westerners call Manchuria. The other category comprises the million and a half square miles commonly called China Proper, a roughly square land mass about half the size of the continental United States. Bounded on the north by the Great Wall, on the west by Inner Asian wastelands and Tibetan highlands, and on the south and east by oceans, this is the historic Chinese homeland.

Two things are especially noteworthy about the geographic situation of China Proper. One is that topography kept China insulated from and generally ignorant about other major centers of civilization until the advent of modern communication and transport techniques. Camel caravans plodded back and forth across the forbidding deserts, steppes, and mountain passes of Central Asia from very ancient times, and seaborne traffic between China and the Indian Ocean originated not later than the time of Christ. But the distances involved are long, and the routes were difficult and dangerous. Geographic isolation must be reckoned a confining factor, and therefore a unifying factor, in Chinese life and history.

It is noteworthy on the other hand that topography fragments China internally. The most prominent divisive element is a mountainous region, with the Tsinling (Ch'in-ling) range at its core, which tapers down across central China from Tibet toward the Pacific coast, separating the Yellow River drainage zone of the north from the Yangtze River drainage zone of the south and the coastal valleys beyond. Both north and south are subdivided into distinctive smaller areas, separated from each other by stretches of low but rugged hills. North China includes a great lowland plain in the east and a highland plateau in the west. South China is fragmented into (1) the Yangtze delta, (2) the central Yangtze basin, (3) the upper Yangtze highland valley of Szechwan province, (4) a cluster of small coastal valleys in the southeastern province of Fukien, (5) the West River drainage zone of the south coast, and (6) the jagged, jungled highlands of the southwest. In this perspective, China's topography lends itself to regional separatism in the fashion of the European nation-states and has been a divisive factor in Chinese life and history.

Some of the differences between north and south derive from differences between China's two great river systems. The Yangtze River, gushing down rapids out of the Szechwan basin onto the sprawling plain of central China, is one of China's great blessings. It is navigable all the way to the Pacific, and its many tributaries give easy access to all surrounding areas, providing a transportation network through which Chinese of the south have traveled and exchanged their goods easily and cheaply. Millions of southern Chinese make their livings on river boats and have no other homes. Water from the Yangtze complex of rivers is always at hand to offset any irregularities of rainfall, and it seldom erupts in damaging floods.

In sharp contrast, the Yellow River in the north has an awesomely malevolent aspect. It brings from Tibet the water on which northern agriculture depends, and it regularly deposits new layers of enriching mud on the North China plain. But these benefits come at a high price. The Yellow River carries a heavier burden of silt than any of the world's other great rivers, and its sedimentation creates shifting sandbars that impede navigation across the plain. It has therefore not been the useful traffic artery that the Yangtze has been for the south. What is worse, the Yellow River has no natural, permanent channel across the plain to the Pacific. It is confined between dikes. Its sedimentation proceeds at such a rate that the river bed rises rapidly, and the dikes must be built higher and higher, until in places the river flows through aqueducts above roof level. When the dikes break, the river inundates thousands of square miles. On receding, it finds a new temporary channel, and the diking begins anew. Cyclically, the Yellow River has even shifted its outlet to the sea from north of the rocky Shantung peninsula to the south and back again; and on the occasions of such major changes of channel its floods have been catastrophic. For such reasons, the Chinese have traditionally referred to the Yellow River as "China's Sorrow."

North-south differentiation also results from, and is accentuated by, the classic monsoon pattern that governs the Chinese climate. In summer currents of warm, moist air move inland from the oceans across China toward low-pressure zones over Inner Asia. They bring saturating rains throughout the south, accumulating to an annual total of about 60 inches along the coasts. But as the air currents move inland

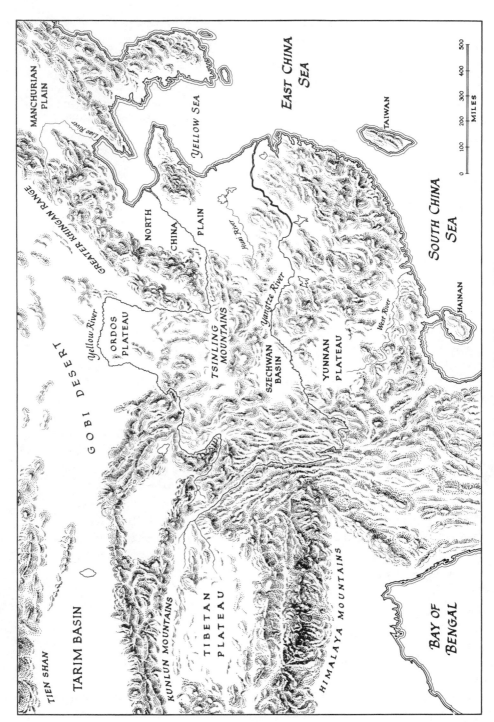

Map 1. Principal geographical features of China

TIEN SHAN

TARIM BASIN

MANCHURIAN PLAIN

GREATER KHINGAN RANGE

Liao River

GOBI DESERT

Yellow River

ORDOS PLATEAU

NORTH

CHINA

PLAIN

Yellow Sea

EAST CHINA SEA

TAIWAN

KUNLUN MOUNTAINS

TIBETAN PLATEAU

TSINLING MOUNTAINS

Huai River

Yangtze River

SZECHWAN BASIN

YUNNAN PLATEAU

West River

SOUTH CHINA SEA

HAINAN

HIMALAYA MOUNTAINS

BAY OF BENGAL

MILES

0 100 200 300 400 500

to the north and northwest, and especially after crossing the Tsinling divide, they have less and less moisture content left, and the land is progressively more arid. In winter a reverse process applies. Cold, dry air currents move outward from Inner Asia across China toward low-pressure zones over the neighboring oceans, bringing little precipitation. Even South China is not entirely shielded from the wintry cold by the Tsinling and other mountains: ice sometimes forms as far south as Canton, in the latitude of Havana. But the south gets some relief from cyclonic storms that bring warmth and rain from over the South China Sea. Thus North China suffers a rigorous climate: relatively dry year-round, alternating between a very cold winter and a very hot summer. The growing season is short, lasting only four to six months. South China, in contrast, enjoys a moderate climate: relatively moist year-round and neither too hot nor too cold. The growing season is long, from six to nine months; most plots regularly produce two crops in succession each year, and some produce three.

In sum, North China is a land of fertile redeposited loess soil, limited and irregular rainfall, dry crops such as wheat and millet, ox-carts and donkeys, extremes of heat and cold, and a brown, barren landscape; whereas South China is a land of rich alluvium, abundant rainfall, paddy rice and myriad fruits, water buffalo, river boats and coolie carriers, moderate variations in temperature, and a green, lush landscape. Nature is harsh in the north and bountiful in the south, and the difference is reflected in the temperaments of the people. It is commonplace for visitors to observe that northerners are stolid and stern and make good soldiers, whereas southerners are volatile and quick-witted and make good businessmen. On a narrower, regional scale, the Chinese stereotype their countrymen just as other peoples do: residents of Shansi province are the canny misers of the Chinese tradition, the Hunanese are flamboyant hotheads, the women of Soochow and Hangchow in the Yangtze delta are China's great beauties, and so on.

Race. Defining race as a matter of physical characteristics alone, and using the simple and common classification of peoples into the three principal stocks called Caucasoid, Negroid, and Mongoloid, the Chinese can consider themselves the only major nation of Asia that is racially homogeneous, for they are uniformly Mongoloid. Moreover, the Chinese throughout most of their traditional history did not even have significant contacts with people who were not Mongoloids like themselves. Until the intrusion of modern Europeans into the East Asian scene beginning in the sixteenth century, all the actors in Chinese history—non-Chinese as well as Chinese—were of one racial stock, so that racial considerations had no place in the Chinese people's conception of themselves as a group different from other groups. Differentiations were made on cultural grounds.

There are nevertheless physical variations among different groups of Chinese, and these fall into the same pattern of north-south differentiations noted in the discussion of topography and climate. Like Mongoloids in general, all Chinese tend to be slighter in bodily structure and shorter in stature than Caucasoids; but the North Chinese are on the whole taller and heavier-framed than the South Chinese. Thus, though all Chinese share the common Mongoloid characteristics of sallow skin, straight black head hair, little body hair, and folded eyelids, the North Chinese are relatively large and sturdy like their northern neighbors in Mongolia and Korea, whereas the South Chinese are characteristically small and wiry like most Southeast Asians and Japanese. Some reasons for these distinctions are to be found in history, as will be noted shortly.

Language and writing. China's racial homogeneity is offset by a marked linguistic diversity. The language spoken by most Chinese is *kuo-yü* (national speech); Westerners commonly call it Mandarin, because it was traditionally the language spoken by officials throughout the country, even if they had to learn it as a second language. Mandarin is the language of all North China and most of the Yangtze region but is not the native speech of Chinese residing in the coastal areas from the Yangtze delta southwestward to Vietnam. It is generally accepted that the coastal speech patterns—Wu, Fukienese, and Cantonese—are not separate languages but are, along with Mandarin, major dialects of one Chinese language, each divisible into sub-dialects. However, the differences in speech—primarily in pronunciation, secondarily in vocabulary, and to a limited extent in grammar and syntax—are so great that the dialects are mutually unintelligible. A speaker of Fukienese cannot converse intelligibly with a Mandarin speaker, or for that matter with a Cantonese speaker or a Wu speaker. Indeed, an inland villager might be unable to make himself understood even in nearby villages.

Linguistic chaos on this scale is of course intolerable in a united modern society. Twentieth-century Chinese governments have prescribed the use of Mandarin in all schools and in mass communication media such as radio and television, and today a large proportion of Chinese from non-Mandarin-speaking areas can consequently communicate in, or at least understand, Mandarin as a second language. (On the pronunciation of Mandarin, see Appendix B, pp. 436-39.)

With some neighboring peoples the Chinese have recognizable linguistic relationships. Chinese, Thai (Siamese), and Vietnamese seem to belong in one language family, which in turn is related to a Tibeto-Burman family; both language families are considered to belong to a language stock called Sino-Tibetan, at a level of relationship comparable to that linking all the Indo-European language families. But there is no discernible linguistic relationship at all between the Chinese and their successive northern neighbors of traditional history, such as the Mongols. The northern peoples belong to a language stock called Altaic, which includes the Turkic, Mongolian, and Tungusic (Manchu) language families and is now thought to encompass even Korean and Japanese. These languages are as unrelated to and different from Chinese as any Indo-European language.

The widespread assumption that Chinese and Japanese are related languages has no linguistic basis. In linguistic analysis, Chinese has four principal characteristics: its words are basically monosyllabic; the words are uninflected, having no variable endings to indicate tense, number, subject or object, and so on; the language abounds in similar-sounding words, or homophones, which are differentiated in part by being pronounced in the varied tones that give Chinese what seems to Westerners a sing-song quality; and the sentences normally follow a word order similar to the English noun-verb-adjective-noun sequence. Japanese differs markedly in all these aspects. What confuses the uninitiated is that Japan early borrowed China's nonalphabetic writing system, as did Korea and Vietnam, all adapting it to their own purposes. Writing systems, however, have no necessary correlation with linguistic relationships. Borrowing Chinese written forms for other languages has no more linguistic significance than the modern use of the so-called Arabic numerals throughout the world.

Westerners have given the term characters to the nonalphabetic symbols or graphs in which the Chinese write. In general, for each word or idea-cluster the Chinese early devised a separate graph. Good Chinese dictionaries list more than 40,000 such graphs, and normal reading competence requires acquaintance with about 5,000. Conventional multi-graph combinations that are in common use add many more

PICTOGRAPHIC FORMS

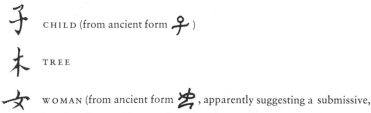

CHILD (from ancient form 孚)

TREE

WOMAN (from ancient form 岜, apparently suggesting a submissive, kneeling figure with arms clasped at the wrists)

IDEOGRAPHIC FORMS

Simple:

一 ONE   二 TWO   三 THREE   上 UP   下 DOWN

Compound:

GOOD (woman and child)   CONTENTMENT (woman under roof)

HOME (pig under roof)   BRIGHTNESS (sun and moon)

A TYPICAL LOGOGRAPHIC FORM

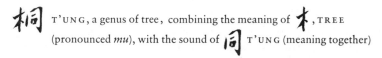

桐 T'UNG, a genus of tree, combining the meaning of 木, TREE (pronounced *mu*), with the sound of 同 T'UNG (meaning together)

The Chinese writing system

thousands of items to the normal reader's vocabulary. Modern Chinese governments have hoped to lessen the difficulties of the writing system, but all they have accomplished to date is the simplification of some of the more complicated graphs. There seems no prospect that Chinese, with its abundance of homophones and its tonal elements among other complexities, can ever be transferred successfully to an alphabetic writing system.

The general nature of Chinese graphs is exemplified in the accompanying chart. There are three basic forms. One is pictographic, a conventionalized picture-symbol of an object such as a tree or a child. The second form is ideographic, an idea-symbol. A few ideographs are simple, directly representational constructions, such as those used for elementary numerals or for "up" and "down." Most are compound constructions, combining two or more pictographic elements in a manner that suggests the idea represented. "Good" combines woman and child; "home" puts a pig under a roof; "contentment" puts a woman under a roof; "brightness" puts sun and moon together. The third form of construction is logographic, representing not ideas but specific words as spoken. The logograph combines a pictographic or ideographic element of relevant meaning with another element whose pronunciation is applicable. In the example illustrated, one element when independently used is pronounced *t'ung*; it does not matter here that its independent meaning is "together." The other element when independently used means "tree"; it does not matter here that its independent sound is *mu*. The logograph signals that it represents a word with a meaning relevant to trees or wood and a sound approximating *t'ung*: specifically, it is the name of the genus of tree called *t'ung*. The great majority of Chinese graphs used throughout history are of this logographic type.

For all its difficulty, the Chinese writing system has been of great service and value to the Chinese. It overcomes all the complexities of homophones, tones, and dialectal variations that characterize spoken Chinese; for the graphs convey the same meanings regardless of how they are pronounced. Thus literate Chinese have been able to communicate in writing even when they could not converse intelligibly, so that the writing system has been the prime culture carrier and a major unifying force in Chinese civilization. Moreover, it has visual aesthetic potentialities that no alphabetic system has, and the Chinese have esteemed great calligraphy as one of their finest arts. Such considerations in some measure offset the practical disadvantages of the system.

Chinese as written can be far more concise than Chinese as spoken. Thus written Chinese at an early time diverged from the patterns of spoken Chinese, if the two ever coincided to begin with; and different styles evolved to suit different genres of writing. Traditional written Chinese, called *wen-yen* (the written word) in contrast to *pai-hua* (plain speech), is governed by rules of grammar unrelated to speech, is very cryptic, and can be elegantly opaque. A major achievement of twentieth-century modernizers has been to popularize the writing of Chinese in pai-hua grammar, which reduces the attainment of literacy for the native speaker to simple memorization of graphs, which is difficult enough. But the bulk of writings produced before about 1920 remain as impenetrable for the modern Chinese as classical Latin is to modern Westerners. Wen-yen has become a specialized field of study, and modern editions of old texts appear with pai-hua annotations and translations. An added difficulty is that, though the Chinese early adopted the convention of putting single dots between graphs to signify pauses or stops, writers used them or not, as they chose, and many a wen-yen text flows along page after page without any form of punctuation. Page format gives no clue that one might be encountering poetry, for poetry was written out in an uninterrupted sequence of graphs, as prose was. Furthermore, with graphs one does not even have the aid of capitalization to signal proper names and the beginnings of sentences. No one need wonder why the Chinese have always esteemed literacy and revered their literary masters.

SOME BASIC CONTINUITIES OF CHINESE LIFE

Fundamental socioeconomic patterns. Families are the core units of traditional Chinese society, and all Chinese have had family names since well before the time of Christ. The family name passed from generation to generation in the male line, as did family property. Property was traditionally divided equally among all male heirs, so that families were regularly fragmented into branches. But the traditional ideal, especially in the later centuries of imperial history, was to keep as many generations together in one household as possible, as an extended family; and the ideal society was envisioned as a vast, interconnected network of extended families in which individuals had secure, well-defined, and gratifying roles and through which their relations with all other members of society were smoothed and buffered. Individual achievements redounded to the advantage of the family as a whole, and individual eccentricities and failures were compensated for by the family as a whole. The individual was never alone in his confrontations with the world at large; he was representative of, responsible to, and supported by his family. The American ideal of rugged individualism was not prized.

The ideal family was a large group held together by the religious sanction of ancestor worship, which made the family an indefinitely perpetuated corporation whose living members were accountable both to forebears and to descendants, and by the socioeconomic sanction deriving from the fact that the family head controlled and was answerable for the activities of all family members. The extended family con-

sisted of a head, his immediate family, and the families of all his male
descendants, ideally with several generations living together in a cooperative household. When the family head died and his property was
divided, his sons became the heads of their own extended families.
Thus the nuclear family—a married couple and their children—were
ideally part of a larger living and working unit, the extended family;
closely related extended families considered themselves a clan or lineage, organized for certain cooperative relationships under a senior
family head serving as clan head; and clans considered themselves related and obligated to all other clans having the same surname, which
were thought to constitute a common descent group. Exogamy was
practiced within the patrilineal lineage: a man might marry a first
cousin on his mother's side, since she bore a different surname, but he
could not marry a woman of the same surname, even if the two families had lived at opposite ends of the country for centuries and had no
traceable blood relationship. Polygamy was acceptable, and though
only one wife was considered the principal or legal wife at any one
time, all offspring born in wedlock were legitimate and were ranked
solely by seniority. Family relationships were projected into more general social relationships by the use of terms like uncle, aunt, and cousin
for neighbors and friends, Father-and-Mother Officials for local magistrates, and the Father and Mother of the People for a ruler.

It is recurringly suggested that in high antiquity Chinese society was
organized on matriarchal lines. Throughout recorded history, however,
women played decidedly subordinate roles in the family and in public;
their status particularly declined in the most recent millennium. Most
families viewed daughters as unwanted burdens. Arranging a reputable
marriage for a daughter required a dowry, and after marriage a daughter contributed only to the welfare of her husband's family. Poor families commonly sold daughters into servitude, prostitution, and concu-
binage, and in particularly hard times female infanticide was widespread. Nevertheless, in spite of their subordinate status and no doubt
because of the humiliations it imposed on them, Chinese women often
developed a strength of character surpassing that of their menfolk.
Both China's own literature and the observations of outsiders testify
that Chinese husbands have been among the world's most henpecked;
and Chinese mothers have notoriously tyrannized over their daughters-
in-law.

The typical family was a farming family living in a village with a dozen or more other, often related families, whose lands were in small, garden-sized parcels scattered in the vicinity of the village. One family's total holdings seldom exceeded three or four acres in recent centuries. On these small plots males of the family tended the crops. Women did some field work but more characteristically spent their time keeping house, tending chickens, and cultivating silkworms or weaving cloth. Hardly an inch of land could be wasted, and no product of the land could be left unused. Even the dead stalks of harvested grain had to be husbanded for fuel to fire the cookstoves and heat the home in winter.

Within sight on the plain or in the valley, normally, were one or two similar villages, and only a few miles away was a market town, with shops and the homes of absentee landlords. Here the farmer sold whatever surplus he might have produced, bought such seeds and tools as he needed, and exchanged greetings and news with his acquaintances. At least during the past millennium the market towns regularly held fairs or festivals, often in a rotational arrangement with nearby towns; and to such fairs traveling merchants brought goods that were not locally produced. At one further remove—perhaps 20 or 30 miles from the most distant farmer in recent centuries—some favorably situated market town had grown into a city. This was the wholesale trading center for the region and also the lowest-level administrative center of anything that might properly be considered formal government.

Unlike the idealized peasant of the Western tradition, the traditional Chinese farmer was not typically self-sufficient and independent. From a remarkably early time, and notably during the past millennium, Chinese agriculture was specialized and commercialized, so that farmers were accustomed to buying and selling in the marketplace. If a farmer, for example, had excellent rice land and lived in a densely populated area where high-quality rice was in great demand and brought a good price, he might devote all his land and all his family's effort to producing rice for sale in the market. For its own consumption, the family might buy poorer quality, cheaper food, perhaps imported from another area entirely. Under other circumstances, even in an area where it was possible to grow two crops of rice a year, a family might grow only one crop and divert most of its efforts to home craft production—of textiles, for instance—if market conditions promised to make such diversification advantageous. In short, the agrarian economy was not a simple, stagnant one; it varied from region to region and from time to time, responding to market and money conditions.

In traditional China throughout history at least 80 per cent of the total population consisted of farming villagers of this sort—living at a bare subsistence level, working hard and imaginatively to sustain that level, exposed to no formal schooling, dependent on the soil and the vagaries of the weather. Of what they thought or felt at any particular point in history very little can now be known. Theirs was a regionally oriented variety of Little Traditions, full of folk superstitions, historical legends handed down by word of mouth, and aspirations dominated by the mere hope of survival. But they were not isolated from the higher culture of the towns.

The remaining 20 per cent or so of the traditional population participated in and partly contributed to the Great Tradition, the homogeneous literate culture. Since the total population was approximately sixty million by the time of Christ and probably reached a hundred million around the year 1100, this group of literate, cultured, town-oriented Chinese was by no means small in absolute numbers. At any time in the last two millennia they outnumbered the total populations of many modern nations of some size and importance. Moreover, society functioned in such a way that town-country dichotomies were minimized. A single conception of good government and a single value system usually pervaded the whole society, from the top to the bottom of the economic scale. Those at the bottom were not cast out, but were embraced into the System. The Great Tradition, consequently, should not be considered a thin veneer under which cowered a mute, downtrodden, resentful mass. The traditional Chinese excelled in many things, but in nothing else so much as in organizing themselves harmoniously.

Frontier relations. The Chinese have not occupied the whole of China Proper from the dawn of history. Rather, they have gradually filled it up by successive expansions out of their earliest known homeland in the North China plain. The China of each successive epoch was therefore a new geographic entity, and Chinese culture as a whole was in some measure transformed accordingly. Assimilation of the Yangtze region was under way well before the time of Christ but was not completed until about the eighth century. The south coastal regions were not thoroughly incorporated until the twelfth century. Assimilation of the southwestern highland of Kweichow and Yunnan provinces was not significantly begun until the fifteenth century and is incomplete even today. Although North China was the dominant economic and cultural zone until the twelfth century, the balance then shifted decisively to the south, and South China has remained economically and culturally preeminent into our own time.

The Chinese did not expand southward into an unoccupied wilderness, nor did they expand American-style by dispossessing unrelated "savages." When a distinctive Chinese civilization first emerged on the North China plain, the southern lands were already occupied by peoples who, as Mongoloids speaking Sino-Tibetan languages, were near relatives of the Chinese and whose level of cultural development was initially not far below that of the Chinese. The Chinese people and culture expanded at the expense of these peoples and their cultures, partly by military conquest and colonization. But part of the process was relatively peaceable assimilation of originally non-Chinese peoples into the expanding Chinese nation. In either case, newly subjugated or assimilated southern peoples did not automatically become North Chinese in their beliefs, customs, and life-styles. Rather, what it meant to be Chinese was transformed with each new expansion, as new peoples brought elements of their non-Chinese life-styles into the mainstream of Chinese civilization. Thus China's expansion southward came about by a progressive enrichment of the original Chinese people and their culture. This aspect of Chinese history accounts for many of the cultural, temperamental, physical, and linguistic variations that abound among the modern Chinese.

The Chinese refer to themselves as the Han people, after the name of an early dynasty. They knew the early aboriginal peoples of South China by many tribal names; the most common collective terms were Man and T'ai. Not all of the aborigines were subjugated or assimilated by China. Those who most vigorously opposed becoming Chinese migrated away from the advancing Chinese civilization and stubbornly developed their own related but autonomous civilizations as the Vietnamese and Thai peoples. Those who remained in China Proper without becoming Chinese found themselves pressed into less and less desirable lands. The culture gap widened, and they became fragmented, ever more disadvantaged "natives." There was almost no year in recorded history when some such group was not fighting the Chinese. Aborigines were occasionally exterminated in large numbers, but for the most part the Chinese tried to appease them while steadily encroaching on their lands and exploiting them in other ways.

By the twentieth century the aboriginal tribespeople of the south and southwest had ceased playing a significant role in Chinese history. They remain today, however, as still-unassimilated minorities known by such names as Miao, Yao, Chuang, Lolo, and Moso. In recent centuries they have been tolerated as more or less autonomous wards of the state, and twentieth-century Chinese governments have tried to protect and foster their local cultures. One especially interesting minority people are the Hakkas, who are widespread in the south and southeastern coastal areas. They are thought to be twelfth-century migrants out of North China who insulated themselves from the surrounding population and clannishly preserved many of their "pure" old-style North China ways.

Although the Chinese from an early time tried to maintain political control over northern Vietnam and periodically sent military expeditions into Burma because of border problems, the southward expansion of the Chinese nation eventually stopped at the natural southern frontiers of modern China Proper. In the thirteenth century and again in the fifteenth century, Chinese naval expeditions were sent abroad, in the latter case dominating the Indian Ocean and reaching the east coast of Africa; but the Chinese made no effort to incorporate overseas territories into their nation. Nevertheless, individual Chinese in large numbers have migrated overseas from the south coastal areas, and in the twentieth century they have been economically influential minorities in every country of Southeast Asia.

On its northern frontier traditional China confronted an altogether different situation. The peoples to the north, though racially kin to the Chinese, were not linguistic relatives but speakers of the wholly unrelated Altaic languages. Moreover, their way of life as pastoral nomads and the life-style of the agrarian Chinese were mutually unassimilable and therefore mutually antagonistic. Through much of history the nomadic horsemen of the northern and western steppes and the sedentary Chinese engaged in a seesaw struggle to determine who would prevail. The nomads had the short-term advantage of mobility, which enabled them to amass overwhelming striking power at any point along the frontier on short notice. The Chinese farmers had great difficulty in maintaining horses and cavalry skills, and on expeditions into the steppes they required enormous supply trains. But in the long run they had a staying power that counterbalanced the striking power of the nomads. Thus dominance passed from one side to the other and back again, until the introduction of modern cannon on the frontier in the eighteenth century tipped the balance permanently in China's favor and led to Chinese incorporation of Sinkiang and Mongolia.

The peoples of the north were not nomads in the beginning, nor

were the earliest known Chinese wholly agrarian and sedentary. Both
originated as migratory peoples who combined hunting and herding
with primitive farming. The emergent Chinese in the North China
plain became steadily more agrarian. But the northern steppes did not
favor agricultural development, and the northern peoples gradually
found it advantageous to devote themselves more and more to pastoral life, perhaps in part because of progressive desiccation. Horse
nomadism appeared only in the ninth or eighth century B.C. and did not
attain its full development until the fifth or fourth century B.C. It was
only then clear that the two ways of life had diverged totally. From that
time on, northerners were not merely non-Chinese awaiting assimilation
like many of the peoples of the south. They had become a force threatening China's existence, and the defense of the northern frontier became a major, continuing concern of the Chinese nation.

China's successive southward expansions were in part reactions to
pressures generated in the north by successive nomad confederations.
It was the natural ambition of every nomad khan to loot the cities of
North China and if possible control them politically. Inevitably, some
nomadic invaders remained and became Chinese; and thus each intrusion left a residue of new blood and new cultural elements in North
China, just as each Chinese expansion southward absorbed new blood
and cultural elements into the Chinese mainstream. On the other hand,
some northern nomads, failing to gain dominance over China or finding themselves pressed by groups to their north, migrated westward
across Central Asia to become the Huns and Turks of European history, just as some of the original inhabitants of South China migrated
out to become the Vietnamese, Thais, and Burmese of Southeast Asian
history.

National unity and dynastic cycles. Internally, Chinese history was,
among other things, a long struggle to attain and recurringly to regain
political unity. The geographic diversity of China Proper and the cultural and linguistic diversity of the ever-changing Chinese people have
not lent themselves to a natural, easily maintained national unity.
Rather, they provide forces that have easily torn the nation into separatist fragments. Regional warlordism flourished periodically throughout history.

The classic cycle has been for a strong man to win control of all
China by military means and to pass his leadership on to his eldest
son. The vigor of the founding emperor, and often the consolidating

successes of his son, established a pattern of dynastic institutions that stabilized the nation and perpetuated peace and prosperity for generations after them. But later emperors of the dynasty grew up in the palace, pampered by sycophantic palace women and eunuchs and insulated from the harsh realities of the world outside. On coming to the throne, they were often ineffective and irresponsible. Meanwhile, conditions of life changed more rapidly than governmental institutions and policies could be modified to cope with change. In time, the state mechanism was insufficiently responsive to new national needs, and regional warlords—domestic rebels or invaders from the north—fragmented the state and precipitated chaotic civil wars. Eventually one contender put down all others and established a successor dynasty, inaugurating the same cycle of consolidation, stabilization, stagnation, and eventual fragmentation and chaos all over again.

Changes of dynasty cannot all be explained by this model, of course; and not all changes of dynasty coincided with important changes in the overall development of Chinese civilization. But the dynastic cycle was an important element in the traditional Chinese view of history, which seemed to be an inexorable progression from strength to weakness, from centralization to decentralization, from order to chaos, from unity to fragmentation, over and over. That some dynasties nevertheless endured for three centuries and more testifies to the remarkable success the Chinese achieved in constructing stable social and governmental systems.

PART ONE

The Formative Age

Prehistory-206 B.C.

1. General History

STONE-AGE cultures that were ancestral to Chinese civilization were scattered across North China by the beginning of the second millennium B.C. By 1500 B.C. interaction among them had generated a monarchy called Shang, which was dominated by a chariot-riding warrior elite, practiced a high-level bronze technology, and used the earliest known form of the Chinese writing system. The Shang state was overthrown about 1122 B.C. by frontiersmen from its western periphery, who established the longest-lived dynasty of Chinese history, the Chou dynasty. The Chou rulers inaugurated a feudal age by parceling out the conquered territories among relatives and allies. The Chinese nation expanded throughout North China and began to assimilate the Yangtze River regions of the south, and Chinese culture matured into enduring patterns that were to become the idealized models for the rest of history. Royal authority waned after several centuries of stable consolidation, and steadily intensifying rivalries among great frontier lords culminated in endemic civil wars from the fifth century B.C. on. Rapid political changes produced and were further accelerated by socioeconomic changes, technological changes, administrative changes, and ideological changes. Chinese civilization was undergoing a thorough transformation.

The western frontier state of Ch'in (from which Westerners derived the name China) eventually subdued all rivals and by 221 B.C. consolidated a greatly enlarged China under a centralized, totalitarian government. Soon after the death of the first Ch'in emperor in 210 B.C., however, the new order broke down, and China was ravaged by civil wars again.

PREHISTORY

In the beginning, a Chinese legend relates, the cosmos was a gas that slowly solidified into a colossal stone. Out of a cosmic egg was born a creature named P'an-ku, who lived 18,000 years, growing at a rate of ten feet a day and spending his time chopping the stone into two parts, one of which became heaven and the other earth. When P'an-ku completed his labors and died, his eyes became the sun and moon, his expiring breath the atmosphere, his bones mountains, his flesh soil, and his blood rivers and oceans. The fleas and lice on his body were ancestors of all living creatures on earth. (See Fig. 38, p. 367.)

This is one of several P'an-ku tales about the origin of the universe that began to appear in Chinese literature in the early centuries of the Christian era. It is noteworthy that until then the Chinese felt no need to explain the creation of the universe and the origin of mankind. Among Chinese of the formative age, the cosmos was accepted as a given, requiring no explanation. What did require explanation was the development of civilization. Consequently, the early Chinese peopled high antiquity with rulers who were culture heroes, inventors of the cultural and technological elements that characterized China's historic way of life. Here, too, there is a noteworthy omission. There is no suggestion in the early legends of any hero who led the Chinese to China from elsewhere. It was taken for granted that the Chinese originated in China—specifically in the central Yellow River region where the loess highland of the west meets the lowland plain of the east. The Chinese are perhaps unique among the world's major peoples in that their early traditions include neither a creation myth nor epic legends about ancient folk migrations.

The most ancient culture heroes spoken of in early records are the Three Sovereigns, a group composed of Fu-hsi (Ox-tamer), whose reign supposedly began in 2852 B.C. and who is credited with the domestication of animals and the institution of family life; Shen-nung (Divine Farmer), who reigned from 2737 and is considered the inventor of the plow and the hoe, the inaugurator of settled agriculture, and the initiator of public markets; and Huang-ti (Yellow Emperor), in whose reign from 2697 wooden houses, silk cloth, boats, carts, the bow and arrow, ceramics, and writing were introduced. Huang-ti reportedly fought and won a great battle against "barbarians" somewhere in modern Shansi province, and after his victory was accepted as national leader by tribes throughout the Yellow River plain. Some Chinese writers suggest that China's history as a nation actually begins with Huang-ti.

Huang-ti was the first of a legendary sequence of rulers known as the Five Emperors, who added more elements to the developing civilization. The fourth and fifth emperors, Yao (r. 2357-2256 B.C.) and Shun (r. 2255-2205 B.C.), are especially esteemed. Yao devised a calendar by which agrarian work could be regulated, espoused moral cultivation through proper use of ritual and music, and created a rudimentary central government. Ignoring his own unworthy son, he searched throughout the empire for a virtuous man to succeed him, and on finding such a successor shared rule with him during his last 28 years. The successor, Shun, was a poor peasant distinguished initially only by his widespread reputation as an obedient, devoted son. His blind father and scheming stepmother punished him regularly and on several occasions tried to kill him, to benefit his spoiled half-brother, but Shun always forgave them and persisted in being a filial son and loving brother. When brought to eminence, he fulfilled every expectation of a model ruler.

The reigns of Yao and Shun, according to the legends, were troubled by great floods. After several major water-control efforts had failed, Shun called on an official named Yü to drain the waters. Yü traveled throughout the empire dealing with the floods for more than a decade, so single-mindedly zealous that on three occasions he passed by his home and heard his wife and children weeping in loneliness but would not pause long enough even to greet them. He successfully dredged channels through which the floodwaters drained out to sea, thereby creating the major rivers of North China. Shun then named Yü to succeed him and shared rule with him for 17 years. As ruler, Yü was benevolent and beloved. After his death the people ignored the successor he had designated and turned to Yü's own son for guidance and adjudication of disputes. The son was eventually prevailed upon to become ruler himself, and China's first dynasty was thus created. Yao, Shun, and Yü are collectively called the Three Sages, and the dynasty that began with Yü's reign (2205-2198 B.C.) is called Hsia.

According to tradition, the Hsia rulers advanced civilization in many ways, but finally the throne came to a tyrant named Chieh. In 1766 he was deposed and exiled by a subordinate called Ch'eng T'ang (T'ang the Successful), who founded a new dynasty, the Shang, which resumed the development of civilization. Finally, however, the throne passed to a tyrannical, self-indulgent, militaristic ruler heedless of wise counsel, named Shou, and like Chieh he was overturned by a subordinate. Thus began the Chou dynasty in 1122 B.C. The Hsia, Shang, and Chou dynasties are commonly referred to as the Three Dynasties.

The historicity of the Three Sovereigns, the Five Emperors, the Three Sages, the Three Dynasties, and other aspects of the legendary past were not questioned through most of China's imperial history. The virtuous conduct and benevolent policies of Yao, Shun, Yü, T'ang, and the Chou founders were grand themes of traditional literature and provided models for traditional education, both official and popular.

Twentieth-century archaeologists have verified, in a most impressive way, what China's written traditions tell about the Shang dynasty. Archaeology has also thrown much light on pre-Shang evolution in China, but the findings so far cannot be correlated with the written record. It seems probable that archaeological evidence will one day identify Hsia with some neolithic culture of Shansi province; and it may become possible to suggest that such legendary culture heroes as Shun and Yao and perhaps even Huang-ti were dimly remembered early chiefs of other North Chinese neolithic cultures. But for the time being, at least, archaeology reveals a different and more believable pre-Shang development in North China than do the legends just summarized.

The oldest clear evidence of humanlike occupants of China comes from a hillside cave near a village named Chou-k'ou-tien, southwest of modern Peking. The evidence dates from at least 200,000 and perhaps more than 500,000 years ago, and consists of bone fragments of some 40 individuals, including 14 skulls. The remains suggest a proto-human or hominid creature with a mature stature of about five feet, erect posture, cranial capacity about halfway between the great ape and modern mankind, a low skull vault and a bony forehead ridge protruding out over the eyes, a receding chin, a brain capable of speech, hunting and nut-gathering habits, a knowledge of fire, and strong head-hunting and cannibalistic inclinations. The type is called Peking Man (*Sinanthropus pekinensis* or *Pithecanthropus pekinensis*) and is clearly related to a type found in Java (*Pithecanthropus robustus*). It represents one of the earliest known stages of development toward modern humankind, and it is of special interest because its teeth include shovel-shaped incisors, a characteristic of the modern Mongoloid race.

Archaeological evidence indicates that from the time of this Old Stone Age creature, who lived in an interval between ancient glaciations, through the remainder of the glacial ages and on into the early post-glacial age, North China witnessed a very slow evolution of Neanderthal-like types, with fully matured *Homo sapiens* of the Mongoloid race finally appearing perhaps 20,000 years ago. During the later stages of this development at least, parts of South China were occupied by protohumans with Negroid racial characteristics and a somewhat less advanced technology in stone tools than developed in the north. All East Asian stone-age technologies, however, are of distinctive chopping-tool types that differ from the technologies of prehistoric Europe and Africa.

About 12,000 years ago the whole of China progressed from paleolithic to neolithic cultures, characterized by ceramics and the beginnings of agriculture. The central Yellow River area—where the modern provinces of Honan, Shansi, and Shensi meet—was one core area of development from the fully migratory hunting and food-gathering life to a less migratory, more settled life combining hunting, herding, and farming. The neolithic culture that first appeared in this area is called Yang-shao, after the name of one of its earliest excavated sites in Honan province. It is represented in more than 1,000 excavations in the highland loess plateau extending westward into Kansu province, and reveals many regional variations. Its most notable general characteristic is hand-molded pottery of red, black, and gray clay with painted decorations in red or black pigment. The painted pottery people clustered in small villages—of about 100 houses at most—sited on terraces overlooking river valleys; but no group remained in one location very long. Their principal crop was millet; their principal domesticated animals were dogs and pigs; they hunted with bows and arrows and spears; they wove baskets and made cloth of hemp and silk. They used a great variety of tools made of stones, bones, and antlers. They buried their dead respectfully, believed in an afterlife, and practiced fertility rites. Their culture reached its peak of development about 3000 B.C.

The Yang-shao painted pottery culture was gradually displaced by —or perhaps generated—another neolithic culture that is most closely associated with the lowland North China plain. It eventually overspread all of China Proper except the southwest. Like the Yang-shao culture, it had many regional variations. This culture is known as Lung-shan, after its earliest excavated site in modern Shantung province; and its best-known characteristic is wheel-made, unpainted black pottery of a thin, hard texture and with a burnished, lustrous surface. The black pottery people had larger and more permanent settlements than the painted pottery people. They lived in walled communities built on low terraces or mounds in the plains of the Yellow and Yangtze rivers, along the coasts from Manchuria almost to Vietnam, and even in the highland northwest where the Yang-shao culture had once prevailed. They cultivated rice as well as millet, domesticated cattle and sheep as well as dogs and pigs, produced and used a greater variety of building and agricultural tools than their Yang-shao predecessors, and revealed greater status and class differentiation in their burial patterns. Occupational specialization had developed significantly. Their religion seems to have emphasized ancestor worship rather than fertility rites, and they engaged in divination by manipulating so-called oracle bones, an established practice of the later Shang civilization. The widespread Lung-shan black pottery culture reached its peak about 2000 B.C., and it is clear that the Shang monarchy emerged out of a Honan branch of it.

SHANG (1766 B.C.?-1122 B.C.?)

Shang civilization is now revealed in dozens of archaeological sites across North China, from the western edge of the Yellow River plain to its eastern extremity in Shantung province. The core area is northern Honan, particularly an arc stretching from the modern cities of Loyang and Chengchow south of the river northward across the river to An-yang. Near Loyang are the remains of a primitive Shang city that might have been the first Shang capital, which early legends report was established in that region by T'ang the Successful. The city of Chengchow lies atop other remains, now systematically unearthed, of what must have been the second Shang capital of legend—Ao. Early historians reported there were five Shang capitals after Ao, but only the last of these, Yin, can so far be identified without question. It is one of 17 major sites of the fully matured Shang civilization in the An-yang area, at a place known throughout history as Yin-hsü (the ruins of Yin). Here the last 12 Shang kings resided for a total of 273 years beginning about 1395 B.C. The whole dynasty is often called Yin after the name of this last capital.

Urban civilization developed in China about 1,000 years later than in Mesopotamia and perhaps 500 years later than in the Indus River valley of the Indo-Pakistan subcontinent. There can be little doubt that some elements of the older civilizations to the west found their way by diffusion to China. The earliest Shang excavations at An-yang revealed what seemed like a life-style far removed from the underlying Lung-shan culture and suggested that Shang civilization may have been imported full-grown into China from outside. However, the more recent discoveries at Loyang and Chengchow demonstrate clear stages of a continuous development from Lung-shan into ever more mature Shang. The conception of an independent emergence of civilization among the North Chinese cannot now be seriously questioned.

Shang civilization was not characterized by population density and urban concentrations on a scale comparable to those of Mesopotamia and the Indus River valley, but the Shang cities were large and multifunctional, and the Shang population was differentiated and stratified by rank, status, and occupation. Each capital had a central core of large public buildings and altars that was clearly the living area of a substantial ruling class. The buildings had raised, pounded-earth foundations inset with large stones and bronze castings in symmetrical patterns, which served as bases for wooden pillars that supported roofs; one of these foundations is 26 feet wide and 92 feet long. Surrounding this central administrative and ceremonial core were workshops of bronzesmiths, potters, stonecarvers, and other artisans; clusters of farmers' houses, which were small and semi-subterranean; and burial grounds.

At An-yang are 11 large tombs that are almost certainly the resting places of the Yin-era kings (excluding the last, who reportedly died in his burning palace). Each tomb is a large square or oblong pit some 30 feet underground, carefully laid out on a north-south axis, measuring from 40 to 60 feet in diameter, and enclosing a wooden burial chamber. The pit was reached by sloping ramps on two sides or sometimes on all four sides, up to 100 feet in length. The tombs give evidence of human sacrifice; large numbers of "accompaniment burials" of warriors and workmen have been found both in the pits and along the ramps. (See Fig. 3, p. 60.)

No evidence of a city wall has yet been found at An-yang, but at Chengchow there was a substantial pounded-earth wall some 30 feet high and 65 feet wide, thickening at the base to more than 100 feet in places, and totaling almost four and a half miles in length. This wall enclosed only the central administrative-ceremonial area. From the scattered excavated remains at An-yang it is clear that the entire community incorporated at least 16 square miles. In short, the Shang capitals were not small-scale settlements.

In addition to large cities, three things especially differentiate Shang civilization from the preceding neolithic cultures: horse-drawn chariots, a high-order bronze technology, and a fully mature version of the Chinese writing system.

War seems to have been the principal occupation of the chariot-riding ruling class, which regularly called out commoner draftees in groups of 1,000, 3,000, or 5,000 for expeditions against surrounding non-Chinese "barbarians." The ways in which chariots were used in the fighting are not clear. Battles seem to have been man-to-man melees, joined with spear and bow and fought by aristocrats and commoners together. The Shang bow, made of wood, bone, and horn, was of the compound sort that later came to be the standard weapon of the steppe nomads and was known to Westerners as the Turkish bow. Such bows are much more powerful than the ones traditionally used in the West; they commonly have a 160-pound pull and have been known to kill at a range of 200 yards. When Shang aristocrats were not warring they engaged in great hunting expeditions, probably as much for sport and military practice as to accumulate game for food.

Bronze, produced by specialized, probably hereditary craftsmen serving the ruling class, seems to have been used more for ceremonial than for utilitarian purposes. Manufactures certainly included weapons, armor, and chariot fittings, but the most abundant and striking products were magnificent cups, goblets, steamers, and cauldrons in a great variety of shapes and sizes, ranging up to 1,500-pound units. These were normally cast in clay molds, in sections that were then fitted together so perfectly that modern archaeologists long thought they must have been cast as single pieces by the lost-wax method. Brief writings are sometimes found inscribed on interior bottom surfaces. In large part, Shang bronze vessels are in forms that derive directly from Lung-shan and even Yang-shao pottery forms; various three-legged forms were popular in all these periods. Some of the Shang vessels were evidently used for libations in religious ceremonies, but many were buried in the larger tombs, no doubt filled with wine and food for the nourishment of the spirits of the dead. Pottery vessels, of a characteristic dull gray color and in some cases glazed, were also buried in tombs.

Shang scribes kept court records written with brushes on slips of bamboo or wood that were bound together in the fashion of modern

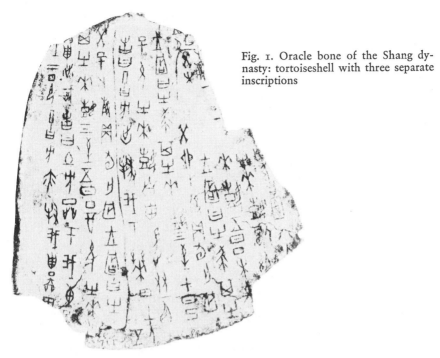

Fig. 1. Oracle bone of the Shang dynasty: tortoiseshell with three separate inscriptions

vertical-slat screens. These perishable materials have long since disappeared. However, excavations at An-yang have yielded great royal archives of oracle bones. These are turtleshells and shoulderblades of cattle and other animals that were used in divination and stored by court diviners. For divination, a small pit was dug partway through the bone or shell, and then a heated metal point was applied to the bottom of the pit. The bone or shell cracked to form a lopsided Y, with one line running straight through the pit and another angling out from its center. The two cracks indicated to the diviner an affirmative or negative response to his question. More than one divination pit appears on many bones and shells.

The archives at An-yang yielded more than 100,000 of these oracle bones, on about 20,000 of which the diviners had inscribed their questions or notations with styluses (see Fig. 1). A common formula is: "Date. The diviner X asks on behalf of the king, . . ." Typical questions are: "Will the king's child be a son?" "Will it rain?" "Will tomorrow be good for hunting?" "The king has a headache. Has he offended ancestor X?" "Will the king have a comfortable night?" "Is the long drought caused by ancestor X?" "If we raise an army of 3,000 men to drive X away from X, will we succeed?" "Were the rituals and sacrifices acceptable?" Many of the oracles seem to have concerned reports to the spirits rather than questions—for example, about the outcome of a battle or a hunt.

The oracle bone inscriptions are in the oldest known form of Chinese writing, and equating the crude graphs with their modern equivalents has been one of the great scholarly achievements of our time. Not only has this endeavor shown that in Shang times the writing system had already developed all the pictographic, ideographic, and logographic principles that characterize the later writing system; it has revealed most of what is now known about Shang history, administration, culture, and religion.

The Shang state was a monarchy in which the throne passed from elder brother to younger brother as often as from father to son. The king was served by officials whose titles indicate at least rudimentary differentiation and specialization by functions. Officials apparently belonged to a hereditary class of aristocrats, possibly related to the king, and particular offices may have been inherited. The kings waged war far afield in North China against non-Chinese "barbarians," who usually are depicted as troublesome raiders, and some of the late Shang kings campaigned southward along the coast toward and perhaps into the Yangtze River regions. The integrated Shang state, however, cannot have extended far beyond the Yellow River banks across the North China plain, though it exchanged limited trade and diffused its cultural influence afar in all directions. Of anything that might be called Shang political history, virtually nothing of significance is known; and whether Shang China was a slave society or a rudimentary feudal society is a matter of controversy among modern scholars.

WESTERN CHOU (1122 B.C.?-771 B.C.)

The people called Chou, who overthrew the Shang state in about 1122 B.C., were not barbarous non-Chinese invaders. Like the Shang people themselves, they were Chinese-speaking descendants of Lungshan neolithic peoples. For centuries they had migrated about the westernmost agricultural basin of North China, the Wei River valley of modern Shensi province. However, they were frontiersmen who did not originally take part in the rise of a bronze-age civilization in Honan; and even at the time of their conquest they were considered semibarbarous "country cousins" by the Shang ruling class. In pre-conquest times the Shang king conferred the title Chief of the West on one of their leaders, and according to tradition, a Shang noblewoman was given him in marriage. The Chou peoples were early allied with, and probably intermarried with, proto-Tibetan tribesmen called Ch'iang, who occupied much of the western frontier of China Proper. The Shang rulers feared and hated them so much that Shang armies often hunted down Ch'iang as if they were animals. It could well have been astute diplomacy on Shang's part to cultivate the emerging Chou statelet as a buffer and stabilizing influence in the west.

Early Chou history, even long after the conquest, is little clearer than Shang history. But some credence is given to legends that a chief named T'ai led his people away from barbarian pressures into the heart of the Shensi basin, began to develop Shang-style agriculture, and built a city in an area called the Plain of Chou, whence comes the name of the state and dynasty. It was his son and successor who reportedly married a Shang noblewoman. Their marriage produced an unquestionably historical figure, King Wen (the Accomplished or the Cultured), who appears in early writings as a paragon of benevolence and wisdom. King Wen apparently conceived the ambitious plan of undermining Shang authority and began making the alliances with neighboring chiefs that eventually made conquest possible. According to one tradition, his activities so disturbed the Shang court that he was imprisoned at Yin but ransomed by his supporters at great cost.

King Wen's son, King Wu (the Martial), came to power about 1133 B.C. and built a new capital east of the old one, located near what is now the city of Sian and called Hao. In the ninth year of his reign, after continuing his father's consolidating efforts, he launched an invasion of Shang. He was driven back, but two years later, in 1122, he attacked again. Legends hold that his 50,000 troops were opposed by a massive Shang army of 700,000 men, but the Shang people were so unhappy under the last Shang king that his soldiers offered little resistance, and many joined King Wu's campaign. The Shang ruler, Shou, retreated into his palace, set it afire, and died in the flames. The Chou bias in this account is evident; the great disparity in the opposing armies, certainly, is not to be believed. But there was some kind of battle, and the Chou forces prevailed.

Tradition does not accord to King Wu the lovable qualities of his father, but he is revered as a strong and stern ruler who quickly restored order. Rather than obliterate Shang entirely, he left the royal Shang heir as nominal ruler of Yin city, apparently to continue sacrificing to the powerful spirits of the former kings; but he assigned two or three of his own brothers to keep Yin under close control. Then King Wu apparently returned to his western capital, Hao, and there he died in 1116, still relatively young.

King Wu had toppled the Shang monarchy, but he had by no means taken control of the whole eastern plain that the Shang kings had dominated. There is reason to believe that King Wu and many of his adherents had no greater ambition than to loot the Shang capital, or perhaps by killing the king to avenge some insult. Tradition gives credit to King Wu's brother Tan, called the Duke of Chou, for having a greater vision and for laying the institutional basis for the long-lived Chou dynasty. When later Chinese praised the early Chou sage-kings, they normally had in mind King Wen, King Wu, and the Duke of Chou.

When King Wu died, his son, King Ch'eng, was a child. One uncle, the Duke of Shao, was chief overseer of the Chou homeland in Shensi; and the Duke of Chou was his counterpart on the newly conquered eastern plain. The Duke of Chou promptly assumed power as regent over King Ch'eng, and as promptly his brothers stationed at Yin joined the Shang heir in a rebellion to restore the old order. Brotherly jealousy was probably involved, and there seems to have been a widespread expectation that the Duke of Chou would usurp the throne from his young nephew. The Duke of Chou reacted quickly and effectively. He put down the rebellion, executed the Shang heir and one of his own rebellious brothers, and conducted a series of expeditions eastward to bring the whole of the Yellow River plain under control. It is claimed that in this process he destroyed 50 statelets and established 71 new administrative units in their places. Then he built a new city at modern Loyang, near the western end of the plain, to serve as an auxiliary Chou capital from which the east could be administered. Many former Shang aristocrats were moved there from Yin, which was leveled. A new Shang scion, with a more trustworthy Chou duke as his guardian, was established in a statelet called Sung, south of the Yellow River in eastern Honan. This accomplished, the Duke of Chou voluntarily gave up his extraordinary powers after seven years as regent. He had persistently lectured his nephew on the responsibilities of ruling, and King Ch'eng ruled effectively until 1079 B.C., by which time a distinctive Chou political and social order had been stabilized throughout North China.

The Chou realm was never a wholly unified state. The royal court

extended its sovereignty over the eastern plain by delegating authority to members of the royal family and favored adherents, who took
garrison troops and established walled forts amidst the original inhabitants of the east. In some instances, local chiefs were accepted as
newly submitted Chou supporters. As has been noted, descendants of
the Shang rulers were allowed to retain a small territory. In this way
there came into existence a scattering of city-states or statelets on the
plain, from which military and political control gradually spread over
the surrounding farming villages. The eastern plain experienced what
amounted to a military occupation by Chou and allied armies, and the
earliest Chou rulers were quick to punish any local leaders who defied
them and were careful to oversee their regional delegates.

Commanders of the regional city-states, like members of the royal
court, were given graded titles of rank, which are normally rendered
in English as duke, marquis, earl, viscount, and baron. Although the
title duke was formally reserved for royal sons, almost all regional lords
were commonly referred to, at least occasionally, by that title. Collectively, they were called "the various marquises" (chu-hou); most of
the early statelets were ranked as marquisates.

Because of the many resemblances between the Chou system and
some varieties of feudalism in medieval Europe, Westerners and modern Chinese usually refer to the Chou dynasty as a feudal age and consider "the various marquises" feudal lords. Insofar as fiefs and vassalage
can be considered the essential ingredients of a feudal political organization, the Chou system was indeed feudal. But there were distinct
differences between the Chou system and the much later feudal systems
of medieval Europe. Probably the most noteworthy of these was that,
despite at least proto-contractual arrangements between the Chou lords
and vassals, the Chou ruling class was principally unified by kinship
ties. Where none existed, family relationships were arranged by mar-
riages. Thus all the feudal lords were expected to accept the king as
head of a vast extended family and to feel themselves beholden to the
Chou ancestral spirits as its founders.

As decades and centuries passed, these early kinship ties naturally
loosened; the feudal lords became steadily more identified with their allocated territories and less awed by the kings. This was true even among
the smaller statelets of the central plain such as Sung (descendants of
Shang) and Lu (descendants of the Duke of Chou). It was especially
true of the larger peripheral states: Chin in modern Shansi, Yen in the

region of modern Peking, and Ch'i in the Shantung promontory in the east. Among the 200 or so Chou statelets that had been created by the eighth century B.C., there were still, in addition, enclaves of unassimilated non-Chinese who were not part of the feudal order but had military and sometimes diplomatic contacts with the Chou court and the feudal lords. In the west and central upland areas were many tribes collectively called Jung. Various so-called Ti peoples were scattered in the north, and "barbarians" collectively called I occupied much of the east coastal region. Southern non-Chinese at this time were lumped together under the name Man. A political entity called Ch'u confronted the Chou realm on the south, sprawling throughout the central Yangtze River valley. Its chiefs called themselves kings, though by the eighth century B.C. they allowed the Chou rulers to consider them part of the feudal order. Beyond Ch'u was a less developed political entity called Wu in the Yangtze delta region, and a Yüeh state existed in modern Chekiang province farther south.

For three centuries after the conquest of Shang, Chou rulers generally maintained order in North China and expanded their realm, but not without troubles and mishaps. King Chao (r. 1053-1002 B.C.) repeatedly campaigned southward into the Yangtze drainage area and died on his last expedition. Fascinating legends cluster about his son, King Mu (r. 1002-947 B.C.), who appears to have been a compulsive campaigner and adventurer. One group of legends indicate that he campaigned afar in Central Asia and visited with a so-called Queen Mother of the West (Hsi Wang Mu), of whom nothing further is known but whom nineteenth-century European missionary-scholars diligently tried to identify with the Queen of Sheba. By the ninth century B.C. regional lords were beginning to ignore their obligations to the Chou court and were fighting among themselves; and, perhaps taking advantage of the declining stability of the Chou realm, non-Chinese on all sides were now seriously harassing the frontiers. King Li (r. 879-828 B.C.) reportedly led 14 armies against "barbarians" to the south and southeast but could not defeat them. King Hsüan (r. 827-781 B.C.) fought defensive wars against non-Chinese of the north through much of his reign, and in 771 his son, King Yu, was killed and the capital city, Hao, was overrun and sacked by northerners. Tradition blames this disaster on King Yu's infatuation with a concubine named Pao Ssu. He often lit beacon fires signifying distress, but only because Pao Ssu delighted to see the royal armies assemble in full array. His officers tired of this game, and when invaders actually appeared King Yu's beacon signals were ignored.

It was now decided that the site of Hao was too exposed and vulnerable to assaults from the frontier. The royal heir and those courtiers who survived the disaster abandoned the city and designated the eastern auxiliary capital at Loyang as the new royal capital. This marks a major turning point in Chou history. The preceding period is called Western Chou to differentiate it from the later Chou reigns at Loyang. The period from 770 B.C. to the end of the dynasty in 256 B.C. is called Eastern Chou.

EASTERN CHOU (770 B.C.-256 B.C.)

The end of the Western Chou era in 771 B.C. signified the end of the real power of the Chou kings and ushered in an age when powerful regional states were the main focuses of interest on the stage of Chinese history. The statelets of early Chou, especially those on the peripheries, had grown into major territorial powers, and many of their rulers had greater economic and military strength than the king, now dependent on a small royal domain around Loyang. The old royal domain in Shensi had been entrusted to the feudal lord of Ch'in, previously a small fief in northern Shensi. Ch'in rapidly became a western counterpart of Chin in the north and Ch'i in the east. By 700 B.C. these three North China states and the semi-Chinese state of Ch'u in the south were the principal centers of power in China. Between them, on the central Yellow River plain, the royal Chou domain was one of several cultured and prestigious but powerless statelets. The great lords gave lip service to the Chou king, but little else.

The subdivision of the Eastern Chou period from 722 to 481 B.C. is called the Spring and Autumn era after the name (Ch'un-ch'iu; Spring and Autumn) of the preserved chronicles of the small state of Lu, which record notable events throughout China between these dates. But the era happens to have a character all its own, of guarded sparring for advantage among the regional states large and small, in shifting alliances. The decline of the royal authority left China effectively leaderless, and the states struggled to preserve the status quo. None was powerful enough to win over all others, but several were powerful enough to disrupt the existing order. Thus the Chou kings continued to reign by default, while each feudal lord was master in his own state. Wars were fought among the states, though not very vigorously and with few drastic consequences. Struggles primarily involved diplomatic maneuvering, and the arts of interstate diplomacy were studied earnestly and practiced with finesse.

Out of the political maneuvering of the eighth and seventh centuries B.C. there developed a remarkable new institution called the hegemon (*pa*), which gave to the Spring and Autumn era much of its unique quality. This was a device to offset the ineffectiveness of the Chou kings without challenging their sovereignty. It originated in reaction to the aggressiveness of Ch'u against the small states of the central plain in the 680's. The threatened central states turned for protection to Ch'i in Shantung. Ch'i had a stable, strong economy and a sound military organization, and its able ruler, Duke Huan (r. 685-643 B.C.), profited from the counsel of a shrewd administrative expert named Kuan Chung. Ch'i was the most respected power in the north at the time. At the appeal of his neighbors, Duke Huan convened a conference of the central states in 681, at which a mutual-defense treaty was signed and sanctified with appropriate sacrifices and oaths. A follow-up conference the next year, attended by more lords, was presided over by an envoy from the royal court. All of the central and eastern states now found it advantageous to join the league, and at a conference in 678 they formally designated Duke Huan hegemon, to preserve peace and the honor of the Chou king. Duke Huan served the league well through the remainder of his reign, convening conferences irregularly as circumstances warranted, defending member states from raids by Jung and I tribesmen, and keeping Ch'u at bay. In 656 Ch'u even signed a peace treaty and agreed to send regular tribute to the Chou court, thus for the first time submitting to vassalage in the Chou feudal order.

After Duke Huan the institution of hegemon was never again so important, but it was perpetuated for some 200 years, and interstate conferences were held periodically. There was only one worthy successor to Duke Huan, Duke Wen of Chin (r. 637-628 B.C.), who won a decisive victory over Ch'u in a famous battle at Ch'eng-p'u in modern Shantung province in 632. For this feat, the reigning Chou king personally carried his congratulations to the duke and named him hegemon. The position of hegemon thereafter remained nominally with the dukes of Chin until the institution faded away in the late fifth century B.C.

Chin, in modern Shansi province, had a divisive clannish tradition that well suited its hilly topography, and it was often so weak internally that it could not give effective leadership to the central states. Ch'u repeatedly gained actual supremacy over the northern plain; Ch'i occasionally reasserted itself; and in the sixth century B.C. the western state of Ch'in, hardly more assimilated to Chinese civilization than

Ch'u, entered the struggle for influence on the plain. Sometimes Ch'i joined with Chin to oppose Ch'u. Sometimes Ch'u and Ch'in collaborated against Chin. Sometimes Chin and Ch'u were in an unstable alliance against Ch'in. Chin's internal weaknesses led to destructive civil wars that divided it into three new states by 453 B.C. A duke of Chin survived as a protected client of one of these new states until 403, when the Chou king formally recognized the tripartite division of Chin. This left Ch'in and Ch'i in the north and Ch'u in the south as the dominant powers.

In the early years of the Spring and Autumn era, interstate warfare was rather polite gamesmanship. Actual fighting seems to have been limited and the casualties few. Outmaneuvered lords were shamed, but their status in the Chou political order was not substantially altered. The art of diplomacy was supreme. During the fifth century B.C., however, the political climate changed. Wars were no longer gentlemanly jousts in any sense; the predominant concern was raw military power. The states now went to war in deadly seriousness, casualties were heavy, and the defeated lords lost their states and often their lives.

The intensification of war continued into the Warring States era, named after the book *Chan-kuo ts'e* (Intrigues of the Warring States) and considered to begin with the formal disappearance of Chin in 403. The number of contending states had been reduced, and wars among them became steadily more destructive. The chief contenders are called the Seven Powers: primarily Ch'in in the west, Ch'i in the east, and Ch'u in the south; secondarily Yen based on modern Peking and the three states that had formerly constituted Chin—Chao, Han, and Wei. Yüeh in the Yangtze delta played an important role intermittently and was effectively subjugated by Ch'u in 333 B.C.

War was perpetuated because tradition already demanded that all Chinese be unified and because almost every lord aspired to become the great unifier. There was no escaping attack. It was win or lose, absorb or be absorbed, kill or be killed; the chaos could not be resolved until one state eliminated all rivals. There were peace treaties, shifting alliances, exchanges of hostages, revivals of hegemon-style conferences, and other efforts to restrain the fighting, but to no avail.

It was a time of rapid and confusing change in almost all aspects of life. The early Chou religious sanctions had given way as soon as it became apparent that having powerful ancestors did not assure success or provide protection in war. As the prestige of the Chou kings de-

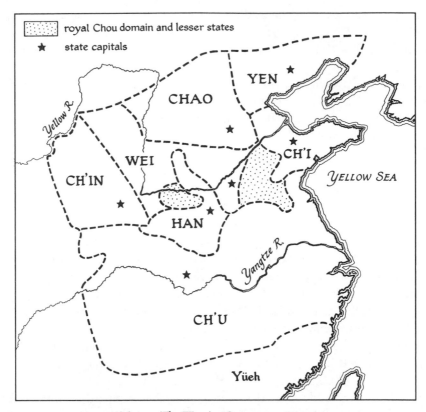

royal Chou domain and lesser states

★   state capitals

YEN

CHAO

Yellow R.

WEI

CH'IN

CH'I

YELLOW SEA

HAN

Yangtze R.

CH'U

Yüeh

Map 2. The Warring States, c. 300 B.C.

clined in the national realm, the positions of feudal lords in their separate states were imperiled. The collapse of Chin into three antagonistic
clan-dominated states might well have been followed by a comparable
fragmentation of Ch'i, which suffered much internal strife in the fifth
century; but Ch'i's imminent collapse was forestalled in 391, when a
ministerial family seized power, deported the duke, and reorganized
the state with its own supporters. There were similar usurpations in
other states; some lords became the puppets of ministerial regents.
Generally, the lords were losing control over their noble ministers.
Then, as wars became more intense and deadly, the noble class as a
whole lost prestige. One's pedigree counted for less and less. What
became increasingly important was one's actual capability, and men
began rising from commoner status to positions of political importance on the basis of their merits and achievements. At the same time,
the intensification of war demanded greater centralization of power

in the states. Thus, ironically, the positions of the regional lords were strengthened anew.

Changes in the art of war contributed to the political and social ferment. The Yangtze delta and the marshy coastal districts between the Yangtze and Yellow rivers did not lend themselves to charioteering; the southeastern states of Wu and Yüeh rose to eminence with infantry armies. When well organized and disciplined, they proved quite able to cope with chariot-riding noblemen. Likewise, the mountainous terrain of Shansi province made Chin and its successor states rely heavily on organized infantry, and they never fared badly in military competition with other states. The mere fact that chariots were expensive and easily damaged made them less and less practical as the scale of warfare grew. Through the Warring States era the chariot steadily declined in importance, so that by about 300 B.C. infantry masses, reportedly in hundreds of thousands, constituted the armies that states hurled against each other. In such circumstances noble birth was no advantage, and noble upbringing may have been an actual handicap on the battlefield.

Meantime, non-Chinese peoples of the far north and west had been undergoing their slow transition into full horse nomadism, and in the fourth century B.C. the northwestern frontier states found themselves confronting the skilled cavalry tactics that were thereafter the specialty of the steppe peoples. By the turn of the century the north Shansi state of Chao had introduced cavalry into its own army. Ch'in soon followed, and in the next century cavalry became a standard auxiliary arm of all Chinese armies. This development was the final blow to the prestige of the charioteering nobleman. Meantime, too, the crossbow and iron weapons, which had been introduced in the fifth century B.C., added to the increasing deadliness of war.

Since the states now engaged in wars fought mainly by infantry masses, it became important to every ruler that he have large numbers of fighting men at his disposal, that their morale be high, and that supplies be sufficient for their needs. Although population statistics are not available for this early age, all the evidence suggests that despite war the Chinese population grew very rapidly during the Warring States era, reaching perhaps fifty or even sixty million. Large areas were newly brought under cultivation, especially in such frontier states as Ch'in, Ch'u, and Ch'i; and agricultural production must have increased greatly, particularly after the development of large water-control and irrigation projects, which had begun to appear in the seventh century. If the lords were to have willing fighters and producers, they had to give thought to the well-being and happiness of their subjects. Traditional class distinctions inevitably became blurred. The leveling of society was perhaps most facilitated by the gradual dying out of early Chou feudalistic land-tenure arrangements. Rulers found that freehold farmers worked more zealously than land-bound serfs, and when called to arms they fought more willingly and successfully.

In addition to good troops and adequate supplies—indeed, to ensure having them—states needed all the managerial talents they could produce or attract. They vied with one another in courting experts and technicians of every sort, and in this atmosphere ambitious intellectuals traveled about among the states offering panaceas to eager patrons. What the Chinese subsequently called "the Hundred Schools" of philosophy flourished. Notable among them were moralistic Confucianism, naturalistic Taoism, and the teachings of governmental efficiency experts that are usually grouped together under the rubric Legalism. In all manner of ways the early Chou socioeconomic order and the value system associated with it were being transformed.

The political history of the Warring States era is complex and confusing. For 100 years and more, the pendulum of success swung erratically among the poles of power—Ch'i and Ch'in and Ch'u. In 335 B.C. regional lords began calling themselves kings; soon every lord was a king, and when the last Chou king was deposed and his domain absorbed by Ch'in in 256, the event was hardly noted. In 323 Ch'in and Ch'u made a peace treaty that seemed to promise the quick extermination of Ch'i, but within four short years Ch'u was organizing an alliance against Ch'in. By 302 it seemed that Ch'in, Ch'i, and Ch'u would divide the nation among them equally, but in 297 Ch'in captured the Ch'u king and pressed on so successfully across Ch'u territory that the central and northern states were provoked into a grand alliance to curb Ch'in. In 285 everyone, including both Ch'in and Ch'u, combined against Ch'i, leaving it so battered that it was temporarily absorbed by its northern neighbor, Yen. So it went, back and forth year after year. Ch'in gradually emerged as the strongest of the states, and in a series of campaigns from 231 to 221 B.C. it destroyed and absorbed its opponents one by one. Ch'u fell in 221, and when the Ch'in armies then turned northward, Ch'i surrendered without a fight, and all China was united.

THE TRIUMPH OF CH'IN (221 B.C.-206 B.C.)

The rise of Ch'in to power parallels in many ways what can be guessed about the rise of Chou almost a millennium earlier. Ch'in arose on the westernmost fringe of the Chinese world, toughened itself in centuries of fighting non-Chinese tribes in its rear, assimilated many Jung tribesmen into its population, and was little restrained by the institutions or the genteel qualities that were fostered among the Chou aristocrats. As the Chou people had earlier been "country cousin" frontiersmen of the Shang world, now Ch'in was the tough, crude, treacherous bully of the Chou world. In 260 B.C., when Ch'in defeated the Shansi state of Chao, it slaughtered the whole surrendered Chao army, reportedly totaling 400,000 men, in the supreme atrocity of a long Ch'in record of brutality.

Among the important reasons for Ch'in's rise to power was its strategically advantageous geographic location. Its home territory in modern Shensi province and the territory it absorbed in modern Szechwan province in 316 B.C. are the two most nearly impregnable natural sanctuaries in China Proper, well insulated from the east by mountains and gorges. Shensi has easy access to the North China plain through Yellow River passes, and Szechwan has equally easy access to the central Yangtze River valley; yet topography makes intrusion from the east difficult in each case. The Ch'in heartland was never itself a major battleground. In contrast, Ch'u was particularly vulnerable to attack by Ch'in from the western uplands of either Shensi or Szechwan, and Ch'i occupied an exposed plain without any natural defenses to the south, west, or north. Of the major contending states, Ch'in clearly had the advantage of location.

Geography also gave Ch'in economic advantages, which it exploited expertly. The Shensi valley was renowned in early times as having the most productive soil in all China, and Ch'in was one of the first states to develop widespread irrigation systems. The annexation of Szechwan gave Ch'in another rich agricultural basin and excellent resources in minerals and lumber. Because of its frontier location and its semibarbarous heritage, Ch'in had never been as saturated with Chou feudal customs as the central states, so that it must have been relatively easy for Ch'in, in the fourth century B.C., to be a leader in the general movement from serfdom to freehold farming. Finally, despite its ruthless reputation, Ch'in was attractive to emigrants from the war-torn central states because of its internal stability and security; and Ch'in welcomed immigrants to help develop its agriculture. Ch'in thus built a strong, stable agricultural base and accumulated abundant grain reserves. When its final campaigns to unify China began in the 230's B.C. Ch'in is estimated to have controlled one-third of all the land then under cultivation in China and one-third of China's total population.

Ch'in was also, and by far, the most aggressive of the contending states in attracting talented administrators from outside its borders, in part because, unlike other states, it did not hesitate to give them positions of responsibility and power. One of these, Kung-sun Yang from the neighbor state of Wei (often called Lord Shang), served as chief counselor at the Ch'in court from 356 to 338 B.C. and is given much credit for Ch'in's subsequent strength. He instituted and rigorously carried out Legalist policies, concentrating state efforts on improving agriculture and public order. He transformed serfs into tax-paying freehold farmers, instituted a centralized bureaucratic form of administration, grouped all families into small mutual-surveillance units, imposed harsh laws, and rewarded informers. Another emigré, Lü Pu-wei, originally a merchant in Honan, served Ch'in as chief counselor from 250 to 237 B.C. A subject of Ch'u named Li Ssu became an influential adviser at the Ch'in court in 237 and eventually, as chief counselor, was principal architect of the Legalist system that Ch'in imposed on all China after 221 B.C.

Chief credit for the Ch'in unification of China belongs to King Cheng, a vigorous and ambitious man who succeeded to the Ch'in throne in 247 and led Ch'in through its successive victories to the conquest of all China. He is known to history primarily by the epithet Ch'in Shih Huang-ti, that is, First Emperor of Ch'in. On becoming ruler of the whole Chinese world, he decided that king was no longer an appropriate title and devised a new one, Huang-ti, by combining two terms previously reserved for gods and mythical heroes. This title was used by subsequent rulers throughout imperial history; Westerners render it emperor. By calling himself First Emperor and ordaining that his successors should be called Second-generation Emperor, Third-generation Emperor, and so on, Shih Huang-ti demonstrated his confidence and that of his Legalist advisers in the endless self-perpetuation of the Legalist state machine they had created. Because his rule was harsh, because he persecuted Confucians whose intellectual descendants dominated subsequent history-writing, and because his policies ended in total failure almost immediately after his death in 210, the First Emperor appears in traditional Chinese history as a cruel and despicable tyrant. By any standard, he was not a model ruler. But he was a remarkable, powerful man who left his mark on Chinese history for all time and achieved what all Chinese considered a historical necessity, unification of the Chinese world.

The outstanding achievement of Ch'in as a national dynasty, which makes the short period of Ch'in supremacy a major watershed in Chinese history, was defeudalization—that is, centralization of Chinese government in a nonfeudal, nonhereditary, bureaucratic administration. All the old feudal states were abolished, and the Ch'in pattern of freehold farmers was extended throughout China. On the advice of his Legalist counselor Li Ssu, the First Emperor even avoided the employment of his sons and other relatives in government. The unified empire was divided into 36 (later 42) administrative districts called commanderies, and these were subdivided into counties, which have remained into our own time the basic units of Chinese local administration. Counties were responsible to commanderies, and commanderies were responsible to a central government at the Ch'in capital in Shensi under the direct supervision of the emperor.

Centralization called for and led to standardization. The regionalism that flourished in the last Chou centuries had been accompanied by diversification of such things as weights and measures, coinage, the axle widths of vehicles, and even script. The Ch'in government prescribed new, universal standards in all these realms and punished local innovators for treason.

Standardization of thought was an important goal in Legalist doctrine and in Ch'in policies. Philosophical thinking was considered detrimental to the efficient working and fighting that the state required of its subjects, and thinking could lead to treasonable questioning of state policies. The Ch'in state therefore prohibited philosophical disputation of the sort that had flourished in the Warring States era and particularly forbade any praising of the past or criticizing of the present. In 213 B.C. all writings other than official Ch'in historical chronologies and utilitarian treatises on divination, the practice of agriculture and medicine, and the like were collected for burning. All literature of the past was preserved in the imperial library for consultation by government authorities as required, but nowhere else. Because intellectuals found it hard to change their ways, the emperor in 212 B.C. reportedly executed 460 scholars and had them buried in a common grave as a warning against further defiance of his orders. Even the crown prince was not exempt from these strictures: he was banished to the northern frontier for protesting these policies.

Aggrandizement of the throne and the capital was another notable Ch'in policy, clearly related to the centralization of power. An elaborate, magnificent new palace was built for the emperor, and he repeatedly made grand tours of the empire, parading in great pomp to overawe his subjects. In 221, 219, and 213 B.C. wealthy or formerly noble families were moved from their homes throughout the empire to residences in the capital, in part so that they might be kept under careful surveillance and in part to add luster to the life of the capital. In one of these resettlement programs alone, some 120,000 families were reportedly transplanted. The construction of a great tomb for the First Emperor was begun in his lifetime on a lavish scale and at lavish cost, but with great secrecy. After his burial there it was widely rumored that hundreds of laborers and guards had been buried alive with him, and that ingenious devices had been installed to kill any intruder. The tomb was covered with a great mound that was made to resemble a natural hill.

Large-scale construction projects of other sorts were also undertaken. A network of roads 50 paces wide was built connecting the capital with every part of the empire so as to facilitate the First Emperor's inspection tours and give the imperial armies quick access to any trouble spot. Waterways were improved. The Ch'in official Li Ping constructed a marvelously engineered irrigation system in the Chengtu region of Szechwan that has been maintained in service up to the present time. Other Ch'in engineers constructed a canal that connected a Yangtze River tributary to rivers flowing south to modern Canton, facilitating the shipment of supplies to Ch'in armies in the far south. The Ch'in general Meng T'ien, who had been prominent in the wars of conquest, was set to work consolidating the walls the northern states had built for defense against northern nomads, thereby creating the famous Great Wall stretching from Kansu province in the west to the Pacific coast. This great engineering feat was achieved at a reported cost of the lives of one million laborers.

Such vast projects were made possible largely by harsh enforcement of Ch'in's all-embracing laws. Hundreds of thousands of subjects were

Fig. 2. Rubbing from a Han tomb relief sculpture illustrating an attempted assassination of the First Emperor of Ch'in prior to his unification of China. The emperor-to-be, on the right, holds aloft a jade disk symbol of royal authority. His attacker, on the left, has just thrown a dagger with such force that it has penetrated a pillar.

convicted and sentenced to forced labor. Other common punishments included such horrors as being branded, having one's nose or feet cut off, being buried alive, being boiled to death in a cauldron, and being torn apart by chariots tied to one's four limbs.

In addition to conquering the traditional Chinese world, now including the Yangtze River valley, Ch'in sent armies to subjugate the sprawling Yüeh state along the southern coasts. The campaign against Yüeh was difficult and prolonged, primarily because the Yüeh peoples learned not to oppose Ch'in forces in formal battle and relied on guerrilla tactics to keep Ch'in garrisons and administrative centers off balance and on the defensive. It was not until 210 B.C. that Ch'in considered the far south pacified. Even then, the Ch'in commanderies and counties on the south coast, nominally incorporating territories as distant as the Hanoi region of Vietnam, were little more than isolated outposts; the southern peoples were by no means assimilated or firmly controlled.

The First Emperor also sent armies campaigning northward into Inner Mongolia, where the first great confederation of Altaic-speaking nomads, the Hsiung-nu, was just forming. The Ch'in court was too preoccupied with consolidating its control of China Proper, however, to pursue a vigorously expansionist policy in the north. It was content to keep the Hsiung-nu out of raiding range, beyond the Great Wall that was coming into being.

In carrying out its pacification and centralization policies within China, the Ch'in government destroyed all city and other local walls that could have helped local separatist movements, and confiscated all weapons of war that were not needed by Ch'in's own armies. Surplus metal weapons were melted down and recast into huge cauldrons and monumental statues to adorn the First Emperor's new palace.

The First Emperor was a very superstitious person. After surviving three attempted assassinations, he became obsessed with the fear of death and began cultivating magicians, fortune-tellers, and alchemists who promised to produce for him elixirs of immortality. Administration was left largely in the hands of the counselor Li Ssu and an influential eunuch named Chao Kao. The emperor died in 210 B.C. while traveling in search of new elixirs, leaving a will that gave the throne to his banished eldest son. Li Ssu and Chao Kao suppressed news of the emperor's death, forged an edict ordering both the crown prince and the general Meng T'ien to commit suicide, and then produced a false will entrusting the empire to the late emperor's second son.

The Second-generation Emperor was a weakling who quickly fell under the complete dominance of Chao Kao. Chao intrigued against Li Ssu and soon had him imprisoned, tortured, and put to death. Then Chao poisoned the Second-generation Emperor in 207 and enthroned a son of the late crown prince, who soon managed to have Chao put to death. But by this time the empire was in a state of collapse, and at the very beginning of 206 the king (who had apparently not dared take the title emperor) surrendered to rebels.

It is ironic that Ch'in was undone by the harshness of its laws, in which the Legalists put such faith. The spark that set Ch'in's empire aflame with rebellion was struck by a commoner of the Ch'u region named Ch'en She. Put in charge of a group of draftees mustered for service on the northern frontier, Ch'en was delayed by heavy rains and realized that his contingent would miss its prescribed rendezvous with similar groups. Under Ch'in law, the penalties for such minor lapses were severe, and no extenuating circumstances were considered. Ch'en persuaded his small following that they might as well be outlaws as convicts. They became a robber band, and Ch'en grandiosely proclaimed himself king of Ch'u. To his surprise, thousands of malcontents rallied to his support, and similar uprisings occurred throughout the empire.

Ch'in generals rushed hither and thither trying to quell the ever-spreading rebellions, and though they caught and executed Ch'en She, the uprisings grew beyond their control. Knowing well what punishments awaited them for their failures, the generals began defecting and joining the rebel cause. A great coalition of rebels emerged, nominally giving allegiance to a scion of the old Ch'u ruling family. One army of this coalition entered Shensi and occupied the Ch'in capital in 207-206 B.C. Then, with Ch'in disposed of and unlamented, the rebels began quarreling among themselves. China was plunged once more into chaotic civil war among rival contenders for control of the disintegrated empire.

2. State and Society

To a degree seldom approached in other civilizations, the Chinese have been spellbound by their conceptions about "the ways of antiquity." Throughout imperial history—and even into the present—Chinese involved in public affairs have based their proposals and arguments about how things should be on the way things were, supposedly, in antiquity. This tendency, which was already evident in the oldest times, was strengthened because so very little factual information survived from the formative age. The endemic, destructive wars of the late Chou centuries, the confiscation and burning of books by the Ch'in dynasty, and the renewed civil wars that brought Ch'in down, in which the imperial palace and its well-stocked library were destroyed, wiped out much of China's accumulated writings about the past. Later scholars and statesmen were wont to fill gaps in the record with speculations that were shaped to serve the purposes of their own times and circumstances. What has been written about the formative age by later Chinese, generation after generation, consequently fills rooms, if not whole buildings. But questions about the authenticity and reliability of writings surviving from the formative age itself arose soon after the Ch'in collapse and have troubled scholars ever since. Whole works attributed to the pre-Ch'in age have been denounced as later fabrications. Some texts that are generally accepted exist in variant versions, and others have sections that are considered late interpolations.

Detailed information about governmental operations and social usages in the early Chou period is provided in two works that were traditionally believed to have been written by the Duke of Chou in the twelfth or eleventh century B.C. The *Chou-li* (Chou Rituals), notwithstanding its title, is a description of governmental organization; the *I-li* (Propriety and Ritual) is something like a book of etiquette for court gentlemen. Specialists generally believe that neither could actually have been written before the fourth or third century B.C.; the works seem to be attempted reconstructions in the chaotic Warring States era of what things must have been like, or should have been like, many centuries earlier. They cannot be relied on to reflect the conditions of the times in either the early Chou or the Warring States era, though they can be used by specialists to throw some light on aspects of both periods. Unfortunately, archaeological remains such as inscriptions on early Chou bronze vessels, while exposing the general unreliability of such texts, do not in themselves provide sufficient details for full reconstruction.

The student of history is thus forced to consider the political, social, and economic institutions of the formative age—the matrix from which later institutions developed—from two points of view. On one hand, it is important to try to understand what actually happened, and how and why it happened. On the other hand, it must always be kept in mind that traditional Chinese accepted such texts as the *I-li* and *Chou-li* as reliable descriptions surviving from a golden age of social stability and good government in the remote past—as evidence of those "ways of antiquity" that they felt obliged to emulate. What they believed was true of antiquity, whether it was objectively true or not in the light of modern scholarship, was always a force in the shaping and reshaping of institutions throughout Chinese history.

GOVERNMENT

By the end of the formative age the major tensions that were to characterize Chinese governance thereafter had been clearly exemplified. China had experienced extremes of centralized and decentralized government, and it had been governed by a hereditary nobility and a nonhereditary bureaucracy. Its accumulated experience provided no acceptable, stable resolution of such polarities but yielded a number of guiding principles that most later Chinese accepted without question.

Organizational structure. The *Chou-li* does not purport to describe governmental organization in China during Shang and earlier times. On the basis of archaeological remains and intimations in early writings, we can do little more than assume that in prehistoric China hunting leaders and warrior chiefs exercised their powers with minimal, ad hoc organizational apparatus, but it is quite evident that Shang China developed a fairly sophisticated governmental system to cope with the size of the state and the complexity of its activities. Shang oracle bone inscriptions abound in titles, but not in data about the functions associated with them. The abundance of identifiable titles nevertheless suggests that the Shang central administration was relatively large and recognized the principle of functional differentiation. By Shang's Yin stage, moreover, there were at least 25 outlying localities or regions that were administered on the king's behalf. Although the administrators bore titles that later, in Chou times, identified feudal lords, the Shang monarchs thought of their state as a centralized one. Oracle bones frequently make reference to the conduct of "my affairs" and the naming of persons "to assist me" in particular governmental activities, and the Shang kings clearly accepted responsibility for defense of rather distant frontiers and for punitive expeditions against rather distant "barbarians." Since eminent title-holders, whether in the central administration or the outlying regions, were all members of a privileged class of hereditary nobles, the Shang state can reasonably be considered a centralized monarchy with strong feudalistic characteristics.

What the *Chou-li* and other late idealizations ascribe to the early Chou era is an elaborate form of centralized feudalism. By these accounts, regional states were graded in proportion to their size and distance from the royal capital, the regional lords had administrative staffs whose size and functions were prescribed by the king, and the king entrusted the central administration to six dignitaries: a minister of heaven, responsible for general policy recommendations; a minister of earth, responsible for education; a minister of spring, responsible for court rituals; a minister of summer, responsible for routine administration; a minister of autumn, responsible for punishments; and a minister of winter, responsible for logistical aspects of government, including large work projects. Each minister supposedly had a prescribed staff of hundreds of subordinates, carefully graded in rank and with responsibilities minutely differentiated. Whereas the king reportedly controlled six armies, the regional states had three, two, or one in proportion to their rank and size; similarly, in contrast to the six ministers who served the king, regional lords were served by three, two, or one.

As a matter of historical fact, the early Chou government seems to have been centralized in conception and, somewhat weakly, in aspects of actual administration. All regional lords originated as appointees of the king, and they remained such at least nominally until almost the very end of the dynasty. In relation to the royal court, they were more independent than later prefects and county magistrates but something less than viceroys—certainly not the autonomous territorial rulers that they became by the middle Chou centuries. The lords were assigned to (and later, inherited) fiefs called *kuo*, a graph depicting a walled and guarded area. The term refers both to the fortified town where the lord resided and to the surrounding territory that the town dominated. Lordly titles were used so indiscriminately that there could not have been a clear rank order among them. However, the small "central states" (*chung-kuo*, which late in history came to mean China as a whole, the Middle Kingdom) of the Chou heartland were the most cultured and prestigious.

The power of the early kings over the regional lords was manifested in several ways. The lords were expected to visit the royal court in demonstration of their loyalty, probably at prescribed intervals; to submit symbolic tribute as well as substantive revenues; and to provide military support for the king on request. Their heirs had to be confirmed by the king. Their fiefs were visited by royal inspectors, who in some instances remained as long-term residents. Regional lords who were remiss in submitting revenues were rebuked, and royal agents were sent out to expedite the payment of arrearages. The lords had limited military responsibilities; their main task, it appears, was to maintain local order. Defense of the whole Chinese realm was recognized, as in Shang times, to be the king's responsibility, and standing armies under his control were garrisoned throughout the country— supported, no doubt, by revenues collected from nearby lords. According to tradition, there were 14 of these royal armies, six based in the Chou homeland in the west and eight scattered over the eastern plain. Frontier wars against non-Chinese "barbarians" were fought by the king's armies hundreds of miles from the royal capital, often under his personal command. The unchallenged early Chou doctrine was that "all land is the king's land, and all people are the king's subjects."

Officials of the royal Chou court, and of each feudal lord on a lesser scale, fell into two categories, the more prestigious known collectively as ministers (*ch'ing*) and great officers (*ta-fu*), the others as plain warrior-officials (*shih*). They bore a bewildering variety of titles, sometimes held several titles concurrently, and sometimes performed duties having no discernible relevance to their titles. In short, there was no highly sophisticated, hierarchical differentiation among them of the sort described in the *Chou-li*.

These early Chou patterns of governance endured into the Spring and Autumn and the Warring States eras, though real authority passed to regional lords after the eighth century B.C. and government offices proliferated and became more specialized. Governance remained highly personal in its style. In 536 B.C., the central state of Cheng promulgated a complete code of laws, the first to be mentioned in Chinese history. It was cast in bronze for all to see, despite vigorous arguments by ministers at the Cheng court that the code would confuse the people and tempt them into wrongdoing. This was perhaps the beginning of the trend toward centralizing and bureaucratizing authority within states, increasing efficiency and production, and standardizing administrative procedures that culminated in the conquest of all China by the Legalist-inspired state of Ch'in, which undertook to make government not only impersonal but mechanistically automatic.

The organizational transformation wrought by Ch'in has two major aspects: (1) the emergence of a clear tripartite division of governmental functions and (2) the division of China into centrally controlled administrative districts rather than feudal fiefs. It should not be supposed that a new kind of government burst on the Chinese scene suddenly and full-blown with the Ch'in unification. States had been creating new administrative structures and policies that foreshadowed the Ch'in imperial system throughout the last half of the Chou dynasty under the leadership of able reform ministers such as Kuan Chung in seventh-century Ch'i, Shen Pu-hai in fourth-century Han, and Kung-sun Yang in fourth-century Ch'in. Many elements of the new design seem traceable to the great southern state of Ch'u, which enjoyed remarkable stability in its royal family and its ministerial ranks even in the Warring States era and was renowned at the time for its effective administration. But it was King Cheng of Ch'in (later First Emperor) and his adviser Li Ssu who brought selected new elements together into an integrated, well-articulated governmental system applicable to the whole of China. They were ahead of their time. China was not yet ready, psychologically or sociologically, for so sophisticated a system to succeed. However, Ch'in established the organizational standards that successive dynastic governments were to strive to realize.

Ch'in's tripartite division of governmental operations was reflected in the organization of its central government. The most prominent office was that of chief counselor (*ch'eng-hsiang*); there was provision for two such officials, one "of the left" and one "of the right." The chief counselors were charged with general administrative supervision and had a staff of subordinate secretarial aides who processed documents. Military affairs were under the jurisdiction of a grand marshal (*t'ai-wei*); his principal duty was to aid the emperor in directing four generals (*chiang-chün*), whose commands were differentiated by the locational designations front, rear, left, and right. The third top-echelon ministerial office was that of censor-in-chief (*yü-shih ta-fu*); he assisted the chief counselors and supervised a staff of investigating censors, who were expected to keep all governmental activities under surveillance and to impeach wayward officials. A host of lesser offices had charge of palace maintenance, imperial ceremonies, imperial carriages and horses, governmental treasuries, capital and palace guards, and the like, presumably under the supervision of either the chief counselors or the grand marshal.

There were two levels of regional and local administrative units that replaced the traditional feudal fiefs. The higher echelon consisted of commanderies (*chün*). The term has a clear military denotation, but administration of each commandery seems to have been shared by a civil governor and a military governor, and all commanderies were occasionally inspected by touring investigating censors. These units, which increased in number from an initial 36 to a final 42, were subdivided into counties (*hsien*) and coordinated county-level administration in accordance with policies emanating from the central government. County magistrates were all-purpose local representatives of the emperor. The Chinese subsequently designated this form of centrally controlled local administration a *chün-hsien* system, in contrast to decentralized, feudalistic systems, which are called *feng-chien*, two terms that were used separately in Chou times with the sense of to enfeoff.

Personnel. The transition from decentralization to centralization in governmental organization was accompanied by a decisive change in the character of governmental personnel. In the Chou system, as in the Shang state, the ruling class consisted of a hereditary elite: not only ministers and great officers, but ordinary warrior-officials as well, comprised a nobility that monopolized office-holding. They were compensated for service with grants of manors, in a subinfeudation process. Many particular offices passed directly from father to son. There is no reliable evidence, however, about details of personnel administration in Chou times.

As has been noted in Chapter 1, the political and social ferment of the last Chou centuries thoroughly undermined the principle of heredity, and Ch'in put into practice a nonhereditary, bureaucratic system of personnel management. All members of the governmental staff, including the executives of the commanderies and counties and perhaps lesser functionaries as well, were considered imperial appointees serving at the emperor's pleasure. Inheritance of office was specifically renounced. Persons were recruited for service largely at the recommendation of officials already on duty, and there was some means of certifying the qualifications of proposed candidates, though there is no evidence that formal written examinations were used this early. All officials were subject to merit evaluations, and were promoted, demoted, or dismissed in accordance with the assessment of their performance. If an appointee did not serve well, those who had recommended him for service were blamed, but how systematically they were made to share the punishments of their protégés is not clear.

In addition to regular civil and military officials, eunuchs played prominent roles in Ch'in times, as under many later dynasties. In Chinese practice extending back into the Chou era, eunuchs were created by the total removal of the external genitals, usually as a state punishment; and they then became personal attendants of the rulers and their harems of consorts and concubines. Ordinarily, no uncastrated male beyond the ruler's immediate family was ever permitted inside the residential quarters of a Chinese palace. A eunuch consequently had unequaled opportunities to win a ruler's favor by catering to his private needs and whims, and once in favor, eunuchs found it easy to insinuate themselves into influential roles even in government—as confidential adviser to the ruler if nothing more. The regular officialdom distrusted and resented palace eunuchs as interlopers who were not subject to any normal bureaucratic constraints; yet officials often had no alternative, especially in dealing with notably strong and notably weak rulers, but to tolerate and even make allies of eunuchs in the interest of orderly administration. The unstable and eventually disruptive alliance in Ch'in times between the eunuch Chao Kao and the chief counselor Li Ssu foreshadowed "eunuch troubles" that recurred in the imperial ages to follow.

Some general principles. Of the assumptions and beliefs about government that had become widespread in China by Ch'in times, none is more noteworthy than what is called the doctrine of the Mandate of Heaven (*t'ien-ming*). This is rooted in religious notions introduced into the Chinese mainstream by the Chou peoples: that the cosmos is dominated by an impersonal but all-powerful Heaven (*t'ien*), that no man rules except by the Mandate of Heaven, and that the ruler is entrusted with responsibility for "all under Heaven" (*t'ien-hsia*). It is this last term that the Chinese traditionally used when referring to their country as a whole; outsiders usually render it as the empire. The Chou king (and every subsequent ruler) was commonly spoken of as the Son of Heaven, though there was no implication that he was a living deity.

The Duke of Chou tirelessly lectured the conquered Shang peoples about the Mandate of Heaven, telling them that the Chou leaders had no selfish wish to aggrandize or glorify themselves by attacking Shang but had no choice in the matter once Heaven commanded them to punish Shang. He advised the newly subjugated peoples to abide by Heaven's decision and pointed out to them firmly that he was prepared to make them do so if need be. The Duke of Chou understood, and emphasized to the young king for whom he acted as regent, the double-edged implications of the new doctrine. Chou could not retain its primacy, he warned, unless its kings conscientiously ruled in such fashion as to remain in Heaven's good graces, and to do that they must rule fairly and benevolently. Thenceforth no Chinese ruler was invulnerable to challenge, and any challenger proved the validity of his claim merely by succeeding. Changes of dynasty were thus not complicated by legalistic quibbles over legitimacy. The doctrine of the Mandate of Heaven was solidly established before many decades had passed, and it remained thereafter the cornerstone of all Chinese political theory.

Other principles that had been firmly established by Ch'in times were:

1. The Chinese world should be united under a single Son of Heaven, and his control should be effectively centralized.

2. In order to govern well, rulers need and should heed capable, wise ministerial advisers. This doctrine was asserted vigorously by the Duke of Chou; failure to heed his officials was one of the great offenses ascribed to the last Shang king in early Chou writings. Officials and influence-seeking intellectuals of the late Chou centuries, Confucians and Legalists alike, quite naturally supported this idea, and the increasingly deafening chorus made it a cardinal principle of Chinese governance.

3. Government exists to provide peace and order. In the Warring

States situation, the immediate goal of many rulers and statesmen was victory in war, to be sure. But it was not common after Shang for Chinese to glorify martial exploits; men were most praised for their non-military virtues. From the early Chou decades there existed a clear, forcefully stated and reiterated concept that Heaven willed mankind to live together in harmonious cooperation and in harmony with the cosmic universe. It was the responsibility of the Son of Heaven to see that such a condition was achieved.

4. Government should be humane and paternalistic, giving a high priority to fostering the welfare of the people. This paternalistic aspect of traditional Chinese governance is often ascribed to the influence of Confucian thinkers of the late Chou centuries, and they did indeed emphasize it. But the concept was proclaimed at the beginning of the Chou dynasty, perhaps as a pragmatic propaganda device to appease and conciliate the subjugated peoples, whom the Chou rulers could not expect to keep under control by military force alone. It was accepted that "Heaven sees and hears as the people see and hear"—that Heaven's favor or disfavor manifested itself in public opinion. The hard realities of politics in the Warring States era lent new significance to this ancient credo. Intense interstate competition forced rulers to treat their people well lest they defect and migrate. Realizing that morale was as great a source of strength as wealth and arms, some Warring States rulers manipulated tax remissions, amnesties, and public entertainments with the shrewdness of modern politicians. Ch'in, after its victory, neglected popular welfare; the fact that its empire soon disintegrated only strengthened the old conviction anew. The founding emperors of later dynasties were often reminded, "You may have conquered the empire on horseback, but you cannot govern it on horseback." Ruthlessness always had to be masked as benevolence.

5. The scope of government was all-encompassing. As Sons of Heaven, the rulers of China in Chou and later times were considered wholly responsible for whatever happened "under Heaven." It followed that peace and order could not be their sole concern. Indeed, even if the country prospered, their duty was not discharged; morality had to be ensured as well. Thus what modern Westerners think of as welfare-state ideas were commonly preached, accepted, and put into practice in Chou China. The ruler was administrator, military leader, judge, manager of the economy, priest, educator, and moral exemplar. His responsibility was total. Accordingly, his authority had to be unlimit-

ed; and the Chinese polity came to be organized in such a way that the ruler's authority was totalitarian in practice, in the sense that no aspect of life was considered immune to his control, should he choose to exert it.

SOCIETY

Two fundamental aspects of traditional Chinese social organization that matured in the formative age are (1) the conception that the patrilineal family is the basic cohesive unit in society and that blood kinship is the social tie of highest importance, and (2) the conception that members of society are naturally and properly differentiated in classes that are honored and rewarded in proportion to the value of their contributions to society.

How early the familistic patterns and ideals described in the Introduction came into existence in China is not clear. The importance of kinship is reflected early in history by the practice of ancestor worship by the Shang and Chou ruling families and by numerous historical anecdotes. In the late sixth or early fifth century B.C., for example, when a man from an outlying region bragged that his countrymen were so public-spirited they would inform on their own fathers, Confucius, a native of the Chou heartland, responded that his own countrymen were so virtuous they would do their utmost to conceal their fathers' offenses.

Through the Chou dynasty the nuclear family was apparently the basic organizational unit among commoners. But among the nobility of the early Chou centuries the social unit that mattered most was the larger common descent group. Great care was taken to differentiate between men of direct royal descent and those of collateral and unrelated clans. As time passed and the population grew and scattered, emphasis naturally shifted to lineages—the different branches of the larger clans. By the Spring and Autumn era the lineage was the predominant social unit and had great political influence. One spoke, for example, of the Sung (state) lineage of the Chi (surname) clan, much as Americans today might speak of their Johnson friends in Ohio and their Johnson friends in California. In the Spring and Autumn era clans were well-organized groups whose heads controlled clan affairs, spoke for the clans, and inherited clan properties and official privileges. At this point, the power of the clans often rivaled that of the great regional lords. It was among such clans that the powerful northern state of Chin was divided in the fifth century B.C., and it was clan heads who thereafter commonly deposed regional lords or assumed dictatorial regencies over them.

The clans effectively shattered themselves in the prolonged, destructive wars of the Warring States era, and what power they retained was blotted out in the Ch'in unification of the country. Clan organization or anything resembling it was anathema both in Legalist principle and in Ch'in practice. Ch'in even attacked small-scale extended families by doubling taxes on households where more than two mature sons lived with parents; its aim was to fragment society into nuclear family units, which could not hope to oppose state authority. Moreover, Ch'in organized families on nonkinship lines into mutual-surveillance, mutual-responsibility teams of fives and tens, to establish loyalty to the state as the supreme value.

Meantime, however, such works as the *I-li* had come into existence, obviously idealizing the clan dominance of society in the Spring and Autumn era and projecting their idealizations back to the founding of the Chou dynasty. Despite all Ch'in's efforts, the classic principles of family organization and family loyalty described above had become an ineradicable part of the mainstream of China's social development.

The late traditional view was that Chinese society comprised four classes of people, ranked according to their social value as follows: scholar-officials, farmers, artisans, and merchants. Several things are noteworthy about this categorization. It exalts government service above all other occupations and accords no place or prestige to groups that cannot be clearly related to government interests, such as religious devotees or public entertainers. It exalts scholastic achievement but co-opts intellectuals automatically into government service. The extent to which the classes were rigidly exclusive and self-perpetuating was arguable in theory and varied in practice: upward mobility between the farming class and the scholar-official class was seldom discouraged and often encouraged; but status as an artisan and particularly as a merchant was usually disesteemed and often inescapable. Farming was exalted as the essential productive contribution to life (the "root" activity), but craft and mercantile occupations were unessential, unproductive, and frivolous ("branch" activities), and mercantile activities in particular were considered exploitive and demeaning. It is noteworthy that the stratification scheme attributes no social value to wealth or military valor, except as they might be coincidental to status as a scholar-official. The scheme reflects the conservative, agrarian-oriented

Confucian value system that was theoretically paramount throughout most of China's imperial history, and it also reflects strong state-oriented interests.

As in the case of the extended family ideal, the degree to which this stratification scheme resembled reality at any point in Chinese history is questionable; society changed over time. But the scheme developed to full maturity in the formative age, and behind it lie some interesting historical mutations regarding the rigidity of class differentiations, the openness of society to the movement of individuals from one class to another, and the criteria by which social value was measured.

It is credible that, as modern Communist historians commonly insist, the migratory peoples of China's prehistory who mixed hunting and herding with primitive transient farming had a tribal, egalitarian social structure. But archaeological discoveries, particularly of burials, suggest that status differentiation steadily intensified from Yang-shao into Lung-shan times as communities became more settled and agrarian, and that the society of Shang China was sharply stratified in three groups. The dominant group was an elite class of chariot-riding warriors principally including the royal family. These were hereditary nobles or aristocrats who no doubt served as officials but who can have had little interest in scholarship or culture. Living under their dominance were commoners, including artisans and peasants, about whose social relationships almost nothing is known, and slaves, who were numerous and whose status was clearly that of chattels. Slaves were in large part war captives; some were probably convicted criminals. They are sometimes depicted toiling in fields or craft workshops with leashes around their necks, under the control of whip-wielding overseers.

The Shang practice of sacrificial burial illustrates the great gap that must have existed between the nobility and the lower classes. Evidence of sacrificial burials has been found under the foundations of buildings and altars at An-yang and, most abundantly, in the royal Shang tombs (Fig. 3). More than 2,000 victims have been unearthed, more than 200 of them in one tomb alone. Some victims were apparently buried alive; others had been decapitated, and their heads and bodies buried separately. There could have been only random, minimal opportunities for upward mobility in such a society. Since polygamy was prevalent among the nobility, and since the Shang state could hardly have supported a steadily multiplying leisure class, at least some offspring of the

Fig. 3. Above: Shang tomb under excavation at An-yang, showing the central burial chamber and two of the four ramps leading into it. Below: skeletons unearthed in a Shang tomb.

nobility and even of royalty must have slipped regularly into commoner status.

In general, Shang patterns of social stratification were perpetuated by the Chou conquerors, except that slavery was less prominent throughout the Chou dynasty than it had been in Shang times. In the early Chou reigns, as could be expected in any conquest situation, social mobility was far from uncommon, both upward and downward. Especially because of the new emphasis on primogeniture, younger sons of upper-class families may have slipped into commoner status more easily than their Shang counterparts had.

After the early Chou decades, social status became more rigidly heredity-bound. It became customary, not merely for kings to confirm an heir in his father's fief, but for kings and regional lords alike to grant new fiefs with accompanying inheritance rights. By the Spring and Autumn era almost all offices of significance were monopolized by clans, were occupied for life, and were transmitted hereditarily. Meantime commoners had stabilized in the role of land-bound serfs, working manorial fields for their overlords and being transferred with the land with every new enfeoffment. Artisans carried on their specialized work in the fortified towns where the nobility resided and probably enjoyed higher status and greater social privileges than the peasantry. As the population grew, a merchant class gradually appeared in a relatively autonomous status, outside the rigid feudal hierarchy but not disesteemed. Merchants were information-bearers who were to be tolerated and even patronized; some regional lords used them as diplomatic spies.

The intensification of war in the Spring and Autumn era and then the Warring States era totally undermined the rigid feudal order, as has been noted in Chapter 1. Ability counted for more and more, inherited status for less and less. There was rapid turnover in ministerial offices, and by the third century B.C. the great clans that had monopolized such offices in Spring and Autumn times were hardly even represented in them. Serfs were becoming freehold farmers, and merchants were becoming wealthy and powerful. The commoner Shen Pu-hai served as chief counselor of the state of Han from 351 to 337, the merchant Lü Pu-wei served as chief counselor of Ch'in for many years until ousted in 237 and driven to suicide in 235, and there were many others like them. Social status had become fluid and transitory. When Ch'in unified China in 221 B.C., it deliberately destroyed traditional patterns of social stratification. It is not clear to what extent society outside Ch'in had already become open—rapid mobility had surely eroded class barriers everywhere—but Ch'in finished the job. Its policy of granting status and rewards solely on the basis of individual achievement, counting heredity for nothing, created an open social situation that not only was unprecedented but was probably never achieved again in China.

The official class deserves special attention here because it is in relation to this class that the criteria of social value were most notably transformed in Chou times. The Chinese term shih apparently originated as a general designation for able-bodied young men. By the mid-Chou period it meant more specifically a fighting man, and later writers used it to apply to the aristocratic warrior elite of Shang as well as early Chou times. Since these chariot-riding warriors had aided the Shang and Chou kings in governing, the term came to have the dual meaning of warrior-official. During the social upheavals that culminated in the Warring States period, these functions drifted apart: generals and ministers were no longer necessarily interchangeable. The term shih attached itself increasingly to the meaning "official," and philosophers of the Warring States era borrowed it to apply to the emerging intellectual elite. It was in this transition that the shih was accorded social primacy, the term having been shorn of the hereditary and military senses that had earlier been of its essence. Depending on context, shih now meant official or intellectual. Although the full maturing of the term into the sense scholar-official was yet to come, achievement rather than pedigree, and increasingly nonmilitary achievement in particular, had already attained preeminence among the criteria that measured social value.

It is noteworthy, finally, that merchants, whose social status had risen dramatically during the Warring States era, were condemned as a class by the Ch'in dynasty. Ch'in, esteeming only war and agriculture, considered mercantile activities unproductive and disruptive of state order. It was the Ch'in policy to gather up merchants along with vagrants and other undesirables to serve as colonists on the far south coast.

THE ECONOMY

Out of the mixed hunting-herding-farming life of neolithic times the Chinese gradually developed into a settled, agrarian people; the transition was well under way in the Shang period and was completed in the

Chou dynasty, when technological advances stimulated the expansion and intensification of agriculture. Farming villages clustered ever more populously around walled towns from which regional lords ruled their territories, and in the towns craft production and trade became ever more specialized and diversified. In both towns and countryside, feudal economic relationships gradually changed into free ownership and entrepreneurship, and there were the beginnings of a money economy.

Agrarian development. Unlike the United States and much of Western Europe, China is not richly endowed with arable land. Modern China Proper, approximately the extent of the continental United States, is not a small territory; even the China of Chou times was a considerably larger territory than modern France. But China has much more topographic variety than either the United States or France, and even in late imperial times only about 20 per cent of the total Chinese land surface was under regular cultivation. The steady expansion of the Chinese people and their agrarian way of life was therefore not a sprawling out over a vast plain such as the American Midwest. It was a hopping from one settlement area to another, scattered in valleys or on small plains. Between these areas are unsettled, uncultivated hilly regions or marshlands.

This kind of topography lends itself naturally to a compartmented, manor-like pattern of agricultural organization, and both written traditions and archaeological discoveries suggest that it was in manorial settlements that the early Chinese organized themselves, certainly in Chou times and probably in the preceding Shang period. Population and the agrarian economy expanded as regional lords gained control over scattered pockets of aboriginal settlers or drove aborigines away and replaced them with millet- and wheat-planting colonists.

One of the most influential traditions handed down from the Warring States era is the notion that in the early Chou golden age agriculture was organized in what is called the well-field (*ching-t'ien*) system. The name comes from the Chinese graph meaning a well (*ching*), which is a ticktacktoe design defining nine equal areas. It was reported that early Chou manors were laid out in that pattern, with eight families of serfs living in the central plot (which presumably had a well) and working it communally to provide revenue for the overlord, and with each family working one of the eight surrounding plots to provide for its own needs. So neat a land-tenure and taxation scheme is obviously an idealization and could never have been widespread. But the scheme is so simple and appealing that every agrarian reformer of Chinese history from the time of Christ into the twentieth century has been inspired by it, and utopian thinkers have given it credit for the equitable harmoniousness that they ascribe to the golden age. Whether or not it even faintly resembles the manorial system that must have existed in early Chou times, no doubt in many local variations, is simply not known.

What is known, and what has been repeatedly emphasized in the preceding pages, is that whatever sorts of feudal manors did exist in early Chou times did not survive the wars and general social turbulence of the last Chou centuries. Feudal serfdom gave way to freehold farming. The transition was completed in the Ch'in unification of China and Ch'in's attempted standardization of Chinese life in all its aspects. The Ch'in ideal was a classless society of tax-paying, service-rendering farmer-soldiers who could rise and fall in state favor, and thus in economic status, in accordance with their individual achievements—in agriculture or in war. The change produced a classic land-tenure problem that plagued economic planners throughout the remainder of Chinese history into our own times. In a society of freehold farmers, some prosper and some do not. The prosperous become landlords, the luckless become tenants, and all sorts of inequities and exploitive situations arise, provoking discontent and rebellion. Whether large-scale landlordism and widespread tenant-farmer distress existed in Ch'in times and contributed to the rapid Ch'in collapse is not clear; but such problems were to loom large very soon.

The population growth and increasing agricultural production of Chou times can be attributed in part to territorial expansion, but the intensification of agriculture after the middle Chou centuries must also be taken into account. Water-control projects such as diking would seem natural and inevitable in the Chinese geographic setting and may have been part of the Shang scene, though available evidence is not persuasive on this point. Systematic irrigation appeared in mid-Chou times and thereafter became steadily more common. Fertilization became common in the same period, as did field rotation, which regularly left some fields fallow to regain their productive capabilities. After mid-Chou times, also, animal-drawn plows came into use. Next to irrigation, however, the most important technological development in agriculture of the whole Chou epoch was probably the introduction of iron farm implements in the fifth century B.C. These not only made plowing more effective, but also facilitated the clearing of new ground for cultivation. By the end of the Chou dynasty, in these various ways, the essential technological elements of traditional Chinese farming had fully matured, to be further refined in the succeeding ages.

As a corollary of the steady development of an agrarian economy, hunting and herding became steadily less important aspects of Chinese life in the formative age. As late as Shang times, cattle, sheep, and goats contributed importantly to the economy, but by the end of the Chou dynasty expanding agriculture left no room, literally, for grazing herds, and the Chinese had settled into the scavenger-breeding patterns that characterized them subsequently: animal husbandry concentrated on plow oxen, pigs, and chickens. Hunting had similarly declined in economic importance. The great hunting expeditions in which Shang and early Chou nobles had engaged, partly for sport and military practice but no doubt partly also to provide food, had faded into dim memories by late Chou times, and thereafter hunting was a negligible factor in the Chinese economy.

Commercial development. From a remarkably early time the Chinese traded on some basis with the other developing peoples of continental East Asia. In the Shang period commodities were used that must have come to the North China heartland—and in such quantity that there must have been a regular supply channel—from the distant southwest (the tin for Shang bronzes) and the far southern coasts of the South China Sea (cowry shells and certain kinds of turtleshells). During the Chou dynasty, and particularly in its last centuries, craft production and both local and interregional commerce developed substantially. Those advances are evidenced particularly in the development of iron technology, the growth of cities, and the use of money.

Iron deposits are found in many localities throughout China, and their exploitation began not later than the fifth century B.C. Iron rapidly became sufficiently abundant that it was used in the manufacture of farm tools as well as weapons. Both iron-tipped wooden tools and fully iron tools were made, in types that were remarkably uniform throughout the country. Great smelters reportedly employed more than 200 workmen, and ironmongers were prominent among the rising new class of rich merchants. What is more, the Chinese of the Warring States era knew how to make cast iron—a full millennium before cast iron replaced wrought iron in Europe. All iron implements that have been found in Warring States excavations are of cast iron, not wrought;

and deposits of hundreds of molds for iron casting have been unearthed. Iron tools of the formative age are not very sturdy and did not wholly replace bronze, wood, or still more primitive tools even in the most densely populated areas; but the iron revolution had a solid beginning, and the making and selling of iron wares had become a big business by early Chinese standards.

Pre-Shang neolithic settlements, though in some cases quite large, can hardly be thought of as towns or cities. The Shang cities whose remains have been discovered were notably more advanced, being multifunctional settlements that served as administrative centers, religious centers, and in some measure craft centers. This pattern was also characteristic of the early Chou cities, which were walled forts occupied by regional lords together with their noble adherents and such artisans as they required. The cities remained essentially administrative and religious centers. But in the Spring and Autumn era, and more intensively in the Warring States era, cities began to grow as industrial and commercial centers. Early Chinese records indicate that 11 cities were considered very large in the Warring States period. Their size is best suggested by the only population estimate dating from that age, which indicates that there were 70,000 households resident in the Ch'i capital, Lin-tzu in modern Shantung province, and that its streets bustled with traffic. Public amusements were provided, and specialized craftsmen offered their shoes, clothing, tools, and other products in shops and markets, for which designated areas of Warring States cities were set aside. Wholesale brokers in grain and salt reportedly kept a sharp eye on price fluctuations in the city markets.

Money became a significant factor in the expanding Chinese economy. Barter was the general basis of economic life throughout the whole formative era; even centuries later official salaries, among other things, were defined and partly paid in grain. But by the late Chou years money was the basis on which large-scale interregional commerce developed. The earliest known monetary units used by the Chinese were cowry shells, which Shang and early Chou kings presented as rewards to their followers in decimal units, tied together on strings. In the early Chou period standardized bolts of silk and graduated amounts of grain began to be used as common units of exchange. Jade, pearls, pieces of metal, leather, dogs, and horses were often used as kinds of commodity money.

Fig. 4. Inscribed coins of the Warring States period. Top: knife money. Bottom, left to right: round coin with square hole, spade money, round coin with round hole.

Cast metal coins came into use not later than the fifth century B.C., apparently produced first by private merchants to simplify their inter-regional dealings. Soon the regional states were producing official coins of bronze (Fig. 4). The earliest bronze coins fall into two categories of shapes called spade coins and knife coins because they were minia-ture reproductions of these tools. Most bore inscriptions identifying the cities, and later the states, that issued them, and they were pro-duced in various denominations, sizes, and weights. The wide circula-tion of such coins is evidenced by the hoards of coins from all areas of China that have been found in some excavated Warring States sites, and the abundance of coins in use is indicated by Ch'in's once offering a reward of one million coins for the capture of a renegade. Supple-menting the prevalent knife coins and spade coins, Ch'in introduced round coins with square holes in the middle, suitable for stringing on cords; and such coins, weighing about half an ounce, were made stan-dard for all China after the Ch'in unification. Eventually, a string of 1,000 of these coins became a standard monetary unit, theoretically equal in value to one bushel of grain or one standard bolt of silk.

The governmental, social, and economic changes of the formative age naturally triggered, intensified, and shaped each other, and after the early Chou centuries the pace of change accelerated steadily. In the Warring States era especially, the institutional patterns of Chinese life were unstable and fluid to a degree that the Chinese were not to experience again until our own time. Thinking men such as many of those discussed in Chapter 3 obviously thought their world was collapsing into chaos; nothing approaching an acceptable normalcy could be foreseen. But from the fifth through the third century B.C. the Chinese were in fact building, testing, and rebuilding new institutional frameworks that would make the following imperial order an enduring one.

3. Thought

O F THE MANY forces that have shaped and reshaped Chinese civilization over the centuries, none was more profoundly influential than the native ideological traditions that developed during the formative age. The political and social turmoil of the last Chou dynasty centuries in particular stimulated Chinese to philosophical reflection. Their attention was attracted, not toward grand speculations about Truth or other abstractions, but toward very practical consideration of this life, in this world—analyses of and prescriptions for living in a society that everyone agreed was sick. It is worth noting at the outset that the Chinese did not sink into despair; they did not seek consolation in notions that reality lies somewhere beyond this tawdry world, and that all will be set right in the afterlife. Rather, they were uniformly optimistic, believing that this world and this life are all that matters, and that something can be done to improve them. Analyses and prescriptions differed, however; and thinking stabilized in three main currents —Confucianism, Taoism, and Legalism.

These three currents or schools of early Chinese thought have different points of view and emphases, but they are not mutually exclusive. Confucianism focuses on man in his social and political relationships, Taoism on man's status in the larger cosmic sphere, and Legalism on state administration. The writings of all three schools were read by educated Chinese throughout subsequent history, and Chinese were influenced by them all, variably according to circumstances. Confucianism and Taoism are so complementary that it is almost axiomatic to say that traditional Chinese were Taoist in private and Confucian in public; and it might well be added that any Chinese who entered government service also inevitably became, by that very act, in some measure Legalist.

A word of warning about terminology is in order here. Confucius and his immediate followers had such prestige in traditional China that modern writers commonly refer to Confucian China and the Confucian state system when what is intended is "traditional China, in which the Confucian value system was predominant" and "the traditional Chinese state system, which officially espoused Confucian doctrines." Such usages obscure the fact that the prevalent social and political doctrines of imperial times were mixtures of elements from all three ancient ideological currents—and, as time went on, elements from other currents as well. What is casually referred to as Confucianism in traditional times was a highly eclectic set of ideas, significantly different from what Confucius himself taught. Moreover, as Chinese history unfolded and conditions of life changed, prevailing ideological currents changed also—from century to century, generation to generation, even decade to decade—as Christianity, for example, has changed from epoch to epoch. It should be kept in mind, therefore, that what Confucius taught and what later Confucians of any age thought and practiced are by no means the same thing.

It should be noted also that at the root of all Chinese thought is the conception that the cosmic universe is one entity, without either a beginning or an end, which is not divisible into natural and supernatural realms. Chinese believed that the cosmic universe has three principal elements or forces: Heaven, Earth, and Man. Of these, Heaven is paramount, corresponding in status to the supreme deity in other religious traditions. It is all-powerful and can be worshiped, but it is not anthropomorphic. Originally, the Chinese assumed that an anthropomorphic deity did exist. In Shang times it was called Shang-ti. The concept of Heaven (t'ien) was introduced by the Chou peoples, who used it interchangeably with the Shang deity Shang-ti until the latter faded from religious thought.

All things in the traditional Chinese cosmos function in accordance with Tao, which resembles what Westerners think of as laws of nature. Tao is not a deity and cannot be worshiped. In nonphilosophical use the term means a path or a way. In cosmological use it is *the* Way, the process by which the cosmos operates. It functions through the interaction of two opposed but complementary and inseparable forces, Yang and Yin, which are perhaps most usefully compared to the positive and negative poles of an electrical system. Yang is associated with the sun, light, and warmth; Yin with the moon, dark, and cold. Yang is male, Yin female. Everything acts by an alternation of Yang and Yin forces; Yang is naturally ascendant in certain circumstances and times, Yin in others. When the natural alternation of Yang and Yin is aborted, the result is inappropriate and might be harmful or otherwise disadvantageous; but no question of good or bad arises in any absolute, abstract sense.

The universe, in the traditional Chinese view, is inhabited by many kinds of spiritual beings. Among them are spiritual essences of natural phenomena such as stars, mountains, rivers, trees, and rocks, and many anthropomorphic deities associated with particular localities or particular kinds of spiritual power. Most familiar are ancestral spirits. The human soul was thought to consist of two parts. At death, one part sinks into Earth; if irritated for any reason, it can reappear as a capricious, often malevolent ghost (*kuei*). The other part of the soul rises into Heaven and joins the host of spiritual beings (*shen*) already mentioned. Both eventually dissolve into undifferentiated cosmic matter, but for an indeterminate prior time both exist as creatures of the universe that do not significantly differ from living humans except in their physical qualities. They can influence affairs in the physical world; demonic ghosts can even take possession of human beings and cause them to do things contrary to their normal wills and natures.

In the Chinese conception, man is part and parcel of the universe in the same sense that Heaven is or the various spiritual beings are, and he copes with the various forces in the universe as best he can, in much the same manner as he deals with other humans. It was the ruler's responsibility to deal with such great forces as Heaven and Earth on behalf of all mankind, but every human deals with lesser spiritual forces as his resources permit, to placate those that might work to his disadvantage and to encourage those that might help him. The traditional Chinese therefore engaged in divination, made sacrificial offerings, communicated with spirits through mediums, bought charms and amulets from shamans, and especially worshiped and propitiated their own ancestral spirits, considering them the most likely sources of good luck and protection.

In finding ways to cope satisfactorily with the universe, the Chinese have traditionally resorted to local cults of all sorts. One prominent type of religious practitioner is the geomancer, an expert in determining the advantages and disadvantages of locations for buildings and graves, so that they benefit from and do not disrupt the functioning of natural forces; his science is called *feng-shui* (wind and water). A book that has great religious prestige is the *I-ching* (Classic of Changes), which originated as a diviner's handbook and early acquired commentaries that made it a cosmological treatise of awesome obscurity. Its core is a set of eight trigrams representing all possible combinations of unbroken lines (Yang: —) and broken lines (Yin: --):

≡ ☷ ☵ ☲ ☳ ☶ ☴ ☱

These trigrams are paired in every possible combination to form 64 six-line forms commonly called hexagrams, and specialists use cryptic statements that were anciently associated with each hexagram for interpretive applications of many sorts. The *I-ching* is used on the simplest folk-culture level for fortune-telling and on the highest intellectual level for gaining somewhat mystical insights into the nature and workings of the cosmos.

Since the Chinese conceive of the universe, seen and unseen, as a single integrated organism, they are not inclined, as most Westerners are, to think in terms of contending, antagonistic polarities such as natural versus supernatural, life versus death, us versus them, this versus that. The Chinese think inclusively, not exclusively. Everything belongs, in its appropriate form and role and on its appropriate plane, in one undivided cosmic universe. Moreover, since the Chinese are polytheistic rather than monotheistic, they are generally uncomfortable with absolute distinctions between good and bad, right and wrong, true and false. They easily accommodate seeming contradictions, and they generally consider it unreasonable to differentiate between "true gods" and "false gods." They have consequently not fought holy wars or gone on crusades; they have felt no compulsion to take holy writ to the benighted heathen; and they have not experienced either the agony of sin or the ecstasy of salvation. Their attitude toward life and the universe has on the whole been eminently rational.

THE HUNDRED SCHOOLS

The intellectuals who wandered about China seeking office and influence during the late Spring and Autumn era, and most conspicuously in the Warring States era, produced a broad spectrum of ideas ranging from the most concrete to the most abstract, from the most practical to the most theoretical. The abundance and variety of their ideas prompted later Chinese to refer to them as the "Hundred Schools" of thought.

Among the most practical of the early Chinese thinkers were military experts, of whom the best known is Sun Wu, a legendary general of questionable historicity who is the reputed author of a remarkable book dating from the fourth century B.C., entitled *Ping-fa* (The Art of War). Reportedly a native of Ch'i who was entrusted with command of the armies of the Yangtze delta state Wu, Sun Wu is commonly called Sun-tzu, "Master Sun," and the book is sometimes called merely the *Sun-tzu*. The work deals analytically with total war in the modern sense and is well known in military academies throughout the world today. It discusses how to organize a state for war, how to evaluate terrain and to choose among various offensive and defensive strategies accordingly, how to maintain sound logistical services, how to wage psychological warfare, how to discover and take advantage of the enemy's weaknesses by the use of spies and saboteurs, and other equally sophisticated problems. Its most fundamental principles are (1) that deception is the key to success in war, and (2) that the greatest generals are those who can overcome the enemy without fighting. This work was the first in a series of military classics that Chinese produced over the centuries, and by far the most astute, systematic, and influential of them all.

No less practical, considering the nature of political life in Warring States times, were rhetoricians who taught the arts of persuasion, particularly in interstate diplomacy. Representative of their preoccupations and methods is the work for which the age was named, *Chan-kuo ts'e* (Intrigues of the Warring States). Although the book may not have been compiled until as late as the second century B.C., it contains rhetorical exercises that were apparently used in the preceding centuries to train men in the subtle skills of diplomatic intercourse. Its anecdotes take the form of historical narratives, in which regional lords are advised how to survive or succeed in critical situations hypothetically confronting their states. Among the diplomatic gambits espoused are so-called horizontal alliances and vertical alliances. The first envisaged east-west cooperation between Ch'in and Ch'i in the north to foil Ch'u in the south, the second north-south cooperation between Ch'i and Ch'u against Ch'in in the west. Rather cryptic general principles of diplomacy are regularly stated and illustrated in anecdotes, but no coherent theory of interstate relations is presented. The book is not a milestone in the development of Chinese thought; it is most esteemed for its lively narrative style, its often humorous stories, and its witticisms.

At the theoretical extreme were logicians or dialecticians who engaged in hair-splitting disputes, often with no discernible relevance to any practical concerns. They apparently adorned every lord's court, but they are represented for the most part only in scraps of references in the writings of other thinkers. Teng Hsi (d. 501 B.C.), from the central state of Cheng, was renowned for concocting paradoxical quibbles that helped his friends win litigations; he may have been China's first professional legal counselor—a type of career that was suppressed by the later imperial state system. Another famous early dialectician was Hui Shih (380-300 B.C.?), a native of Sung who became chief counselor of the state of Wei, for which he is reported to have devised a law code. Hui Shih is credited with formulating a set of paradoxical propositions that demonstrate the difference between abstract logical absolutes and concrete realities, and suggest that concrete realities are without exception relative (large from one point of view, small from another) and changeable.

A new level of abstract thought was achieved by Kung-sun Lung (320-250 B.C.?), of the northern state of Chao, to whom is attributed a short treatise entitled *Kung-sun Lung-tzu*. Whereas Hui Shih seems to have been fascinated by the relativity of reality, Kung-sun Lung was preoccupied with the terminology in which reality is symbolized, and particularly with seeming paradoxes deriving from the logical extensions of nominal categories. According to one famous anecdote, while riding horseback one day he was stopped by a gatekeeper, who told him that horses were not allowed beyond. Kung-sun announced, "This is a white horse, not a horse!" and brazenly rode on. One of the most famous passages in the *Kung-sun Lung-tzu*, indeed, is a discourse on the proposition that "a white horse is not a horse," which emphasizes that "horseness," "whiteness," and "white-horseness" are mutually exclusive logical categories. The book consists of a series of such paradoxical propositions, which come close to logical argument in the ancient Greek mode.

Although Teng Hsi, Hui Shih, and Kung-sun Lung had influence on other thinkers of some major schools and can be considered to have sharpened the rationality of Chinese philosophical thought generally, their way of thinking did not find a place of its own in the mainstream of ideological development. They were not concrete and practical enough to suit the general Chinese temperament. Their type of disputation seemed frivolous quibbling, playing with words rather than contributing to solutions of China's troubles.

CONFUCIANISM

Confucianism in its original form was a set of ethical and political doctrines, with minimal religious substance, articulated in the teachings and writings of three men known to Westerners as Confucius, Mencius, and Hsün-tzu. In the Chinese tradition Confucianism was known as the school or doctrines of the *ju* (pronounced much like "roo"). Ju is a rather baffling term. It seems originally to have meant weakling or perhaps more nearly a genteel, nonviolent man. Some specialists think it refers to descendants of the priestly diviner class of Shang times. Whatever its specific reference, it must have been used to denote a nonmilitary group distinct from the early Chou warrior-official class (shih); and it probably became attached to Confucius and his followers, perhaps by some of their opponents in ridicule, because they were the least military-minded of the early Chinese philosophical groups.

Confucius. Confucius was born in 551 B.C., a generation before the Buddha in India, and died in 479, a decade before the birth of Socrates in Greece. His name was K'ung Ch'iu, and Chinese refer to him as K'ung fu-tzu, Master K'ung, *fu-tzu* being an elegant variant of tzu, master. From K'ung fu-tzu modern European missionaries devised the latinized form Confucius.

Confucius was a native of the small state of Lu in modern Shantung province, which was ruled by the descendants of the Duke of Chou. He seems to have been born into a family of low-ranking aristocratic status and for a time occupied a not very important office; but he grew up in rather humble circumstances and acquired a variety of menial skills that were normally scorned by aristocratic gentlemen. He became China's first professional teacher, so far as is known; he took tuition-paying disciples and taught them his views on life and government. Some of his disciples quickly attained eminent posts in feudal state administration. In middle life Confucius spent at least a decade traveling about North China hoping to persuade some feudal lord to put his

Fig. 5. Traditional portrait of Confucius by unidentified artist

principles into governmental practice, but he had no success despite being generally respected. At the end of his life he apparently considered himself a failure.

All that is reliably known about Confucius's thought comes from a single small book called the *Lun-yü*; the title means discourses and is normally translated *Analects*. It is not a systematic treatise on philosophy, nor was it written by Confucius himself. It is a collection of Confucius's sayings that appear to have been remembered and passed along by his disciples until they were gathered up into a single compilation, probably not many decades after his death. Most Westerners on first encounter are astonished to find it an unorganized jumble of "The Master said's," resembling nothing so much as the ruminations of a cracker-barrel philosopher. There is normally minimal, if any, context in which to fit the sayings, and sections of the work offer lists of disjointed statements such as "If the mat is not straight, he does not sit," which some specialists interpret as descriptions of Confucius's personal habits and others as Confucius's prescriptions about what a proper man should or should not do. Specific aspects of Confucius's thought are therefore subject to dispute, and the basic principles that guided him must be pieced together out of such fragmentary passages.

As he appears in the *Lun-yü*, Confucius was a very human person, by no means saintly. He was often disappointed with his disciples and lamented that he seemed destined never to get the right sort of students. He could be short-tempered and rude, as when he encountered an old acquaintance who had never amounted to anything: "Growing old and not dying is just being a pest," Confucius exclaimed, and he hit the poor fellow on the shin with his cane. He could also be calculatingly rude, as when he declined an invitation on the plea of illness, then played his zither and sang loudly so his host's departing messenger would know he was not ill at all. Confucius was also more than a little sorry for himself at not getting an influential position. On at least two occasions disciples were hard put to restrain him from taking service with petty rebels, despite their bad reputations; Confucius wanted to believe that if given any sort of chance he could create "a new Chou in the east," and he resented being treated "like a gourd that is fit only to be hung on the wall and is never put to use." Moreover, there is a sanctimonious quality about the ways in which he consoled himself: "I do not mind not being in office; I am concerned about being qualified for office. I do not mind that no one gives me recognition; I seek

to be worthy of recognition." Even his frequent self-deprecatory statements have a somewhat sanctimonious ring: "The Master said, Am I
one who has knowledge? I have no knowledge. If anyone questions
me I just talk things out from beginning to end." "The Master said,
I am not one who was born with knowledge. I am just one who esteems
the old ways and pursues them zealously." For all this, he had a strong
sense of humor, was fond of teasing his disciples, and could appreciate
a joke on himself.

    Not only was Confucius a very human person; he was a great human
being. His impact on China was neither that of a dazzling intellectual
nor that of a radiant prophet. He was certainly not a strongly religious
man in the usual sense. When asked about the spirits he said, "Being
unable yet to serve men, how can one serve the spirits?" Being asked
about death, he said, "Not yet understanding life, how can one understand death?" He was, however, a dedicated, indefatigably concerned
man, whom the Chinese revere because of his insistence that human
beings are social and moral creatures capable of living on a higher
plane than animals—and should try to do so simply because they know
they ought to. Confucius did not presume to be a moral law-giver; all
he expected was that people should care about the quality of life and
should ask themselves at every turn, "What is the right thing to do?"
"The gentleman," he said, "is as concerned about what is right as the
petty man is about what is profitable." He did not threaten worldly
failure or otherworldly damnation, and he promised no rewards beyond the gratification of doing what one knows is right and not simply
"herding together like the birds and the beasts."

    One of Confucius's contributions was to give new, moral meanings
to terms that had long been familiar in the Chou feudal system. The
terms shih (warrior-official) and *chün-tzu* (son of a ruler) were common general designations for the old militaristic, hereditary elite class.
Confucius transformed them to mean men of moral worth, regardless
of birth, and implied that such men deserved to be the social and political elite. The transition is quite similar to the change in meaning of
the word gentleman, which once referred simply to a man of gentle
birth. Another term, li (ritual), had come to mean the ritualistic etiquette that was cultivated by the aristocratic class. Confucius broadened
it to mean social and moral propriety based on full-hearted sincerity.
Into the cosmological term Tao, the Way, Confucius also injected a

strong moral content, making it "the moral Way" ordained by Heaven. In Confucius's ethics a proper gentleman devotes himself to the earnest cultivation of the inner qualities, especially sincerity, that enable him to act in accordance with li and thus to help make the Tao prevail.

Confucius's social morality is rooted in what some call the Silver Rule: "Don't do to others what you yourself would not like." It is significant, and characteristic of Confucius, that this injunction is put in negative terms. The Golden Rule ("Do unto others . . .") Confucius would have considered aggressive, presumptuous, and certainly "not li." The same restrained unaggressiveness pervades Confucius's political thinking. He emphasized government for the happiness and welfare of the people, but implemented primarily by example rather than by law. His concept of proper government is perhaps best summarized in his belief that "the gentleman's essential quality is like wind, the common people's like grass; and when the wind is on it the grass always bends." He was persuaded that the people would irresistibly follow and emulate a truly benevolent ruler, no matter whether he ordered them about or not, whereas they would not obey the laws of any ruler who was himself not a proper moral exemplar. "The Master said, If one leads them with administrative measures and uses punishments to make them conform, the people will be evasive and will have no sense of shame; but if one leads them with virtue and uses propriety to make them conform, they will have a sense of shame and will come up to expectations." When a clan head who was de facto ruler of Lu asked Confucius's advice about dealing with widespread thievery, Confucius courageously retorted, "If only you were not avaricious yourself, they would not steal even if you paid them to."

Confucius declared himself a transmitter of the old ways fostered by the Duke of Chou, not an innovator. He deplored the deterioration of old standards and people's inability to know their proper places and to behave as they ought to. In his view a proper man had no choice but to work tirelessly for what was right and, if need be, to sacrifice his life "for the Tao." He would not be discouraged. As a disciple said, "The gentleman's function in government is to put into effect what is right. As for the fact that the Tao does not prevail, he is fully aware of that!" Confucius's epitaph might well be the comment made about him by a contemporary who had obviously despaired of society: "Is he not the fellow who knows it is impossible but still works at it?"

Mencius. The rather vague principles of propriety and benevolence that Confucius espoused could have been lost in the philosophical ferment of the following centuries had they not been championed by two brilliant intellectuals, Mencius and Hsün-tzu. Mencius—the name is an early modern latinization of Meng-tzu, Master Meng—lived from about 372 to about 289 B.C. His name was Meng K'o, and he was a native of the tiny fief of Tsou, a neighbor of Lu and Ch'i. Like Confucius, he came from an aristocratic family; but unlike Confucius, he was, in temperament and in practice, a thoroughgoing aristocrat himself. He was an only child reared by a widowed and doting mother, who saw to it that he got a good education. As a grown man, he was lavishly devoted to her, and on her death he mourned and buried her with such extravagance that his own disciples were embarrassed enough to chide him. In everything he was extravagant and arrogant. He traveled about with a huge entourage of disciples, supported and entertained by a succession of feudal lords who were intimidated by his manner and his reputation. He was probably the most erudite man of his age. He knew this, and he made the most of it.

The book in which Mencius's thought is preserved, simply called *Meng-tzu*, is in the form of anecdotal memoirs and was probably compiled or at least edited by Mencius himself in his old age. It is no more a systematic philosophical treatise than the *Lun-yü* is, but a collection of reports on what must have been the highlights of Mencius's career as a debater and counselor. In it he is never seen at a disadvantage or at a loss for words; he always skewers his adversaries with devastating rhetorical skill; and he says audacious things to rulers that make them "turn color" in pent-up irritation or helplessly "look this way and that, and then speak of other things." The give-and-take of argumentation is reproduced in detail, and in a literary style that traditional Chinese considered exemplary expository prose.

Mencius offered no apologies for his extravagance and arrogance, which were sometimes challenged. On the contrary, he believed and stated forthrightly that it was natural and proper for Brain to govern Brawn and for Brawn to support Brain. The counterbalancing virtue in Mencius is that he brilliantly and eloquently argued for benevolence in government and for the egalitarian doctrine that every man has the potentiality of becoming a sage.

Mencius expounded Confucius's views about benevolent government primarily by arguing that it was a matter of enlightened self-interest for a ruler to treat his people well. He seems to have believed sincerely that if a truly benevolent lord were to appear, people would flock to him from all over China and he would win the empire by default. In concluding a long lecture to King Hui of Liang, he said:

Your dogs and pigs feed on the food of your people, but you are unaware that you should restrain them. On your roads are people starving to death, but you are unaware that you should open your granaries. When people die you say, "It is not my fault; it is the year!" How does this differ from stabbing a man to death and then saying, "It is not my fault; it is the sword!" If your majesty would stop putting blame on the year, people from throughout the empire would come to you at once.

In other words, Mencius recognized public morale to be the proper first concern of every ruler; and he argued that if a people's morale is high they can and will fight off the best-armed enemies, even if they have no more than sticks and stones to fight with. Mencius advocated and explained various social welfare schemes that he thought would build this spirit, and in this connection he provided the earliest known description of the idealized early Chou well-field system, which was discussed in Chapter 2. He also carried the principle of the Mandate of Heaven to its logical conclusion—that it is the duty of right-minded men to overthrow an unworthy ruler. And he told rulers so to their faces.

The egalitarian aspect of Mencius's thought stems from his conviction that in every man's nature there exist the seeds of goodness—good instincts, so to speak—which in the course of normal life become obscured by greed, lust, ambition, and other unworthy impulses, which are also latent in everyone. The Confucian virtues, he argued, "are not fused into us from without; they are securely in us." He considered it man's moral obligation to seek out, through self-cultivation of the sort advocated by Confucius, his "lost child's mind." "Those who follow their great qualities are great men," he said, "and those who follow their petty qualities are petty men." Like Confucius, he recognized no external standard of right. He was somewhat more conservative than Confucius in praising the ways of the ancients and recommending that men follow them, but he insisted that every man must be his own judge of what is right for him, in his particular circumstances. As for why men should strive to be good, Mencius was no more authoritarian than Confucius had been. He expressed the fatalism that is inherent in Confucius's refusal to make promises or threats. "As for accomplishing results, that rests with Heaven. What have you to do with that? Try your best to do good; that is all." Also: "The gentleman merely follows the rules and then waits for his fate." Men can be persuaded to do this, he believed, by being shown that it is through the virtues inherent in their natures that men become truly human. "What differentiates man from the birds and beasts is very small. Ordinary people abandon it, whereas the gentleman cherishes it." A major obligation of rulers, Mencius argued, was to create environments that would encourage and help people to cultivate themselves in this sense.

Hsün-tzu. Whereas Mencius's conception of the essential goodness of human nature has led some specialists to characterize him as a tenderhearted idealist, it is universally agreed that the last great Confucian thinker of the formative age, Hsün-tzu, was an unsentimental, ruthlessly tough-minded rationalist. His characteristic intellectual approach was "Humbug! Let's consider the facts!"

Hsün-tzu's name was Hsün Ch'ing. He lived from about 300 to about 235 B.C., when the turbulence of the Warring States era was approaching its climax in the military conquests of Ch'in. A native of the northern state of Chao, he seems to have spent most of his life studying and teaching in Ch'i. He did less traveling about than either Confucius or Mencius, though on one occasion he did visit Ch'in. When he was approaching old age, he was offered and accepted a post as county magistrate in the southern part of Shantung, which was then under the control of the great southern power, Ch'u. He was the only notable early Confucian who had such first-hand administrative experience, but nothing is known of his actual performance as a magistrate.

Unlike Confucius and Mencius, Hsün-tzu set down his philosophy in very systematic detail in a book called the *Hsün-tzu.* Most of its 32 chapters are well-organized essays on a single topic: self-cultivation, kingly governance, the difference between kings and hegemons, proper ministerial conduct, the recruitment of good officials, military affairs, proper conduct, music, and so on. The book shows enormous erudition and broad interests in practical matters. Most strikingly, it shows a very orderly and perceptive mind. A good argument could be made that Hsün-tzu had the finest mental equipment to be found among all the ancient Chinese philosophers. His thought had great influence in China during the early centuries of the imperial age. Eventually, however, Chinese came to esteem him less and Mencius more. He seems to have been not quite in tune with the developing Chinese character. He had a superb mind but little heart.

Hsün-tzu's interpretation of Confucianism conflicts with that of Mencius on a critical point, the evaluation of human nature. In contrast to Mencius's strong emphasis on the potentiality for goodness in all men, Hsün-tzu suspected that there was very little innate goodness in man. As a matter of fact, he observed that man's nature is dominated by "bad" or uncivilized impulses, and that goodness in the Confucian sense must be learned. Hsün-tzu thought Mencius's views on the "lost child's mind" were just sentimental humbug. That men could be taught he would not deny, however. Thus he was essentially just as egalitarian as Mencius. Since men are equally uncivilized by nature, and since all have the potentiality of learning, he agreed that any man could become a sage. But the methods he prescribed are quite the opposite of Mencius's, and very authoritarian. To become good, in Hsün-tzu's view, one must steep oneself in the precepts and precedents of the great men of antiquity, and above all one must subject oneself obediently to a properly qualified teacher. Perhaps no other thinker ever placed so much emphasis on the important role of the teacher in society.

In his authoritarian way, Hsün-tzu conceived of rules of proper conduct (li) as external standards imposed on people by early sage-kings for the common social good, to restrain men's natural inclinations to grasp for selfish satisfactions, and thus to avoid contention and disorder. Hsün-tzu's conception of social organization and social relationships in general was a thoroughly rational and utilitarian one. Are sacrifices offered to benefit spirits? Humbug! Those who think so, he wrote, are simply ignoramuses. Sacrifices, mourning, and other rituals are desirable, to be sure, but merely because they have social and psychological value: they provide socially useful channels for the expression of emotions, and contribute orderliness and dignity to human relationships. Hsün-tzu himself doubted that spirits exist; he had never seen one.

As for government, Hsün-tzu supported most of the specific social welfare plans advocated by Mencius, and he shared Mencius's conviction that an unworthy ruler should be overthrown. To a greater extent than Mencius, he justified all such views on strictly utilitarian grounds.

The Confucian consensus. As the foregoing discussion has indicated, the early Confucian thinkers were not of one mind on several points.

But they had a common spirit, which can be expressed without too much distortion in seven propositions:

1. The universe and mankind are governed by an impersonal but willful Heaven (t'ien).

2. Heaven wills that men be happy and orderly in accord with cosmic harmony (tao).

3. An ethical and virtuous life is the appropriate human contribution to the cosmic harmony.

4. Virtue (*te*) is developed by and manifested in proper conduct (li). It should be specially noted in this regard that virtue is not something nurtured and secluded in one's secret self; man is only what he does. As Mencius said, "If you wear the clothes of [the sage-ruler] Yao, speak the words of Yao, and carry out the actions of Yao, you will then be a Yao. But if you wear the clothes of [the Hsia dynasty tyrant] Chieh, speak the words of Chieh, and carry out the actions of Chieh, you will then be a Chieh."

5. In important particular crises it is not easy to know Heaven's will or to choose between conflicting values; this is especially the case for a ruler.

6. Proper conduct, especially in important matters, often requires wisdom or sageliness; and this can be acquired only through sober study of the precepts of prior sages and the lessons of history, and through earnest effort to cultivate oneself accordingly.

7. Individual men and human society are perfectible; that is, every man potentially can be a sage, and society potentially can be made harmonious and fulfilling for all.

The ethical system that can be perceived in the early Confucian writings is a complex system, including one set of values or virtues that is externally oriented and a complementary one that is internally oriented. The externally oriented virtues constitute a basic situational ethic that can be charted as follows:

Five Key Relationships	*Appropriate Virtues*
father-son	filial piety
ruler-subject	loyalty
brother-brother	brotherliness
husband-wife	love and obedience
friend-friend	faithfulness

It is noteworthy that family relationships loom very large in the Confucian value system, and also that relationships fall generally into hierarchical superior-subordinate patterns. What is not apparent in this chart, but is an important dimension of the value system, is that all these relationships and virtues were considered to be reciprocal. That is, the father-son obligation does not fall solely on the son, or the ruler-subject obligation solely on the subject; the father is obligated to be a proper father, the ruler a proper ruler, and so on. All these situational values are summed up in two larger conceptions: li, proper conduct; and *jen* (pronounced almost like "run"), for which such awkward but suggestive translations as man-to-manness and humankindness have been proposed, the latter being intended to combine the meanings of human kindness and humankind-ness.

The concepts of li and jen connect the external-oriented virtues with the internal-oriented virtues, which are ethical absolutes. These principally include rightness, righteousness, or duty; resolution or courage; wisdom; sincerity; and a sense of shame.* To manifest all these virtues in proper balance is worthiness, and to achieve perfect worthiness is sageliness. If only a ruler could attain to sageliness, the early Confucians believed, the magnetic force of his virtuous example would so transform the population that social harmony would result without strenuous governmental efforts. What saddened and frustrated the Confucians was that rulers and other members of the elite class would not recognize what to the Confucians was so obvious. Confucius said, "Who can go out except through the door? Why are there none who will follow this Way?" Mencius echoed him: "This Way is like a great road; there is no difficulty in recognizing it! The trouble with people is that they simply will not seek it out."

A last point and one that cannot be emphasized too insistently: despite all its urgings that people should simply do what they know is right, early Confucianism provides no easy solutions for problems that arise when different values conflict. What should one do when being a loyal subject would violate one's filial obligation to one's parents?

---

* The graphs in which some of these virtues are written are peculiarly expressive. Jen is a combination of elements meaning man and the number two; it suggests the relationship between people. Resolution or courage (*chih*) combines "heart" with "warrior-official" and suggests "the heart of a shih." Sincerity (*ch'eng*) combines "speech" with "fulfillment, completion"—"words that are carried out." A sense of shame (*ch'ih*) combines "ear" and "heart," suggesting "listening to one's heart."

How should a filial son cope with a father committed to an unrighteous act? Can it be loyal to disobey what one considers the unwise orders of one's ruler? Early Confucianism does not set forth rules that give sure comfort and guidance in such situations. What it really offers is a challenge: Fret about it! Think it out!

THE SCHOOL OF MO-TZU

Confucianism had an interesting and influential early defector. This was a man of the central state of Sung named Mo Ti, more commonly known as Mo-tzu. He lived in the period between Confucius and Mencius; his approximate dates are 470-391 B.C. Mo-tzu studied under followers of Confucius, but in his time they had fallen away from the spirit of Confucius, settling into comfortable careers as prim specialists in ritual and professional funeral directors. Mo-tzu was disillusioned with them, but he also found himself at odds with Confucius's essential spirit. So he broke away and developed a philosophy and an educational system of his own. He left a book, the *Mo-tzu*, in which he analyzes and offers solutions for the problems of the world in highly logical, systematic essays that set an organizational model for the later Hsün-tzu and reveal great intellectual kinship with the sophistic dialecticians.

Mo-tzu departs from Confucianism chiefly in his militant do-goodism. Confucius may not have known for certain what absolute goodness was, but Mo-tzu knew. For him, anything that helped people preserve themselves or that contributed to the growth of population and wealth or that made for peace in the world was good, requiring no further proof. Anything that had contrary effects was necessarily bad. Mo-tzu's utilitarian standards were coupled with a strongly authoritarian concept of social organization. Society simply could not afford people's judging for themselves what was good and proper. The common good required what Mo-tzu called "identification with the superior." People should be regimented into total obedience to their rulers, and rulers in turn should be totally obedient to Heaven and the spirits. Mo-tzu made of Heaven the closest approximation to an anthropomorphic supreme god found in ancient Chinese thought. He warned that if people persisted in their contentious, destructive ways, Heaven would have every excuse for concluding that humans are troublesome misfits in the universe and would certainly wipe them out.

Human beings are contentious, Mo-tzu believed, because they are selfish, and Confucianism accentuates their selfishness by giving high priority to family relationships and such virtues as filial piety. People would cease being contentious, he argued, if only they would practice what he called universal love—that is, if only they would revere other people's fathers as fully as their own and respect other people's homes, cities, and states as fully as their own.

War was the greatest abomination of all in Heaven's eyes and in Mo-tzu's. Mo-tzu was confident he could persuade rulers that everyone suffers from war, even the victors. Part of his antiwar campaign was to train his followers in the tactics and strategies of defensive warfare; he turned them into a skilled, rigidly disciplined peacekeeping army that he made available to any state threatened by aggression. After Mo-tzu's death, his military organization survived under successive leaders into the early centuries of the imperial age, separated into scattered bands of professional knights-errant who turned over a tithe of their earnings to the central headquarters.

Mo-tzu's social goals were not significantly different from those of the Confucians; he had the best of intentions. Mencius said that if Mo-tzu could have benefited the world by scrubbing the skin off his whole body, he would have done so. But he was impatient and had little faith in man's moral judgment. His philosophical positivism alienated him from the mainstream of Chinese intellectual development, and his writings were almost totally ignored throughout the imperial age. Still, he left his imprint on society: Robin Hood-like knight-errantry remained a somewhat romanticized ideal in the folk culture.

TAOISM

For all their differences, Confucians and Mo-ists alike were earnest reformers, concerned with improving society. Theirs was one predictable reaction to the chaos of the late Chou centuries. Almost as predictable was the reaction of those who became hermits and recluses, questioning the wisdom and efficacy of even struggling to reform society. Confucius repeatedly encountered such skeptics on his travels— men who had retired to the simple rustic life and considered him foolish for not doing the same. In the following centuries such escapism seems to have flourished.

One early representative of this trend was a man named Yang Chu (440-360 B.C.?), of whom almost nothing is known except that he was heroically hedonistic and heroically selfish. Whereas Mo-tzu would have sacrificed himself to benefit the world, Yang Chu's total concern was "What's in it for me?" Mencius reported that if Yang Chu could have benefited the whole world by merely plucking a single hair from his head, he would not have done it. Other references to Yang Chu suggest he felt that life was a swiftly passing succession of potentially pleasant experiences, and that it should be accepted joyously in whatever form it comes and lived to the full.

Development of the escapist point of view, shorn of Yang Chu's hedonism, culminated in the doctrine known as Taoism, whose major works, the *Lao-tzu* and the *Chuang-tzu*, are among the most interesting and most influential writings of the Chinese heritage.

The Taoist texts. The *Lao-tzu* (Master Lao? The Old Boy?) is also known as the *Tao-te ching* (Classic of the Way and of Virtue). It apparently took its present form in the third century B.C. and is probably the work of more than one person. No one can be sure to whom the title *Lao-tzu* refers, though Taoist tradition ascribes the work to an older contemporary of Confucius called Li Erh or Lao Tan, a man of Ch'u. He reputedly served as archivist at the royal Chou court, was visited and honored by Confucius, and in old age disappeared from China traveling westward. Later Taoists even asserted that he made his way to India and converted the Buddha to Taoism.

The *Lao-tzu* has been called the most profound and most beautiful book ever produced by the Chinese. It has been translated from Chinese more often than any other work, and into English more often than anything except the Bible. The translations differ in important ways because the text is open to interpretation. It is short, totaling only about 5,000 words; it is largely in poetry; it abounds in apparent contradictions; and it is cryptic, enigmatic, and paradoxical. From the opening line the reader is in trouble. In crude word-for-word equivalents, the first line reads as follows:

tao   can   *tao*   not   constant/common   *tao*

The Chinese graph tao can be read not only as both "a way" and "the Way"; it carries the meaning "to discuss" as well. For this reason, and because of other complexities, the line can be understood, and has been translated, in quite different ways, with contradictory senses. Does it mean "The way that can truly be considered the Way is not what is ordinarily meant by tao"? Or "The way that can be spoken of is not the constant Way"? Or "The way that can truly be considered the Way

Fig. 6. Traditional woodblock print illustrating a Taoist legend that Confucius and a disciple visited Lao-tzŭ (shown playing a zither) to inquire about proper ritual

is an inconstant (i.e., changing) way"? Chinese grammar permits all these meanings and more, and translators have explored them fully. With whatever meaning the reader may choose to begin, he soon encounters something that makes no sense unless he changes his assumptions. The book is therefore a perennial puzzle. It has always been that to the Chinese, and it will always be that to outsiders. In one unmistakably clear passage, the *Lao-tzu* says, "Those who understand don't talk, and those who talk don't understand." Confucians have delighted in using this epigram to tease Taoists, suggesting that in writing a 5,000-word book, the author of the *Lao-tzu* may have proved that point conclusively.

The *Chuang-tzu* is a longer, prose work attributed to a man named Chuang Chou (369-286 B.C.?), but of him, too, very little is known. He was apparently a man of the small central state of Wei who was well versed in all the intellectual currents of his day but with no urge to take service in government. His book gives evidence of both great intellectual power and great literary skill. Its anecdotes are among the most richly imaginative masterpieces in China's literature. In them Confucians and the dialecticians are lampooned with cutting wit, men with punning names engage in nonsensical harangues, animals and insects converse philosophically, and Chuang-tzu floats around in the air. This is a work of parables, parodies, and fantasies rather than exposition.

The inventiveness of Chuang-tzu's mind is well illustrated in the following short excerpts:

The ruler of the Southern Ocean is Impetuosity, the ruler of the Northern Ocean is Indifference, and the ruler of the Center is Chaos. Impetuosity and Indifference from time to time met one another in the domain of Chaos, and Chaos was a good host to them. So Impetuosity and Indifference consulted about repaying the kindness of Chaos: "People all have seven head-holes for seeing, hearing, eating, and breathing. Chaos alone has none. Let us chisel them in for him!" So they chiseled one head-hole a day. On the seventh day Chaos died.

Once upon a time Chuang Chou dreamed he was a butterfly, and he flew about enjoying himself, unaware that he was Chou. But when he suddenly waked up, he was the same Chou as always. He does not know whether he is Chou and only dreamed he was a butterfly or whether he is a butterfly now dreaming it is Chou. Yet there is a definite difference between Chou and a butterfly. This is what is called a transformation.

A third work that Taoists prize is the *Lieh-tzu*, a short book that has the same rambling, anecdotal, whimsical spirit as the *Chuang-tzu*. It is attributed to a shadowy figure named Lieh Yü-k'ou (450-375 B.C.?) but is certainly a later production than the *Chuang-tzu* and may have been concocted as late as the third or fourth century of the Christian era.

The Taoist consensus. The early Taoists avoided rational exposition and engaged in enigmatic paradoxes and fantasies because their philosophical position, though utterly simple, is unarguable. Taoism is a lyrical, mystical, but by no means irrational advocacy of individualism, quietism, and spontaneity in union with Nature (*tao*). It is the antithesis of moralistic Confucianism. Its basic insight is that Nature is all there is, and its impulse accordingly is to debunk reformism and do-goodism, to renounce the obligations that attach to social relationships and social institutions, and to seek psychological freedom and peace of mind by being oneself naturally and spontaneously. Nature is conceived as all-encompassing, as an impersonal, purposeless cosmos in which everything has its natural place and function; it is what it is for no reason other than that it is what it is, and can only be distorted and misunderstood when it is defined, labeled, or evaluated by standards such as good and bad that do not exist in Nature.

The Taoists consequently say, Let Nature take its course! Be yourself! Relax and enjoy life! The difficulty about this exhortation—and one of the fundamental paradoxes in Taoism—is that striving for anything is unnatural and thus "wrong." Striving, as a matter of fact, is the surest way not to achieve, because Nature balances any thrust with a counterthrust, pendulum-like. One achieves only by non-striving (*wu-wei*, literally, non-action), and there can hardly be anything more self-defeating than trying conscientiously to relax. One can be oneself only by letting it happen naturally and spontaneously.

The true Taoist cannot even urge others to follow Nature's way, because this itself supposes that something should be or should not be, thereby imposing on Nature a value judgment that is unnatural and thus "wrong." As Chuang-tzu pointed out, the duck's legs are short and the crane's legs are long; and to judge that anything in Nature is good or bad—for example, to cling to life and to fear death—is as absurd as to suggest that the duck's legs ought to be as long as the crane's or the crane's as short as the duck's. Whatever is, is natural and thus "good." But even to say so is to depart from the point of view of Nature. Man can therefore only go through his cycle of existence as dispassionately as possible, doing zestfully whatever life calls on him to do but preserving the inner freedom and equanimity of his own natural essence (te: "virtue" in Confucian usage).

Taoism has little to offer in the way of a governmental program; for in the Taoist view government is obviously an obnoxious interference with the operation of Nature. But it may be a man's lot in the natural scheme of things to be a ruler or a minister. If so, according to the *Lao-tzu*, it is to be hoped he will keep the people rustic and simple— "fill their bellies and empty their minds, strengthen their muscles and weaken their wills." By minimizing institutions and laws, the Taoist sage would bring society to a state of primeval innocence in which the interplay of natural forces would be least hindered—for good or for ill as may be, since that is irrelevant.

Taoist strains no doubt stem in part from the naturalistic and animistic religious beliefs of Shang and early Chou Chinese, and they were probably strengthened by China's gradual incorporation of the Yangtze River region in Chou times. South China exhibits nature in a far more mellow and benevolent aspect than North China does, and South China has always contributed more than its fair share of the more wildly poetic, artistic, imaginative qualities in the Chinese heritage, which are usually attributed to the Taoist impulse. It is probably no accident that Confucius, Mo-tzu, Mencius, and Hsün-tzu were all men of the North China plain, whereas most of the early Taoist thinkers were associated with the Yangtze valley state of Ch'u. The eventual merging of the antithetical reformist and escapist strains in the Chinese character has given it admirable poise and resiliency, contributing to the remarkable national endurance or staying power that has served China so well throughout its history. In times of crisis or disaster, while the Confucian part of every Chinese is soberly thinking, This is awful! We'd better do something!, his Taoist part is happily thinking, Such is life! Isn't it marvelous!

LEGALISM

If Confucianism is a doctrine of "ought-ness" and Taoism a doctrine of "such-ness," then Legalism is a doctrine of "must-ness." Neither benevolently reformist nor mystically escapist, Legalism concentrates single-mindedly on what must be done to make the state prosper and survive—and ultimately to unite China. It is rational, cynical, and totally amoral. What it teaches is totalitarian regimentation of society in the service of the state.

Ch'in's excesses and its ultimate failure gave Legalism a bad reputation in traditional China, and modern readers familiar with totalitarian principles and methods may shudder in distaste at some of the cynical statements and implications in Legalist writings. But Legalism does not deserve all the odium that has been heaped on it. Many early Legalists were no different in their point of view than many well-intentioned governmental technicians the world over—the managers, administrative specialists, and efficiency experts who keep governments functioning, and to whom philosophy and morality are often irrelevant.

Legalist practitioners and writers. The earliest notable administrative specialist in China was Kuan Chung, who was chief counselor of the state of Ch'i in the seventh century B.C. and is credited with making Ch'i the strongest and most admired power in his time. To him is attributed the *Kuan-tzu*, a dull, eclectic collection of narratives, dialogues, and essays, some of which deal in the fashion of the later Legalist writers with problems of state administration and interstate competition. This is probably a very late Chou, or possibly Ch'in, compendium of materials from several sources; it has no central focus or systematic emphasis. Another famed early administrator was Shen Pu-hai (d. 337 B.C.), chief counselor of the state of Han. His writings exist only in fragments but suggest that his principal interest was in administrative techniques (*shu*), particularly in the realm of personnel management, and that he was opposed to harsh punishments. Shen Tao of the state of Chao held office in Ch'i about 300 B.C. and is known to have emphasized what Legalists called authority (*shih*), but he left no writings.

The oldest known Legalist tract is the *Shang-chün shu* (The Book of Lord Shang), a short series of topical essays on aspects of government. It is ascribed to Kung-sun Yang (d. 338 B.C.), who as chief counselor of Ch'in established the administrative system that prepared the way for Ch'in's great conquests a century later. He was rewarded for his services by being given a small fief in Ch'in called Shang and is consequently known as Lord Shang and even as Shang Yang. The book was probably compiled shortly after his death, perhaps from some of his own writings; it seems to reflect the spirit of the governmental institutions he established in Ch'in. It heavily emphasizes the necessity of government by law (*fa*) rather than by human caprice, and it is from this emphasis that Legalism acquired its name in common Chinese usage.

The final Legalist synthesis was achieved in practice by Li Ssu (d. 208 B.C.), chief counselor under the First Emperor of Ch'in, and in writing by his contemporary Han Fei (d. 233 B.C.), in a stylish, sophisticated, often witty book entitled *Han Fei Tzu*. Han Fei was a nobleman of the state of Han, which adjoined Ch'in and was its longtime enemy. He wrote his book as a guide for his own ruler but later defected to Ch'in. At first he was warmly received there, but he was later imprisoned and forced to drink poison by Li Ssu, perhaps out of jealousy but ostensibly and perhaps in actuality for fear that he had subversive intentions. It is noteworthy that both Li Ssu and Han Fei had earlier studied under Hsün-tzu, the tough-minded, authoritarian interpreter of Confucianism.

The Legalist synthesis. In its fully matured form as revealed in the policies of Li Ssu and the writings of Han Fei, Legalism incorporates and synthesizes Shen Tao's emphasis on authority, Shen Pu-hai's emphasis on administrative techniques, and Kung-sun Yang's emphasis on law. It is not to be considered a philosophical doctrine in the normal sense; it is a set of Machiavellian guidelines for rulers and ministers. But it does offer a concept of historical evolution that has considerable philosophical interest and is directly opposed to the view of the Confucians and the Taoists alike that "the ways of antiquity" are the best ways. The Legalist attitude is that people are no worse and no better than their ancestors, but that conditions change over time. In antiquity the population was small and there was more than enough land to provide what food was needed; there was consequently little contention and little need for governmental controls. After many centuries, however, the population grew large, and the need for food and other goods exceeded production; therefore competition and contention arose, creating a need for strict controls. In general, governmental policies must always be adaptable so as to deal with new conditions as they evolve. Han Fei illustrated this point in a famous parable:

There was a plowman of Sung in whose field was a tree stump. When a rabbit scampered headlong into the stump, broke its neck, and died, he abandoned his plow and kept watch over the stump, hoping it would get him more rabbits. But he got no more rabbits and became the laughingstock of the whole state of Sung. Now, wanting to apply policies of the former kings in governing people in these times belongs in the very same category as watching over that stump!

In emphasizing authority, the Legalists insist that talent, wisdom, and virtue matter little in government; what matters is power—the authority that enables one to do something. Even the most sagely man can accomplish no good, if he has no position of authority, whereas a scoundrel in a position of authority can do great harm. A ruler or minister must therefore jealously guard what authority is properly his; for it is this that gives him power, not his moral or intellectual qualities.

Administrative technique, in the Legalist conception, is the difficult art of manipulating people by perceiving their particular selfish interests and making it advantageous for them to do what serves one's own interests. Persons in positions of authority cannot trust anyone, even their closest relatives and friends, since human nature is such that even one's wife or son has selfish interests that sometimes conflict with one's own. A superior therefore cannot afford to be candid and friendly toward his subordinates, but must keep them in awed ignorance of his intentions and pit them against one another in such ways as to achieve his own optimum results. Similarly, Legalists advise, subordinates should learn the art of manipulating their superiors to their own ends.

The Legalists conceive of law as the only possible means of ensuring that people, including the ruler, will do what is best for the state. Legalist law is by no means divine or natural law; it is a man-made, all-encompassing system that guarantees successful perpetuation of the state, generation after generation endlessly, whether sages or fools come to the throne. Laws must be promulgated clearly and in sufficient detail to apply to every conceivable eventuality, and they must be enforced so promptly and so unwaveringly that enforcement appears automatic and in fact becomes virtually automatic. It is not enough to punish those who harm the state. Those who benefit the state must be rewarded, and rewards and punishments should both be exaggerated. Thus people can be made to want to do whatever the state's interest might require of them. In modern terms, the Legalists believed that people could and should be programmed computer-style to do what is good for the state. They believed that this is the only way a state can survive. Sage-kings may indeed appear from time to time, they admitted; but to let the fate of state and society rest on the expectation that every ruler would be a sage is pure and simple stump-watching.

Some modern specialists call these authoritarian thinkers Realists rather than Legalists, because the reality of late Chou China was such that order and central control could be achieved only by unsentimental harshness as practiced successfully by the state of Ch'in in conquering all of China. Ch'in's fate, however, demonstrated that Legalism was not a realistic program for China after all. When Ch'in collapsed there was still no commonly accepted ideology on which to build soundly for the future.

4. Literature and Art

THE CORPUS of literature left from the ancient formative age, including the philosophical writings discussed in Chapter 3, is the part of the ancient heritage that traditional Chinese most esteemed. It became the subject matter of traditional education, so that literate Chinese of all later eras memorized it, revered it, and pored over it in search of inspiration and guidance, with an intensity seldom approached by even the most ardent neoclassicist of the Western tradition in his devotion to ancient Greek and Latin writings. The arts of China's antiquity were not so conspicuously influential in later times, but they include some magnificent achievements, especially in bronze casting, that are admired throughout the world today.

The study of all ancient Chinese literature is complicated by problems of authenticity and dating, which so preoccupied Chinese of the imperial epoch that text-oriented classical scholarship flowered, and little attention was given the literary qualities of the ancient writings. The fact that the ancient writings were used intensively for didactic purposes, so that their meaning was emphasized far more than their form, also contributed to the general neglect of their literary qualities. Problems of dating and authenticity arise because no Ch'in or pre-Ch'in copy of any ancient piece of literature survives. In the formative age writing was done on slats or slips of bamboo, which were tied together side by side and rolled scroll fashion into bundles, or on lengths of silk cloth, which were similarly rolled; in either case the scroll, called a *chüan*, was a chapter-like unit without any prescribed length. Such materials are of course highly perishable. Moreover, the transmission of the scrolls was seriously disrupted by the Ch'in policy of burning books and by the destruction of the Ch'in imperial library in 206 B.C.

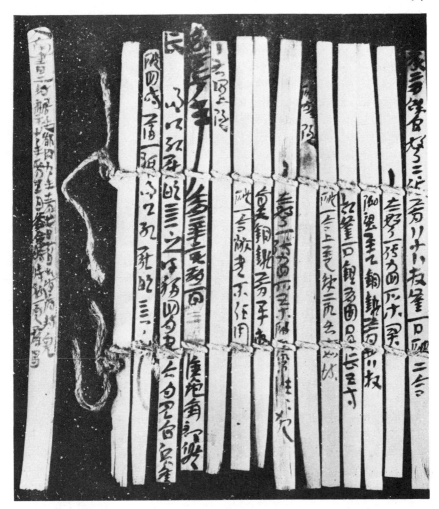

Fig. 7. Han document on wooden slats: part of an inventory of weapons from the late 1st century A.D.

Precisely because of these disasters, however, the reconstitution of old texts became an obsessive intellectual enterprise in post-Ch'in times, and throughout the imperial epoch scholars worked very carefully to verify and correct the transmitted texts.

PROSE

Early in the post-Ch'in imperial age, when Confucianism came to be espoused as the orthodox state ideology, some of the texts transmitted from the formative age were chosen for official canonization as the Five Classics (*ching*). The term ching literally denotes the vertical threads, or the warp, on a loom, through which other threads are woven horizontally, as woof; it suggests a basic matrix of any sort. The works originally designated in this way were esteemed by Confucians as the literary cornerstones of Chinese civilization. They were:

1. *I* (Changes) or *I-ching* (Classic of Changes). As has been noted in Chapter 3, this work originated as a cryptic diviner's handbook but by early imperial times had acquired commentaries that lent it mystical cosmological significance. It has no interest as literature.

2. *Shu* (Writings) or *Shu-ching* (Classic of Writings) or *Shang-shu* (Ancient Writings). This is a collection of disjointed documentary pieces, mostly harangues and exhortations, which are attributed to kings and ministers from the ages of the legendary rulers Yao and Shun down through the first three centuries of the Chou dynasty. All of the documents purporting to relate to the pre-Chou era are highly suspect, believed to be productions of Chou times and perhaps of very late Chou times. The early Chou materials, on the other hand, are generally believed to be genuine, and they make up more than half the bulk of the collection.

3. *Shih* (Songs) or *Shih-ching* (Classic of Songs). A collection of China's earliest poetry, it will be discussed later in this chapter.

4. *Ch'un-ch'iu* (Spring and Autumn Annals). This is a chronicle of events from 722 to 481 B.C., written from the point of view of the state of Lu and believed by traditional Chinese to be compiled and edited by Confucius to indicate his value judgments about historical events and personages. Its year by year, month by month, day by day entries are laconic in the extreme: "There was a great drought." "Wu Te of Ch'u led an army that joined Ch'in in attacking the state of Cheng and laid siege to Lun-shih city." "Marquis I-wu of Chin died." "The sun was eclipsed." "The Duke met with the Marquis of Ch'i, the Duke of Sung, the Marquis of Ch'en, the Marquis of Wei, the Earl of Cheng, the Baron of Hsü, and the Earl of Ts'ao at Hsien." The *Ch'un-ch'iu* early acquired three commentaries that attempt to explain the hidden meanings thought to lie in such terse entries. Two of these, the *Kung-yang chuan* (Commentary of Kung-yang) and the *Ku-liang chuan* (Commentary of Ku-liang), are of little literary interest. They are merely entry by entry explanations of what the commentators (both unidentifiable) thought Confucius meant to convey, in the way of praise and

blame, by variations in terminology. The third commentary, the *Tso-chuan* (Commentary of Tso), differs from the others in important ways: besides occasional remarks about the terminology of the main chronicle, it provides long, vivid narrative accounts of events that are merely summarized, in the fashion of newspaper headlines, in the main text; it provides narrative details about many events that are not even mentioned in the *Ch'un-ch'iu* itself; and it carries its narration 13 years beyond the end of the *Ch'un-ch'iu*. For such reasons, specialists generally believe the *Tso-chuan* was originally an independent narrative history of the Spring and Autumn era that someone cut up and spliced onto the *Ch'un-ch'iu* with appropriate editing. Also of unidentifiable authorship, the *Tso-chuan* is one of China's greatest literary masterpieces.

5. *Li* (Rituals) or *Li-ching* (Classics of Rituals). This is not in fact a single work but three books in one category, all compiled late in the formative age but attributed to much earlier times. One is the *Chou-li* (Chou Rituals), which, as was noted in Chapter 2, is an elaborately detailed description of how government was organized in early Chou times but is obviously a late idealization. The second, also mentioned in that chapter, is the *I-li* (Propriety and Ritual), supposedly a description of the Chou code of gentlemanly conduct; it includes, for example, an exhaustive description of just how an archery contest should be organized and conducted, and prescriptions about which words and actions are appropriate for each stage of a diplomatic mission from one feudal ruler to another. The third of the "three Rituals," which exists in two versions, is the *Li-chi* (Ritual Records), a heterogeneous collection of treatises on funerals, mourning, sacrifices, weddings, banquets, and similar matters. Much of the *Li-chi* purports to be pronouncements of Confucius, but this attribution is as unreliable as the traditional attribution of the *Chou-li* and the *I-li* to the Duke of Chou. Whatever their origins, some essays in the *Li-chi* are rhetorical gems and have philosophical significance.

More than a millennium after the canonization of the Five Classics, four works from the ancient formative age were officially elevated to equally exalted status, as the Four Books. They are the *Lun-yü* (the *Analects* of Confucius), the *Meng-tzu* (the book of Mencius), and two short essays embedded in the *Li-chi*—the *Ta-hsüeh* (The Great Learning) and the *Chung-yung* (The Doctrine of the Mean). The Chinese also sometimes speak of the Thirteen Classics, a catchall reference to the Five Classics, the Four Books, the three commentaries to the *Ch'un-ch'iu*, and China's earliest known dictionary, a lexicon called the *Erh-ya* that was produced in the early imperial age.

In addition to these classical texts, prose writings that have come down from the formative age notably include the philosophical works of Mo-tzu, Hsün-tzu, the Taoists, and the Legalists mentioned in Chapter 3; two late histories or pseudo-histories, *Kuo-yü* (Discourses of the States) and *Chan-kuo ts'e* (Intrigues of the Warring States); and a chronicle of questionable reliability called *Chu-shu chi-nien* (Bamboo-Book Annals), written in the cryptic style of the *Ch'un-ch'iu* but covering a much longer time span, from the legendary Yellow Emperor down to 298 B.C. All except the last-named item have considerable literary interest.

Exposition. Exposition is the prose art that was most fully developed in ancient China. Even the earliest writings, such as those in the *Shu-ching* attributed to the first Chou centuries, reveal stylistic vigor and finesse. One example is a harangue addressed by the Duke of Chou to Shang loyalists after he had put down their rebellion, destroyed their old capital, and resettled them at the new city of Lo, modern Loyang. He reviews for them—not for the first time—the history (as interpreted by the Chou conquerors) of how Hsia rule degenerated and was succeeded by that of Shang in obedience to Heaven's Mandate, and how Shang rule similarly degenerated until the Chou people hesitantly accepted Heaven's Mandate to punish the tyrannical last Shang king. He rebukes the Shang loyalists for their refusal to abide by Heaven's will and concludes with the following clear warning:

O, if you numerous officials cannot persuade yourselves to consider my commands sincere, you will then find that you cannot be obedient. All the people will say, "We will not obey"; you will become negligent and perverse, grossly violating the king's orders. Then your numerous regions will bring on themselves the wrath of Heaven, and I shall have to inflict Heaven's punishments, scattering you far from your lands. . . . It is now a new beginning for you. If you cannot be respectfully peaceable, then lay no blame on me!

The expository tradition was further developed in the later Chou philosophical writings. The *Mo-tzu*, the *Meng-tzu*, the *Hsün-tzu*, and the *Han Fei Tzu* show a particularly high order of rhetorical skill, offering sustained argumentation of great rationality. The following excerpt from the *Hsün-tzu* is not unrepresentative of the formal, disciplined, almost rhythmic **argumentative** style that was commonly employed:

When his horse is uneasy harnessed to a carriage, a gentleman is not comfortable in the carriage; just so, when the common people are uneasy under an administration, a gentleman is not comfortable in his post. When a horse is uneasy harnessed to a carriage, nothing is as good as calming it; just so, when the common people are uneasy under an administration, nothing is as good as being kind to them. Recruit the worthy and respectable. Appoint the sincere and respectful. Promote filial piety and brotherliness. Care for the orphaned and widowed. Aid the impoverished. If such is the case, the common people will be comfortable under the administration. If the common people are comfortable under the administration, only then will the gentleman be comfortable in his post. It is traditionally said, "The ruler is like a boat; the common people are like water. It is water that supports the boat, and it is also water that overturns the boat." This is my point. Therefore, if a ruler of men desires contentment, nothing is as good as governing peacefully and loving the people; if he desires glory, nothing is as good as promoting ritual and respecting his officers; and if he desires esteem, nothing is as good as honoring the worthy and employing the capable. These are the great principles of the true gentleman.

Argument by analogy, as evidenced here in the references to horses and carriages and boats and water, was especially favored by early Chinese writers and became a standard rhetorical device in Chinese prose of the whole premodern period. An equally common rhetorical device in traditional Chinese writing is apparent in both of the preceding selections. This is what is called the chain syllogism (if A then B, if B then C, and so on), which gives to Chinese argumentation a strikingly different quality than is found in Western argumentation derived from the classical Greek syllogism (if A is B and B is C, then A is C). The most famous set of chain syllogisms in Chinese, summing up the Confucian emphasis on rule by virtuous example, appears in the late Chou essay *Ta-hsüeh*, which was eventually to be canonized as one of the Four Books:

Growing things have roots and branches, and human affairs have endings and beginnings. If one knows what should be put first and what should be put last, then he is near to the Way. The ancients who wished to shine their bright virtue throughout all under Heaven first set in order their states. Wishing to set in order their states, they first regulated their households. Wishing to regulate their households, they first cultivated their persons. Wishing to cultivate their persons, they first rectified their minds. Wishing to rectify their minds, they first made their intentions sincere. Wishing to make their intentions sincere, they first extended their knowledge. The extension of knowledge lies in the investigation of things. Things being investigated, then knowledge is perfected. Knowledge being perfected, then the intentions are made sincere. The intentions being made sincere, then the mind is rectified. The mind being rectified, then the person is cultivated. The person being cultivated, then the household is regulated. The household being regulated, then the state is set in order. The state being set in order, then all under Heaven is at peace. From the Son of Heaven down to the common people it is uniformly so: for all, cultivating the person is to be considered the root. It is false that the root can be in disorder and yet the branches can be in good order. It has never been that what should be emphasized can be deemphasized and that what should be deemphasized can be emphasized.

Expository skills are perhaps most elaborately developed in the *Chan-kuo ts'e*, a compilation of anecdotes about late Chou interstate diplomacy. Although traditionally believed to be a compendium of historical documents akin to those in the *Shu-ching*, the *Chan-kuo ts'e* seems to be a compendium of rhetorical exercises illustrating what might have been said, or what should have been said, in known historical situations. These "persuasions" commonly set forth various alternative courses of action that are open to rulers, discuss their advantageous and disadvantageous possible consequences, and conclude with recommendations. They are often long and complex arguments, stating general principles and illustrating them with allusions to earlier history. Although the arguments often reek of cynical opportunism, they have great rhetorical power; and they have served as models for much of China's later expository writing.

Narration. Historical narration was not as developed as exposition in the formative age. The *Ch'un-ch'iu* and *Chu-shu chi-nien* are barebones chronicles and no more. Fuller narrations occur in the *Tso-chuan*, *Kuo-yü*, and *Chan-kuo ts'e*, but their narrative portions are most often simple transitional passages connecting expository passages in which historical personages are made to anticipate, plan for, report on, interpret, celebrate, or lament events. The narratives of the *Tso-chuan* in particular are nevertheless esteemed as stylistic marvels— terse, straightforward, and dramatic. The compactness and forcefulness of its style can perhaps be recognized, even in translation, in a brief selection from one of its most renowned accounts. This tells of events leading up to, during, and resulting from the Battle of Ch'eng-p'u in 632 B.C. The powerful, still only partly Sinicized southern state of Ch'u had massed all its forces for a campaign into the Yellow River plain and had the capital of the Sung state under siege. Duke Wen of Chin (here entitled marquis; soon to be proclaimed hegemon by the Chou king) rallied an army representing the northern states of Ch'i and

Ch'in as well as his own Chin forces to raise the siege and drive Ch'u back into the south. On the day of the climactic battle:

> The Chin army took up a position north of the ruined village Hsin. Hsü Ch'en, aide in command of the Third Division, was poised opposite [Ch'u auxiliaries from] Ch'en and Ts'ai.
>
> [On the Ch'u side] Tzu-yü commanded the Central Division, augmented with six companies from Jo-ao. "After this day," he announced, "there will be no more Chin!" Tzu-hsi commanded on the left flank, Tzu-shang on the right.
>
> Hsü Ch'en, his chariot horses draped in tiger skins, charged against Ch'en and Ts'ai. Ch'en and Ts'ai fled the field, and the whole Right Division of Ch'u collapsed.
>
> [Meantime, on Chin's right flank] Hu Mao brandished a couple of battle flags but then withdrew, and Luan Chih also pretended to retreat, dragging branches behind his chariots [to raise a dust screen]. When the Ch'u Left Division charged pell-mell after them, Yüan Chen and Ch'üeh Chen attacked it from one side with the First Division and the marquis's personal troops, and then Hu Mao and Hu Yen swung the Second Division around to attack Tzu-hsi from the other side. The Left Division of Ch'u collapsed.
>
> The whole army of Ch'u was thus routed in disgrace. Tzu-yü's Central Division was not destroyed, but only because he held it back out of the battle. [He was promptly dishonored and committed suicide.]
>
> The Chin army occupied the Ch'u camp and fed on its victuals for three days and then on the fourth day withdrew.

More representative of the *Tso-chuan* style, showing its heavy reliance on exposition in direct quotations, is the following complete entry under the year 593 B.C., when Ch'u was again rampaging northward, again had the Sung capital under siege, and again was opposed by a duke of Chin (who from the days of Duke Wen inherited the title of hegemon):

> Sung sent Yüeh Ying-ch'i to report its plight to Chin. The Marquis of Chin intended going to its rescue. But his counselor Po-tsung said, "That would be inappropriate. The ancients had a proverb: 'However long one's whip, it will not reach the horse's belly.' Heaven now favors Ch'u, so that it is irresistible. Can Chin, even with all its power, go against Heaven? . . . Your lordship should wait."
>
> So Chin desisted. Nevertheless, the marquis dispatched Hsieh Yang to persuade Sung not to surrender to Ch'u by saying, "All the Chin armies are being called up and will be coming!" However, the intervening state of Cheng captured Hsieh Yang en route and handed him over to Ch'u. The Viscount of Ch'u offered him a generous bribe to change around his intended announcement, but he would not agree. After repeated refusals, however, he consented.

So they put him up on a high-turreted chariot, from which he could communicate by shouting at the Sung defenders. What he did then was carry out the orders of his own ruler.

The Viscount of Ch'u, fully intending to put Hsieh Yang to death, sent him this message: "You gave us your word but violated it. Why? We did not break faith. It is you who spoiled things, and you will promptly be punished."

"I have heard," Hsieh Yang responded, "that what makes it possible for a ruler to give orders is his righteousness, and what makes it possible for a subject to obey orders is his faithfulness. The faithful carrying out of righteous orders is a great advantage, and anyone who can govern so that this advantage is not lost, and thus preserve his state altars, is a genuine master of the people. But righteousness cannot be served by two standards of faithfulness, and faithfulness cannot serve two sources of righteousness. Your lordship's bribing me only shows ignorance of the nature of orders. I would have given my life rather than violate the orders that I left with. How could I have been bribed! I gave in to your lordship only in order to carry out my orders. Having carried them out in the face of death satisfies me that I am a faithful subject of my ruler. I am fulfilled, and though I now die what more could I seek?"

The Viscount of Ch'u set him free to go home.

The outstanding characteristics of the *Tso-chuan* style—a minimum of description, a focus on individual participants in events, terse statements of what they did, and detailed reconstructions of what they said —were emulated by most later Chinese narrators.

Fiction. Nothing that can be considered a substantial work of prose fiction, a wholly imaginary tale presented as such, is preserved from the formative age, and there is no clear evidence that there even existed in those days the kind of professional storyteller who flourished in imperial times. However, most of the stylistic qualities that make good fiction were fully developed. The *Shu-ching* includes one early Chou piece, the "Chin-t'eng" (The Metal-Bound Coffer), that would qualify as a well-plotted short story except that it is presented as history. It relates that soon after Chou's conquest of Shang, when King Wu fell dangerously ill, the Duke of Chou inscribed a prayer to the royal ancestors pleading that he be taken to Heaven in King Wu's place so that the consolidation of the expanded kingdom might proceed uninterrupted. The king recovered. Later, after he died and the Duke of Chou made himself regent for the young King Ch'eng, the court was shaken with rumors of possible usurpation, the duke was temporarily out of favor, and the kingdom was battered by endless storms and other natural disasters. Then the young king by accident discovered a lockbox containing the duke's earlier prayer on behalf of King Wu. The king and court were ashamed of themselves for questioning the duke's loyalty to the throne, the duke enjoyed greater prestige than ever, and Heaven showed its pleasure by providing a bounteous harvest.

Many short entries in the *Tso-chuan* have equally fictional qualities, and many philosophical writings of the later Chou centuries abound in highly imaginative fables and anecdotes. The *Chuang-tzu* is particularly rich in this regard, as was noted in Chapter 3. But probably no work contributed more to China's later fictional development than the *Chan-kuo ts'e*. Its accumulation of "persuasions by analogy" is a treasury of witty anecdotes, on the order of the following two examples.

Lord Meng-ch'ang, a minister in the state of Ch'i, had in his entourage an unconventional, unpredictable fellow named Feng Hsüan. Learning that Feng possessed some knowledge of mathematics and accounting, the minister thought to make use of him by sending him to collect unpaid debts from the villagers of his hereditary fief, called Hsüeh.

"I should like to go," said Feng Hsüan. So he got ready his wagons and supplies and carried away the debt-tallies. As he left he said, "After the debts have been collected, is there anything I should buy with them for you?"

"Oh, anything that you see my household is short of," Lord Meng-ch'ang said.

Feng Hsüan hurried to Hsüeh and had the local authorities summon all the residents who were indebted to come and match their tallies. When all were matched, he took it upon himself to order that what was owed should be given back to the people, and then he burned all the tallies. The residents cheered for his lordship.

Feng Hsüan drove hastily back to the Ch'i capital and early in the morning demanded audience. Lord Meng-ch'ang was taken aback by his urgency but put on cap and gown to greet him.

"Are the debts all collected? Why have you come back in such haste?"

"They are all collected."

"What have you bought with them for me?"

Feng Hsüan said, "Your lordship told me, 'Anything that you see my household is short of.' By my reckoning your lordship's mansion has plenty of gems and treasures; dogs and horses fill up the outbuildings; and there are a lot of beauties in the women's quarters. The only thing your household is short of is righteousness. So I bought your lordship some righteousness."

"How can one buy righteousness!" Lord Meng-ch'ang exclaimed.

"Well, your lordship possesses this little fief called Hsüeh. You do not cherish and love its residents but only exploit them for profit. So I took it upon myself to issue an order for your lordship giving what was owed back to the people, and I burned the tallies. In that way I bought your lordship some righteousness!"

Lord Meng-ch'ang was furious. "All right, then!" he said. "Go away."

A year or so later Lord Meng-ch'ang had occasion to appreciate Feng Hsüan's work. He was relieved of his ministerial post and forced to go live off his fief. The residents of Hsüeh came miles out of the village to welcome him with cheers, whereupon Lord Meng-ch'ang said to Feng Hsüan, "Today I can see the effects of that righteousness you bought for me."

❧

Chao was going to attack Yen when Su Tai, on Yen's behalf, said to King Hui of Chao, "En route here today I crossed the River I. A mussel there had just opened up to bask in the sun when a snipe pecked its innards. The mussel sprang its shell shut, clamping the snipe's beak. The snipe said, 'It is not raining today, and if it does not rain tomorrow there will be a dead mussel here.' The mussel said to the snipe, 'I am not opening up today, and if I do not open up tomorrow there will be a dead snipe here.' Neither was willing to let go, so a fisherman was able to catch them both. Now Chao is going to attack Yen. But Yen and Chao will withstand each other for a long time, distressing a lot of people. I am afraid mighty Ch'in may turn out to be the fisherman! I wish your majesty would think about it carefully."

"A good point," King Hui said, and he ceased his preparations.

POETRY

Chinese of the formative age set great store by music, dancing, and singing, not only in the folk culture but in the highest levels of society as well. It was thought that ritualistic musical performances at court and in public contributed to cosmic harmony and stimulated morality, and that folk songs were gauges of public morale. Certain kinds of music were thought licentious, at least among Confucians. The Chou kings reportedly sent officials touring throughout the kingdom at regular intervals to collect and write down the songs people were singing; and music masters were among the respected dignitaries at Chou-era feudal courts.

Since no system of musical notation existed in China until a much later time, it is not possible to reconstruct tunes of the Shang and Chou periods. But a well-developed musical theory already existed, providing a five-tone cyclic scale that became the basis for all later Chinese music. There was a wide variety of instruments, including drums, bells, sets of stone chimes, ocarinas, multiple-tubed flutes, and several kinds of stringed instruments. Court orchestras were large; there is one reference to as many as 300 players. In ritual performances these orchestras accompanied dancing groups that commonly consisted of six lines, or ranks, of six dancers each, or even eight lines of eight each. Dancing involved movement of the head, arms, and upper torso—no doubt in what modern Westerners would consider a Balinese style—as much as of the legs and feet, and dancers commonly carried and waved feathered wands.

From the beginning, as in other cultures, Chinese poetry had a close relationship with music, and throughout history poetic styles and genres changed as ever newer types of musical instruments and melodies were introduced. Most poetry was originally meant to be sung, or at least chanted in semimusical fashion. Even in modern times, long after the tunes had been forgotten, old poems were chanted by traditional scholars in ritualistic performances. Some prose compositions have traditionally been recited in comparable fashion as well.

Poetry is scattered in much of the narrative or anecdotal prose of ancient China. Some of it duplicates poems found in a collection that as early as Confucius's time had become part of the common heritage of all educated Chinese. This was known simply as the *Shih* (Songs) in Chou times but subsequently came to be called the *Shih-ching*. According to tradition, the 305 poems in the *Shih* were selected for preservation by Confucius from a collection of more than 3,000 songs that had been gathered together by a music master of the state of Lu. That Confucius did know and esteem the *Shih* is well established by references in the *Lun-yü*. That he had anything to do with collecting or editing it, however, seems unlikely.

The *Shih-ching* is generally conceded to be the greatest single literary monument left from China's formative age, and no work is cited more regularly in later Chinese literature of all sorts. More than half of its bulk is made up of folk songs, no doubt edited into literary form; the remainder consists of formal odes or hymns that were used on ceremonial occasions in the feudal courts. The poems are normally in four-word lines grouped into two or more stanzas, four-line stanzas being most common. Rhyme occurs in many patterns: *a b c b*, with the last words of the second and fourth lines rhyming, is common; *a b c a*, with the last words of the first and fourth lines rhyming, is not uncommon. Internal rhymes also frequently occur. Although there was no prescribed standard for meter and rhyme, these were clearly recognized to be the essential poetic elements. The monosyllabic character of the Chinese language naturally discouraged such metrical feet as iambs (da-DA) or dactyls (DA-da-da); poetry in the *Shih* has a steady metronomic beat: DA-DA-DA-DA.

In addition to meter and rhyme, the unidentifiable poets who are represented in the *Shih* were adept at alliteration, at the duplication of words for emphasis, and at refrain-like repetitions of lines. They also made much use of metaphors, commonly drawn from nature, to symbolize or contrast with the emotions being expressed by the singer. The poems are characteristically short and compact, but their subject matter is wide-ranging, touching on many aspects of everyday life and expressing sentiments about love, work, war, and great men. Some are joyous, some sorrowful. Following are some examples of folk songs that deal with courtship and marital love.

O Please, Young Chung

O please, young Chung,
Don't burst into our village!
Don't crash through our willows!
Would I care about such things?
I'm afraid of Father and Mother.
I may indeed love you, Chung,
But what Father and Mother might say
Is still to be dreaded.

O please, young Chung,
Don't burst over our wall!
Don't crash through our mulberries!
Would I care about such things?
I'm afraid of Elder Brothers.
I may indeed love you, Chung,
But what Elder Brothers might say
Is still to be dreaded.

O please, young Chung,
Don't burst into our courtyard!
Don't crash through our sandalwoods!
Would I care about such things?
I'm afraid of the gossip of others.
I may indeed love you, Chung,
But what others will gossip
Is still to be dreaded.

The All-Day Wind

The all-day wind is piercing.
When he looks at me, he smiles,
But he talks with scorn and laughs haughtily.
Deep in my heart I grieve.

The all-day wind is dusty.
Kindly, he agrees to come,
But he neither goes nor stays.
Sad and anxious are my thoughts.

The all-day wind is gloomy,
And not a day passes but is gloomy again.
Awaking, I do not sleep;
Yearning, I only whimper.

How gloomy is the dark!
How ominous is the thunder!
Awaking, I do not sleep;
Yearning, I only imagine.

My Lord Is on Army Duty

My lord is on army duty.
There's no knowing for how long.
When will he come?
The chickens have nested in their crannies;
It's the end of the day.
The cows and sheep have come in.
But my lord is on army duty.
How can I not worry about him?

My lord is on army duty,
Not for a day or a month.
When shall we be together?
The chickens have roosted on their perches;
It's the end of the day.
The cows and sheep have come in.
But my lord is on army duty.
If only he doesn't hunger and thirst!

Some folk songs, like the next one, apparently accompanied everyday farming chores.

Reeds

We gather up the reeds;
O yes, we gather them.
We gather up the reeds;
O yes, we have them.

> We gather up the reeds;
> O yes, we strip them.
> We gather up the reeds;
> O yes, we rub them clean.
>
> We gather up the reeds;
> O yes, we bundle them in our aprons.
> We gather up the reeds;
> We tuck our aprons under our belts.

Religious sentiments commonly expressed in early Chou writings are represented in the following ceremonial hymns:

We Bring Offerings

> We bring our offerings,
> Both sheep and cattle.
> May Heaven honor them!
>
> We pattern after the rites of King Wen,
> Daily pacifying the four regions.
> O blessed be King Wen!
> May he be pleased and receptive!
>
> Let us day and night
> Dread the majesty of Heaven
> And thus be preserved.

Silken Robes

> Silken robes so new and straight,
> Conical caps so neatly adorned,
> From the hall we move on to the altar,
> From the sheep we move on to the cattle.
> Tripods, cauldrons, and flagons,
> Rhinoceros-horn goblets so curved,
> Fine wines so mild.
> No loudness, no haughty airs.
> O may we be blessed by the ancestors!

Some of the poems in the *Shih* have a more personal character, such as the lament of a dismissed official translated below. In later centuries, Chinese scholars liked to interpret such poems as political allegories masking denunciations of historical personages who are now impossible to identify.

The North Gate

> Sent away out the north gate—
> My sorrowing heart is heavy.
> I am ruined and impoverished,

But no one appreciates my distress.
It is all over!
It is actually Heaven's doing;
How can I explain it?

The prince's business entangled me,
And administrative problems increasingly beset me.
When I came home from afar,
My kinsmen all rebuked me.
It is all over!
It is actually Heaven's doing;
How can I explain it?

The prince's business was thrust upon me,
And administrative problems increasingly burdened me.
When I came home from afar,
My kinsmen all ridiculed me.
It is all over!
It is actually Heaven's doing;
How can I explain it?

Poetry of a distinctly different style and form occurs in another ancient collection called the *Ch'u-tz'u* (The Elegies of Ch'u). The poems therein date from the late Chou centuries and in some cases from Ch'in and even immediate post-Ch'in times; and as the title indicates they represent a South China tradition. About half of them are attributed to the only identifiable poet of the whole formative age—a member of the royal clan of the great southern state of Ch'u—named Ch'ü Yüan. Because of his uprightness, tradition relates, Ch'ü was victimized by slanderers, estranged from his king, and finally banished from court. In shame and grief he committed suicide by drowning, sometime between 298 and 265 B.C. He became the hero of both a literary cult and a folk cult; China's famous dragon-boat festivals in the Yangtze valley are symbolic efforts to recover Ch'ü Yüan's corpse from the river.

The songs or elegies in the *Ch'u-tz'u* differ from those in the *Shih-ching* in several ways. They are characteristically very long by *Shih* standards; emotions are expressed more directly and much more verbosely; adjectives and adverbs heap up in rich, lavish descriptive passages; there is an abundance of sensuous and erotic imagery. In sum, the *Ch'u-tz'u* poems are lush and ornate in contrast to the compactness of the *Shih*'s; and above all they exude a moaning, lugubrious quality that is alien to the *Shih*. Ch'ü Yüan's own poems are thought to have been written during his exile. They are characteristically self-righteously sorrowful, expressing the outrage of an honest man who is not appreciated by his ruler. The *Ch'u-tz'u* poems are also in different metrical patterns than are found in the *Shih*. Lines commonly run to six- and seven-word lengths. Some words are clearly unstressed (DA-DA-DA-da-DA-DA), and in some poems the meaningless syllable *hsi* is regularly inserted into lines, like "fa-la" in old English ballads. The rhythms suggest that the poems were sung to a quite different music than predominated in North China.

The longest and most famous poem in the *Ch'u-tz'u* collection is a narrative recital called the "Li-sao" (Encountering Sorrow), ascribed to Ch'ü Yüan. Speaking entirely in the first person and in mystical symbolic language, the poet sings of his virtues, his ruination by slanderers, his hatred of wickedness, his travels to a variety of heavens and fairylands in quest of goodness and appreciation, and his anguished frustrations. The general flavor of the poem is illustrated in the following excerpts from David Hawkes's translation:

> Many a heavy sigh I heaved in my despair,
> Grieving that I was born in such an unlucky time.
> I plucked soft lotus petals to wipe my welling tears
> That fell down in rivers and wet my coat front.
> I knelt on my outspread skirts and poured my plaint out,
> And the righteousness within me was clearly manifest.
> I yoked a team of jade dragons to a phoenix-figured car
> And waited for the wind to come, to soar up on my journey.
>
> . . .
>
> The age is disordered in a tumult of changing:
> How can I tarry much longer among them?
> Orchid and iris have lost all their fragrance;
> Flag and melilotus have changed into straw.
> Why have all the fragrant flowers of days gone by
> Now all transformed themselves into worthless mugwort?
> What other reason can there be for this
> But that they all have no more care for beauty?

Several items in the *Ch'u-tz'u* collection are shamans' songs addressed to gods or goddesses. One of the more famous songs of this type is the "Chao-hun" (Summons to the Soul), which is at least symbolically addressed to the departing soul of a sick king. It warns the soul of the natural and supernatural horrors that await it wherever it might wander and then describes in elaborate and luscious detail the delights it can enjoy if only it will return—delights of the court, the garden, the table, and especially the bedchamber, as in the following excerpt, again from a David Hawkes translation:

Many a rare and precious thing is to be seen in the furnishings of
    the chamber.
Bright candles of orchid-perfumed fat light up flower-like faces that
    await you;
Twice eight handmaids to serve your bed, each night alternating in
    duty,
The lovely daughters of noble families, far excelling common
    maidens.
Women with hair dressed finely in many fashions fill your
    apartments,
In looks and bearing sweetly compliant, of gentleness beyond
    compare,
With melting looks but virtuous natures and truly noble minds.
Dainty features, elegant bearing grace all the marriage chamber:
Mothlike eyebrows and lustrous eyes that dart out gleams of
    brightness,
Delicate colouring, soft round flesh, flashing seductive glances.

      . . .

O soul, come back: Why should you go far away?

The different poetic strains represented in the *Shih-ching* and the
Ch'u-tz'u—it would not be stretching things too much to consider them
literary dimensions of the conflict and complementarity between sober
Confucianism and playful Taoism—were soon to merge and give to the
poetry of the imperial era its great variety and vivacity.

THE ARTS

Chinese of the imperial era considered paintings and porcelains to
be their greatest art products, and statuary was esteemed in a special,
secondary category, being associated chiefly with Buddhism. The art
historian finds none of these art forms represented significantly in the
ancient formative age. Rather, antiquity offers genres that were later
respected as skilled craft work but not fine art—unglazed pottery, jade
carvings, lacquerware, and bronze castings. This is a realm in which
archaeologists and cultural anthropologists are more at home than art
historians are. Yet it includes, in its bronzes, a unique and exquisite art
form that cannot properly be considered anything except a fine art.
There is nothing of comparable quality in the productions of later
bronzesmiths, in China or elsewhere.

Ancient Chinese artisans in bronze produced a great variety of
things, including weapons, chariot and harness fittings, and mirrors.
Their most noted and prized products, however, are sacrificial vessels
that were used in rituals and buried with the important dead. Such ves-

sels have been collected and catalogued by Chinese connoisseurs for at least the past 1,000 years, and hundreds of them are now scattered in museums and private collections around the world. They have been analyzed into more than 30 separate shapes, and their variations in decor have been sorted out so minutely that specialists can now date a vessel almost to the decade on stylistic grounds.

Common shapes of ancient bronze vessels include hollow-legged tripod cookers, four-legged cauldrons, covered and uncovered steamers, deep bowls, shallow basins, dishes perched atop tall stems with flaring bases, kettles, covered and uncovered gravyboat-like pourers, narrow bottle-shaped goblets, bucket-like containers with swinging handles, cups, and vases. They are usually grouped in fewer categories according to their presumed uses: for cooking food, for serving food, for serving and drinking wine, and for storing, serving, or drinking water. Vessels of the Shang period seem primarily to have been intended for sacrificial use, which did not prevent the sacrificers from banqueting on what remained after the ancestral spirits had partaken of the "spirit" of the food and drink offered them. After the mid-Chou period, however, shapes of vessels became so ornate as to rule out almost any conceivable use except as decorations.

On the basis of stylistic criteria, early bronze vessels are assignable to three main periods: (1) Shang and early Chou, which witnessed the rapid rise and perfection of bronze artistry; (2) middle Chou (tenth century to sixth century B.C.), a time of artistic degeneration; and (3) late Chou (sixth century to third century B.C.), when there was an artistic renaissance, especially in South China, though not a complete recovery of the Shang and early Chou bronze mastery. Bronzes of the first period are sometimes decorated over the whole surface and sometimes only in well-defined circling bands. The decoration is rather restrained on the whole, normally providing a background of repetitious geometric patterns or spirals, from which animal forms emerge in low relief. The shape and decoration of a vessel are characteristically integrated into a cohesive aesthetic whole that has an overall effect of elegant daintiness, despite the large size of some vessels. Middle Chou bronzes, in contrast, have an effect of coarseness, bulkiness, awkwardness, and vulgarity. They are often over-decorated with animalistic attachments that distract attention from the vessel itself, or roughened with large, jutting flanges at corners and seams. In the third, late Chou period, bronzes became elegant again—sometimes elegantly or-

Fig. 8. Bronze vessels of the Shang and early Chou periods. Upper left: Shang *kuei.*
Upper right: early Chou *li-ting.* Lower left: Shang *chia.* Lower right: early Chou *fang-i.*

nate and sometimes elegantly refined. Some are inlaid marvelously with
gold, silver, or jade. This late Chou style is sometimes called the Huai
style because its earliest excavated examples came from the Huai River
watershed on China's central east coast.

The most famous decorative motif found on the early bronzes is a
design called the *t'ao-t'ieh.* This is an animal face seen directly from
the front; the animal is sometimes recognizable but is more often stylized to such a degree that it appears to be a fabulous monster. It is
flattened on a side surface or bent round a corner; in either case a

Fig. 9. The *t'ao-t'ieh* design

flange is likely to split it into symmetrical halves, each having a prominent eye button peering straight out. From each side of the face, sometimes in proper proportion and sometimes not, extends a body in perfect symmetry with its opposite. It is as if the carcass had been cut through along the backbone and the two halves had been folded out like wing attachments to the head. The bodies have serpentine, dragonlike qualities, coiling in spirals or geometric twists and turns, and are normally themselves covered with small spiral or geometric designs, sometimes including smaller t'ao-t'ieh. The same t'ao-t'ieh usually appears many times on a vessel. It is a striking, powerful, and unique design. What it represents is not known.

One aspect of early Chinese art that has long intrigued art historians is its alternation between representational and nonrepresentational forms. Art of the imperial era was overwhelmingly representational, though it fluctuated between naturalistic and abstractionist impulses. Art forms of the formative age, on the other hand, are predominantly nonrepresentational, purely decorative. The decor of the early (Yangshao) painted pottery is dominated by whorls and curvilinear geometric patterns. A few representations of fishes, birds, plants, and even human forms have been found on painted pottery, but the inclination of the potter was to stylize them out of all recognition. The later (Lungshan) black pottery, being undecorated, in itself reflects an abstractionist, nonrepresentational spirit. As has been noted above, the same decorative, nonrepresentational character is discernible on the early bronzes: the background for the animalistic forms that appear in relief is normally a dense pattern of geometric meanders, spirals, whorls, lozenges, or fish scales, and such patterns often cover the relief forms themselves. It is noteworthy, too, that over time the animalistic relief forms became increasingly stylized and abstracted, as in the case of the t'ao-t'ieh. Then, in the Warring States period and especially in products of the south, animal and human forms appear in all art forms, even in strikingly naturalistic representations. They are often intermixed with the old, nonrepresentational motifs, but it is clear that the long predominance of geometric and other purely decorative designs was now ending.

PART TWO

The Early Empire

206 B.C.-A.D. 960

5. General History

THE CHAOS into which China was plunged by the collapse of Ch'in in 207-206 B.C. did not last long. In 202 there emerged out of it a new dynasty called Han, which moderated Ch'in's harshness and capitalized on the strengths of Ch'in political institutions to build a new state system that endured until A.D. 220. Han China, contemporaneous with the Roman empire in the West, rivaled if it did not surpass Rome in its achievements. It created a stable aristocratic social order, expanded geographically and economically, and spread Chinese political influence not only into neighboring Vietnam and Korea, but also across Central Asia to the Pamirs. To this day, the Chinese proudly call themselves the Han people. But Han government became corrupt at the center, Chinese confidence waned, and the Han empire, like the Roman empire, was simultaneously invaded by barbarian hordes and an alien, subversive religion. In the Chinese case, these foreign elements were the nomadic Hsiung-nu from Mongolia and Buddhism from India.

In A.D. 220 Han gave way to a long era of political division, during which the Hsiung-nu and other nomad groups gained control of China's homeland in the Yellow River drainage area and Han traditions were perpetuated in the south by ever weaker native dynasties. In all regions semifeudal great families dominated politics and socioeconomic life, and Buddhism became the paramount cultural force at all levels of society. In 589 a northern dynasty, Sui, reunified China Proper and began thrusting China's power outward again. Exhausting its resources in this process, Sui was succeeded in 618 by the T'ang dynasty, which brought China to new peaks of organizational stability, economic and military strength, and cultural splendor.

The seventh and eighth centuries were the zenith of aristocratic dominance and Buddhist influence. T'ang emperors became universal monarchs acknowledged by Turkic khans in Mongolia, and T'ang patterns of civilization were emulated in Vietnam, Central Asia, Korea, and Japan. As in the late Han decades, however, T'ang institutions finally could not cope with changing conditions, and in 907, after long deterioration, the centralized T'ang state broke apart. Regional warlords established separate kingdoms throughout South China, and in the north five short-lived dynasties in succession groped for some formula to renew the lost T'ang glories, threatened and manipulated by new nomadic enemies in Mongolia.

HAN (202 B.C.-A.D. 220)

The uprisings against Ch'in quickly resolved themselves into a struggle between two remarkable men. One contender was Hsiang Yü, a descendant of the old Ch'u feudal nobility; the other was Liu Pang (originally Liu Chi), a coarse commoner. Hsiang's lordly arrogance and battlefield brilliance attracted the original rebel chieftains to him in a coalition designed to unify China under a Ch'u regime. Liu, rising to prominence by persuading the Ch'in capital to capitulate peaceably in 206 B.C., became prince of Han in Hsiang's coalition. Hsiang outraged Liu by vengefully devastating the surrendered capital, and he steadily alienated other supporters by similar cruelties. Liu, in contrast, attracted popular support wherever he went by dealing with his aides and troops fairly and generously, treating defeated enemies with magnanimity, and manifesting sincere concern for the well-being of the people. Hsiang utterly lacked the common touch and, though never defeated in battle, was steadily undermined by his rival; in 202 B.C. he committed suicide in isolated desperation. Liu was then acclaimed emperor of Han.

Former Han (202 B.C.-A.D. 9). Liu Pang, or Han Kao-tsu as he is best known, was the first commoner in Chinese history to fight his way to the throne. For that reason, and because he never lost the earthy crudeness and cunning that are admired by peasants everywhere, he has always held a very special place in the pantheon of Chinese emperors. He is further esteemed for establishing two principles of governance that pervaded Chinese political thought forever after. First, giving credit to his generals and aides for their contributions to his success and acknowledging his own limitations, he insisted that in decision-making a ruler must heed his advisers; and second, reacting against the totalitarian excesses of the Ch'in regime, he emphasized that government exists to serve the people.

Partly because as emperor he was preoccupied with campaigning against challengers among the ranks of his earlier allies, Kao-tsu did not pursue an aggressively expansionist policy and did not initiate major domestic reforms. He moderated the harsh punishments of Ch'in, lowered the tax rate to one-fifteenth of a farmer's crop, and maintained the pattern of governmental organization that Ch'in had established. The one fundamental change he made was to grant most of the eastern half of the empire to his strongest supporters in the form of hereditary princedoms and marquisates. In part he was moved to this action by a realistic estimate that he could not achieve Ch'in-style centralization, but he also had a generous urge to share power with his aides. Kao-tsu's policy in general was to preserve order and let the people recuperate from their sufferings under Ch'in without governmental harassment.

Kao-tsu's laissez-faire style of governing characterized the first 60 years of the Han dynasty. His own reign was short; he died in 195 B.C., still in his forties. His strong-minded widow, Empress Lü, also of commoner origin, was virtual regent for the next 15 years and ruled very conservatively. Kao-tsu's son Wen-ti (r. 180-157 B.C.) and grandson Ching-ti (r. 157-141 B.C.) won renown as paragons of frugality and benevolence. Throughout this half century all high official posts were held by Kao-tsu's trusted aides and generals and their sons. The only significant challenge to the stability of the empire was a domestic revolt of seven imperial princes in 154 B.C., and it was quickly suppressed. After centuries of turbulence, the peaceful early Han reigns gave the Chinese people an opportunity to thrive, and they did so, explosively. The population grew, the economy expanded, and culture flourished. Under Ching-ti taxes were cut in half, to one-thirtieth of the crop. Even so, at the end of his reign state granaries bulged, and the central government had vast cash reserves.

The early Han laissez-faire spirit permitted the development of inequities that many court officials considered intolerable, and their arguments for greater state activism prevailed in the reign of Wu-ti (141-87 B.C.). By this time the rested and prospering Chinese people seem to have been bursting with pride, confidence, and restlessness; and Wu-ti came to the throne as a vigorous young man, intelligent, imaginative, and bold. He reigned longer than any other Chinese emperor until the eighteenth century, and he provided for later emperors a Yang model of aggressiveness to complement the Yin model of quiescence so notably provided by Wen-ti and Ching-ti. This was possible because memories of the overambitious Ch'in regime had now dimmed, and China was economically and psychologically ready to flex its muscles.

For a start, Wu-ti undertook to centralize and extend imperial authority in domestic affairs. Kao-tsu's creation of semifeudal princedoms and marquisates side by side with centrally controlled commanderies and counties of the Ch'in sort had proved troublesome from the outset, and Empress Lü's practice of enfeoffing her own relatives and even favored eunuchs had complicated the situation still more. Though the new lords were court appointees who could be removed at an emperor's whim, and though their domains were managed for them by court-appointed administrators, the lords were often tempted to aggrandize themselves to the detriment of the imperial prestige and sometimes gained great economic power if not political influence. The quick suppression of the princes' revolt in 154 B.C. had not ameliorated the basic problem, but Wu-ti pursued so vigorous a policy of weakening the semifeudal lords that after his reign they were powerless adornments in the state organization. He made arbitrary and heavy financial demands on the lords—for example, by requiring them to offer him gifts of white deerskin of a type available only at the palace treasury at extortionate prices. He also stripped lords of their rank on the slightest pretexts, and transformed their fiefs into commanderies and counties. In a single year, 114 B.C., 104 princedoms and marquisates were thus confiscated. In the long run, Wu-ti's most effective measure against the lords was a decree issued at the beginning of his reign requiring every princedom and marquisate to be divided equally among all male heirs upon a lord's death. In consequence the lordly domains were increasingly fragmented generation after generation.

Another troublesome group that Wu-ti challenged was the merchant class, which had taken advantage of the breakdown of old feudal barriers and of laissez-faire attitudes in the early Han government to build fortunes in fields largely exempt from taxation—in the iron, salt, and liquor businesses, in grain speculation, and in mortgage foreclosures that had driven large numbers of freehold farmers into tenancy and even slavery. Wu-ti attacked these abuses, and drained away much mercantile wealth to the state, by introducing new taxes on mercantile inventories and vehicles, by forbidding merchants to own farming land, by instituting an "ever-normal granary" system whereby the state regulated the supply of grain, and most dramatically by taking over the production and wholesale distribution of iron, salt, and liquor as state monopolies.

Wu-ti was equally aggressive in foreign relations. Late in the Warring States era and especially after the collapse of Ch'in, Chinese renegades established petty kingdoms in many frontier areas—in southern Manchuria and northern Korea, on the southeastern coast, and in the Canton region. The early Han rulers had been content to consolidate their control over the North China heartland and the Yangtze River drainage area, which was only now becoming substantially assimilated into the Chinese mainstream; they considered it a diplomatic triumph when peripheral rulers were persuaded to acknowledge nominal Han overlordship. But the neighbors were unruly from the Han point of view, and Wu-ti undertook to chastise them and assert Han supremacy decisively. In 111-110 B.C. he mounted campaigns to subjugate the Fukien-based state of Min Yüeh and the Canton-based state of Nan Yüeh (Nam Viet), establishing durable Chinese control throughout South China and into modern Vietnam; and in 109-108 he subjugated southern Manchuria and most of Korea. Meantime, other Han armies had gained loose control over the aborigines of Yunnan and Kweichow. All these areas were carved up into commanderies and garrisoned with Han troops, and Sinicization was significantly accelerated, especially in Korea and Vietnam. Overseas contacts began with Japan and some peoples of the South China Sea.

Many of Wu-ti's aggressive policies, in domestic as well as foreign affairs, were designed to strengthen China for a showdown with the Hsiung-nu nomads who threatened the northern and western frontiers. In Kao-tsu's time the Hsiung-nu, under a chieftain named Modok (Mao-tun), were building a confederation that was soon to dominate not only Mongolia, but the Indo-European oasis statelets of Chinese Turkestan as well. Kao-tsu tried to dislodge them from China's northern frontier zones, but after he was lucky enough to escape from a week-long Hsiung-nu entrapment in Shansi in 201, he and his successors pursued a policy of appeasement. They treated Modok and his successors as equals, sent them Chinese princesses and noblewomen as brides, and sometimes dispatched to them gifts of grain that amounted to tribute. Modok arrogantly proposed to the widowed Empress Lü that they marry and consolidate their empires, and later Hsiung-nu unhesitatingly

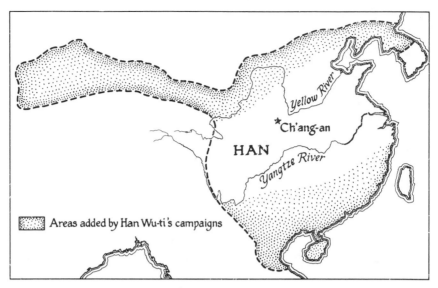

Map 3. The Han Empire, c. 100 B.C.

raided the Han frontiers. Chinese generals seethed in frustration, and courtiers and merchants fretted about the disruptions of caravan trade across Central Asia, which was relied on for such luxury goods as glass and amber and for fine-quality jade, which had important uses in Han symbolism and ritual.* Wu-ti was easily persuaded that appeasement of the Hsiung-nu was a failure, and that military action against them was overdue.

Wu-ti hoped to form an alliance against the Hsiung-nu with the Yüeh-chih, an Indo-European people who had been driven westward out of Kansu by Hsiung-nu pressures. To this end he sent a young courtier named Chang Ch'ien to find the Yüeh-chih and make a treaty with them. Leaving the capital in 139 B.C., Chang was captured by the Hsiung-nu, settled peaceably among them, took a wife, and began raising a family. Only after ten years had passed did he find it opportune to escape and continue his travels. He eventually located the Yüeh-chih beyond the Pamirs in northern Pakistan, but learned that they had no intention of re-involving themselves in East Asian affairs. After being captured again en route home, Chang finally reached the Han capital

---

* State and private interests in mineral resources and luxuries such as pearls and ivory had something to do, also, with Wu-ti's efforts to win control of the southwest and the south coast.

at Ch'ang-an (Sian) in Shensi province in 126. His reports gave the Chinese their first reliable intelligence about Central Asia—and incidentally suggested that trade routes of some sort connected southwestern China with India, giving Wu-ti added interest in bringing the southwest under control.

Meantime, in 133, Wu-ti had launched a series of grand campaigns against the Hsiung-nu that were to absorb the resources and energies of China for the next 18 years. The first target was the Ordos area north of Ch'ang-an in the northern bend of the Yellow River, a natural staging area from which the Hsiung-nu had easily raided the agrarian basins of Shensi and Shansi. The Ordos was cleared by 127, and in the subsequent years Han generals fanned out east and west to drive the Hsiung-nu from Inner Mongolia, Kansu, and Chinese Turkestan. Some 700,000 colonists were settled in the Kansu corridor to Central Asia, and in the farther desert regions the Han armies established military colonies—self-sufficient garrisons of soldier-farmers, with whose support military governors kept foreign rulers in awed submission and the Central Asian caravan routes open. General Li Kuang-li in 104 and 102 B.C. even led forces across the Pamirs into Russian Turkestan, to obtain for Wu-ti a famous breed of "blood-sweating horses" from the inhospitable king of Fergana.

In these ways the empire under Wu-ti's direct rule came to incorporate the whole of modern China Proper, northern Vietnam, Inner Mongolia, southern Manchuria, and most of Korea. In Central Asia, which was not geographically suited to Chinese-style settlement, Wu-ti instituted the pattern of diplomatic relations commonly known as the tributary system. The native rulers of the settlements there were allowed to retain their traditional authority and were protected by China's proconsul-like military governors. In return, they submitted gifts of local products to the imperial court as symbols of their vassalage, came to the capital at intervals to render homage, and left sons at court—nominally to be educated in the Chinese fashion, but also to serve as hostages guaranteeing their fathers' good behavior. This pattern became the basis of China's subsequent relations with all foreign peoples.

Wu-ti's long reign saw a cultural flowering that produced China's greatest historian, Ssu-ma Ch'ien; the most esteemed Han poet, Ssu-ma Hsiang-ju; and the most influential Han philosopher, Tung Chung-shu. Under Tung's influence, the emperor adopted a reinterpreted, eclectic Confucianism as the official state ideology and created a rudimentary national university for the training of Confucian officials. There were also the beginnings of systematic civil service recruitment through recommendations and written examinations. The state was not promptly transformed into a Confucian bureaucracy; throughout Han times a hereditary aristocracy of great landowning families almost totally monopolized political, social, and economic influence. But Wu-ti's initiatives had important long-run consequences.

Wu-ti's reign was the high point of Han power, prestige, and morale. Under his successors, Han armies continued to press the Hsiung-nu. In 73 B.C. five armies collaborated to shatter the reviving Hsiung-nu in Mongolia, and thereafter the Hsiung-nu split into two rival leagues. In 51 B.C. the southern chieftain came to Ch'ang-an to submit as a Han vassal. His counterpart in the north retreated westward, only to be killed in 36 B.C. by a Han force venturing far beyond the Pamirs into the Samarkand region, where it defeated a coalition reportedly including some Roman legionaries. For the most part, however, Wu-ti's successors were undistinguished. They allowed most of his domestic economic controls to lapse, and fell under the influence of powerful eunuchs and imperial in-laws. Nepotism and cronyism flourished at court, and rapacious landlordism was unchecked in the countryside. The imperial family lost its prestige and its nerve; a succession of young emperors who died without natural heirs finally convinced the court that the Liu family had also lost its Heavenly Mandate. After A.D. 6 there was an infant emperor, and China was governed by a regency council until A.D. 9, when a prestigious minister named Wang Mang was induced to take the throne.

Wang Mang (A.D. 9-23). Han Kao-tsu and his early successors had not been committed to any ideology in particular, but in Wu-ti's time Confucianism—much altered by Han interpreters to include numerological and cosmological trimmings—was made the state-espoused dogma and the basis of education for all officials. By the first century B.C. this eclectic Han-style Confucianism was the dominant intellectual current at court, and Confucian-indoctrinated civil servants were laying the foundations for a bureaucratic preeminence in later Chinese administrations. Carried to its logical extreme, Confucianism lends support to the Platonic notion that government properly belongs in the hands of philosopher-kings. Wang Mang's accession is understandable only in the light of this intellectual climate, since he had no military base or following. Originally an obscure provincial member of a powerful family that had repeatedly married its women to Liu-family emperors and princes, Wang gained public attention as a paragon of filial piety, humanitarianism, and other Confucian virtues and as a generous patron of Confucian scholarship. Catapulted by his reputation and family connections into high court posts, he was publicly acclaimed another Duke of Chou and finally took the throne because of popular demand, after repeated protestations of his unworthiness. He called his dynasty Hsin, literally meaning new.

Wang Mang's reign, from A.D. 9 to 23, was a disaster of such proportions that subsequent Chinese historians labeled him a villainous usurper. Rationalizing everything by selected and sometimes spurious classical writings, Wang undertook to reestablish early Chou institutions and to put into practice "genuine" Confucianism. He reorganized the government with archaic titles, vastly increased the semifeudal nobility with Wang-family appointees, tried to restore some ancient feudal powers to the nobility, and made many bureaucratic offices hereditary. He revitalized discriminatory policies against merchant families, forbade the buying and selling of slaves, and tried to alleviate conditions of slavery in general. He revived the ancient doctrine that all land belongs to the ruler, confiscated the properties of great landlords, established an allocation system to provide all adult males with farming plots, and claimed state ownership of mountains, forests, streams, and marshes, which traditionally had been considered public domain. He issued new coinage, reinstituted Wu-ti's "ever-normal granaries" and state monopolies, and introduced new taxes and state controls of marketing and credit. Although most of his changes proved unenforceable and were soon rescinded, his efforts antagonized almost all classes of society; even the Hsiung-nu and the statelets of Central Asia, disgruntled by Wang Mang's changes in their titular status, renounced their vassalage to China.

Almost from the beginning of his reign everything seemed to conspire against Wang Mang, even nature. Aberrations in the weather produced a series of poor harvests; perennial drought settled on the Shensi basin, in which the capital was located; and what was worse, a series of breaks in the Yellow River dikes culminated in A.D. 11 in a vast inundation of the eastern part of the northern plain, with the result that the Yellow River changed its course to run south rather than north of the Shantung peninsula. Uncounted thousands of people were drowned or made homeless refugees. Famine became endemic, state welfare schemes proved inadequate, and food prices skyrocketed. Vagrants swarmed over China and in desperation formed robber bands. By A.D. 18 a great rebellious group called the Red Eyebrows had formed, and by A.D. 22 several Liu-family claimants were in the field. In A.D. 23 rebels broke into the imperial palace and murdered Wang Mang. Order was eventually reestablished by a scion of the Liu family, who reinstituted the Han dynasty in A.D. 25.

The traditional view was that Wang Mang was a callous opportunist whose whole official career was a propagandist sham designed to pave his way to the throne, and that his programs as emperor served no purpose other than to aggrandize and enrich himself. It seems fairer to conclude that Wang was an idealistic intellectual with many genuinely humanitarian impulses who was seduced by political ambition and eventually corrupted by power. He was compulsively attracted to impractical and politically disadvantageous programs, suspiciously refused to delegate authority and overburdened himself with work on details, and on the whole proved to be an inept leader.

Later Han (A.D. 25-220). The restorer of the Han dynasty, known as Kuang-wu-ti, established his capital at Loyang in Honan province, near his own home. For this reason the period he inaugurated is known as the Eastern Han as well as the Later Han era, and the era from Han Kao-tsu to the accession of Wang Mang, during which the national capital had been at Ch'ang-an in Shensi, was retrospectively called Western Han as well as Former Han.

Kuang-wu-ti (r. 25-57) and his immediate successors, Ming-ti (r. 57-75) and Chang-ti (r. 75-88), were vigorous, conscientious rulers under whom China regained stability and prestige. The natural disasters and rebellions of Wang Mang's reign had reduced the population and wrecked agriculture and commerce; but with peace and a revival of the laissez-faire policies of the early Han years, the population and the economy rebounded. Confucian scholars were honored, and scholarship, education, and culture in general flourished. By the end of the first century Chinese life was as affluent and sophisticated as in the best of Former Han times.

The Chinese also fared well in foreign relations during the early reigns of Later Han. The Hsiung-nu, who had once again become a menace in Wang Mang's time, now had internal problems, and in A.D. 50 Kuang-wu-ti allowed a supplicant group of southern Hsiung-nu tribes to settle inside China's traditional border, in northern Shensi and Shansi. By the end of the century, some northern Hsiung-nu had begun the westward migrations that were to carry them into Europe as the Huns of Attila. On other frontiers Han power was reasserted by three of the ablest proconsuls of Chinese history—Ma Yüan (14 B.C.-A.D. 49), who reconquered the south coast and northern Vietnam, and a famous father and son team, Pan Ch'ao (32-102) and Pan Yung (active into the 120's), who reestablished Han supremacy throughout Chinese Turkestan. In A.D. 97 Pan Ch'ao marched an army all the way to the Caspian Sea and from there sent an aide reconnoitering toward the Mediterranean; he reached either the Persian Gulf or the Black Sea before turning back. For the next several centuries camel caravans carried Chinese silks across Central Asia to Rome, and seafarers from Southeast Asia and the Indian Ocean regularly traded in China's southern ports.

After the first century, however, domestic conditions deteriorated very rapidly. As in Former Han times, the government's laissez-faire policies allowed the peasantry to fall under the control of great landowners who, because of their connections at court or in the palace, easily found ways to evade taxes. Many farmers were reduced to virtual serfdom on semifeudal manors, and great families patronized hundreds of retainers euphemistically called "guests" (k'o) and fielded whole armies of private fighting men (pu-ch'ü). Always vulnerable to the intimidation of such local magnates, the remaining freehold farmers found themselves burdened with ever larger shares of taxes and labor obligations to the state. After the middle of the second century, a series of natural disasters added to peasant discontents: there were devastating floods and locust infestations in 175, and in 173 and again in 179 epidemics swept across the empire. Peasants began seeking refuge in Taoist-inspired religious cults, which offered them social welfare programs, mystical faith healing, and alchemical prescriptions that were perhaps effective. By 182 two such groups, the Yellow Turbans in eastern China and the Five Pecks of Rice Band in Szechwan, had huge followings, and in 184 the Yellow Turbans rose in a rebellion that hastened the fall of the already declining dynasty.

The upper classes, though enjoying unprecedented affluence and indulging themselves in amusements and exotic imported luxuries such as new musical instruments from Central Asia and cosmetic powders, were meantime experiencing a crisis of confidence. The buoyant optimism of Former Han Confucianism had been shattered by the Wang

Mang debacle. Kuang-wu-ti fostered a sober, earnest, chastened realism, and this quickly gave way to fatalism, skepticism, and finally escapism. Other-worldly Buddhism, introduced from India about the time of Christ, gradually attracted interest among the curiosity-seeking upper classes, and by the end of the second century a revived philosophical Taoism was beginning to gain currency among intellectuals, as a Taoist popular religion was among the poor.

Political deterioration began with the accession of a minor, Ho-ti, in A.D. 88. Thereafter the dynasty was plagued by a succession of short-lived, weak rulers. The families of dowager empresses manipulated government by palace intrigues and coups. In self-defense young emperors gave more and more power to their most trusted allies, palace eunuchs; and eunuch cliques were soon in open control of many governmental agencies. Civil service officials, trying to maintain governmental integrity, poured out futile criticisms of both the eunuch and the imperial in-law factions; and students being trained for official careers at the national university, whose number had swollen to 30,000, gathered in raucous demonstrations at the palace in support of one "honest critic" after another. Intrigues and demonstrations escalated quickly into massacres. In 159 a eunuch gang in the service of Huan-ti (r. 146-67) slaughtered relatives of the Empress Dowager Liang, and five eunuchs were subsequently ennobled, given large fiefs, and made a virtual council of state. Protests against eunuch dictatorship in 166 resulted in the arrest and imprisonment of more than 200 officials and students. New protests in 169 against the abuses of the eunuch Hou Lan, who had reportedly confiscated houses and fields to build himself ten great mansions and a 100-foot-square mausoleum, led to the deaths in prison of more than 100 "honest critics" accused of forming treasonable partisan cliques. Some 700 other officials and 1,000 students were thrown in prison and tortured.

Generals who were given responsibility for putting down the Yellow Turban rebellion that exploded in 184 made themselves into regional warlords and eventually wrested control of the throne from the palace eunuchs. General Tung Cho (d. 192) seized Loyang in 190, deposed the emperor and installed his own protégé, murdered the empress dowager and an imperial prince, and slaughtered eunuchs wholesale. When a coalition of rival generals gathered to challenge him, he retreated with his puppet emperor westward to Ch'ang-an. There he was soon murdered, and the emperor fell under the control of a general named Ts'ao

Ts'ao (d. 220). Ts'ao, himself the son of a eunuch's adopted son, became protector of the empire and put down the Yellow Turbans. On his death in 220, his son Ts'ao P'ei (d. 226) accepted the abdication of the last Han emperor and established a new dynasty, called Wei. Four centuries of Han rule, which the Chinese have traditionally considered the stable imperial model against which the great dynasties of later ages were measured, thus came to an inglorious end.

THE ERA OF DIVISION (220-589)

Although the Han dynasty was not formally terminated until 220, General Tung Cho's capture of Loyang in 190 threw the empire into confusion and inaugurated four centuries of disruption that have commonly been considered a "dark age" in China comparable to the disintegration of imperial unity in Europe after the fall of Rome.* In social organization and intellectual life there was creative ferment and regeneration, but the political history of the post-Han epoch is a dismal record of disunity, intrigue, strife, and alien encroachments, of which the Chinese have not been proud.

Ts'ao Ts'ao, the dominant figure of the last Han decades, was never able to reunite the empire after the Yellow Turban upheavals of the 180's; for the rest of his life he had to fight against separatist-minded regional warlords. His major effort at reunification ended in one of the most celebrated battles of Chinese history, the Battle of the Red Cliff at Ch'ih-pi in Hupei province in 208, when he was defeated by two rivals. Thereafter Ts'ao consolidated Han control in the north, while his victors dominated the south. When Ts'ao P'ei established his Wei dynasty at Loyang in 220, two southern rivals set themselves up as emperors also—Sun Ch'üan (d. 252), whose Wu dynasty based at Nanking controlled the Yangtze valley and the south coastal regions, and Liu Pei (d. 223), whose Shu Han dynasty based at Chengtu controlled Szechwan and the southwest (see Map 4). The military adventures of Liu Pei and his sworn brothers, Chang Fei and Kuan Yü (both d. 219), originally as lieutenants of Ts'ao Ts'ao and then as his most dedicated antagonists, became one of the great epic legends of China and the inspiration for much later fiction and drama. Kuan, in fact, was eventu-

---

* This period is sometimes referred to as the Six Dynasties era, after the "legitimate" Han successor states with modern Nanking as their capital: Wu (222-80), Eastern Chin (317-420), Sung or Liu Sung (420-79), Southern Ch'i (479-502), Liang (502-57), and Ch'en (557-89).

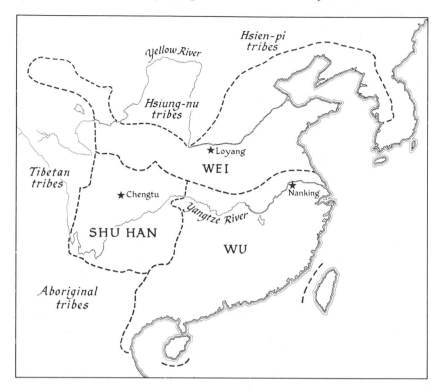

Map 4. The Three Kingdoms, c. 230

ally canonized as China's god of war. The chief counselor in Liu Pei's imperial government, Chu-ko Liang, also attained legendary renown—not as a stolid strongman of Kuan Yü's type, but as a wily strategist who dazzled the Wei armies with his brilliant maneuvers. After Chu-ko Liang's death in 234, Shu Han could no longer compete with its northern enemy and was absorbed by Wei in 263. The conquest of Wu in 280 ended the so-called Three Kingdoms era, to which traditional Chinese gave an aura of knightly derring-do suggestive of the great age of chivalry in medieval Europe.

Meantime, during Wei's struggles with Shu Han and Wu, the prestige of the Ts'ao rulers had been eclipsed by generals of the Ssu-ma family, and in 265 a Ssu-ma had usurped the throne and changed the dynastic name to Chin. For a generation after Chin's defeat of Wu, China was united again, but its unity was fragile. The Chin rulers carried out a neofeudal fragmentation of the empire among their Ssu-ma relatives, and regional princes became almost autonomous satraps. Particularly after 300, regicides and abdications rapidly succeeded one another as princes contended for power. Feudalistic patterns of socioeconomic organization, which had begun to develop in Later Han times, flowered during the civil wars of the Three Kingdoms era and by Chin times produced a society totally dominated by great landowning families, each commanding hordes of serfs, "guests," and private soldiers. The intellectual malaise of Later Han had led to a dilettantism of the most cynical sort among the upper classes; Buddhist thought, art, and architecture were gaining dominance in Chinese culture, challenged by an imitative neo-Taoism. The Hsiung-nu and other northern nomad groups, taking advantage of the disunity and instability of China, increasingly infiltrated the frontier. In 304 a Sinicized Hsiung-nu chieftain declared himself the only legitimate heir to the imperial throne and established a state called Han (later changed to Chao) in Shansi; and from this base the Hsiung-nu sacked Chin's capital, Loyang, in 311, capturing and eventually killing the Chin emperor. The Chin government reorganized itself under a new emperor in the ancient western capital, Ch'ang-an, but in 316 this too was overwhelmed by the Hsiung-nu.

For more than two centuries after Chin's collapse in the north, China was divided into two quite different societies, northern and southern. Refugees from the north set up an Eastern Chin dynasty at Nanking. They made some efforts to recover the lost territories: in 347 they reconquered Szechwan; in 383 they turned back the most threatening advance of alien northerners in a famous battle at the Fei River in northern Anhwei, which was decided more by propaganda and intrigue than by fighting; and in 415-17 they pushed northwestward, regaining access to the Central Asian trade routes through Kansu. But the court continued to be distracted and weakened by factional intrigues, and a series of usurpations created ever weaker successor dynasties—Sung (420-79), Southern Ch'i (479-502), Liang (502-57), and Ch'en (557-89). Under these so-called Southern Dynasties, which considered themselves the champions of Han civilization, the aboriginal peoples and customs of South China were substantially absorbed into the Chinese mainstream, Buddhism gradually became the predominant intellectual and religious force, feudal socioeconomic patterns became entrenched, and the life of the upper classes steadily became more refined and effete. The founder of the Liang dynasty, Wu-ti (r. 502-49), was an especially noted patron of Buddhism and of elegant litterateurs.

In the north, the Hsiung-nu destruction of Chin's capitals at Loyang and Ch'ang-an precipitated the rise and fall of a bewildering array of ephemeral regional states that are collectively called the Sixteen Kingdoms. The proto-Turkic Hsiung-nu were now challenged by other alien groups—proto-Tibetans, proto-Mongol tribes called the Hsien-pi, and separate proto-Turks called the T'o-pa (Toba). There were also occasional Chinese contenders, especially descendants of Chin's frontier governors in Kansu.* In the latter half of the fourth century, the north was temporarily consolidated by a Tibetan general named Fu Chien (r. 357-85), but his Ch'in dynasty disintegrated soon after his ambitious plan to conquer the south was wrecked at the Battle of the Fei River in 383. A more stable unification of the north was achieved by the T'o-pa Turks' Northern Wei dynasty (386-534), the first in a sequence of so-called Northern Dynasties—including Eastern Wei (534-50), Western Wei (534-57), Northern Ch'i (550-77), and Northern Chou (557-81). Farther north, in Mongolia, the dominance of Hsiung-nu, Hsien-pi, and T'o-pa Turks gave way early in the fifth century to a new nomadic empire of the Juan-juan tribes, a mixture of proto-Turk and proto-Mongol elements. Overthrown in 551, the Juan-juan migrated westward and became the Avars of East European history. Their successors in Mongolia were the Turks proper, whom the Chinese called T'u-chüeh.

From Later Han times, and especially after the Hsiung-nu depredations in the early fourth century, large numbers of Chinese migrated out of North China into the Yangtze valley. Those who remained were normally enslaved or made agricultural serfs, to support the invading tribal warriors. Some great landlord families survived by intimidating

---

* The Sixteen Kingdoms, overlapping from 301 to 439, are most conveniently listed in regional groupings by modern province names, as follows. In Shansi and Shensi: Han or Chao (Hsiung-nu, 304-29), Later Chao (Hsiung-nu, 319-52), Ch'in or Former Ch'in (Tibetan, 352-410), Later Ch'in (Tibetan, 384-417), Hsia (Hsiung-nu, 407-31), and Western Ch'in (Hsien-pi, 385-431). In Szechwan: Ch'eng-Han or Shu (Tibetan, 301-47). In Hopei: Yen or Former Yen (Hsien-pi, 348-70), Later Yen (Hsien-pi, 383-409), Southern Yen (Hsien-pi, 398-410), and Northern Yen (Chinese, 409-36). In Kansu: Liang or Former Liang (Chinese, 313-76), Southern Liang (Hsien-pi, 397-414), Later Liang (Tibetan, 386-403), Western Liang (Chinese, 400-421), and Northern Liang (Hsiung-nu, 397-439). For the most part, the designations Former, Later, Northern, and the like are labels subsequently applied by historians to differentiate ruling lineages. But their efforts have not been wholly successful, for there are three units bearing the name Later Liang: the kingdom of 386-403 in Kansu mentioned above, a statelet based at Hankow on the Yangtze from 555 to 587, and a dynasty that governed the whole of North China from 907 to 923. Almost all dynastic titles of the early imperial age were revivals of the names of Chou dynasty feudal fiefs.

the nomads with their cultured manners, and became tutors and administrative specialists for alien rulers. Such families tended to cling tenaciously to the heritage of Han Confucianism, with the result that the intellectual mood of the northerners remained more soberly realistic and moralistic than the southerners'. Like the south, however, the north was thoroughly penetrated by Buddhism, especially in its aspect as a popular religion. Alien rulers were attracted to Buddhism and commonly made it a state religion that gave them status as living Buddhas. The T'o-pa rulers in particular were great patrons of Buddhism.

One reason for the popularity of Buddhism among the alien rulers of North China was that its universalist ethics, in contrast to the particularist ethics of Confucianism, gave the two populations of North China—family-oriented Chinese peasants and tribe-oriented nomad warriors—some basis for common interest and cooperation. The transformation of Chinese civilization into a thoroughly Buddhistic society was perhaps the essential factor promoting the emergence of a revitalized civilization incorporating both Chinese and aliens in a new Chineseness, and allowing the eventual reunification of north and south. Even so, the invading northerners did not easily become Chinese. From the beginning there were nomadic groups that resisted Sinicization in any form. Conflicts between such determined tribal conservatives and advocates of Sinicization account in large part for the instability of the alien northern states in the fourth and fifth centuries. But there could be no real future in North China for invaders who would not accommodate themselves to the geographic and socioeconomic realities of the region. Those tribes that doggedly preserved their alien identities had no choice in the end but to retreat back to the steppes and be absorbed by the Turks of Mongolia. Meanwhile, such advocates of Sinicization as the T'o-pa Turks eventually lost their separate identities as they were absorbed into, and contributed some of their own qualities to, the general North China population; it was their leaders who established the patterns of governmental organization that made possible the stable consolidation of North China coupled with gradual advances in the struggle with the southern dynasties.

SUI (581-618)

The reunification of all China was finally achieved by a Chinese named Yang Chien, whose forebears had long served T'o-pa and Hsienpi rulers. Married to a strong-willed alien noblewoman, Yang became an influential minister at the Northern Chou court and married his daughter to the emperor. When his infant grandson succeeded to the throne, Yang was prevailed upon to take his place; and the Sui dynasty was thus inaugurated in 581. At this time, the south was in extreme disarray. In 555 a northern prince had pressed into the central Yangtze valley and set up a puppet Later Liang state based at modern Hankow, and by the 580's the Ch'en dynasty at Nanking was gravely weakened by court factionalism. The new Sui emperor, known posthumously as Wen-ti (r. 581-604), proved to be a prudent, effective administrator and a skilled propagandist, using Buddhist, Taoist, and Confucian pronouncements and observances to win support in all quarters; and it was not difficult for his forces to subdue Later Liang in 587 and Ch'en in 588-89.

Since there had been no devastating wars anywhere for many decades, both northern and southern Chinese had prospered in peace. Sui Wen-ti's frugal and temperate policies ensured continuing prosperity, and he centralized governmental power to a degree not known in China since the Later Han. The rebuilding of old canals, to link his capital, Ch'ang-an, with the Yellow River in 584, had contributed to his securing stable control of North China, and after the Sui conquest of the south he borrowed on that experience. To improve travel and transport throughout the newly unified empire, he undertook to link the Yellow and Yangtze rivers by building connecting canals among the natural waterways of east-central China. This project, known to Westerners today as the Grand Canal, was completed in 605 by his successor, who subsequently extended the waterways network north to Peking and south to Hangchow. The Grand Canal not only symbolized the political reunification of north and south; it made the growing economic wealth of the south easily accessible to support military and other governmental needs in the north, and it provided a communication channel that facilitated stable reintegration of the divergent northern and southern cultures.

The stability, prosperity, and high morale achieved by Wen-ti were wholly undone by his son Yang-ti (r. 604-18), who brought Sui to an early end, remembered by the Chinese as an oppressive tyranny comparable to that of Ch'in in the third century B.C. Mothered by Wen-ti's strong-willed alien wife, Yang-ti had megalomaniacal qualities reminiscent of the First Emperor of Ch'in, and many traditional historians considered him a complete madman. He reportedly came to the throne by poisoning his father. Then he built a lavish new palace at Loyang and transferred the capital there. While the Grand Canal was still being worked on, he raised new labor levies to rebuild the Great Wall, construct huge grain-storage depots, and build roads from the North China plain to the northern frontier zones. His armies reconquered northern Vietnam and attacked the Cham people farther south, conducted exploratory expeditions to Taiwan, campaigned successfully against the Turko-Mongol tribesmen in Chinese Turkestan, intimidated some Turkic nomads of Mongolia into accepting vassalage, and in three massive efforts in 612, 613, and 614 tried in vain to conquer the Korean state of Koguryo.

Yang-ti's frantic engineering and military activities disrupted the domestic economy and aroused widespread resentment. In 615 his army was humiliated by Turks in the north, and when he personally led a punitive expedition against them in 617, he was almost captured. Domestic revolts sprang up everywhere. Ordering a frontier general named Li Yüan (566-635), the Duke of T'ang, to deal with the aroused Turks, Yang-ti fled to South China and devoted himself to a life of leisure and licentiousness. He was assassinated by a courtier in 618. By then Li Yüan had already renounced his allegiance to Yang-ti and set up a puppet Sui heir at Ch'ang-an, and soon after Yang-ti's death Li accepted his puppet's abdication and inaugurated a dynasty of his own, called T'ang.

T'ANG (618-907)

Under the T'ang dynasty, China combined prosperity, cultural grandeur, aristocratic sophistication, military power, and supremacy in foreign relations to achieve an age of greatness unapproached since Han. The T'ang capital at Ch'ang-an became the world's largest and most brilliantly cosmopolitan city, a mecca to which traders, diplomats, and seekers after culture traveled from Japan, Korea, Central Asia, Vietnam, and the South China Sea, and where Arabs, Persians, Jews, and Christians from the Mediterranean basin were welcomed. Later Chinese esteemed T'ang equally with Han among their greatest dynasties, and T'ang achievements were the models to which all subsequent dynasties claimed to aspire.

T'ang China owed much of its early strength and prosperity to the maturing of institutions that had been developing under the Northern Dynasties and Sui. In addition to a stable, centralized administrative structure, these notably included a civil service system that accommodated the hereditary claims of powerful landowning families and yet advanced the bureaucratic principles of recruitment and evaluation established by Han. Economic inequities were minimized and fiscal stability ensured by an "equal-fields" system of land tenure; the state claimed ownership of all agricultural lands, allocated them equitably on a per capita basis for lifetime tenure, and collected taxes and requisitioned labor services in accordance with head counts. Military strength derived largely from a national militia system called *fu-ping*, which provided a prestigious corps of volunteer career citizen-soldiers, who supported themselves on state-allocated farmland and in rotation served in armies both at the capital and on the frontiers.

The Li family of T'ang emperors in a sense symbolized the changed China, combining new and old elements, that had evolved during the centuries of disunion. On one hand, it claimed descent from the famous Former Han general Li Kuang-li and, beyond him, from the ancient Taoist philosopher Lao-tzu. On the other hand, it had intermarried with alien nobility to such an extent that it could be considered only half Chinese at best by Han standards. Its vigor was best personified by Li Yüan's son Li Shih-min (600-49), known posthumously as T'ang T'ai-tsung, who was the real founder of the dynasty and is generally considered the most heroic ruler of all Chinese history. His leading generals were later deified in popular religion as gate guardians of palaces and temples, and his favorite chargers were glorified by singers and painters.

It was Li Shih-min, then still a youth of seventeen, who provoked his father into renouncing Sui Yang-ti in 617. At that time China swarmed with more than 100 rebellious movements, of which 11 became major challengers to the emerging T'ang regime. For seven years Li Shih-min and his aides battled for supremacy while keeping the Turks neutralized on the northern frontier. Their most decisive confrontation took place near Loyang in the renowned Battle of Ssu-shui, in which the T'ang forces outmaneuvered the far more numerous armies of the Cheng regime of Honan and a northeastern regime called Hsia. Li Shih-min's victory in this battle secured T'ang control of North China; thereafter, resistance in the south was quelled with relative ease. By 624 all major opposition had been subdued, and the new dynasty had won national acceptance by its policies of clemency and amnesty. In that year Li Shih-min disposed of his two brothers, including an elder one who was heir apparent, in an ambush. He was named heir apparent and was given virtually complete governmental authority by his father. Two years later his father formally abdicated in his favor.

Fig. 10. T'ang dynasty painting of T'ang T'ai-tsung, surrounded by female attendants, being carried to greet an envoy from Tibet

As emperor (r. 626-49), T'ai-tsung had still more military successes. A masterful strategist and tactician, he so intimidated the Turks of Mongolia that in 630 they made him their grand khan; he was the first Chinese ruler to attain such power over the northern steppes. Then, with combined Chinese and Turkic forces, he established T'ang authority throughout Chinese Turkestan and across the Pamirs into Afghanistan, driving out the local agents of a Western Turkic empire based in western Inner Asia. The western campaigns of 639-40 and 647-48 also brought Tibet under T'ang suzerainty, and in 648 a small Chinese force crossed the Himalayas from Tibet into northeastern India to chastise a regional ruler who had insulted a T'ang ambassador; the offender was brought captive to Ch'ang-an. In the 640's T'ai-tsung also sent armies against Korea on two occasions, but Korean resistance was so vigorous that the Chinese had to abandon the effort.

Notwithstanding his military achievements, T'ai-tsung has been most esteemed by later Chinese for his conscientious, capable, and benevolent role as civil administrator. He fostered education, welcomed advice, chose able ministers, and delegated authority wisely. In philosophical and religious matters he was interested and tolerant. Though his governmental policies were primarily Confucian, he befriended both Tao-

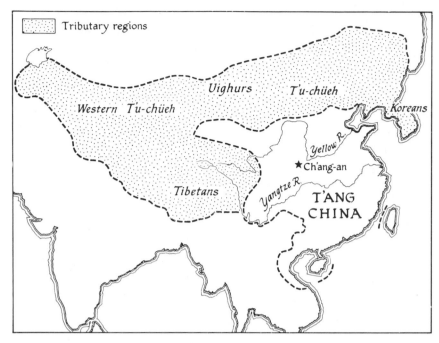

Map 5. The T'ang Empire, c. 700

ism and Buddhism. In 635 he welcomed and built a church for a Central Asian missionary preaching the Nestorian variety of Christianity. In his time China's most famous Buddhist pilgrim, Hsüan-tsang (ca. 596-664), made a historic 16-year journey to India and back and then devoted himself prodigiously to translating the Buddhist texts he had brought back with him, under imperial patronage.

T'ai-tsung's son Kao-tsung (r. 649-83) is best remembered for becoming infatuated with one of his father's young concubines, the Lady Wu. Recalling her from the Buddhist nunnery to which, according to custom, she had retired after T'ai-tsung's death, Kao-tsung allowed her to intrigue and poison her way to the status of empress, and in 660, when his eyesight began to fail, gave her informal regental power. When Kao-tsung died in 683, Empress Wu perpetuated her power by placing first one and then a second son on the throne. Finally, in 690, she deposed the second and took the throne herself, becoming the only woman of Chinese history who formally bore the title emperor. She proclaimed a new dynasty with the venerable name Chou and ruled China until 705, when she was forced to abdicate at the age of eighty.

The Empress Wu was execrated by later Chinese as a despotic usurper of the most ruthless character, and there is no denying that she manipulated the government to suit herself and staffed it with her favorites. All the same, she ruled very capably and maintained China's prestige in foreign relations. In the 660's she and Kao-tsung intervened vigorously in a Korean civil war during which the state of Silla, with T'ang help, forged a united Korea. Chinese authority was established in some Manchurian territory formerly dominated by Koreans. Although Silla was rather aggressively independent, it grudgingly acknowledged T'ang overlordship and was respectful to Empress Wu throughout her reign.

For a few years after Empress Wu's abdication the court was unstable as Li family factions competed for dominance. Then in 712 another great T'ang ruler came to the throne and presided over the greatest cultural flowering China had yet known. This was Hsüan-tsung (r. 712-56), also called Ming-huang, or Brilliant Monarch. A conscientious and able administrator, he purged the bureaucracy of parasites and favorites, reduced court extravagances, made special efforts to keep informed about conditions among the people, abolished capital punishment, and continued to follow the vigorous foreign policy of his predecessors. In addition, he encouraged cultural development in all forms, setting up a long-enduring Hanlin Academy at court to harbor talented scholars and litterateurs, and a music and dance institute to train theatrical performers for palace entertainments. His court was splendidly elegant, and in his reign flourished some of the greatest cultural geniuses of the Chinese tradition—among them the poets Li Po and Tu Fu and the painters Wu Tao-tzu and Wang Wei.

But Hsüan-tsung lived too long for his own good, and for China's. He became dependent on sycophantic advisers and palace eunuchs, and he turned over command of the frontier armies to alien generals of questionable loyalty. Then, in 745, at the age of sixty, he fell in love with the concubine of one of his sons, the deliciously plump young Lady Yang, and became her doting lackey. This was Chinese history's most notorious *femme fatale*, known primarily by her concubine title, Yang Kuei-fei. Soon her relatives monopolized the most powerful ministerial posts, and her favorite general, An Lu-shan (d. 757)—an obese, witty, and audacious Turk—had the run of the palace as her adopted son and commanded the strongest frontier armies on the north.

When officials remonstrated with Hsüan-tsung, he uncharacteristically ignored them and then began punishing them. Administration was neglected, the military establishment began to decline, and border relations deteriorated. In Central Asia the high tide of Arab expansion had already begun encroaching on the most remote T'ang vassal statelets around Samarkand, and in the 740's rebellious Tibetans and Western Turks had to be suppressed. In 747 and 750 Chinese armies crossed the Pamirs to chastise unruly Tibetans who had been raiding Kabul and Kashmir, but in 751 the Chinese were routed by a coalition of Arabs and Western Turks in a momentous battle on the banks of the Talas River near Samarkand, and reeled back across the Pamirs. Closer to home, an aboriginal chieftain in Yunnan declared his independence in 750, established the state of Nan Chao, which lived on for centuries in the southwest, and in 751 decisively repulsed a T'ang punitive expedition. The government's deterioration accelerated, and in 755 General An Lu-shan rose in rebellion. One important consequence was the immediate recall of T'ang's demoralized forces from Central Asia, which thereafter turned increasingly from Buddhism to Islam; Chinese power was not to reappear in the area for six centuries.

The An Lu-shan rebellion, which was not suppressed until 763, was a major turning point in Chinese political history; it began an erosion of T'ang stability that could not be checked. An's forces pillaged Loyang and then Ch'ang-an, while Hsüan-tsung and his court entourage fled southward into Szechwan in an exodus lamented in famous poems and immortalized in famous paintings (see Fig. 11). En route the emperor's palace guard, blaming all the empire's troubles on Yang Kuei-fei, strangled her and tossed her corpse into a ditch; Hsüan-tsung abdicated in shame and sorrow. General An promptly proclaimed himself emperor of a new dynasty called Yen, but he soon became blind and irritable, and in 757 was murdered by his son. The son was then murdered by a subordinate, General Shih Ssu-ming, under whom the rebellious Yen dynasty survived for a time. But Shih was eventually murdered in his turn by a son, and T'ang loyalists managed to restore order of a sort. Meantime, however, opportunists had risen in revolt in many areas, and T'ang's regional governors and commanders, given extraordinary powers to deal with the revolts, had made themselves semiautonomous warlords.

Apart from the high political drama of the An Lu-shan rebellion, it is of major significance to historians because it resulted from, caused, or simply coincided with important changes in Chinese society. Some

Fig. 11. T'ang Hsüan-tsung's flight with Yang Kuei-fei to Szechwan, by unidentified T'ang dynasty painter

institutions had already broken down at this point—among them the fu-ping militia system, which had given way to mercenary armies, and the equal-fields system of land distribution. As the central government weakened, early T'ang restraints on exploitive landlordism, private commerce, and social mobility withered away; and gradually the social and political eminence of the old aristocratic class, the mainstay of early T'ang stability, was undermined by irreversible waves of social change. By the end of the eighth century, trends were developing that would bring about a vastly altered way of life in the post-T'ang age.

A semblance of the earlier political order was finally restored, but the effort required the military help of the Uighurs, a Turkic people who had overthrown the Eastern Turks in Mongolia in 744, and even of some Arab auxiliaries from Central Asia. The restored T'ang court, all its foreign influence having evaporated during the rebellion, was almost a vassal of the Uighur khan. With its domestic authority undermined by the regional warlords who had risen during the An Lu-shan rebellion, the court was further troubled by rampant partisanship among its officials and gradually came to be dominated, even more flagrantly than the Later Han court, by powerful cliques of palace eunuchs. Hsien-tsung (r. 805-20) and Ching-tsung (r. 824-26) were both assassinated by eunuchs, and most emperors beginning with Mu-tsung (r. 820-24) were installed by eunuch coups, to become little more than puppets manipulated by their eunuch attendants.

As years passed there were small-scale rebellions, army mutinies, and new humiliations inflicted by the southwestern state of Nan Chao. Thus for a century after the An Lu-shan rebellion the prestige and authority of the T'ang emperors declined. Nonetheless, the T'ang administrative apparatus preserved an air of normalcy, the economy thrived, and culture flourished, notably producing the great poet Po Chü-i and the moralist and prose stylist Han Yü. There were the beginnings of a Confucian philosophical revival, as Buddhist preeminence began to wane. A vigorous campaign was conducted by the government in 841-45 to reduce the number of Buddhist temples and monasteries and return hundreds of thousands of monks, nuns, and temple attendants to lay life, so that they could be taxed and drafted for state service.

The long twilight of T'ang splendor was finally shattered by another great rebellion, lasting from 875 to 884. Beginning as a popular uprising in drought-stricken Honan, it quickly engulfed most of east and central China and swept on southward to Hangchow and Canton under the principal leadership of a salt merchant named Huang Ch'ao, embittered by his failure to win an official appointment. In 879, when the rebels took Canton, thousands of Moslems, Jews, Christians, and Manichaeans who were engaged in China's thriving overseas trade were slaughtered. Huang then turned his forces northward and in 881 captured Ch'ang-an. As in the time of An Lu-shan, the T'ang court fled south into Szechwan. Huang proclaimed himself emperor of a new dynasty called Ch'i. Turkic forces summoned from the northern frontier finally helped T'ang loyalists to suppress the rebels, and in 884 Huang committed suicide. But the T'ang dynasty thereafter ruled in name only. Generals and governors became increasingly unrestrained, and two strongmen contended for domination of the eunuch-ridden central government. One was Li K'o-yung, a Turkic general who had played a major role in putting down Huang Ch'ao's rebellion; the other was Chu Wen, a Huang Ch'ao follower who had prudently surrendered in time to win honors in helping to suppress his former comrades. By 900 Chu Wen was the foremost warlord of North China, and the dynasty survived on little more than its prestige. In 903 Chu took the imperial court at Ch'ang-an under his protection and slaughtered the eunuchs who had corrupted it for so long. That "protection" extended only to 904, when he transferred the emperor as a virtual prisoner to Loyang, had him murdered, and installed a boy successor. Finally, in 907, Chu Wen accepted his protégé's abdication and took the throne himself. He founded a new dynasty and reigned until his death, in 914.

THE FIVE DYNASTIES ERA (907-960)

For the next two generations the political fragmentation that had begun after the Huang Ch'ao rebellion was fully realized. As soon as Chu Wen proclaimed his Later Liang dynasty, which had its capital at his base of personal power, Kaifeng, rival strongmen in central and southern China dissociated themselves from him and established independent states of their own, each with T'ang-style imperial institutions. The so-called Ten Kingdoms* that rose in defiance of the North China usurper generally enjoyed peace and late blossomings of the T'ang cul-

---

* Among the regional states that appeared in central and southern China, historians conventionally apply the label Ten Kingdoms to (1) Shu (907-25) and its successor (2) Later Shu (934-65) in Szechwan; (3) Nan-p'ing or Ching-nan (907-63) in Hupei; (4) Ch'u (927-56) in Hunan; (5) Wu (902-37) and its successor (6) Southern T'ang or Ch'i (937-75) based at Nanking; (7) Wu-Yüeh (907-78) in Chekiang; (8) Min (907-46) in Fukien; and (9) Southern Han or Yüeh (907-71) based at Canton. The tenth state normally included is Northern Han (951-79) in Shansi, a puppet state of the Ch'i-tan, a powerful nomadic group in the north.

tural tradition. None was militaristic enough to consolidate the south or even to consider attempting reunification of the whole empire. They marked time, as it were, and enjoyed their local prosperity while waiting for the more vigorous warlords of the north to settle China's fate.

Consolidation was far from easy in the north. There five dynasties rose and fell in rapid succession—Later Liang (907-23), Later T'ang (923-34), Later Chin (936-47), Later Han (947-51), and Later Chou (951-60)—as military preeminence passed from one family to another. These northern regimes had no time for cultural pursuits, and little inclination. They single-mindedly concentrated on maintaining their precarious military supremacy. Only a thoroughgoing reorganization of the government could have reversed the long-flowing tide of decentralization and made possible a strong central administration of the sort that had given the early T'ang emperors their great power. But in the best of circumstances, this restructuring of government could not have been accomplished easily; and Five Dynasties rulers were not favored by circumstances. To their north a new nomadic power had risen—the proto-Mongol Ch'i-tan (or Khitan), who consolidated a federation of tribes on the northeastern frontier in 905. The Ch'i-tan khan Yeh-lü A-pao-chi in 916 declared himself emperor; his state soon adopted the dynastic name Liao. In 937 the Ch'i-tan helped a protégé establish the Later Chin dynasty at Kaifeng. In recompense, Later Chin ceded the whole Peking region to Liao and began sending the Ch'i-tan annual gifts of cash and silk. The second Later Chin ruler, by refusing to acknowledge Liao overlordship, provoked a long war that ended in his ruin. The Ch'i-tan occupied Kaifeng and ruled North China in 946-47, but withdrew when it became clear that permanent control would require a greater effort than they could then mount. Thereafter North China dynasties did not challenge Liao's pretensions, and most of modern Hopei province remained attached to the Ch'i-tan empire in Mongolia.

To tenth-century Chinese, the situation must have seemed ominously like the final breakup of the Han empire, and they had every reason to expect that, in the pattern of post-Han developments, they were entering a sad and long new age of political disunion and alien intrusions.

6. Government

DURING the millennium-long early imperial age, from the beginning of the second century B.C. into the tenth century A.D., the ancient Chou feudal era was idealized into a golden age whose best qualities the Chinese perennially hoped to recover. Conversely, both the Warring States era, with its separatist rivalries, and the Ch'in dynasty, with its totalitarian ruthlessness, became nightmares whose recurrence was dreaded. But there could be no real return to the governmental patterns of the past, for good or ill, since new territories, peoples, life-styles, ideas, and economic elements were constantly being absorbed or accommodated, and the problems China confronted were never quite the same as those encountered before.

The great institutional challenge of the new age was whether or not some form of government, avoiding excesses of the Ch'in sort, could establish equitable social, economic, and military controls nationally under centralized management. The challenge was not successfully met. China was a conglomeration of great families manipulating social, economic, and political power rather than an integrated nation, even in long periods of political unity and cultural glory such as Han and T'ang. On balance, decentralization prevailed, and the personnel of government were predominantly of aristocratic background and temper. From Han into T'ang times, nevertheless, there were major steps in the direction of centralization of authority and of bureaucratic dominance.

ORGANIZATIONAL STRUCTURE

As has been observed in Chapter 5, the Han dynasty generally perpetuated the governmental structure that Ch'in had initiated. Thereafter all imperial governments resembled a pyramid, with the emperor at the apex and groups of ever more numerous agencies in central, regional, and local strata under him, each level of the pyramid having three faces —one for general administration, one for military command, and one for censorial surveillance. It would be grossly misleading to suggest that there were clear divisions of governmental powers, since all power emanated from the emperor; but there was a relatively clear differentiation of functional responsibilities.

In Han times, as in Ch'in, the top-echelon triumvirate of ministerial dignitaries comprised a chief counselor (*ch'eng-hsiang* or *hsiang-kuo*), a grand marshal (*t'ai-wei*), and a censor-in-chief (*yü-shih ta-fu*). The post of grand marshal became honorific and nonfunctional very early, and the censor-in-chief served as an associate chief counselor, normally succeeding to the chief counselorship when it fell vacant. In practice, therefore, the chief counselor directed the national government as a kind of chief of staff or prime minister for the emperor. He presided over a number of central government agencies. Notable among them were the offices of "the nine chief ministers" (*chiu-ch'ing*), high-ranking dignitaries who constituted a kind of imperial household administration. They were in charge of imperial rituals, palace maintenance, palace guards, the imperial stable, the capital police, the imperial commissariat, and the like. One chief minister, always a member of the imperial family, was responsible for supervising and keeping genealogical records on the imperial clansmen. Two others were in charge of revenues and disbursements, one for the palace and one for the officialdom. In less prestigious but more substantially functional roles, 13 department heads were responsible for routine administration; their duties were divided quite rationally into fiscal affairs, judicial affairs, military affairs, and the like. Important policy questions were often submitted to court conferences of all the chief ministers and other court dignitaries. Such conferences were assembled on the emperor's order and were presided over by the chief counselor, who reported both majority and minority views to the emperor. Although final decision-making power rested with the emperor, the tradition established by Kao-tsu (r. 202-195 B.C.) called for emperors to heed their advisers; and chief counselors were particularly prestigious and influential as the acknowledged leaders of and spokesmen for the officialdom in general.

Gradually, however, the Han chief counselor's influence with the emperor was undermined. Chinese generally referred to the officialdom at large as the outer court in an effort to distinguish it from the em-

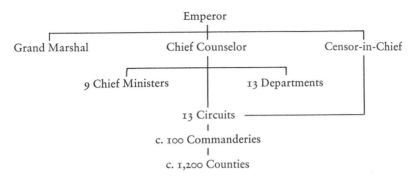

Basic governmental organization in Former Han times

peror's "inner court" of consorts and personal attendants. Since the outer court's principal concern was the governance of the country as a whole and that of the inner court merely the personal care of the emperor, relations between the two groups were unavoidably strained at best. In early Han times, when Kao-tsu's generals occupied the high ministerial posts and relations between palace and government were relatively informal and close, a number of regular officials were assigned to the palace as stewards and chamberlains. These included a group called masters of writing, who handled the emperor's personal correspondence and served as secretarial intermediaries between the emperor and the chief counselor. By the reign of Wu-ti (141-87 B.C.) eunuchs were again, as in earlier times, the only males allowed to attend the emperor in private; the masters of writing then gravitated to the outer court, and eunuch secretaries called palace writers became new inner-court buffers. Soon their agency also gravitated to the outer court, to be staffed by regular officials. Inexorably, the masters of writing and the palace writers successively took over some of the chief counselor's functions, and by the end of the Former Han era in A.D. 9 the chief counselorship had become no more than a status symbol. In Later Han times general administration was managed by three agencies that had all originated in the inner court: the Department of State Affairs (*shang-shu sheng*; department of masters of writing), the Secretariat (*chung-shu sheng*; department of palace writers), and the Chancellery (*men-hsia sheng*; department of personal attendants). By now the post of censor-in-chief had, like those of chief counselor and grand marshal, been transformed into a purely honorific sinecure. The military establishment had been divided among generals who were an-

swerable directly to the emperor, and censorial surveillance was directed
by the man occupying the one-time palace position of assistant to the
censor-in-chief, now removed to the outer court like the masters of
writing and the palace writers before him.

The consequence of these institutional changes was to weaken the
whole outer court in its relations with the throne and the inner court.
The outer court no longer had an unchallenged leader with prestige
and power comparable to the early Han chief counselor, and cliques
of officials gathered around spokesmen called "honest critics" in factional struggles to win imperial favor. This instability in the outer court
permitted the rise to power of inner-court elements—first empresses
and then eunuchs. In the Han dynasty's last decades, when the general
Ts'ao Ts'ao (d. 220) was de facto ruler, one of the ways in which he
tried to rebuild a strong central administration was to revitalize the
post of chief counselor and take it for himself.

While the throne's predominance over the outer court was being
strengthened by the changes just described, the capital was strengthening its predominance over local administrations. The basic Han pattern
of local administration was that inherited from Ch'in, of regional commanderies and their subordinate counties. Each commandery governor
and county magistrate was responsible for all aspects of government in
his territorial jurisdiction and accounted for his actions in annual reports to the capital. Each had a staff that normally included a military
commandant, and all areas were subject to intermittent inspection tours
by investigating censors from the capital. As was noted in Chapter 5,
there were hereditary princedoms and marquisates as well as directly
administered commanderies and counties in the first Han decades, but
by the end of Wu-ti's reign they were little more than commanderies
and counties under different names, and fully centralized government
was achieved for the first time since Ch'in. Besides reducing the feudalistic princedoms and marquisates to insignificance, Wu-ti tried to
strengthen the central government's authority over the commandery
governors. He divided the empire into 13 circuits or regions (*chou* or *fu*)
and assigned to each a censor as circuit inspector (*tz'u-shih*) to check
and report on the performance of the commandery governors in his
jurisdiction. As time passed, the inspectors became ever more powerful
regional supervisors, moving far beyond the limited purpose Wu-ti had
had in mind and achieving a still greater coordination of local governments under the central government. In Later Han times, however, the

institutional development came full circle: the regional supervisors became in effect regional governors, agents of a regional separatism that fragmented the empire.

The late Han patterns of organization persisted, with minor changes, in the following centuries. The embattled, conservative southern dynasties clung to them as evidence of their proclaimed legitimacy, and the mostly alien northern dynasties copied them in efforts to assert their own legitimacy, and because they provided the only working models of large-scale government at hand. Outer-court officials steadily gave ground to the circles around the throne, and regional governorships became the institutional bases from which princes and great land barons launched attempts at usurpation.

The prestige of the officialdom and the power of the central government over regional authorities began to be restored in the middle of the sixth century under Northern Chou, a development that contributed greatly to Sui's reunification of the empire in the 580's. Continuing the Sui trends, T'ang achieved a stable new balance of power between the inner and outer courts and between the central and regional administrations.

The T'ang central government manifested the traditional tripartite structure. There was a staff of generals who commanded the imperial armies; a Censorate that was somewhat more elaborate than its Han antecedent; and for general administration, a mature complex of the three agencies that had developed in mid-Han times: the Department of State Affairs, the Secretariat, and the Chancellery. These agencies now had towering prestige, in part because the founding genius of the dynasty, T'ai-tsung (r. 626-49), served as president of the Department of State Affairs before accepting the throne from his father. It became the T'ang custom for the highest ranking officials of the three agencies to meet daily with the emperor as a Council of State, in which all major policy decisions were reached. The participating officials, collectively known as grand councilors (tsai-hsiang), served as a not insignificant check on the autocratic caprices of the early T'ang emperors. Their prestige and authority derived in some part from a T'ang principle that every imperial edict had to be authenticated by the seals of the Secretariat and the Chancellery.

The T'ang Secretariat and Chancellery were essentially advisory bodies and had small staffs. It is commonly suggested that the Secretariat was the channel through which the officialdom submitted its reports and requests to the emperor in the form of memorials, and the Chancellery the channel through which imperial decisions were promulgated to the officialdom in the form of edicts, proclamations, and orders. The two agencies worked in such close coordination, however, that their functions were virtually inseparable.

The Department of State Affairs was the operating arm of the government, a huge bureaucracy incorporating both the old "nine chief ministers" of the Han system (in somewhat altered form) and a raft of new, highly specialized agencies. Along with these, and at the core of the Department's administrative apparatus, was a group of six ministries, each with an array of specialized subordinate bureaus. These six ministries—of personnel (*li-pu*), revenue (*hu-pu*), rites (*li-pu*), war (*ping-pu*), justice (*hsing-pu*), and works (*kung-pu*)—remained until the end of China's imperial history the administrative heart of every central government, the place where all the routine business of the empire was transacted. With their emergence, the T'ang central government looked far less like an imperial household administration than its Han predecessor had. A detailed manual prescribing and describing the functions of the ministries, entitled *T'ang liu-tien* (The Six Canons of T'ang), was prepared in Hsüan-tsung's reign; it was the fullest treatise on government since the ancient *Chou-li*, and is considerably more reliable.

Counties (*hsien*) remained the local base of the governmental hierarchy, but the commanderies of the Han days had long since passed from the scene, and the counties were now directly subordinate to the nominal descendants of the old regional governors (*chou tz'u-shih*). Over the centuries these officials had become so numerous and their territorial jurisdictions had become so small that they posed no threat to the central government. For the T'ang period the terms prefect and prefecture are commonly used.

Structural changes do not account for the ultimate deterioration of the T'ang outer court in its competition with the inner court; the Council of State was simply corrupted and made a captive tool of the inner court—first by flagrant favoritism under Empress Wu (r. 690-705), then by mixed favoritism and nepotism in the late years of Hsüan-tsung (r. 712-56), under the influence of the notorious concubine Yang Kuei-fei. Thereafter the grand councilors were no match for the powerful generals and influential eunuchs who manipulated the emperors, and the frustrated outer court contributed to its own deterioration by indulging in partisan factionalism.

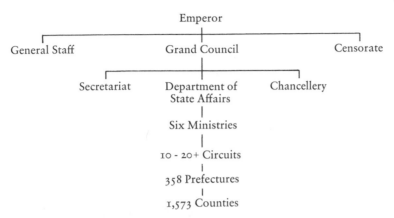

Basic governmental organization in T'ang times

As for relations between the central and local governments, the T'ang rulers followed precisely in the path of their Han predecessors, allowing regional coordination to evolve into regional autonomy in their efforts to cope with the great An Lu-shan rebellion of 755-63. In 711 the empire's prefectures had been grouped into ten circuits (*tao*), each headed by a coordinating commissioner, who was permanently stationed in the circuit. The number of circuits soon grew to 15 and finally to more than 20. In Hsüan-tsung's time, these commissioners became circuit controllers (*chieh-tu shih*), combining civil and military responsibilities. From there they made the full transition to all-powerful regional governors in the confusion brought on by An Lu-shan's rebellion. The regions they controlled remained semiautonomous satrapies as the T'ang central government deteriorated, and out of them grew the independent regional kingdoms of the post-T'ang Five Dynasties era.

PERSONNEL

The notion that government officials should be chosen on the basis of merit rather than birth, which had gained currency in the Warring States era and had then been established as a firm principle by Ch'in, was not easy to champion after the Ch'in debacle. The ideal survived, but in considerably modified form. From Han through T'ang times merit commonly meant good breeding, and access to office was for the most part limited to men who by their learning and conduct demonstrated commitment to the value system of the dominant social class of large landowning families. Although men of relatively obscure origins repeatedly rose to eminent government positions, the normal thing was for the sons and protégés of the well-to-do to monopolize government offices. Imperial princes and empresses' relatives were often particularly favored in the assignment of powerful posts. Ancient Chou titles of nobility were granted as badges of high imperial favor and were normally transmitted hereditarily. Members of the titled nobility did not necessarily perform any governmental functions, but they received government stipends and were considered available for official appointment. Moreover, officials of the higher ranks automatically earned so-called protection (*yin*) privileges, which guaranteed one or more sons eligibility for official appointment. Some officials were able to nominate their own successors and to make their offices hereditary; and well-to-do men were often permitted or even encouraged to contribute to the emperor's or the state's coffers by purchasing official status and appointments. Only in the military service were there always clear opportunities for men to rise by merit alone, and even there eminence was by no means restricted to the meritorious. Among both military and civil officials, nepotism and cronyism were widespread.

Early imperial China is nevertheless famous, and deservedly so, for instituting and systematizing rational, merit-oriented techniques for the recruitment, placement, and evaluation of government officials that had no counterparts elsewhere until very recent times. This extraordinary accomplishment can be fully appreciated only if one remembers that the British civil service, which became justly famed throughout the world, did not come into existence until the nineteenth century, and that early proposals to create it were denounced as insidious plots to "Chinesify" England.

Developing from experiments with bureaucratization in pre-Han China, especially in the Ch'in dynasty, recruitment procedures became systematic in early Han times. The earliest known date of significance is 196 B.C., when local officials were called on to recommend "worthy and talented" men for appointments. Then in 165 B.C. a call was issued for high officials of the central government and local authorities—princes, marquises, and commandery governors—to recommend men who were capable of "speaking out forthrightly and remonstrating without inhibition," and the emperor personally gave written examinations to all recommended candidates. These precedents established the two principal characteristics of the Han recruitment system that then matured—recommendations and confirmatory examinations. A third major element appeared about 124 B.C., when local governments were called on to recommend promising youths to study under a group of scholars called Erudites (*po-shih*), each a specialist in one of the Five Classics, who served as advisers in the central government. Thus came into existence a rudimentary national university, which subsequently played a major role in preparing men for bureaucratic careers. From an original complement of 50 students the enrollment increased apace, to reach 3,000 by the end of the first century B.C. In Later Han the student body swelled to 30,000 youths, most of whom seem to have been roisterous evaders of military and other state service.

Detailed descriptions of the Han personnel-recruitment system are not provided in early Chinese writings, but its general outlines are clear. There were two types of recommendations, one for study in the national university and one for direct appointments. Students, after unspecified periods of discipleship under the Erudites, sometimes graduated into status as supernumerary court gentlemen without regular assignments but available for irregular, temporary service when they were needed. Others returned to their homes at the end of their studies in the hope of getting staff appointments under commandery governors or county magistrates. In either case, they were eligible to be recommended for direct appointments by the central government, as were all low-ranking government personnel and qualified persons not yet in service. Some calls for such recommendations were issued irregularly, most often in reaction to natural portents such as eclipses or earthquakes, or when a new emperor came to the throne. Commandery governors were the principal recommenders, and the qualities desired in recommendees were usually specified in such vague terms as "worthy gentlemen," "learned scholars," "straightforward critics," "morally correct men," "men qualified to care for the people," "men of extraordinary talents," "men of righteous conduct," and so on. Beginning in Wu-ti's time, calls for recommendations were issued annually as well, and each commandery was required to submit one or two names; in these cases "filial and honest" men were normally asked for. Early in Later Han annual quotas were set requiring commanderies to submit one name for every 200,000 residents; 200 or more names were regularly forwarded each year.

When candidates for appointment appeared at the capital, they were questioned by senior officials, sometimes orally, but apparently more often in the world's earliest known written examinations, which were sometimes checked by the emperors. On confirmation, recommendees might be appointed directly to office or might join the pool of court gentlemen awaiting appointments, who sometimes numbered 1,000 or

Fig. 12. Officials as portrayed on Han dynasty painted tomb tiles (detail)

more. After Wu-ti's time, and throughout Later Han, most middle- and low-ranking officials, and some of the most eminent as well, had gone through one or another of the recommendation processes, and it can fairly be said that China was administered by literate, bureaucratic careerists.

The Han recommendation system did not create open competition for official status; commandery governors were not likely to recommend men without good family connections. Moreover, the requirement of literacy excluded all but the well-to-do, since education was not widespread and books, existing only in manuscript form on bundled-up wooden slips or on bolts of silk, were not widely accessible. However small the social base from which officials were drawn, the recruitment system was nevertheless a remarkable institution, one that at once provided a regular supply of literate, reputable men for office and ensured that all parts of the country were represented in the officialdom.

In Han times appointments to all offices throughout the country were not centrally controlled. Commandery governors and county magistrates were themselves appointed by the central government, and a "rule of avoidance" applied to such posts, forbidding service in one's native area. But these local authorities customarily selected their own subordinates, as did many officials in the central government. All offices were graded by annual salaries reckoned in piculs of grain (a picul being about 133 pounds, or a bushel). The chief counselor's annual salary was 10,000 piculs, but the normal salary range was from 2,000 down to 100 piculs. Salaries were paid partly in grain and partly in equivalents of silk or cash.

Once appointed to an office, a man served on probation for a year; if he performed satisfactorily, the appointment was then made permanent. Every third year officials submitted efficiency ratings on their subordinates, which led to salary adjustments and occasionally to promotions, demotions, or dismissals. Aged officials were regularly retired from service, sometimes with pensions.

All these elements of Han personnel administration survived in the post-Han centuries, but the recommendation system was substantially altered in the confusion of the Han collapse in the third century. As a result of the Yellow Turban rebellion and the wars between Ts'ao Ts'ao and his rivals, the population was considerably reduced, there were great migrations, and society was being rearranged in neofeudal relationships. In an attempt to regularize the recruitment and evaluation of officials in so unstable a time, Ts'ao Ts'ao's government sought out a notable "worthy" in every region, designated him senior rectifier (*ta chung-cheng*), and required him, with the assistance of junior rectifiers (*hsiao chung-cheng*) in local areas, to rate on a nine-grade scale of excellence all men of his region, in or out of office, deemed qualified for government service. Appointments were reshuffled accordingly. This nine-grade (*chiu-p'in*) system, intended to be a one-time expedient, was adopted by almost all the dynasties in the post-Han era of division. The rectifiers were inevitably the creatures of the predominant great families of their regions, and their periodic ratings naturally perpetuated the influence of the great families in government.

A few changes in personnel administration were made by some of the later northern dynasties as they strove to consolidate their rule. In the 570's, the Northern Ch'i dynasty asserted its right to fill many local offices that had traditionally been controlled by regional governors; and the Sui dynasty went still further, vesting in its central government the power of appointment to all offices held by regular officials. Sui also laid the foundation for the full-fledged system of personnel recruitment by examination that matured in early T'ang times, and for which T'ang is normally given full credit.

The T'ang system of personnel administration was a major advance in bureaucratic professionalism from the Han level. T'ang opened the doors to officialdom much wider, and nominees for examinations came regularly to outnumber the successful candidates by as many as a hundred to one. The prestige of office was an enormous incentive to education. Although paper was invented in Later Han times and was used increasingly thereafter, books were still not abundant in the seventh and eighth centuries. But great families assiduously collected manuscript libraries and hired tutors; the government sponsored schools at the prefectural level; and ironically enough, Buddhist monasteries, as part of their broad social welfare programs, educated promising young men in the Confucian classics so they could compete in the civil service examinations. The literate class expanded, and even men who failed in the examinations could usually find employment as clerical subofficials in government or as private tutors.

Many examination candidates came from two national universities, one at Ch'ang-an and one at the auxiliary capital, Loyang; admission to both was restricted almost entirely to sons of the nobility and the bureaucracy. Other examination candidates were accepted on the recommendation of their prefects, after preliminary screening in examinations at both the county and the prefectural level. Examinations at the capital led to what Westerners commonly call doctoral degrees. Five types of examinations, and correspondingly different degrees, were offered annually throughout the T'ang dynasty. One examination called for the demonstration of pronounced literary talent; it led to the "presented scholar" (chin-shih) degree. A second tested classical scholarship. The other three, significantly less esteemed, were on law, calligraphy, and mathematics. Still other types of examinations were given irregularly or for only short periods. For a time in the eighth century there was even an examination on Taoism. All the recruitment examinations were managed by the Ministry of Personnel in the Department of State Affairs until 736, when the responsibility was passed to the Ministry of Rites in recognition of the prestige of the recruitment system as a symbolic ritual of state.

Success in an examination gave one official status and rank in the civil service but did not automatically entitle one to an appointment. Assignments were handled in a separate process by the Ministry of Personnel, and applicants included not only those who had just earned their degrees, but also lower-ranking officials whose terms of appointment had expired and other men who were considered eligible, such as the sons of officials entitled to the traditional "protection" privilege. Once a year the Ministry of Personnel called for all qualified men to present themselves for consideration. The Ministry tested each applicant's calligraphy and his ability to compose an essay on a practical administrative problem. Then it judged his personal appearance and his manner of speaking. Finally, it checked his dossier for evidence of virtuous conduct, talent, and zeal. When this procedure was completed, each acceptable applicant was asked to indicate his preferences for appointment, these were compared with known or expected vacancies suitable to the rank of the applicant, and the Ministry then sent a slate of nominations to the Chancellery. If the Chancellery approved, it presented the nominations to the emperor. After new appointments were proclaimed, the appointees formally expressed their thanks in imperial audience before taking up their assigned duties.

Appointments had been permanent in Han times but were now limited to three-year periods. To be reemployed, officials had to apply to the Ministry of Personnel and repeat the procedure just described— perhaps several times before attaining sufficient rank to be exempted. While on duty, every official was evaluated by his superiors in an annual efficiency report that was deposited with the Ministry of Personnel and consulted in connection with reassignments.

All officials were now ranked in nine grades, which determined salaries; and all offices were similarly ranked. By accumulating favorable evaluations in the annual ratings and in the reappointment process, an official could steadily rise in rank, receive higher salaries, and move up the hierarchy of government agencies into ever more prestigious posts. But progress was slow. A first-time applicant commonly had to wait two or three years for a suitable vacancy, and qualifying for reassignment did not necessarily bring immediate reappointment. Even now, in the higher offices a good record did not count as much as good family connections, so that the T'ang government never attained a wholly bureaucratic, nonaristocratic character. After mid-T'ang times, however, all the apparatus was at hand to permit the bureaucratic dominance of the later imperial age.

CENSORS

Repeated references to censorial officials in the foregoing pages should not lead to the conclusion that China's early imperial government employed specialists to burn objectionable books or act as watchdogs over public morality. To be sure, since the emperor was considered "the father and mother of the people," all officials were expected to share his responsibility for giving moral leadership and punishing immorality. The censorial officials, however, had a more specifically defined responsibility—to ensure that government functioned as intended. Though commonly called the "ears and eyes of the emperors," they were far more than secret police, and though also called "legal officials," they had very limited judicial powers. They were regular members of the civil service who, when assigned to the Censorate, had the sole prescribed function of maintaining surveillance over all governmental operations for the purpose of impeaching officials who violated laws, administrative regulations, or traditional moral standards. Because the censors had the right to submit their impeachment memorials directly to the throne, bypassing routine communication channels, they enjoyed considerable independence of action and high prestige. They were not immune from punishment if their memorials offended an emperor; but it was normally in his interest not to intimidate his censorial inspectors, and it was popularly considered outrageous for a conscientious censor to be punished for doing his job.

From Ch'in and Han times on through T'ang, censors were administratively organized into a metropolitan Censorate (*yü-shih t'ai*, literally Tribunal of Censors). But in the T'ang system the censorial service had even greater autonomy, for the censor-in-chief was no longer associated with the general administration hierarchy, as in the Han system.

In addition to the censors proper, whose responsibility was to maintain surveillance over the officialdom at large, imperial governments traditionally included officials with titles suggestive of censorial functions: remonstrators, reminders, rectifiers of omissions, and supervising secretaries. In Ch'in and Han times, these titles were honorifics, given to high-ranking dignitaries as symbols of their worthiness to be companions and mentors of the emperor. But by T'ang times officials with such titles were regular members of both the Secretariat and the Chancellery, assigned to keep watch over the conduct of the emperor himself and the flow of documents to and from the throne. They were expected to remonstrate with the emperor about his faults and shortcomings. Some of them even exercised a sort of veto power over imperial edicts and other pronouncements, since they were authorized to return for reconsideration any decree they judged improper, either in substance or in form. This routine control over imperial pronouncements, coupled with the customary requirement that all imperial orders had to be authenticated by the Secretariat and the Chancellery before they could be carried out, provided incomplete but not insignificant checks on imperial autocracy.

Particularly strong-willed emperors of the early imperial age, such as Han Wu-ti and T'ang T'ai-tsung, could use censors to help intimidate the officialdom much of the time. Most emperors, however, were too heavily dependent on the support of powerful kinsmen and the great families that dominated the officialdom, even with the increasing bureaucratization of the government, to behave arbitrarily. The institutionalization of remonstrance functions by T'ang times further ensured that the emperor, though something more than first among equals, normally fell far short of being a despot.

LAW

Like the censorial system, traditional Chinese legal practices and conceptions about law deserve special attention, since they differed in notable respects from Western counterparts. Chinese law was always merely an instrument of government; it was not thought to have divine sanction, nor was it considered an inviolable constitution. It was part of, and inseparable from, routine administration. There were no provisions limiting state authority, and there was no church or independent judiciary before which the state could legally be called to account. Laws were promulgated for one purpose only—to spell out what kinds of behavior the state wanted its subjects to avoid and what it would do to them if they misbehaved. The code was implemented and enforced primarily by county magistrates, who were the emperor's all-purpose surrogates in dealing with the people at large. They served as investigators, prosecutors, defenders, juries, and judges all in one. Though doubtful cases were often passed up the administrative hierarchy to the Ministry of Justice or even to the emperor for decisions, and serious sentences were normally reviewed by higher authorities before being carried out, the magistrate of original jurisidiction still had awesome punitive powers that he could exercise without challenge.

Rule by law in this form derived from the ancient Legalist conception of statecraft. The early Confucians distrusted rule by law, preferring that society be brought into accord with the will of Heaven—that is, into harmony with the cosmos—by adherence to ethical principles (li; ritual or propriety) as exemplified in the behavior of rulers and officials.

But in the large, complex empire that China became in Han times even Confucians conceded that laws were unavoidable for governance. Indeed, the Confucian officials became assiduous codifiers of law, but they infused much of their own philosophy and spirit into their legal systems. Whereas in the Legalist view laws should be both rigidly egalitarian and rigidly enforced, the laws promulgated under Confucian influence from Han times on were relativistic and conditional. Murder, for example, was never simply murder, to be punished ruthlessly in every case. It all depended on who murdered whom, and under what circumstances. The relationship between the parties, and the moral obligations deriving from it, determined the degree of guilt. Thus, if a father killed a son because of unfilial conduct he might be applauded, whereas if a son killed his father it was considered a most heinous offense regardless of the circumstances; even the plea of accident had no force. An even more clearly Confucian principle is discernible in the T'ang law that prescribed the death penalty for anyone who conceived a child during a period of mourning for a parent. Handling legal cases was by no means easy for a magistrate. It was up to him to ferret out all the circumstances, motivations, and consequences of a crime, to make a judgment, and to assign a penalty that was equitable and supported public morality. Quibbles about the letter of the law were not important.

Of the Han law code, only remnants survive. Its general pattern was apparently followed by the many dynasties of the era of division. The earliest code that is still known in full is the T'ang code promulgated in 653, which was reportedly based on the Sui code. It has 501 articles, grouped under 12 headings:

1. Terms and principles
2. Prohibitions concerning security of the imperial palace
3. Administrative regulations
4. Family and marriage
5. State stables and treasuries
6. Coercive treatment of others
7. Violence and theft
8. Conflicts and contentions
9. Deceptions and frauds
10. Miscellaneous statutes
11. Arrests and escapes
12. Trial and imprisonment

The state was little concerned with what modern Westerners call civil law, relying instead on family heads and village elders to enforce local customs. If a civil litigation was brought before a magistrate, he was expected to try to find an equitable resolution, but all parties were likely to be punished in some measure for failing to resolve the matter themselves in a spirit of harmonious cooperation.

Even in Han times, despite efforts to moderate the harshness of the Ch'in period, statutory punishments were cruel. Death penalties were carried out by beheading or by chopping the offender in two at the waist. In the case of treason or some equally serious crime, all the offender's relatives might be put to death as well—partly to diminish the possibility of vengeance. Mutilation was prescribed for lesser offenders —tattooing, amputation of the nose or the feet, or castration. Terms of hard labor on state construction projects such as roads, walls, and canals were common for the most minor offenders. Imprisonment was not a regularly prescribed punishment, but accused persons were imprisoned and sometimes manacled while awaiting trial, and witnesses as well as the accused were commonly beaten with rods during interrogation. For officials, the usual punishments were fines, dismissal from service, or exile to some distant and disagreeable place, such as the malarial south coast. The sentences of officials and persons of means were sometimes commuted to the payment of fines.

By the T'ang dynasty statutory punishments had come to be graded in five categories: death by strangulation or bisection; exile from home to a distance of 2,000, 2,500, or 3,000 Chinese miles (*li*, about one-third of an English mile); hard labor for one, two, or three years; beating with heavy bamboo rods, from 50 to 100 blows; and beating with light bamboo rods, up to 50 blows. As in Han times, commutation to fines was often possible for people of status or wealth.

THE MILITARY

As a practical matter, the authority of China's imperial state system rested on a military base. Dynasties were always anxious about potential military challenges from within and without, and dynasties became great and durable only to the extent that they achieved tight centralized control over military forces. But it was not easy to determine what kind of military system best served China's purposes. Three types of forces were always needed. The frontier zones, especially on the north and northwest, required permanent garrisons to fend off aggressive nomads; the national capital required large forces to protect the throne against surprises and enhance its awesomeness, yet flexible enough to be sent campaigning afar when circumstances warranted; and local governments required forces for routine police activity and for small-scale campaigns against local bandits. In meeting these needs, the state faced a dilemma. Amateur citizen-soldiers, who were least likely to create internal control problems, could prove ineffective in battle, but skilled professionals, who could be expected to be effective in battle, might also be difficult to control internally. On balance, early imperial China was committed to the citizen-soldier ideal, but only in early Han and early T'ang times did the system function well.

In the Han militia system, all males were registered for military service on attaining the age of twenty and were considered eligible for service between the ages of twenty-three and fifty-six. In theory every male was required to participate in military training at home under the military commandant of his county for one month every year, after the autumn harvest; and in the course of his lifetime to serve one year in guard units at the capital plus three days in the frontier garrisons. Such a system was unworkable in practice, especially in its provisions for frontier service, even though the military spirit was strong through the first century or so of Han rule. It quickly became common for "substitute money" to be levied on draft-eligible men, with which volunteers—or draftees too poor to pay—were paid for a year or more of duty on the frontiers and even in the capital guards. In Later Han local militias were abolished, no doubt to prevent the local and regional warlordism that nevertheless flourished by the end of the second century A.D.

In addition to the basic service requirements described above, the

Fig. 13. Rubbing of Han dynasty relief inscription: "Battle on a Bridge"

Han citizen-soldiers were subject to call-ups for local emergencies and for distant campaigns under generals delegated from the court. For some campaigns, the Han court also requested volunteers, and individual generals sometimes raised their own armies with court authorization. In time the whole military establishment became professionalized. Mercenaries staffed the capital guards, and alien tribes were hired to protect the frontier marches. Regional governors and great families had their own mercenary followings. The citizen-soldier ideal and the high military morale of early Han disappeared.

During the post-Han era of division mercenaries in the service of great families were prevalent in the south, while in the north nomadic tribesmen were the elite standing armies of the conquest dynasties, supported by revenues extorted from the Chinese peasants. But in the middle of the sixth century the Western Wei dynasty, in an adaptation of traditional Hsien-pi tribal organization, instituted a new militia system. Every family with more than two sons had to send one male for permanent service in one of the 100-odd garrisons (*fu*) scattered throughout the state, distributed for command purposes among 24 armies. The militiamen themselves, but not their families, were exempt from taxes and other labor levies. Their essential needs were provided for by the state, but the garrisons were expected to become self-sufficient by farming state-assigned lands in intervals between military activities.

This fu-ping system, originally intended to separate elite fighting men from the farming population, evolved through Sui into a new citizen-soldier system in T'ang times. The T'ang militia system differed from the Han system principally in that it was not based on universal conscription for short terms of service but provided elite career soldiers who performed agricultural work to support themselves insofar as possible. Especially in the early T'ang decades, militia service was highly esteemed; well-to-do families were ambitious to get militia posts for their sons. Young men were chosen for service at the age of twenty-one on the basis of their physical fitness and respectable family backgrounds. They manned more than 600 garrisons, clustered primarily in the region of the T'ang capital at Ch'ang-an and the auxiliary capital Loyang and near the northern frontier. They remained on duty until retirement at the age of sixty. In rotation, on a schedule that took account of each garrison's distance from the capital, groups of militiamen were sent to the capital for a month of service in the imperial

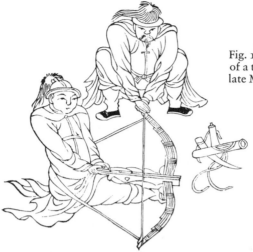

Fig. 14. Traditional woodblock print of a two-man crossbow team. From the late Ming encyclopedia *Wu-pei chih*.

guards. In another rotation, the garrisons dispatched men to serve for three years in the frontier units; and as need dictated they sent contingents to join in special campaigns.

In addition to the imperial guards provided by the militia system, there was a standing army at the capital—the Northern Army, which served as the emperor's personal force. It originated as the army with which the T'ang founders rose against Sui, and through the seventh century it was replenished with sons of the nobility. The Northern Army came to have the highest military prestige and, as a permanent body of professionals, was the core of T'ang battle strength into the eighth century. Militiamen on duty in the capital guards suffered in comparison and gradually were transformed into servants of court dignitaries. Militia service then came to be avoided, and by 749 militia strength and prestige had so declined that no more militiamen were called for capital duty.

The militia system lingered on, but even its role in support of the frontier defenses declined. The state had to resort to conscription to maintain its frontier forces at full strength and finally, by the middle of the eighth century, had come to rely on permanent frontier armies of mercenaries, recruited in large part from friendly alien tribes. The development of such armies under circuit controllers (*chieh-tu shih*) made possible the devastating rebellion of An Lu-shan in 755-63 and led to regional warlordism thereafter. Meantime, eunuch-controlled palace armies rose to prominence in Ch'ang-an, undermining the prestige and strength of the Northern Army and setting the stage for the late T'ang tragedy of eunuch dominance in the capital coupled with warlord separatism in the hinterland.

The early imperial age did not witness any innovations in the arts of war comparable in importance to the cavalry and crossbows of the Warring States era. The only major technological advance was the introduction from the steppes of the stirrup, which greatly facilitated mounted archery. It came into use perhaps as late as the fifth century, after light cavalry had already been the principal striking force in East Asian armies for a millennium. The crossbow remained the supreme Chinese weapon through the T'ang dynasty, though gunpowder was known well before that and was widely used in fireworks.

A more noteworthy development occurred several hundred years earlier, with the penetration into South China. As the Chinese moved into this area they had to adapt themselves to marine warfare. When Han Wu-ti suppressed Nan Yüeh in 111-110 B.C., his victory at Canton was achieved by a flotilla sent from the Yangtze delta. During the civil wars of Ts'ao Ts'ao's time and in the Three Kingdoms era that followed, river battles were common and often decisive; and both Sui and T'ang employed naval forces in their military operations against Korea. From Han times on, in short, China's military forces regularly included a naval arm.

For all the important developments in civil service techniques and the repeated attempts to attain the ideal of a military establishment consisting of citizen-soldiers, the most highly esteemed and rewarded careers through most of the early imperial age were in the military, not the bureaucracy. Both early Han and early T'ang exuded a notably militaristic spirit. Even in T'ang Hsüan-tsung's heyday the civil service by no means became predominant in government, and after the An Lu-shan rebellion militarism was rampant. In a word, the widespread modern notion that traditional China esteemed only genteel pursuits is simply mistaken, so far as the early imperial age is concerned.

7. Society and the Economy

CHINA'S INABILITY to sustain a unified, centralized state system throughout the early imperial age is hardly to be wondered at. What is remarkable is that political unity was maintained for such long periods under the Han and T'ang dynasties. The successive Chinese governments of these times faced problems of a scale and complexity beyond the imagining of European statesmen until modern times. They were confronted continuously on the north and northwest by hostile and powerful aliens, against whom they had to mount defenses that drained them of manpower, fiscal resources, and managerial expertise. China was also constantly expanding southward into unaccustomed terrain and accommodating new peoples and life-styles quite different from those of the original homeland in North China, while the character of life in the original homeland was itself being repeatedly transformed by alien intrusions. Political cohesion could hardly be expected amid such socioeconomic diversity, change, and confusion. That unity was achieved at all testifies to the extraordinary Chinese genius for social engineering and to the importance of the halting development of a nationally recruited civil service bureaucracy composed of men with a common educational background and a common commitment to Confucian principles of governance; for there was no socioeconomic basis for integrated nationhood.

The diversity of peoples and local customs had to be tolerated even by China's most insistent centralizers and standardizers. The tentacles of dynastic administrations never extended directly down below the county level, and county magistrates were responsible for populations ranging from twenty thousand up to hundreds of thousands. The people themselves had to be counted on, therefore, to implement state policies in ways that were appropriate in local circumstances, as well as to maintain local order, settle petty disputes, and manage small-scale water-control systems and other communal enterprises. The Ch'in precedent of organizing people into mutual-responsibility groups of five and ten households was consequently perpetuated by later dynasties in one form or another. Han village headmen (called *san-lao*; thrice-aged) were officially sanctioned and honored, and nomadic tribal backgrounds seem to be reflected in the system of "three chiefs" (*san-chang*) —a hierarchy of chiefs of 5, 25, and 125 households—that was common beginning with the Northern Dynasties. By T'ang times, and possibly much earlier, merchants and artisans were separately organized into guilds (*hang*) or under state-sanctioned foremen. In similar patterns, the non-Chinese within the empire—nomadic peoples settled in the frontier zones, southern aborigines, and even Arab traders residing in T'ang China's southern ports and other commercial centers—were generally allowed to follow their own ways of life under headmen of their own choosing, who were expected to perform the functions of Chinese village headmen, serving as intermediaries between the people and the state governmental apparatus.

POPULATION

One of the primary functions of the village headmen and their counterparts in other communities was to submit regular reports to county magistrates on population and landownership, which were the foundations of the state revenue and service levies. Local control over these procedures made national censuses inevitably inaccurate. Underreporting was prevalent, partly because this helped localities to minimize their tax and service obligations, and partly because the system could not keep accurate account of the splitting off of new families from old ones, the in-migration of settlers, and the opening of new territories. Even so, the surviving census records are more illuminating than comparable records kept elsewhere in this epoch, and they reveal that demographic change was a major aspect of social history during the early imperial age —a cyclical growth and shrinkage of the registered population, coupled with massive relocations of people.

From the Warring States era through the T'ang dynasty it appears that the Chinese population repeatedly approached and fell back from a maximum of about sixty millions. Steady, continuous growth was prevented in part by recurrent droughts, floods, and other natural disasters; but the major population declines seem to have resulted, directly and indirectly, from the wars that swept over China periodically. The

population loss was particularly severe in the last years of the Warring
States era, in the civil wars that followed the collapse of Ch'in late in
the third century B.C., again in the transition from Wang Mang to Later
Han early in the first century A.D., in the Han collapse at the end of the
second century, during the Hsiung-nu invasions of North China in the
fourth century and the general turmoil that followed, in the course of
the An Lu-shan rebellion in the eighth century, and in the rebellions and
warlordism of the T'ang decline late in the ninth century.

During the peaceful Former Han years, the population grew to a peak
registration of 59,594,978 in A.D. 1. The rebellions that overthrew Wang
Mang were reported by contemporaries, no doubt with gross exaggeration, to have reduced the population to one-tenth its former size; but
by 140 the national census reported 49,150,220, and in 157 the population reached a Later Han peak of 56,486,856. The extent of the devas-
tation that followed the Han collapse beginning in 190, when widespread cannibalism was reported, is indicated by the sharp drop in total
population under the Chin dynasty: at the height of its centralized
power in 280, only 16,163,863 people were registered. After the vicissitudes of the long era of division, population registration climbed
under Sui to 46,019,956 in 606, and leveled off at around fifty million
under T'ang in the eighth century. For 753, shortly before the outbreak
of the An Lu-shan rebellion, the census recorded 9,619,254 households
and 52,880,488 persons. Immediately after the rebellion, in 764, the
central government could account for only 2,900,000 households and
16,900,000 persons—the round numbers suggesting estimates rather
than actual counts. Thereafter the registered T'ang population never
again reached even five million households.

Not only did the population diminish in times of trouble; it shifted
geographically. Throughout the whole early imperial age the general
trend of movement was from the northwest (Shensi and Shansi) to the
southeast (the central Yangtze valley and the Yangtze delta region).
Notable secondary trends show people migrating into Szechwan in west
central China and into the northeastern region of modern Peking and
southern Manchuria. Nevertheless—and notwithstanding the massive
migrations out of North China during the era of alien invasions and occupations—the north remained the dominant population area from Han
into at least mid-T'ang times. As late as the 730's the population ratio
was about two to one in favor of the north. The T'ang circuit called Honan, which incorporated the whole south bank of the Yellow River

across the northern plain into modern Shantung, was the most populous, with a registration of 11,278,695; and the circuit called Hopei, the comparable territory north of the Yellow River, followed closely, with 10,230,972. The much vaster southern circuit of Chiang-nan, stretching south of the Yangtze from Szechwan to the Pacific Ocean and incorporating all of the south except modern Kwangtung, Kwangsi, and Yunnan, had a total registered population of only 10,559,728. The imbalance is equally revealed in the distribution of densely inhabited urban areas. Of the 26 most populous prefectures in T'ang China, only six were in the south—all clustered in the rich lower Yangtze triangle including modern Nanking, Shanghai, and Hangchow. Only after the An Lu-shan rebellion devastated the Yellow River plain did the Yangtze valley and the southern areas beyond begin to approach something near population parity with the north.

URBANISM

Urbanization itself was a prominent aspect of social development from Han into T'ang times. The urbanizing trend of the Warring States era seems to have stabilized in Former Han; in both periods there were a dozen or so well-known towns, but few of these could properly be called cities. The most populous city was the capital, Ch'ang-an, which was a bustling, exciting metropolis surrounded by a thick wall some 16 miles in circumference. The city was crisscrossed by broad avenues running north-south and east-west. The city wall was breached on each of its four sides by three great gates, each wide enough to allow the simultaneous passage of four carriages and topped with a defense tower. The residences of the well-to-do commonly enclosed gardens that offered country-like seclusion and had second stories that gave panoramic views. Mercantile activities were confined to designated market areas scattered through the town. A large imperial park, including a zoo, lay just outside the city's west wall. In A.D. 1 the capital prefecture had a registered population of 246,200; probably some 80,000 people resided within the walls. The Later Han capital, Loyang, was not much smaller than Ch'ang-an even in early Han times and probably grew much larger in the second century A.D. A third populous center was Chengtu in Szechwan.

The growth of urbanism in Chinese life by T'ang times is evidenced by the fact that in the early eighth century all 26 of the largest T'ang prefectures had registered populations of over half a million. Ch'ang-

Fig. 15. Han tomb figurine of dancing drummer

an prefecture had swelled to two million registered inhabitants. Loyang and Ta-ming in Hopei each exceeded one million, and Chengtu fell just short of a million. Tientsin, ranking ninth, had 825,705 residents; Soochow ranked nineteenth with 632,650, Hangchow twenty-first with 585,963. The mid-T'ang ranking does not include among the empire's large prefectures either the great southern port of Canton or the inland entrepot of Yangchow, at the confluence of the Yangtze and the Grand Canal, though Arab visitors wrote admiringly of their metropolitan glories. Yangchow, which was the headquarters of the nationwide water-transport system, must have grown tremendously after the An Lu-shan rebellion.

Ch'ang-an in T'ang times was unquestionably the most populous, most cosmopolitan, and most brilliant city in the world. Rebuilt several times since Former Han, it now enclosed within great walls some 30 square miles, including an outer city, an administrative quarter that was a small city in itself, and a palace compound that was almost a city-in-a-city. The outer city contained 106 separately walled wards, two large market areas, and hundreds of temples, mostly Buddhist. The resident population within the walls was about a million, and the city always thronged with visitors from afar—horsemen from Mongolia, camel drivers from Central Asia, holy men from India, Arab traders from the

Persian gulf, Malay adventurers, and Korean and Japanese monks, diplomats, and students. Musical troupes, jugglers, acrobats, dwarfs, and blacks from distant realms amused the crowds at the city's fairs; sing-song girls enlivened its eating and drinking houses; and exotic wares from much of Eurasia, as well as specialty goods from every region of China, were sold in its markets.

The cosmopolites of Ch'ang-an were fascinated by foreign things, and adopted one outlandish fad after another—in music, dancing, cos-

Fig. 16. T'ang palace concert, by unidentified painter of the Five Dynasties era (detail)

tume, food and drink, hairdressing, makeup, pets, and slaves. The same cosmopolitan spirit infected other T'ang cities and left its mark on subsequent urban life in China. It was apparently in faddish imitation of a popular court toe-dancer that Chinese women, in the post-T'ang Five Dynasties era, inflicted on themselves the torture of foot-binding, which literally crippled all upper-class women into the twentieth century; and it may have been some Islamic influence of late T'ang times that caused upper-class Chinese to begin isolating their women in the harem-like privacy that also became part of Chinese tradition, though not rooted in either Han or nomad customs.

GREAT FAMILY DOMINANCE

The transformation of ancient China's warrior shih class into a scholar-bureaucrat shih elite, which had an auspicious beginning in the pre-Han centuries, progressed only spasmodically in the early imperial age. As has been observed repeatedly in the preceding chapters, Chinese society was dominated by hereditary great families from Han through T'ang times.

The Han elite differed from the old Chou nobility in that its status was only partly based on birth, the obvious exception being imperial relatives. Many men rose to social prominence from commoner status, especially through military achievements. Moreover, though prominence once achieved was transmitted hereditarily, social position was lost very easily, at a ruler's whim. None of the descendants of the lords created by Han Kao-tsu, for example, were noblemen at the end of the Former Han period. The members of the new elite also differed from the Chou nobility in that they did not necessarily have governmental roles, though in practice they virtually monopolized government offices and their continued eminence depended in substantial part on their having at least nominal status in the officialdom. In short, the Han elite was not a nobility of birth; it was an aristocracy of wealth and political influence. In some cases, political influence produced wealth; in others wealth produced political influence. The two elements were inseparable. The elite's political influence was most securely rooted in the control of military forces, governmental or private; and its wealth was most securely rooted in landownership.

The great families of Han times were not really groups of relatives. As a matter of fact, the Ch'in dynasty's policy of trying to destroy the great lineages and extended families of the Chou tradition was continued under the Han dynasty. Relatives were actively discouraged from living together in extended families; for even three generations to live together in one household was considered remarkable in Later Han. The great Han family was something like a business company. The components of such a unit typically included (1) a wealthy, politically influential landowner; (2) his immediate family and household, including concubines, servants, and slaves; (3) his agricultural estate, probably including some scattered plots worked by tenants but ordinarily consisting mainly of a large, consolidated tract worked by serf-like indentured peasants and often partly by slaves; (4) a host of "guests" (k'o), ranging from astrologers and scholarly protégés to political spies and assassins; and (5) an army of private fighting men (pu-ch'ü), who often manned castle-like fortifications that defended the estate from intruders. "Guests" and private fighting men were attached to the household by pledges of allegiance; they could be given away as gifts but not sold, and they were free to renounce their allegiance to one patron and offer themselves to another. Peasants on an estate seem to have been bound to the land, usually by contracts that theoretically allowed them to regain their freedom. Slaves were openly bought and sold, but the proportion of slaves in the population seems to have been far smaller than that in ancient Greece and Rome, and Han estates did not resemble slave-worked plantations.

Especially in Later Han and Three Kingdoms times, a great family of this type was a colossal enterprise. It might control thousands of acres, incorporating dozens of farm villages, mines and workshops, mills, and other industrial and commercial enterprises. Its "guests" might number in the hundreds, its slaves in the thousands, and its fighting men in the tens of thousands. By any standard it was fabulously rich. One local land baron of the Three Kingdoms period is known to have given his daughter a bridal dowry of 1,000 slave girls sumptuously garbed in silk. The Han empire clearly fell far short of the social ideal that had evolved in pre-Han thought—a prosperous free peasantry governed by an intellectual elite.

Feudalistic social patterns became still more pronounced under the Northern and Southern Dynasties. This development was a predictable response to the political fragmentation of the times, and it naturally only accelerated that fragmentation. In the south people clustered around strong local leaders for protection against the successive waves of migrants fleeing the north and the aboriginal southern tribes whose territories the Chinese were encroaching on. Chinese who remained in the north similarly clustered together to defend themselves against nomadic invaders and the widespread brigandage that arose as traditional government broke down. Meanwhile, the invading nomads gradually became new types of Chinese. In both north and south society was atomized in hostile geographical enclaves, so that no government of the period was more than a patchwork of local baronies, and within these enclaves the people became ever more rigidly bound into hereditary status. Later Chinese scholars have sometimes gone so far as to compare Chinese society in the era of division with the caste society of India.

During the fourth and fifth centuries a large proportion of China's population, north and south alike, sank into a debased state, though probably not quite what could be called a caste. This huge category included not only serfs on the large estates, bondsmen of other sorts, and outright slaves, but also various disesteemed occupational groups such as shamans, medical practitioners, and entertainers. The respectable citizenry had shrunk to a few remaining freehold farmers and artisans, supplemented in the north by tribal warriors of alien origin; the thriving Han mercantile class had all but disappeared in the resurgence of local autonomy and local self-sufficiency. Atop the social hierarchy was a greatly transformed elite designating itself the shih class. Among its many disparate elements were some descendants of the great families of Han times, many militaristic opportunists who were little better than brigands, and the tribal nobility of the northern invaders. Upward social mobility came to be prohibited by custom and perhaps by law, as was intermarriage between classes or even between subgroups within classes. Since no one but a proper shih could be considered for official appointment and its privileges, hereditary claims to shih status were carefully guarded by great families and carefully scrutinized by governments. Genealogical scholarship consequently flourished. All the great families traced, or claimed to trace, their lineages back to important officials, preferably of the Han dynasty.

Several forces worked against this rigid social stratification. The spread of Buddhism, with its emphasis on compassion, eventually provoked a sentiment against the ill treatment of the common people; and Buddhist monastic establishments offered increasing numbers of people a respectable and secure social status outside the established hierarchy —to the point where governments were finally impelled to restrict their growth. The traditional tribal egalitarianism of the nomadic invaders, the vigorous efforts of the later Northern Dynasties to expand their political control, and the new civil service procedures that were developed under the Sui and T'ang dynasties all contributed to a weakening of class discrimination and to the emergence of a fresh new respect for individual human dignity, which became a prominent characteristic of T'ang China.

The T'ang social order was more open than any since Former Han. The prospering of commerce in the now-centralized empire offered new opportunities for social mobility, and the lot of the common man improved. But T'ang society was no more egalitarian than Han society had been. Wealth and political privilege remained the monopolies of a relatively small group of estate-owning lineages or clans, among which it was now commonplace for three or more generations to live in one household. The T'ang government itself compiled great lists of the empire's recognized shih families, prefecture by prefecture. Some lineages or clans, which for centuries had dominated central govern-

Fig. 17. Pottery models of T'ang court ladies playing polo, in red pottery with traces of polychrome pigment

ments, enjoyed empire-wide prestige. Others had only regional or local influence. An individual shih might in fact be impoverished. No matter; as a shih by birth he had state recognition, good connections, and the esteem of other members of the elite.

Especially in the earliest T'ang years, the T'ang elite prominently included northern aristocrats of the same mixed Chinese-Turkic bloodlines as the T'ang emperors themselves. These were characteristically hard-drinking, hard-riding fighting men who hunted with falcons on their country estates and whose women played polo. But the T'ang elite did not consist entirely of such hearty roisterers. Shih descended from the more effete aristocrats of the Southern Dynasties had strong intellectual and cultural interests, and intellectual activities were fostered by the personnel-administration procedures developed by Sui and T'ang. Nevertheless, the heritage of the northern aristocrats gave the whole T'ang age a spirit more akin to that of Han than to that of the later Chinese dynasties.

The gradual, partial professionalization of the civil service in T'ang times inevitably eroded the long-enduring principle of hereditary claims to social status and office. But it was the shock of the An Lu-shan rebellion in the eighth century, followed by the warlordism of the late T'ang and Five Dynasties eras, that finally undermined the socioeconomic as well as the political power of the hereditary aristocracy. The tumultuous ninth and tenth centuries cleared the way for the rise of the social structure that was to characterize the later imperial age, exalting nonhereditary shih who were genuine scholar-officials.

AGRICULTURE

Severe economic inequities naturally accompanied the social inequities described above, and during the early imperial age Chinese governments struggled imaginatively to counteract the trends that made the rich richer and the poor poorer. Their motives were partly idealistic —to reestablish the harmonious society that was thought to have existed in antiquity. But their concerns were also very practical and hardheaded. The concentration of great wealth in private hands under any circumstances was always considered a threat to the centralization of political authority and to the adequacy of state revenues, and widespread poverty always created a popular unrest that threatened political stability and even dynastic survival. It was in the state's interests to capture economic surpluses for its own purposes on one hand, and on the other to do away with the grosser imbalances between rich and poor so as to maintain social order. Since society remained over-whelmingly agrarian, the greatest challenge for government was to de-vise a reasonably equitable system of land distribution.

Once the old Chou feudal patterns had been abandoned in favor of freehold farming and the unfettered sale and purchase of land on the open market, the small peasant class quickly fell into trouble. Con-temporaries estimated that the typical peasant family of early Han times, consisting of a married couple and three children, might own and farm 100 *mou* of land* and produce an annual harvest of about 100 piculs, or bushels, of grain, supplemented by beans or other vegetables and hemp or silk floss with which to weave cloth. Assuming each family member consumed, on average, less than a quart of grain daily, the family's food needs amounted to at least half its production. The pre-scribed land tax—one-fifteenth of the crop at the beginning of Han, but only one-thirtieth after the 150's B.C.—should not have been a major household problem if fairly administered. But there were other, heavier burdens. Besides a cash outlay in the form of a head tax of 120 copper coins per adult and 23 coins per child, the family's male members had to fulfill the military obligations described in Chapter 6 (during which period of service the citizen-soldier supplied his own food). In addition, every adult male was required to work without pay for one month each year on local construction projects or in other menial tasks under gov-ernment direction. The farmer's subsistence was therefore precarious at best. When any sort of disaster struck, the small farmer had few choices. He could mortgage his farm and postpone ruin for a time. He could go into trade, but without capital the outlook was bleak. He could take up banditry. The most likely way out in the end was to sell his land to some local man of means and become a tenant farmer, or if all else failed, to sell his dependents and himself into slavery. Thus men with money—officials and merchants—became large landlords. Landowning was an excellent investment because rents were commonly half the crop. In addition, the monied property owners often had enough political in-fluence to get their landholdings exempted from taxes.

The well-to-do were of course not self-sacrificing rescuers of the im-poverished; they were often aggressive, coercive exploiters. It was not difficult for a large landlord to gain sufficient control over water re-

* The basic unit of land measure, the mou, was about one-sixth of an English acre; 100 mou made a *ch'ing*.

Fig. 18. Han dynasty pottery mortuary models of farmhouse and human figures, including a farmer pounding grain beside a large millstone watched by a dog and two domestic fowl

sources to starve out small neighbors, or to enclose marshes and hills that were traditionally considered state domains and were relied on by the poor for fuel-gathering, fishing, and hunting. Particularly after state authority weakened significantly in Later Han, the bullying retainers of local magnates freely indulged in kidnaping and pressed peasant families into serfdom or slavery. It also became common for peasants to commend themselves and their households to a powerful land baron in order to evade state exactions or gain protection from bandits or rebels.

Early in Wu-ti's reign (141-87 B.C.), conscientious officials at court began complaining about the plight of the peasantry and urging reforms. Occasionally thereafter the government remitted taxes in times and areas of widespread natural disasters. (Tax remissions remained the standard relief measure in all subsequent dynasties.) The government also occasionally resettled the landless on undeveloped lands, provided seeds and tools for the impoverished, undertook canal-building projects to improve irrigation, and tried with other kinds of stopgap measures to alleviate the worst distress. But it did not face up to the basic problem of inequitable land distribution until 7 B.C., when 30 ch'ing (3,000 mou, or about 500 acres) was established as the maximum amount of land any one family could possess. This rule was not enforced. The visionary usurper Wang Mang (r. A.D. 9-23) then proclaimed the nationalization of all land and ordered that large estates be broken up and redistributed to the poor. He also ordered the freeing of all slaves. Neither plan could be implemented, primarily because the men called on to enforce the reforms were precisely those most disadvantaged by them. Both plans were abandoned even in principle after two or three years. The founder of the Later Han dynasty was himself a man of the local landed elite, and neither he nor his successors initiated any land reforms. Great family estates grew still larger, and fewer and fewer peasants managed to remain independent.

The drastic population decline at the end of Han alleviated the land pressures on the survivors, and at the beginning of the third century the dictator Ts'ao Ts'ao vigorously resettled landless and uprooted peasants as tenants of the state on abandoned land so as to create a reliable revenue system and stabilize society. State tenants paid rents that were higher than the taxes on private farms, but these exactions were not as exploitive as the demands made on the serfs of the great family estates, which continued to thrive without governmental interference. The Southern Dynasties generally followed Ts'ao Ts'ao's precedent, providing different forms of relief when independent farmers encountered some disaster and resettling new destitute groups as state colonists in new territories. Taxes and rents from state tenants were gradually increased to meet the increasing needs of the extravagant southern courts.

In the north invading tribal chieftains comfortably adapted themselves to the late Han and post-Han patterns of great family estates, so that North China peasants in the era of division were as thoroughly transformed into serfs and slaves as their compatriots in the south. But in the fifth century the T'o-pa rulers of the Northern Wei state, who laid the foundations for so much of the stability and strength of Sui and T'ang, initiated land reforms with two goals in mind. For one thing, they wanted to increase the amount of land under cultivation and thus grain production. For another, they wanted to bring powerful landlords under firmer state control. Therefore in the 480's they adopted a series of measures that combined elements from the well-field system attributed to antiquity, the Han administrative tradition, and the state-tenancy system that had developed in the south. The result, which persisted into T'ang times with modifications, was called the equal-fields (*chün-t'ien*) system.

Reform is perhaps an inadequate word, for what the T'o-pa rulers attempted was a fundamental restructuring of the land-tenure system. All families were now proclaimed to hold land only by allocation from the state, and tenure was generally limited to the lifetime of the recipient. The allotment to which any family was entitled depended on the number of its adult and adolescent males, its slaves, and its oxen. Because the cultivation of mulberry trees for sericulture is a long-term venture, households were allowed small supplementary plots for this purpose, which could be transmitted hereditarily. Upon the death of any male, a suitable portion of his family's allotted land reverted to the state for reallocation. On the assumption that all males now had equal shares of land, land taxes were abolished and state tax and service levies were based exclusively on male head counts. Thus a genuinely equitable system of land distribution and taxation was theoretically achieved, in the spirit of the well-field tradition.

In practice, some of the T'o-pa reforms were purely nominal. Local chieftains, who had previously been unsalaried, were now given Han-style status as commandery governors and state salaries, varying according to the extent of their domains. What had been the great personal estates of these land barons were now designated state-owned lands, but the revenues from them went into the same purses as before, simply redesignated as salaries. The amount of land that supported each dignitary was supposedly limited in accordance with his rank, though the available evidence suggests that excess holdings were not confiscated. As for the very poor, they were still settled as colonists on uncultivated land, in the Southern Dynasties pattern.

The equal-fields system in its mature form, in the early T'ang reigns, theoretically provided that at age sixteen every male received an allotment of 80 mou owned by the state and could inherit a maximum of 20 mou as well, and that all males up to age sixty paid an identical tripartite tax: an amount of grain equivalent to a land tax or rent (*tsu*), variable forms of payment in lieu of labor service (*yung*), and a fixed amount of cloth (*tiao*). On reaching the age of sixty, a man's land allotment dropped to 40 mou, and he was exempted from the tsu-yung-tiao tax. A widow was entitled to 30 mou, or 50 if she was the head of a household; but she was exempt from taxes. Townsmen such as merchants and artisans and Buddhist and Taoist monks were all entitled to small plots. Officials were granted very large, inheritable tracts according to their rank, and in addition while on duty had control of the lands attached to their posts, which provided part of their salaries. In theory, reallocations were made annually by county magistrates through village headmen, balancing out new claims against reversions. In heavily populated regions, less-than-standard allotments were provided for, on a fixed scale; and variations in other local conditions were taken into account, especially in frontier regions.

Although one could hardly expect that so idealized a system could have been applied successfully and uniformly throughout the empire, available evidence indicates that into mid-T'ang times it was enforced vigorously in North China, where the peasantry's circumstances were significantly improved. The fact that land was scarcest where the population was densest was a disadvantage that no planner could wholly overcome. Moreover, in allotting generous parcels to persons of official status—and even of purely honorific status—the system perpetuated the privileges of the favored few. Successive emperors repeatedly compromised the system still further by granting large tax-exempt tracts to their special favorites even in the most densely populated areas, and the government did not vigilantly protect peasants from infringements and encroachments by the influential. Buddhist establishments were commonly granted large tracts by devout rulers and were then allowed to enlarge them endlessly by accepting gifts of state-allocated lands from hard-pressed farmers, who then became tenants on Buddhist estates and in this way managed at once to evade all state tax and service levies and to forestall the encroachments of influential private estate-builders. For all these reasons, and especially because of population growth, the equal-fields system steadily deteriorated.

From an early date in the T'ang period the national tax system was supplemented by a variety of small levies. They are noteworthy here only because they established two important precedents. These levies, which were the only taxes imposed on landless townsmen such as merchants, were generally based on households and graded by appraised wealth. Thus the principle of progressive taxation was established: the rich not only paid more tax, but paid at a higher rate. The supplementary levies also included a small tax at a flat rate per mou, from which no one was exempt, which was intended to support granaries for public relief. Thus the principle of a standard land tax was established.

These precedents led to a historic fiscal reform designed in 780 by a noted administrator named Yang Yen (727-81), which rescued the T'ang state from the accumulated abuses of the equal-fields system and the decentralization of authority after the devastating An Lu-shan rebellion.

Yang Yen's reform of 780, initiating what was called a two-tax (*liang-shui*) system, did away with all of the old taxes and imposed a consolidated tax payable in two installments, in summer and autumn (hence the name), and comprising two elements. One was a levy on each household, graduated according to the number of persons included and the appraised value of all household property. In recognition of the steadily increasing importance of money in the economy, this levy was made payable in copper coins, or *cash*.* The other was a levy on all land under cultivation, payable in grain. In neither case was there a standard nationwide rate. Imperial negotiators worked out with each regional governor what his region's total tax quota should be and what proportion of it should be sent to the capital, what proportion should be retained for prefectural needs, and what proportion should be made available to the regional government. Thus local tax rates varied, to fulfill the somewhat arbitrarily negotiated regional quotas. Only in this way did the T'ang central government succeed in getting revenues from all parts of the country during the last half of the dynasty, when central political control gradually disintegrated.

The Yang Yen plan benefited the state by giving it a stable revenue, but the new system represented a total retreat from the long-established doctrine that the state was responsible for rectifying inequities in land distribution. The two-tax system was a realistic acceptance of the fact that the equal-fields system was no longer workable. In short, it was a restoration of the early Han laissez-faire policy. The principle of private ownership prevailed, and the peasant was again thrown directly into unequal competition with great landlords. Although the ideal of the well-field system was far from dead in Chinese minds, the great age of land-distribution experimentation was over. The two-tax system, because it served state needs, remained the basis of Chinese fiscal administration into the sixteenth century.

---

* Throughout the early imperial age the standard unit of metallic money was a single-denomination copper coin. Modern Westerners traditionally have called such Chinese coins *cash*.

COMMERCE

Commerce flourished in Han and T'ang times in spite of, not because of, governmental policies. The combination of Confucian and Legalist attitudes that served as the dominant state ideology throughout the early imperial age was overwhelmingly anticommercial. To Confucians, the profit motive of merchant life corroded personal morality and impeded social harmony. To Legalists, mercantile activities were basically nonproductive if not counterproductive, did not increase state wealth and power, and drained into private hands economic surpluses that the state should rightfully control. Governments of the early imperial age therefore considered private commerce something to be watched with care, discouraged, and suppressed if it thrived too flagrantly.

From the beginning of the Han dynasty on, merchants as a class were subject to discriminatory sumptuary laws. They were forbidden to wear silk clothing, ride in carriages, and carry weapons, and in principle though hardly in practice they were not allowed to own agricultural land. Their sons and grandsons were disqualified from official appointments, recommendations, and examinations. They were permitted to set up shops only in certain market areas of towns, where officials were delegated to supervise them closely and prevent them from using irregular weights and measures or committing other frauds. Almost all these restrictions were enforced only sporadically, but it was not until after mid-T'ang times that they seem to have been ignored consistently. In the last T'ang century mercantile life gradually developed the freer patterns that would predominate in the later dynasties: the scattering of shops out of designated urban market zones, the flourishing of regional trade centers, and the emergence of distinct marketing areas within counties in which villages exchanged goods at rotational fairs.

Merchants of the early imperial age were also subjected to heavy direct and indirect taxes. Governments often acquired needed commodities, especially for out-of-the-way frontier garrisons, by procedures euphemistically called "harmonious purchases." These were government purchases in bulk at arbitrarily fixed low prices, amounting almost to confiscatory requisitions. Sales taxes and taxes on mercantile goods in transit were common—imposed not only by central governments, but also, from time to time, by local governments and even important landowners.

On many special occasions governments called on wealthy merchants to make large "contributions" to the state coffers. One of the most drastic sequences of measures against merchants was pursued by Han Wu-ti in the second century B.C. In an effort to replenish his treasury, drained by his many costly military campaigns, Wu-ti imposed new taxes of 120 *cash* on each merchant boat and 240 *cash* on each merchant wagon, offered handsome rewards to informers who reported evasions, and confiscated all possessions of offenders. Then he required all merchants to submit inventories of their entire stock and pay ad valorem taxes on their total wealth—and again rewarded informers and confiscated the possessions of evaders. These laws were enforced so stringently that the imperial treasury was enriched and the merchant class all but ruined.

In a more fundamental manifestation of anti-mercantile attitudes, all traditional Chinese governments barred merchants from certain money-making ventures that have commonly been open to private exploitation in other societies. Many of the commodities needed by the government itself were not bought from merchants but were manufactured in government-owned workshops. These enterprises notably included shipyards, armories, and other sorts of armament works; military equipment and weapons were products from which private entrepreneurs were never allowed to make fortunes.

In addition, it was early taken for granted that the state had a special responsibility to regulate the marketing of such essential goods as grain, salt, and iron. The most notoriously wealthy men of the Warring States era and the earliest Han decades were grain speculators; and the trade in salt and iron—most prominent among the commodities that were in demand everywhere but were not naturally available everywhere— was highly susceptible to private manipulation. In Han Wu-ti's reign public outrage against the flagrant profiteering in these products coincided with the state's need for new revenues, and the emperor's fiscal administrators—themselves recruited from the mercantile class despite the dynasty's prohibitions against merchants holding official positions— brought together isolated precedents from pre-Han experiments into a sophisticated complex of market controls that had no systematic counterparts outside China until state socialism and welfare-state practices developed in the very modern West. The Chinese system that stemmed from Wu-ti's measures had two main components. One was a group of indirect controls collectively called the ever-normal granary system; the other was a system of direct controls through regulated monopolies. Both systems were perfected by Sang Hung-yang (143-80 B.C.), a merchant's son who was brought into palace service at the age of thirteen because of his mathematical wizardry, eventually rose to the eminent post of censor-in-chief, and became a virtual fiscal dictator in Wu-ti's last decades.

The ever-normal granary system was intended to stabilize supplies and prices of market commodities—particularly grain, but some other goods as well—making private speculation unprofitable. Government agencies throughout the empire, under central direction, bought up surplus grain whenever and wherever there was an abundance, thus preventing severe declines in market prices, and conversely sold government-stored grain whenever and wherever the market supply was inadequate, thus preventing severe price increases. Although the government now had to bear the cost of storing grain for extended periods and transporting it from place to place as regional markets fluctuated, it was able to offset these expenses by selling when prices were rising and buying when prices were falling, and in fact—under Sang Hung-yang's astute management, if not at all other times—made very substantial profits. Such was Wu-ti's intention, at least in part. In effect, the state captured the profits that had previously gone to private speculators.

The state monopolies were also profitable, though consumers perhaps suffered less than when they were at the mercy of private manipulators. The state did not directly engage in the manufacture of salt and iron but rather licensed the manufacture of these products under its own supervision and made its agencies the sole lawful distributors. This effectively put a stop to the excessive profiteering of the past, and such profits as were made under the new plan accrued directly to the state. The salt and iron monopolies were so successful from the state's point of view that monopolistic controls were similarly imposed on the liquor trade. Unlike salt and iron production, however, liquor production was so fragmented and localized that national controls proved unenforceable, and the project was quickly dropped.

The state's entry into the marketplace was not unopposed. There were widespread complaints, particularly about the salt and iron administration. In 81 B.C., not long after Wu-ti's death, 60 scholars from throughout the country were summoned to a court conference to discuss with Sang Hung-yang and other high officials the merits and demerits of the monopolies and a broad range of other governmental policies. A scholar named Huan K'uan took notes at the meeting and wrote a digest of some of the exchanges—*Yen-t'ieh lun* (Discourses on Salt and Iron)—which reveals earnest, idealistic "country Confucians" pitted in unequal debate against Legalistically inclined, tough-minded, and quick-witted administrators such as Sang. Against the Confucians' suggestion that the monopolies put the state in improper competition with common people in the marketplace and fostered greed, Sang and his colleagues argued that the monopolies and other measures were necessary to produce revenues for the state's frontier defenses against the Hsiung-nu. The scholars retorted that military strength was un-availing unless rooted in national morality, and that if only rulers and ministers cultivated themselves so as to exude moral virtue the Hsiung-nu would clamor to submit and there need be no wars. It was one of the most classic confrontations on record between Confucian and Legalist attitudes in a real historical context.

The court conference did not result in any immediate changes of government policy. In the last Former Han decades, however, the early laissez-faire attitudes became prevalent again, and Wu-ti's economic controls for the most part lapsed. The reformist usurper, Wang Mang, tried to revitalize and even expand them—to achieve centralized state control of the exploitation of all natural resources and the marketing of all commodities. He also tried to create a state monopoly of credit by offering loans to the needy at low interest rates, financed by an income tax levied on merchants and artisans. These plans failed as did his other reforms, and the Later Han dynasty made few efforts to re-assert governmental influence on industry and commerce.

Sang Hung-yang's fiscal innovations had a lasting legacy, however, just as the ideal of the well-field system persisted. Most of the dynasties that followed Former Han maintained some parts of the ever-normal granary system. The tax-supported relief granaries of the T'ang dy-nasty, mentioned earlier, were one example. Recurringly, also, dynasties revived state monopolies of one sort or another—particularly of salt. After the An Lu-shan rebellion in the eighth century, the T'ang fiscal administrator Liu Yen (715-80) so skillfully revived and managed the salt monopoly that its revenues alone provided more than half of the tottering central government's income until the two-tax system, insti-tuted 17 years after the end of the rebellion, provided a sound new basis of regular revenue. Liu Yen's system made state employees of all salt producers, and state agencies sold salt to merchants with a substantial tax added to its price. Iron was not monopolized by the T'ang state, but in its last century T'ang tried to reestablish the old Han liquor monopoly—and to monopolize the tea business as well. Neither effort was successful.

In keeping with their domestic policies, the Chinese dynasties of the early imperial age did not generally encourage foreign trade. It was not considered either proper or safe for Chinese to have private intercourse with uncivilized peoples; indeed, unofficial travel beyond the frontiers was often deemed treasonable. But some commercial interchanges were unavoidable, since foreigners from all sides sought such Chinese products as silk, ceramics, and coins; and Chinese governments found that giving the Hsiung-nu and other hostile neighbors opportunities for peaceful trade was one way to lessen the danger of raiding forays. From Han times on, therefore, it became standard practice for Chinese and neighboring peoples to trade their wares at frontier markets under government sponsorship and supervision. Tributary missions from vassal states were commonly allowed to include traders, who thus gained opportunities to do business in the capital markets. No doubt a large proportion of what the Chinese court chose to call tributary missions were in fact shrewdly organized commercial ventures by foreign merchants with no diplomatic status at all. This was unquestionably the case, most notably, with a group of traders who appeared on the south coast in 166 A.D. claiming to be envoys from the Roman emperor Marcus Aurelius Antoninus (An-tun to the Chinese).

Foreign trade was of course not merely a grudging concession to foreigners. Chinese merchants were never inclined to bow submissively to restrictive laws, and frontier officials could often be bribed to ignore violations. Moreover, as has already been noted, exotic things from afar fascinated upper-class Chinese, especially in T'ang times, and Chinese rulers were as enchanted as anyone else with the rare and costly things that came to the country through trade or tribute—gold, jade, furs, spices, and strange animals and birds, to name a few. And one trade item above all the Chinese desperately needed—horses. Try as they might to maintain pasturages or devise other schemes that would ensure a regular domestic supply of horses for use in the endless conflicts with the northern nomads, the Chinese seldom had as many military mounts as they wanted or required without relying on foreign suppliers. In this regard if no other the successive Chinese dynasties regularly pursued aggressive trading policies. Fortunately for China, some nomads were almost always willing to provide horses for the Chinese to use against other nomads, and even when most united and hostile the nomads so desired Chinese grain, silks, and eventually tea that they could be persuaded to provide the horses China was sure to employ against them. Fortunately for China, too, the Koreans were usually on friendly terms and could supply good horses. All frontier trade in horses was normally monopolized by the government.

The ingenuity of Chinese craftsmen and engineers and the continuing commitment of all Chinese dynasties to development combined to keep the country on a course of general economic progress through the vicissitudes of the early imperial age. Irrigation, intertillage, double-cropping, and improved crop rotation practices increased agricultural productivity. Breast-strip harnesses for horses, ox-drawn plows, wheelbarrows, water-powered mills, crude sowing machines, simple draw-looms, and other labor-saving devices, some of which were adopted in China as many as ten centuries earlier than in Europe, also helped to increase production. Iron technology improved with the spread of bellows-fanned furnaces, and iron weapons and implements became ever more commonplace. State-sponsored canal- and road-building projects improved transportation and communication—sometimes dramatically, as in the opening of the Grand Canal in Sui times. The economy did not wholly rise above the barter level; even through T'ang times rents, taxes, salaries, and wages were commonly paid at least in part in kind, usually grain or bolts of silk. But copper coins (cash) in strings of a thousand served as the basic monetary standard from Han through T'ang, and by late T'ang merchants were using bills of deposit and credit that foreshadowed paper money.

In the paraphernalia of everyday life China was revolutionized between the beginning of Han and the Five Dynasties period. No early Han Chinese ever burned coal, wrote on paper, saw printing, sat at a table on a chair, drank tea, or rode in a sedan chair—activities that were all commonplace in tenth-century China. In its material and technological richness, T'ang life had no equal anywhere in the world.

8. Thought

THE POLITICAL and social concerns that preoccupied early Confucian and Legalist thinkers slipped out of the philosophical realm into the realm of practical statecraft once China had been successfully unified under the Han dynasty. With political stability at last achieved, many intellectuals devoted their energies wholly to administrative routine, court politics, and institution-building of the sort discussed in Chapter 6. When not directly engaged in government, men of predominantly Confucian inclination busied themselves in reconstituting and reinterpreting the canonical writings of antiquity or in historical scholarship (considered in Chapter 9), in both pursuits striving to evaluate and influence their time by reference to the standards of the past.

Metaphysical and cosmological thinking, which had seemed rather capricious aberrations in pre-Ch'in times, now surged into the mainstream of China's intellectual history. Even conservative Confucians turned their attention to vague questions about the nature of the cosmos and mankind's place in it, and Taoism gained increasing influence both as a philosophy and as a popular religion. Then, in late Han times, Buddhism, imported from India, caught the Chinese imagination, and in the post-Han centuries it so altered Chinese life that the process has been called the Indianization of China. Yet there never developed in China a Buddhadom akin to Christendom in Europe. After centuries of absorption and adaptation, Chinese Buddhism reached its apogee in the mid-T'ang period, and then began giving way to the first stirrings of a new Confucianism that would dominate the later imperial age.

HAN ECLECTICISM

Han Kao-tsu and his immediate successors were anything but ideologues. In government, while finding it prudent to avoid the harsh excesses of Ch'in, they adopted Ch'in's Legalist-based organizational structures and administrative practices. By personal inclination they were largely Taoist—or at least eager devotees of occult superstitions that were increasingly being associated with Taoism. For Confucianism they had no special fondness. Kao-tsu early in his career did not bother to conceal his contempt for the dour liturgists who then passed as Confucians, though he grudgingly came to realize that some of the ritualism they esteemed was essential to the dignified management of his imperial court and government. He commissioned Confucians to draw up a court ritual that might restrain his hard-drinking, rowdy followers from such pranks as hacking away with their swords at the columns of his new palace. It is one of the great ironies of Chinese history that Han Wu-ti, one of the more Legalistic rulers of the whole imperial age, pronounced Confucianism the ideological basis of imperial rule, banned all but professed Confucians from state service, and established a wholly Confucian curriculum for the national university he founded in 124 B.C. to train officials. He did so under the influence of the leading Confucian scholar of the time, Tung Chung-shu (c. 179-104 B.C.), who wedded original Confucian emphases with the eclecticism that was prevalent in his time.

Early Han eclecticism consisted of Taoist mysticism and naturalism mixed in with every myth and superstition of any currency. Eclectic tendencies had appeared in several late Chou works, notably the collection of miscellaneous essays called *Li-chi* (Ritual Records). Eclecticism also abounds in the so-called wings, or appendixes, to the ancient *I-ching* (Classic of Changes), which were apparently still being written in the second century B.C. The extremes of eclecticism seem to have been reached in a group of works, now almost entirely lost, that were written in Han times as complements to the ancient classics, known collectively as *wei* (woof), as opposed to the classical *ching* (warp). Later scholars eventually denounced them as occult absurdities, but they apparently reflected a world view that was almost universal in early Han.

The world view of intellectuals now incorporated not only the old seminaturalistic, semimystical notion that the cosmos is ordered by Yang and Yin forces, but also the related belief that all things are constituted of Five Elements (*wu-hsing*)—wood, metal, fire, water, and earth. These fundamental substances too are dynamic forces, which come into cosmic predominance one after another in a predictable cyclical progression that supplements the seesaw functioning of Yang and Yin. Wood is shaped by metal, metal is melted by fire, fire is put out by water, water is channeled and contained by earth, earth is broken by wood, and so on; just so, each element is "produced" by its predecessor and then yields to its successor in the sequence. The Five Elements were thought to correlate metaphysically with the seasons, the principal grains and domestic animals, the primary colors, musical notes, tastes and smells, planets, imperial dynasties, directions, and almost all other things that can be grouped appropriately. In a different system of metaphysical correlations, Yang and Yin were also related to the eight basic trigrams of the *I-ching* (see the diagram, p. 72). By means of all these complicated numerological correspondences, Han scholars sought to understand, analyze, and categorize every aspect of their world, and thus to find ways to conform to the cosmic harmony of the universe.

Tung Chung-shu. One early attempt at synthesizing all these systems is a work called the *Huai-nan tzu*, a predominantly Taoist compendium by scholars at the court of Liu An, prince of Huai-nan (d. 122 B.C.). But the most influential synthesis by far was that of Tung Chung-shu, whose adaptation of numerology and cosmology to Confucianism is best revealed in a book of essays called *Ch'un-ch'iu fan-lu* (Deep Significance of the Spring and Autumn Annals). One of its emphases is the glorification of man's role in the cosmic scheme:

As for the human body, the head is large and round, resembling Heaven. The hair resembles stars and constellations. The ears and eyes are penetrating, resembling the sun and moon. The nose and mouth exhale and inhale, resembling wind currents. The intestines are perceptive, resembling the spiritual intelligences. The stomach and womb fill up and empty, resembling the material phenomena.... The correspondences of Heaven and Earth and the complementarities of Yin and Yang are regularly fixed in the human body. The body is like Heaven; their numbers are comparable, and so their fates are intermingled. Heaven shapes the human body with the numbers of the full year. Thus the 366 [sic] small joints correspond to the number of days, and the 12 large joints correspond to the number of months. Inside are the five viscera, corresponding in number to the Five Elements. Outside are the four limbs, corresponding in number to the four seasons. The opening and closing of the eyes correspond to sunrise and sunset. The firmness and softness [of bone and flesh?] correspond to winter and summer. Grief and happiness correspond to Yin and Yang. The mind engages in reckoning, corresponding to numerical measurements. For conduct there are principles and rules, corresponding to Heaven and Earth. These are all manifested subtly but pervasively in the body, living jointly with humans like a pair of dolls [?]. In whatever can be numbered, there is a correspondence of numbers; in whatever cannot be numbered, there is a correspondence of categories. Everything fits together so as to correspond to the unity of Heaven.

Such tortuous, pseudoscientific reasoning is typical of early Han philosophical thought in general.

Tung harmonized the contrasting views of Mencius and Hsün-tzu regarding human nature in such a way as to give Wu-ti and his successors a respectable ideological basis for the new imperial order. Tung insisted with Mencius that human nature has the potential for goodness in it, but like Hsün-tzu he believed that goodness must be developed by practice, especially of the basic virtues of human-heartedness (jen), righteousness (i), and wisdom (chih). What guides man in this direction, Tung believed, is necessarily the influence of the ruler, since the ruler is the personification of Heaven's will, if not of Heaven itself.

The appeal of Tung Chung-shu's cosmological exaltation of kingship to Han rulers needs no explaining; in the imperial system that had emerged his assumptions could hardly be denied, and they were reiterated by rulers and officials alike throughout subsequent imperial history. It is noteworthy, however, that in accepting the sublime status Tung conferred on them, emperors also had to accept the corollary, humbling concept that the improper use of imperial power disrupted cosmic harmony. As Tung wrote: "When the world is in disorder and the people are perverse, or when the ruler's will is erratic and his moods are rebellious, then the transforming influences of Heaven and Earth are obstructed, natural forces produce evil portents, and harm ensues." Tung considered strange astronomical happenings in particular to be warnings of Heaven's displeasure and large-scale natural disasters such as floods and droughts to be punishments inflicted by Heaven for failure to heed its warnings. These punishments were further thought to be omens that Heaven was withdrawing its mandate from the ruling family.

In the orthodox imperial ideology that stemmed from Tung's eclectic Confucianism, officials relied on astrology to interpret Heaven's moods and thus to evaluate the propriety of emperors' public and private acts. Criticisms based on astrological interpretations often drove emperors to prostrate themselves in penitence at the altar of Heaven outside the capital, taking upon themselves the blame for whatever in the human realm had provoked Heaven's wrath. Thus the power of being the Father and Mother of the People was in considerable measure offset by the awesome responsibility of being the Son of Heaven.

Classical scholarship. The eclecticism of Tung Chung-shu and other early Han thinkers partly reflected a passion for books that was becoming a predominant characteristic of upper-class life, stimulated by the loss of many early writings in Ch'in times and in the Ch'in-Han transition. The recovery or reconstitution of the lost works took on the character of a national crusade, and led by extension to efforts to synthesize the ideas they contained.

Some Ch'in copies of old texts had survived one way or another. Other ancient writings were reproduced from memory by elders who had studied them in pre-Ch'in times. All the texts that circulated in early Han times were consequently written in the script that had been made standard by Ch'in. From time to time later, especially in the first century B.C., texts came to light that were written in pre-Ch'in scripts; one, for example, was discovered in the wall of a house that had supposedly belonged to Confucius. The early Han texts came to be called "new text" versions to differentiate them from the later, "old text" discoveries; the versions often varied substantially. In general, the "new text" versions inclined toward a numerological and cosmological eclecticism not found in the "old text" versions. Scholarly controversies about the authenticity of these texts raged throughout Han times and sporadically thereafter, even into the twentieth century. Controversial textual variations account in part for the difficulties modern scholars have in using the writings attributed to antiquity.

Authenticity was not the only problem. Over the centuries the Chinese language had changed so greatly that the ancient texts required much clarification. Scholarly attempts to cope with this problem produced the early lexicon, *Erh-ya*, which was perhaps prepared as early as pre-Han times; and in A.D. 100 a scholar named Hsü Shen compiled China's first real dictionary, *Shuo-wen chieh-tzu* (Words Explained), which explained the pronunciations and presumed meanings of more than 9,000 characters. Thereafter, lexicography became a continuing, prolific activity among Chinese scholars throughout history. Hsü Shen's *Shuo-wen chieh-tzu* is a particularly noteworthy landmark in the history of Chinese cultural development because to some extent it arrested the rapid changes in meanings of characters that had been occurring earlier, just as Ch'in's standardization of Chinese script had arrested changes in the form of characters.

The efforts to clarify ancient writings also produced—in much greater volume—learned commentaries in which scholars explained obscure words or passages, discussed their reasons for preferring one reading over another, and sometimes rearranged passages to make sense out of otherwise inexplicable sequences. (Since books still existed primarily in the form of wooden slats laced together, it was not difficult for slats to get misplaced.) In the process, probably in the first century A.D., Han scholars invented the world's first footnotes.* Among the more renowned annotators were Ma Jung (A.D. 79-166), the earliest scholar ambitious enough to write commentaries on all the Five Classics, and Cheng Hsüan (127-200), whose perceptive insights into ancient textual obscurities have been admired and relied on by almost all subsequent scholars.

Han scholarship produced important new works as well as explanations of old ones. The most influential, a brief treatise of unknown authorship called *Hsiao-ching* (Classic of Filial Piety), espouses Hsün-tzu's authoritarian form of Confucianism and extols filial piety as the root of all other virtues. Known from early Han times, *Hsiao-ching* became the traditional introduction to classical learning for all Chinese youths. Another esteemed work of Han scholarship is *Shan-hai-ching* (Classic of Mountains and Seas), a collection of essays on famous places that inaugurated a long series of descriptive geographical writings, which constitute a substantial category of traditional Chinese scholarly literature.

Han bibliomania so infected the Chinese spirit that throughout subsequent history Chinese intellectuals learned their classics by heart, wrote ever newer and more complex commentaries on them, brought classical allusions into their discourses on every subject, and in general steeped themselves in the classics as assiduously as the most devout European Christians ever submerged themselves in Scholasticism.

---

* The early practice was to copy out the text being discussed and at appropriate intervals to insert one's explanatory comments in smaller script. Later, to make it easier for readers to distinguish text from commentary clearly, scholars compressed their notes into double columns of small characters inserted into the vertical single columns of large characters in which the main text was written. This practice continued into the twentieth century.

Fig. 19. Scholars collating Chinese classic texts: detail of a 10th-12th century copy of a painting traditionally attributed to the Sui-T'ang era

Later Han pessimism. Tung Chung-shu's philosophy was a systematic expression of the fundamental optimism that predominated in early Han times. It was accepted that Heaven rewarded good and punished evil, that Heaven's will could be understood through astrology, and that men could shape and change the course of events by suitably virtuous conduct. But after the disastrous usurpation of Wang Mang, who had been considered a paragon of virtue, this optimism waned, and as conditions worsened during Later Han it gave way to skepticism, fatalism, and finally nihilistic escapism. Most Confucians seem to have given up political philosophizing for textual scholarship.

One early spokesman of the new mood was Wang Ch'ung, a petty official of the first century A.D. An iconoclastic debunker of prevalent superstitions, Wang combined a healthy Taoist naturalism with rationalistic realism in the style of Hsün-tzu. He ridiculed the idea that man has a special place in the cosmos and can influence events, and especially the idea that Heaven requites good and evil appropriately. He believed only in chance, or in a kind of fatalistic predestination:

The men who manage affairs may be wise or stupid; but as for the disasters or blessings that ensue, some are lucky and some are unlucky. What one undertakes may be right or wrong, but the rewards or punishments that one gets are matters of chance.

If one is fated to be rich, he will on his own emerge from impoverished status and succeed. If one is fated to be poor, he will on his own fall from wealthy status into danger.

When the world is well governed, this is not the achievement of worthies and sages; and decay and ruin are not brought about by a lack of the Way. If a state is destined for decay and disorder, worthies and sages cannot make it prosper; and if the time is ripe for good government, evil men cannot cause disorder. Whether the world is well ordered or disordered is a matter of the time, not of policies; whether a state is safe or endangered is a matter of its destiny, not of its doctrines; and whether there are worthy or unworthy rulers or enlightened or unenlightened policies cannot change things for better or worse.

Wang Ch'ung was followed by a succession of writers who complained about the extravagance of the rich, the indolence of the powerful, and the general ineffectiveness of government. As Han continued to deteriorate, some thinkers began to revive Legalist arguments for strong laws, strict enforcement, and harsh punishments. Thus Ts'ui Shih (c. 110-70), in his treatise *Cheng-lun* (On Governance), combined lip-service to Confucianism with thoroughly Legalist arguments such as the following:

Laws that serve the state are like medical treatment [*li*; putting in order] for the human body. If it is at peace, it is nourished; if it is sick, it has to have remedies applied. Now penalties and punishments are the medicines of disorder, virtue and education the daily nourishment of order. But attempting to get rid of troubles by means of virtue and education would be like attempting to cure sickness by prescribing a rich diet. Dealing with a peaceful situation by means of punishments and penalties would be like nourishing [a healthy body] with medicines.

Men of Legalist bent gained increasing prominence at court as conditions continued to worsen. Their influence was shown, for example, in the Chin law code of 268, which is no longer extant but reportedly had 2,926 paragraphs of statutes pertaining to every imaginable crime. By then, however, political philosophy had been entirely abandoned;

the Chinese intellectual world was dominated by the escapism of a resurgent Taoism and the salvationism of a newly arrived Buddhism.

Philosophical Taoism. The so-called Neo-Taoism movement of Later Han took two forms. One was a kind of Taoist revisionism, which by harmonizing the Taoist spirit with Confucian social and moral doctrines made it possible for Chinese of subsequent centuries to bear normal social responsibilities while retaining spiritual detachment and a measure of individualism. The other form was an outburst of hedonistic nihilism in the third and fourth centuries. Both forms contributed to the so-called pure conversation style of discourse, an apolitical, metaphysical, dilettantish mode that prevailed among intellectuals through the long era of division, especially in the south.

The chief revisionists were Wang Pi (226-49), a brilliant annotator of the *I-ching* and the *Lao-tzu*, and Kuo Hsiang (d. 312), whose commentary on the *Chuang-tzu* made its wilder flights of fantasy almost understandable. Both honored Confucius as China's foremost patron saint, intimating that as a fulfilled Taoist he could dispense with mystical profundities and concentrate on externalizing the Taoist spirit in the world of practical affairs. They introduced a number of new concepts and terms that later Confucians were to find handy, and also popularized the idea that absolute reality is nothingness (*wu*), which became the Taoist counterpart of Buddhism's eternal Buddha spirit.

Kuo Hsiang's commentary on the *Chuang-tzu* makes explicit and emphasizes that the ancient Taoist concept of nonaction (*wu-wei*) means taking no unnatural or inappropriate action:

Now, the workman does not act to cut down the tree; his action lies in using an ax. The ruler does not act to manage affairs personally; his action lies in using ministers. If ministers are able to manage affairs personally, and the ruler is able to use ministers; if the ax is able to cut down the tree, and the workman is able to use the ax—if all do what they are properly able to do, then Heavenly principles are manifested spontaneously; it is not a matter of taking action. If, on the other hand, the ruler does the ministers' work, then he denies his rulership; and if ministers take over the ruler's powers, then they deny their ministership. Therefore, each should perform his own function, and then superiors and subordinates will all be successful, so that the principle of nonaction will be attained.

Nonaction does not mean folding the hands and being silent. It is simply that one should always do what is natural; then a person is content with his nature and his fate. If one cannot avoid [being a ruler], one should not act oppressively with severe punishments; one should simply embrace the Way, cherish simplicity, and tolerate any extreme that is inevitable. Then everything in the world will fulfill itself.

The basic Taoist goal of being content with oneself and letting Nature take its course is further emphasized:

Now, sorrow and pleasure arise from losing and getting. A scholar who understands the Mysteries and harmonizes with the Transformations is always content with the times and always comfortable in making necessary accommodations. In quiescence he is at one with the creative processes. Wherever he goes, he is not self-conscious. What is to be got, what lost? What dies, what lives? Since he accepts whatever he is given, sorrow and pleasure have no way to get mixed into the matter.

The Taoist notion that rulers should appoint ministers and leave governing to them naturally appealed to Confucian bureaucrats, and it accounts in part for the tradition, originating in early Han, that government policies and undertakings were initiated by ministers in memorials to the throne, not by emperors acting without ministerial advice.

The revisionists were traditionally called "discoursers on profundities." Their hedonistic contemporaries have often been called the "lyrical" or "romantic" Taoists. The most celebrated of them were the Seven Sages of the Bamboo Grove, led by a scholar, poet, and master lute player named Chi K'ang (223-62). Instead of accepting social responsibilities and government appointments as Wang Pi did, they persuaded themselves that the way to preserve moral integrity was to evade every duty, flout every convention, and indulge every whim, be it sensual or intellectual. One of the Seven was always attended by a servant carrying a jug of wine and a shovel, so that his master might take a drink whenever he thirsted and might be buried on the spot if he happened to fall dead. Another, having walked a great distance to a friend's house, turned on his heel without even saying hello and returned home; when asked why, he explained with a shrug that he went because he felt like it and came back home because he wanted to. The group regularly gathered in a bamboo grove outside Loyang to admire the beauties of nature, drink, indulge in witty "pure conversation," compose poems, make music, or meditate. Their days commonly ended in a nearby tavern, where they drank themselves into a state of spiritual communion with the Tao.

Not long after these Taoist bon vivants there appeared a less blithe spirit, Pao Ching-yen (fl. c. 300?), who carried the antiestablishment strain in Taoism to an anarchistic extreme. Believing that all men were created equal, he denounced government as a device by which the strong and clever dominate the weak and ignorant masses:

The Confucian literati say: "Heaven gave birth to the people and then set rulers over them." But how can High Heaven have said this in so many words? Is it not rather that interested parties make this their pretext? The fact is that the strong oppressed the weak and the weak submitted to them; the cunning tricked the innocent and the innocent served them. It was because there was submission that the relation of lord and subject arose, and because there was servitude that the people, being powerless, could be kept under control. Thus servitude and mastery result from the struggle between the strong and the weak and the contrast between the cunning and the innocent, and Blue Heaven has nothing whatsoever to do with it.

Pao Ching-yen's views were swallowed up in the pure-conversation dilettantism of his time, when intellectuals were not inclined to take any mundane matters seriously enough even to be anarchists.

Religious Taoism. Meanwhile, on a different level of intellectual sophistication, a hodgepodge of ancient folk superstitions and cults were coalescing into a Taoist religion. Local cults had existed since prehistoric times, and in the Warring States era shamans, sorceresses, magicians, medicine men, and seers were found at every feudal court. They drew heavily on the more mystical Taoist writings, notably the *Chuang-tzu.* By Han times, when philosophical Taoism had become almost dormant, popular Taoism flourished as a catchall movement embracing many occult arts that shared the common goal of physical immortality. Legends were already accumulating about men who had attained the status of immortals.

One group of cults, originating in Shantung, focused on legends about a magical island called P'eng-lai somewhere in the ocean to the east. It was thought to be inhabited by immortals, and cultists believed that by visiting P'eng-lai they could achieve extraordinary longevity or procure an elixir of immortality. In the fourth century B.C. some coastal lords reportedly sent maritime expeditions in search of P'eng-lai. The First Emperor of Ch'in certainly did so, and for centuries many East Asians thought the Japanese were descended from one group of youths he had sent abroad. The P'eng-lai cults faded away in Han times, but they left a legacy in later Chinese myths, poems, and art.

Another group of Taoist practitioners were alchemists. According to tradition, alchemy originated with an intellectual of the fourth century B.C. named Tsou Yen, who is also credited with the doctrine of the Five Elements referred to above. The earliest alchemical experiment of which there is a reliable historical record was made under the sponsorship of Han Wu-ti in 133 B.C. It was an unsuccessful effort to make gold out of cinnabar, the work of one Li Shao-chün, a many-faceted magician who was believed to have visited P'eng-lai and gained immortality. The oldest extant alchemical treatise, an appendix to the *I-ching*, is attributed to Wei Po-yang of the second century A.D. but may date from the next century. It describes the marvelous powers of many famous elixirs and how they can be produced, but unfortunately in terminology too strange to be understood.

Alchemy continued to be practiced throughout the early imperial age. However questionable its premises, its results were by no means negligible. Taoist experiments initiated Chinese chemistry, mineralogy, and pharmaceutics, and produced various dyes, alloys, and porcelains as well as the compass and gunpowder. But Taoist alchemists were not interested in generalizing their methods and observations. For this reason, and because China's best minds were normally preoccupied with other intellectual pursuits, Chinese alchemy was never transformed into science.

Still another major Taoist cult was devoted to yoga-like hygienic disciplines designed to extend youthfulness and prepare the body for immortality. The principal techniques of this cult were abstention from certain kinds of food, respiratory and gymnastic exercises, and trance-like meditation. In Han times these practices, which derived from the cults of ancient shamans, became intermixed with Yang-Yin and other numerological and cosmological systems. For a time it was believed that the path to immortality lay through long dietary preparation, sexual strengthening (sometimes by continence, sometimes by excesses), and finally intense concentration yielding the "inner vision" by which, in trances, one could see and communicate with each of the human body's 36,000 "interior gods." In Han and later times some Taoist groups indulged in mass sex orgies, in which Yang and Yin forces were thought to be brought to maximum efficacy. But by the end of the T'ang dynasty Taoist beliefs about hygiene were mellowing, eventually to produce various dietary principles and the mild gymnastics widely known as *kung-fu* (literally, work) that have been practiced by all classes of Chinese into modern times.

Out of the Taoist cult eclecticism of Han times there developed in the second century A.D. a most remarkable phenomenon: a faith-healing, drug-dispensing, polytheistic Taoist church practicing congregational worship, preaching salvation through immortality, and eager to establish its own state and fight for it. It had two branches, one based in Shantung in the east and the other in Szechwan in the west. Both were dominated by hereditary theocrats surnamed Chang, who were perhaps related. The Shantung group's doctrine was called the Way of Great Peace, and that of the Szechwan group the Way of the Five Pecks of Rice, after the dues collected from the household of each devotee. The Shantung group's influence spread so rapidly that the Han government took steps to suppress it, whereupon in 184 the church's adherents, donning yellow turbans for identification purposes, openly rebelled. So began the Yellow Turban uprising that precipitated the decline of the Han empire. The Szechwan church rebelled separately in the same year.

Though the two rebellions were finally put down, organized Taoist religion survived. In competition with Buddhism in the era of division, its high priests gradually developed monastic practices and substituted social welfare activities for militancy. New deities were constantly added. By T'ang times Confucius had joined Lao-tzu in the Taoist pantheon, and a supreme being, the Jade Emperor, was thought to preside over all the deities ranged in a graded hierarchy of multi-tiered paradises corresponding to the T'ang imperial government. There were also multi-tiered hells attended by demons. Every household had a kitchen god (or stove god), who reported on its activities to the Jade Emperor during the New Year season. Taoist festivals abounded in every locality, and some were observed nationally. Hereditary Taoist priests attended local shrines everywhere, selling charms and talismans and exhorting people to virtue in the same tones as Confucian magistrates and Buddhist monks. Great Taoist monasteries competed with Buddhist establishments for the patronage of the elite and the donations of the lowly.

The Taoist church superstructure lasted only until the upheavals of the late Han. Thereafter, religious Taoism was practiced in contradictory ways in autonomous monasteries and shrines. The most prestigious Taoist establishment eventually came to be a monastery based in the mountains of Kiangsi, presided over hereditarily by a family of Changs who claimed descent from the Han founders of the church;

they have commonly been called Taoist popes. Their establishment was disrupted by civil wars in the early 1930's, but a Taoist pope of the Chang family remains active in Taiwan today.

Biographies of Taoist immortals were included in an encyclopedia of folklore called *Feng-su t'ung-i* (Compendium of Customs), written about A.D. 175 by Ying Shao. A proper Taoist hagiography, *Lieh-hsien chuan* (Biographies of the Various Immortals), appeared in the third century, impossibly attributed to a famed scholar of the first century B.C. It had many sequels through the ages. By T'ang times a considerable corpus of Taoist religious literature had accumulated, and a collection resembling the Buddhist canonical writings subsequently appeared as the Taoist Tripitaka (*Tao-tsang*).

After the classical *Lao-tzu* and *Chuang-tzu*, the single most famous Taoist work—and the most useful reference on Han and immediate post-Han Taoism—is *Pao-p'u-tzu* (The Master of Preserving Simplicity), a compilation of all things Taoist by a fourth-century scholar named Ko Hung. Although he had an active civil and military career, Ko's great passion was to become a Taoist immortal, and he recorded everything he could learn about the process. His work is in two parts, one on social and political matters, the other on alchemy, which was clearly his first interest. He describes pills that confer immunity to fire and water, and others that enable people to disappear at will, fly, assume any desired shape, raise the dead, achieve position or wealth, and even expand their vocabularies effortlessly. Despite such extravagances, Ko Hung's work shows a strikingly scientific temperament. It was his greatest regret—and perhaps China's great misfortune—that he never had the money to set up a laboratory and conduct experiments.

The influence of the Taoist religion has been immense. It was an integral part of daily life in China from pre-T'ang times into the twentieth century. As sincerely as many modern Westerners read their horoscopes in newspapers and almanacs, even the most sophisticated Chinese believed in Taoist prognostications and sorcery. Indeed, many an eminent Confucian official believed without question that certain Taoist hermits in the famous mountain retreats had lived for hundreds of years. That they ultimately died made no difference, for immortals were expected to pretend to die so as not to confound lesser folk; and it was often reported that when an immortal's grave happened to be opened nothing could be found in the coffin but a stick of wood or a heap of discarded clothes.

BUDDHISM

Like Christianity and unlike Confucianism, Buddhism is a world religion. It appeals to individuals regardless of the social and political orders in which they live, enjoining its believers to adhere to a strict moral code and promising them personal salvation in an eternity divorced from the burdens and sorrows of this life. Its basic philosophical assumptions, its church organizations and monastic communities, and its dazzling public ceremonies were all far different from anything conceived of by China's ancient thinkers. From unspectacular beginnings in Han times, Buddhism rapidly developed a stunning, explosive impact on the Chinese tradition and was the most dynamic intellectual and religious force in Chinese life during the post-Han era of division and the remainder of the early imperial age.

Original Buddhism. The founder of Buddhism, named Siddhartha Gautama but known universally as the Buddha (the Enlightened), was the son of a petty warrior king in northeastern India, born late in the sixth century B.C. In his time Indian thinkers were creating a tradition of intense religious devotion that gave India its enduring reputation as "a God-intoxicated country." Their early consensus, which provided many of Buddhism's basic assumptions, included the conviction that individual beings pass through endless reincarnations (*samsara*) shaped by their cumulative records of good and bad deeds (*karma*). The goal of life is the "snuffing out" (*nirvana*) of the forces propelling one from existence to existence by learning that one's spiritual essence, Atman, is the same thing as the cosmic essence, Brahma, which is the only true reality and in contrast to which the whole of the material world is an illusion.

In the prime of life the Buddha gave up worldly things and plunged into the religious exertions that absorbed his intellectual contemporaries. But it was only after he finally abandoned his ascetic strivings toward Truth and sat down under a tree in disillusioned relaxation that he experienced a flashing revelation of the nature of life and the path of release, and knew that he would not be born again. For the rest of his long life he traveled about northern India preaching his doctrines and winning converts. He organized his followers into monastic communities constituting a church (*sangha*), and he taught them the law or discipline (*dharma*) of being good monks. By the time of his death the fundamental Buddhist confession had been established: "I take my refuge in the Buddha; I take my refuge in the dharma; I take my refuge in the sangha."

The Buddha won converts in part because it is clear that his was an electric personality. But he also had a superb intellect, and his conception of the human condition was at once breathtakingly brilliant and utterly simple. Its essence is: There is no Brahma; there is no Atman. What keeps you in this world of illusion, propelling you from one life to the next, is no more than your own craving for existence and for self-ness. If you really want to get off the merry-go-round of endless suffering and rebirth, then realize you are on it only because you want to be. To get off, all you have to do is let go!

Becoming enlightened by realizing these Buddhist truths, the convert attains a state of serene indifference, unconcerned whether he lives or dies, completely without attachment to life or to any of the things that he encounters in life. He knows that for him the cycle of births is at an end, that life has been fulfilled, that all that should be done has been done. When he dies, he enters a final state called *paranirvana*. This state, the Buddha insisted, is entirely beyond human comprehension, beyond any distinction between existence and nonexistence, and therefore indescribable; but it is an enhancement and a realization, not extinction.

Original Buddhism offered the hope of salvation only to people able to renounce the world and become monks living under strict discipline —in the Buddha's phrase, "wandering lonely as a rhinoceros." Laymen were encouraged to abide by the Buddha's ethical commandments as best they could so as to earn monkhood in future incarnations, and to help the monks by giving them food and more substantial donations. This is the form of Buddhism that spread from India to Ceylon, Burma, and Thailand, where it still thrives. It is known as Theravada Buddhism, the Doctrine of the Elders.

Another form of Buddhism developed in India not long after the Buddha's death and eventually spread northward into Central Asia and thence toward China. The Buddha himself was exalted into the status of a supreme godlike spirit very much like Brahma or the traditional popular Christian concept of God. He was transformed into an eternal Buddha spirit, and nirvana became a uniting of the individual self with the eternal Buddha spirit in everlasting bliss. Another characteristic of the new Buddhism was the belief that some saints, deliberately choosing not to enter the final bliss of paranirvana, stayed behind to help others along the way. Such saints, called bodhisattvas, eagerly wait to be

Fig. 20. Colossal Buddha statue at Yün-kang

personal saviors for the devout, presiding over paradises that are thought of as way-stations along the road to full Buddhahood. People who are favored by a bodhisattva can gain temporary respite from the sufferings of reincarnation by entering into such a paradise when they die. For most believers, this is the supreme religious goal; the concept of paranirvana fades into remoteness.

Followers of this new form of Buddhism called their doctrine Mahayana, the Great Vehicle (that can carry everyone to salvation), in contrast to the older form that emphasizes monastic life, which Mahayanists know by the disparaging term Hinayana, the Lesser Vehicle.

Buddhism in China. Unreliable traditions have it that the Later Han emperor Ming-ti (r. A.D. 57-75), in consequence of a dream, sent ambassadors to India in search of a mighty sage, and that they returned with China's first knowledge of Buddhism. More trustworthy evidence suggests that Buddhism was already known in China by Ming-ti's time —that his brother Prince Ying of Ch'u in northern Kiangsu was in fact a generous patron of both monks and laymen. By the second century A.D. Buddhism was an intriguing novelty in Chinese intellectual circles; by 166 both Taoist and Buddhist religious altars had been established in the Han palace, in consonance with the eclectic spirit of the time; and by the end of Han, Buddhist communities were scattered about North China and in parts of the south. In the Three Kingdoms era the rulers of Wei in the north and Wu in the Yangtze delta were considered converts, and by the beginning of the fourth century Buddhism was solidly established at all levels in Chinese life.

Both forms of Buddhism, Mahayana and Hinayana, were brought to China by missionaries, either overland from Central Asia or via Vietnam by monks from India and Ceylon traveling in trading ships. Those best known to history were the translators of Buddhist canonical writings (*sutras*)—a long succession beginning with a Parthian called An Shih-kao in Chinese, who arrived in Loyang about A.D. 148 and lived there for 20 years translating and teaching. In the earliest centuries the movement was wholly foreign-dominated; it was generally considered improper for a Chinese to become a monk. Chinese nevertheless were attracted to monasticism, and when a Hsiung-nu ruler of the Later Chao state in the north proclaimed in 335 that native converts might adopt monastic life, he was merely confirming a practice that had already become common. Thereafter native monks gradually became the leaders of Chinese Buddhism, and Chinese pilgrims to India competed with in-migrating missionaries in introducing new sutras.

One of the most famous foreign translators and innovators was Kumarajiva (344-413), a Central Asian who headed a government-sponsored translation bureau in Ch'ang-an beginning in 401; his translation of the sutra "The Lotus of the Wonderful Law" (or simply "The Lotus Sutra") has been the single most influential book in East Asian Buddhism. Another, equally renowned foreign teacher was Bodhidharma, who in the sixth century introduced the practice of wall-watching as an aid to concentrated meditation and is considered the inspiration of the Ch'an sect of sudden enlightenment (best known to Westerners by its Japanese name, Zen).

Among the more famous Chinese pilgrims was Fa-hsien,* who be-

* On taking monastic vows Chinese Buddhists abandon their original names and take religious names with appropriately auspicious meanings, usually in two characters. Fa-hsien's name means Illustriousness of the Law.

tween 399 and 413 traveled overland from North China to visit all of Buddhism's holy places in India, sailed to Ceylon and then to Java, took a trading ship bound for Canton that was blown far off course in a storm, and finally landed on the coast of Shantung. Fa-hsien was the first Chinese pilgrim known to have reached India and returned. He spent his remaining years translating the texts he had brought back with him. The most famous pilgrim of all was Hsüan-tsang (c. 596-664), already mentioned in Chapter 5, who traveled overland to India and back between 629 and 645 and then devoted himself to prodigious translation work. Both Fa-hsien and Hsüan-tsang left records of their travels that have great historical value.

Buddhism gained acceptance in China in the beginning as a strange variant of religious Taoism, since there were some superficial resemblances, notably in their common disdain of worldly power and their emphasis on the goal of inner contentment. Like Taoists, the early Buddhist missionaries were not averse to practicing rain-making and other shamanistic magic; such skills, combined with their objectivity as political and military advisers, were particularly helpful in gaining them the patronage and protection of alien rulers in the north. Moreover, in Buddhism's early centuries in China it was taught and explained to Chinese largely in the metaphysical terminology of the Taoists. Translators deliberately combed the *Lao-tzu* and the *Chuang-tzu* for analogies they could use to suggest Buddhist concepts that were utterly foreign to the Chinese tradition. One of Kumarajiva's great contributions in the fifth century was to shed this camouflage of Taoist terms and provide accurate translations of Buddhist terms that preserved their full foreignness.

Late Han China was as ripe for Buddhist salvationism as it was for Taoist escapism, and the flourishing of Buddhism during the era of division paralleled that of Taoism. In intellectual circles, Buddhists participated zestfully in the "pure conversation" movement; among the masses they preached the immortality of the soul rather than emphasizing the physical self, as the Taoists did. In its competition with Taoism Buddhism had two notable advantages. For one thing, its ethical teachings, though conflicting at points with Confucian doctrines, were of a high order of respectability and did not shock Chinese conservatives as some of the orgiastic Taoist practices did. Moreover, whereas Taoism offered only newer and newer interpretations of the *Lao-tzu* and the *Chuang-tzu*, Buddhism benefited from the continuing vitality of the religious movement in India, which regularly produced exciting

Fig. 21. Colored and gilded wood statue of the bodhisattva Kuan-yin from the 12th or 13th century

new canonical texts that reinvigorated the movement in China. It is noteworthy that as Indian Buddhism declined, eventually to disappear entirely from its homeland a thousand years ago, Chinese Buddhism too began to lose its intellectual force, eventually to join and in some degree merge with Taoism in an eclectic national popular religion.

Meantime, the Chinese had developed a number of Buddhist sects. Many of these were based entirely on single texts and had only fleeting significance, but four principal sects endured to become the major pivotal forces in the continuing Buddhist movement, not only in China, but in Korea and Japan as well. Though all are considered Mahayanist sects, they honor the early sutras on which Theravada, or Hinayana, Buddhism is based. They regard the Hinayana texts as the Buddha's introductory-level teachings and the numerous later Mahayana sutras as his highest-level, final teachings. This tolerance has been carried over into their own relationships, which have always been characterized by considerable interaction and little hostility; the Chinese penchant for eclecticism and syncretism prevailed. Two of the sects, T'ien-t'ai (Heavenly Terrace, named after its mountain headquarters in Chekiang) and Hua-yen (Garland), have been heavily doctrinal and scholastic for the most part; they have been conservative movements attempting to consolidate all the canonical concepts into a unified system that categorizes the different stages of Buddhist teaching and the different levels of Buddhist truth. They developed staid intellectual followings but never generated the popular or intellectual excitement that attended the two other major sects, Ching-t'u and Ch'an.

The Ching-t'u (Pure Land) sect is a populist, devotional form of Buddhism that preaches salvation by faith. The Pure Land is a Western Paradise presided over by the bodhisattva Amitabha (A-mi-t'o-fo), attended by the Goddess of Mercy, Kuan-yin (Fig. 21); and sectarians aspire to be admitted to the Pure Land paradise after death. They worship congregationally and practice good works, but what matters most is the sincerity of their belief in Amitabha and in his desire to help them. They devote themselves to earnest meditation to achieve such sincerity, and they believe that a single sincere utterance of the name Amitabha is sufficient to guarantee them entry to paradise. Simple believers mutter Ambitabha's name over and over daily in the hope that at least one of these utterances will be heard and accepted as a sincere avowal of belief. Statues of Amitabha and Kuan-yin came to be fixtures in almost all Buddhist establishments and in private homes, and scenic views of the Western Paradise came to be a favorite motif of painters and muralists.

Ch'an or Zen (literally, meditation) in its mature form was developed primarily by an extraordinary Chinese monk named Hui-neng (638-713), who was traditionally considered the Sixth Patriarch of the sect. It seems to be a fusing of the original Buddhist conception of enlightenment with elements from the Taoist philosophical tradition. Ch'an monks do not withdraw from worldly affairs; they are traditionally the only Buddhist monks who do not beg but work for their own livelihoods. They prefer nonintellectual, nonscholastic, simple workmen's tasks, and are often very gifted artisans. Though they practice meditation, they do not believe that meditation leads to insight; they insist that meditation *is* insight. They disdain bookishness and both learning and teaching in the normal sense. Indeed, they ridicule the very process of reasoning, emphasizing the need to transcend rationality and prepare themselves for an immediate intuitive perception of reality.

Ch'an masters, either in delight or in outbursts of anger according to their impulses, give irrelevant and irrational answers to questions and torment their disciples with paradoxes and conundrums (*kung-an*), such as "What is the sound of one hand clapping?" Enlightenment, in the Ch'an view, is merely to be fully, unselfconsciously aware of the Here and Now; and it comes unpredictably in a sudden, spontaneous flash— perhaps triggered by something as simple as tripping on a pebble, hearing a strange birdsong, or contemplating a teacup. One must therefore prepare for enlightenment by being receptive to whatever might happen and responding to it spontaneously, neither regretting or savoring anything that has passed nor hoping for or dreading anything that is to come. In direct contact with reality without the distortions imposed by intellectualizing, the successful Ch'an devotee attains the detachment advocated by the Buddha, an enviable peace of mind, and—though Ch'an does not stress this—the certainty that he will not be reborn. The object is to live and not to strive, even for nirvana.

In addition to the Buddha, the bodhisattva Amitabha, and the Goddess of Mercy, Kuan-yin, the pantheon of popular Buddhism notably includes Maitreya (Mi-lo-fo), thought to be a Buddha who has yet to appear and who when he comes will create a paradise on earth. He is normally portrayed as a big-bellied, laughing scamp; figurines of him are found in gift shops throughout the world. By T'ang times popular Buddhism also included a semisecret cult known as the White Lotus

Society, whose messianic preachings later helped fan the flames of many peasant rebellions. The Society was usually able to rally mass support instantaneously with pronouncements that Maitreya had materialized or was about to materialize.

The voluminous Buddhist canonical and exegetical writings in Chinese are known collectively as the Tripitaka (*Ta-tsang*, the Great Treasury); the earliest collection was prepared in 581. There is also an extensive Buddhist hagiographic tradition, beginning with *Kao-seng chuan* (Biographies of Eminent Monks), written by Hui-chiao in the sixth century.

Chinese reactions against Buddhism. Buddhism did not win favor and flourish in China without opposition. There were many aspects of Buddhist doctrine and practice that were at odds with the evolved national character of the Chinese. Buddhist pessimism about this life in this world conflicted with the fundamental optimism and this-worldly emphases of both the Confucian and the Taoist philosophical traditions; celibacy and monasticism conflicted with entrenched Chinese familism and views about social harmony. Such tensions persisted unresolved even though Buddhists in China found some ways to accommodate their beliefs to Chinese traditions—for example, by advocating the moral virtues of Confucianism, including filial piety. Moreover, Buddhists inevitably aroused jealousy among religious Taoists, with whom they competed directly for elite patronage and mass support, and among Confucian officials, who resented any political influence achieved by either Buddhists or Taoists. Surprisingly, even xenophobic arguments were raised against Buddhism from an early time: it was repeatedly insisted that Buddhism could have no truth to it because it was not of Chinese origin. Most difficult of all, probably, was the conflict of interest that unavoidably existed between both Buddhists and Taoists on one hand and all those concerned with the practical functioning of the Chinese state, on the other, over the monasticism that withdrew individuals from the normal controls of the integrated political and social order.

One of the more bizarre aspects of Buddhist history in China is the long controversy that raged between Buddhists and Taoists over the relative priority in historical time of the Buddha and Lao-tzu. In India, little attention was paid to historical record-keeping, so that establishing dates for the life of the Buddha has had to be a matter of guesswork. At the same time, as was noted in Chapter 3, there is no evidence in

China that a person named Lao-tzu ever existed at all, let alone of the intriguing tradition that in his old age he traveled beyond China's north-western frontier, never to be heard of again. This story nevertheless inspired an ingenious Chinese named Wang Fu, who lived in the early fourth century, to write a book called *Lao-tzu hua-hu ching* (The Classic About Lao-tzu's Civilizing the Barbarians), which reappeared in several versions, to be serious irritants to Chinese Buddhism for the next thousand years. Its basic thesis is that Lao-tzu, on departing China, traveled across Central Asia into India and there either (1) magically transformed an accompanying disciple into the historic Buddha, (2) converted the Buddha to Taoism, or (3) became the Buddha himself, depending on which version of the text one reads. Buddhists fought this Taoist attack primarily by moving the life of the Buddha back to earlier and earlier times, and Taoists responded in kind by reassigning dates to Lao-tzu. The controversy was aired in formal court conferences in 520 under the sponsorship of the T'o-pa Northern Wei dynasty and again in 568 under Northern Chou, but though Taoists were regularly chided and chastised for their contentiousness, the Buddhists were unable to suppress Taoist claims on Lao-tzu's behalf until the thirteenth century.

Confucians were on the whole more rational in their criticisms of Buddhism. They occasionally argued on doctrinal grounds that the Indian notion of karma was invalidated by the Chinese doctrine of the Mandate of Heaven; and they joined with Taoists in arguing against Buddhism simply because it was non-Chinese. (Still, the Confucians never carried the alien argument to the same insulting extremes: the Taoists went so far as to assert that the Indians, being naturally evil, needed a doctrine like Buddhism to reform them, whereas the Chinese, being naturally good, had no need for reform but merely needed Taoism to bring their natural goodness to fulfillment.) The Confucians' most insistent arguments were thoroughly practical ones: that Buddhism drained the people of their all-too-inadequate funds and made them crave what they were not destined to have, that it undermined the social order by destroying families through monastic celibacy, and that it undermined the state by withdrawing monks and nuns from productive economic life and exempting them from taxation, labor service, and military conscription. The same arguments of course could be, and were, leveled against religious Taoism; but when Chinese rulers came to be annoyed with Buddhism it seems ordinarily to have been because favored Taoists provoked them using the Confucians' arguments, and Taoism was not adversely affected.

The conflict between religion and state was recognized early in China, but in late Han and immediate post-Han times governments were generally so weak that rulers seem to have seen the church less as a threat than as a useful prop; and Buddhists found it easy to maintain the independence of their monks from any earthly authority. In 340 some officials at the Eastern Chin court at Nanking challenged the principle of exempting monks from rendering ritual homage to the emperor, but the emperor confirmed their traditional autonomy. In 403, when the question was again raised at court, a famous early Chinese monk, Hui-yüan (334-416), successfully argued that the church claimed no special status for its pious lay converts but had to protect the integrity of its monks, since they could fulfill their vows only by abandoning all worldly affairs. Hui-yüan also managed to prevail against suggestions that the monasteries harbored impious, illiterate monks who should be ousted and returned to lay life. Hui-yüan's conception of the proper relationship between state and religion set the pattern for all the Southern Dynasties, though criticism continued even during the reign of Buddhism's most ardent champion in the south, Liang Wu-ti (r. 502-49), who liked to be called Imperial Bodhisattva. Wu-ti commanded all his court officials to adopt Buddhism, denounced Taoism as a false doctrine, and in 517 ordered the destruction of all Taoist temples. Beyond this, he repeatedly enriched Buddhist monasteries by presenting himself to them as a menial bondsman and then having the state treasury emptied to ransom him.

Although the Northern Dynasties were usually as bountiful in their patronage of Buddhist ascetics as the Southern Dynasties, the Buddhists had notably less independence under the alien northern rulers. More aggressively autocratic than their southern counterparts, the northern rulers never permitted monks and nuns to believe they were anything but subjects. The Buddhists accommodated themselves to the situation by considering the northern rulers living Buddhas, before whom it was natural and fitting that they should prostrate themselves. The form that state-religion relations took in the north was clearly fixed when the T'o-pa Northern Wei dynasty in the 390's appointed a monk to the government as the chief of monks, charged with regulating all monastic activities in the state. In the latter half of the fifth century the northern government even set limits on the number of monks, nuns, and pagodas allowed in each region, according to the population. This pattern was perpetuated thereafter in the north.

In 607, Buddhism was finally brought under genuine state control when the Sui dynasty unequivocally proclaimed that all Buddhists in the newly reunified nation, in the south as well as in the north, must do ritual homage to the emperor and his officials. Sui even prescribed examination and certification procedures for applicants to Buddhist and Taoist monasteries and officially chartered temples. These regulatory practices were continued by T'ang.

State control of religion in the north and ultimately throughout China was not necessarily oppressive, though damaging proscriptions were occasionally imposed. The Northern Wei emperor T'o-pa T'ao (Wei Wu-ti, r. 424-52), who favored Taoism, initiated a sequence of restrictions on Buddhist establishments in 438 that culminated in full-scale persecution from 446 into 452, when all Buddhist monks and nuns were ordered executed, and all Buddhist architecture, art, and books destroyed. In the next century, when the Northern Chou dynasty undertook to reestablish China's classical traditions, both Buddhism and Taoism were under proscription from 574 to 578. All religious buildings, art, and books were ordered destroyed; monastic treasuries were confiscated; and more than three million monks and nuns were reportedly returned to lay status—undoubtedly an exaggeration of vast proportions.

These early persecutions do not seem to have had serious lasting effects in the north, where they solely applied. The policies cannot have been implemented effectively, and after the persecutions new rulers zealously tried to undo whatever damage had been done. Thus the state proscriptions did not impede the progress of Buddhist influence to its peak in the T'ang dynasty. But in the last T'ang century Buddhism was persecuted again, this time on a national scale and with sufficient effect to force it into an economic and organizational decline from which it never recovered. The persecution was provoked by Taoists but was rationalized on grounds commonly argued by Confucians. The persecution was cumulative, progressing through a series of restrictions from 841 to 845, when it culminated in an almost total suppression. The court ordered only one temple to be spared in each prefecture, except that four temples, each with a caretaker staff of 30 monks, were to be retained in each of the two principal cities, Ch'ang-an and the auxiliary capital, Loyang. It was reported that 4,600 monasteries and 40,000 temples and shrines were destroyed; 260,500 monks and nuns and 150,000 bondsmen were returned to the laity; and millions of acres of tax-exempt farmland were confiscated and returned to the tax registers. That the proscription was carried out vigorously, even if not with complete effectiveness, is evidenced in the diary of a Japanese monk, Ennin, who was a traveling student in China at the time. The Buddhist church had simply grown too rich and its tax-exempt, nonproductive devotees too numerous. The hard-pressed T'ang state could tolerate the situation no longer, and Buddhism in its institutional aspects suffered the most damaging blow of its whole history in China.

Even so, state control, persecution, and suppression did not significantly weaken the role of Buddhism at the popular-religion level, where its salvationist preachings continued competing and intermixing with religious Taoism into the twentieth century. Nor could state action of itself diminish the intellectual appeal of the scholastic and meditative sects. However, as has been suggested above, by the end of T'ang, Buddhism had virtually died out in India, supplanted by Hinduism, a more orthodox outgrowth of the ancient Indian traditions; and Chinese Buddhism, though long since thoroughly Sinicized, consequently lost some of its doctrinal inspiration. More important, by late T'ang times Confucianism, which since mid-Han had provided only a widely accepted ethical system, a code of government, and a tradition of textual scholarship, was experiencing the first faint stirrings of revival as a creative philosophical force.

Later Chinese ascribe the beginnings of this revival to an official and litterateur named Han Yü (786-824), who was an innovative prose stylist and an ill-tempered polemicist. One of his most famous writings was a memorial protesting the processional display of a purported bone of the Buddha within the imperial palace; it throbs with xenophobic disdain, as in the following excerpt:

Now the original Buddha was a man of the barbarians. Having no comprehension of Chinese speech and wearing strange garb, he neither spoke nor dressed in accord with the prescriptions of our former kings. He knew nothing of the right relations between rulers and subjects or the natural affections between fathers and sons. If he were to appear in person here today, bearing his country's commission and coming to court in our capital, your majesty might be willing to receive him; but there would be no more than an audience in the Hall for Manifesting Governance, a banquet in the Pavilion for Entertaining Guests, and a bestowal of clothing. Then he would be sent under guard beyond the frontier, so that he might not delude our people. How is it conceivable that now, when he is so long dead, his rotted bone—this inauspicious, odious relic—should be admitted directly into the imperial quarters?

Though much more a polemicist than a philosopher, Han Yü is an important figure in the history of Chinese thought—not because he hated and attacked Buddhism (and Taoism as well), but because he eloquently insisted that the teachings of early Confucianism were the true wellspring of Chinese civilization. He thus foreshadowed, and perhaps in a minor way inspired, the Neo-Confucian movement that was to dominate Chinese intellectual life during the later imperial age.

9. Literature and Art

IN THE REALM of arts and letters, the most renowned achievements of China's early imperial age were in historiography, poetry, and Buddhist-inspired statuary and painting. Ssu-ma Ch'ien and Pan Ku, two Han masters, perfected an integrated, all-encompassing form of historical writing that has no counterpart in other civilizations, and initiated a sequence of dynastic histories that give imperial China a fuller and better organized historical record than exists for any other people over a long time span. Meantime, the writing of poetry was becoming a commonplace part of the lives of all educated Chinese, and new forms of poetry developed in response to new musical styles and other changes in the cultural environment. The fame of the two poetic geniuses of T'ang, Li Po and Tu Fu, has never been surpassed. The artistic traditions of antiquity were overwhelmed in the post-Han era of division by Buddhist themes, which by T'ang times dominated all art forms but then quickly lost their preeminence as the great age of Chinese Buddhism began to pass away. These achievements in literature and art deserve much credit for the gradual development of a durably unified and integrated Chinese civilization, and they were important components of the Chineseness that in T'ang times was admired and emulated in Vietnam, Korea, and Japan.

LITERATURE

Several general considerations about literary developments during the early imperial age are worth emphasizing here. The standardization of the Chinese script by the Ch'in dynasty aided the development of a genuinely national literature through the later ages, much as the universal adoption of Arabic numerals has provided the basis for an international science in modern times. Thus even when China was most divided politically and socially, as in the period of the Southern and Northern Dynasties, and despite linguistic variations that made oral communication impossible, for example, between natives of Ch'ang-an and Canton, educated Chinese everywhere wrote characters in the same forms. Moreover, regional differences in subject matter and rhetorical style were minimized by the rise to prominence of a class of officials who were recruited nationwide on the basis of their expert knowledge of classical writings. Directly or indirectly, the state established norms for formal education everywhere, since education was undertaken primarily and increasingly for the purpose of gaining official status. Hence government officials, deployed nationwide, were the living repositories of the national literary heritage and the principal contributors of new content to it. Their common educational background and common interests gave unity and homogeneity to Chinese literature, whether written and read in Ch'ang-an or Canton. One therefore cannot speak of a Szechwan literature, a Honan literature, or a Chekiang literature as one does of a French literature, an Italian literature, and a German literature. Chinese literature, unlike European literature, was one corpus.

It is also worth noting that since officials and aspirants to officialdom were the arbiters of what was literature and what was not, the songs and tales of the common folk seldom surfaced directly in formal written literature. However, litterateur-officials often imitated—or edited into suitably elegant literary form—those folksongs and legends that pleased them, and thus new literary forms and themes, particularly in poetry and fiction, cyclically moved up the social scale into formal literature. The folk heritage, in short, was a reservoir from which the literature of the elite regularly renewed itself.

As the domain of the official class, literature normally reflected the moral code espoused by the successive dynastic governments. That is, literature was predominantly didactic; it was expected to reflect and reinforce the traditional value system. Though "art for art's sake" was by no means unknown in literature and was not always disesteemed, a work so fashioned was generally considered a somewhat frivolous aberration and symptomatic of moral degeneration.

It will be recalled, as well, that paper was invented in China in the first century A.D. and quickly became the principal material on which writings were circulated. The obvious advantages of paper over silk and wooden slips—cheapness and convenience—were offset to some extent by paper's greater perishability. For this reason, many writings of the early imperial age have been irretrievably lost. Fortunately, the Chinese early began to gather what they considered important writings into anthologies that were carefully preserved; this became a common practice in the Southern Dynasties, and in T'ang times it became fashionable to make collections of the complete works of individual writers. In such anthologies and collections many writings received the special treatment that prevented their being lost and forgotten. The great age of preservation through mechanical reproduction was yet to come, however. Though printing was known in T'ang times, it was not until the later imperial age that literature was regularly printed and thus reproduced in sufficient quantities to ensure its survival.

Historiography. As was noted in Chapter 4, the prestige of historical writing was strongly rooted in China's antiquity, and diverse forms of historical texts remain from the pre-Han era: crisp chronicles, anecdotal narratives, and compendiums of documents. The variety and abundance of historical writings increased immeasurably in the early imperial age.

The earliest major historical work of the age happens also to be the most important. This is *Shih-chi* (commonly though imprecisely known in English as Historical Memoirs), a monumental work in 130 chapters compiled by a father and son who successively held the post of Lord Grand Astrologer at the court of Han Wu-ti. The father, Ssu-ma T'an (d. 110 B.C.), having ready access to the court archives, conceived a plan to write a complete history of the world (the world as known to China and himself, of course) from the beginnings to his own time. The son, Ssu-ma Ch'ien (145-87 B.C.?), toured widely in his youth, saw China's historic places, and talked with people who were steeped in local traditions or had personally participated in the great events of early Han. On inheriting his father's court post in 110 B.C., Ssu-ma Ch'ien carried his father's project to completion—a remarkable accomplishment in any case, but the more so, since he fell into disfavor for defending a general who had surrendered to the Hsiung-nu, was punished by castration, and was forced to spend his last years in humiliating service as a palace eunuch. The resulting work, *Shih-chi*, is a masterpiece of organization and style, and is important in both respects. Its organization set the pattern followed by subsequent writers in producing 25 dynastic histories that present the history of imperial China in unsurpassed detail and uniquely systematic order; and its style has made it one of the most prized works of all East Asian literature, which educated Vietnamese, Koreans, and Japanese as well as Chinese have delighted in reading for relaxation and edification, almost as if it were a novel.

The *Shih-chi* is organized in five main sections:

1. Basic Annals, 12 chapters. Here is presented a cryptic narrative of the principal events of China's political history from the legendary Yellow Emperor down into the reign of Ssu-ma Ch'ien's own ruler, Wu-ti.

2. Chronological Tables, 10 chapters. These are gridded tabulations presenting genealogical data about the successive ruling families, the families of the Chou feudal lords, and the noble families created by Han. The last table shows who held the most important civil and military posts at court, year by year, from the beginning of Han to about 100 B.C.

3. Treatises or Monographs, 8 chapters. These are partly historical, partly analytical essays on eight topics: rituals, music, pitch-pipes (and other pseudoscientific matters), the calendar, astronomy, sacrificial worship, the construction of waterways, and the regulation of the economy.

4. Hereditary Families, 30 chapters. These are collective biographies of the great feudal families of the Chou dynasty, gathering together and expanding on the skeletal data presented in the Basic Annals and the Chronological Tables. Confucius is exalted by having his biography included in this section.

5. Biographies, 70 chapters. These are biographies of people Ssu-ma Ch'ien considered important or interesting, and notably from the Han period. They include not only great officials and generals as might be expected, but a panoply of nongovernmental personalities, the notorious along with the famous—thinkers and poets side by side with rebels, assassins, and rogues. The most eminent personages have whole chapters devoted to them individually, but for the most part subjects are grouped into chapter-length categories, such as the disciples of Confucius. Six "biographies" relate China's historical contacts with non-Chinese: the Hsiung-nu, the various aboriginal tribes of the south and southwest, Central Asians, and Koreans. The final chapter is an autobiographical essay in which Ssu-ma Ch'ien honors his father, outlines his own career, and explains his motives and methods in writing *Shih-chi*.

Ssu-ma Ch'ien's multifaceted, multitextured approach to history was a remarkably original achievement. Without ignoring the chronological flow of events, he stressed the complicated interrelations among them, the evolution of important practices and systems, and above all the importance and fascination of people as individuals. His work is far more than a political chronicle; it is also an institutional history and most importantly, a sourcebook for social history.

Ssu-ma Ch'ien approached the facts of history with a spirit of respect and objectivity. Verbatim quotations from available documentary sources—especially memorials to the throne and imperial proclamations—are freely woven into his narrative, and his personal judgments are clearly labeled and set apart in prologues and epilogues. Yet, like the unknown author of the earlier *Tso-chuan*, he did not let the lack of sources deter him from presenting a narrative with rhetorical flow and dramatic impact. He unhesitatingly invented speeches and dialogues that he felt fitted characters and situations and brought them alive. Similarly, he did not clutter his pages with unimportant minutiae. Especially in the biographies, he gave detailed treatment to characteristic and illuminating episodes and skimmed over the rest. Such stylistic qualities, like his pattern of organization, became guidelines for later dynastic historians; but no successor equaled him as a superb prose artist, whose succinct descriptions, characterizations, and narrations have a forceful directness and an evocative power that readers have savored into our own time.

Something of the liveliness of Ssu-ma Ch'ien's writing is suggested in the following excerpt about the last days of the rebel leader Hsiang Yü (King Hsiang), before he yielded up the crumbled Ch'in empire to the founding emperor of Han. His forces reduced to a small company of cavalry, Hsiang Yü is being hounded by a large Han army and is falling back southeastward toward the Yangtze.

King Hsiang realized there was no escape and said to his horsemen, "Eight years have passed since I rose in rebellion, and I have personally taken part in more than seventy battles. All those I confronted were destroyed; all those I attacked submitted. I have never been beaten, and so I became hegemon over the whole empire. But now I finally come to grief here. This is because Heaven forsakes me, not because of any fault of mine in battle!

"Today I shall certainly perish," he continued. "But I want to fight lustily and win three triumphs for you—breaking their encirclement, beheading their generals, and cutting down their flags—so that you will recognize it is Heaven that forsakes me and no fault of mine in battle."

So he divided his horsemen into four squads, facing out in four directions. The Han army surrounded them, many men deep.

King Hsiang said to his cavalrymen, "Now I shall get a general for you!"

He ordered all four squads to gallop downhill and then regroup in three locations on the east slope. With a great shout, King Hsiang went galloping down; the Han army scattered, and he beheaded a Han general.

At this time the marquis of Ch'ih-ch'üan commanded the cavalry pursuing King Hsiang. When King Hsiang flashed his eyes and roared at them, the marquis of Ch'ih-ch'üan's men and horses were all startled and fell back several leagues.

When King Hsiang rejoined his troops in their three locations, the Han army did not know where he was. So it split into three groups and once more encircled the king's forces. King Hsiang then charged out again, beheading one officer and killing several hundred men; and when he reassembled his cavalrymen, he had lost only two of them. So he said to his men, "What do you think of that?" And they all bowed down and said, "It was as your majesty said!"

Then King Hsiang considered crossing the Yangtze at Wu-chiang into Chiang-tung. The Wu-chiang administrator was waiting with a moored boat. He said to King Hsiang, "Even though Chiang-tung is small, it covers a thousand leagues and has a population of several hundred thousand; it is enough for a king. Will your majesty please hurry to cross? For the time being I alone have a boat. When the Han army arrives it will have no means of crossing."

King Hsiang laughed and said, "Heaven has forsaken me; why should I cross? Moreover, I took eight thousand youths westward out of Chiang-tung, and now I return without a single one of them. Even if the elders of Chiang-tung should forgive me and accept me as king, how could I look them in the face? Though nothing might be said, I would feel shame in my heart.

"I know you, sir," he went on. "I have ridden this horse for five years. It has never met its match, and in one day it once covered a thousand leagues. I cannot bear to destroy it." And he presented it to him as a gift.

Then he ordered his horsemen to dismount, proceed on foot, and engage the enemy with short swords. He himself killed several hundred Han soldiers, but he suffered more than ten wounds about his body. Looking around, he saw the Han cavalry officer Lü Ma-t'ung and said, "Aren't you an old acquaintance of mine?" Lü Ma-t'ung took a good look at him and then beckoned Wang I, saying, "Here is King Hsiang."

"I hear," King Hsiang said, "that Han would buy my head for a thousand gold pieces and a fief of ten thousand households. I shall do you a favor." Thereupon he cut his own throat and died.

The historiographic tradition that Ssu-ma Ch'ien established was carried on in the first century A.D., again as a family enterprise, by a court official named Pan Piao and two of his three children. One son, Pan Ch'ao, earned a name otherwise, as a man of action; his exploits as one of the great Han proconsuls in Central Asia were mentioned in Chapter 5. Pan Ch'ao's twin, Pan Ku (A.D. 32-92), was the family's great historian, and after his death his work was completed by his sister, Pan Chao (A.D. 45-114?), the outstanding female intellectual of early Chinese history. Widowed early in life, Pan Chao became a friend and tutor of empresses and other palace ladies, and wrote a small book of moral admonitions for gentlewomen that circulated widely for centuries.

Pan Ku's classic, *Han-shu* (Book of Han), is a history of the Former Han dynasty, including the reign of the usurper Wang Mang. It has no Hereditary Families section (since Chou-type feudal states no longer existed in Han times), but otherwise follows the organizational pattern of *Shih-chi*, with 12 chapters of Basic Annals, 8 of Chronological Tables, 10 of Treatises, and 70 of Biographies. Among its major innovations were treatises on four new subjects: administrative geography, justice, the Five Elements, and bibliography. The *Han-shu* is important because it was the first application of Ssu-ma Ch'ien's composite organizational pattern to the history of a single dynasty, and because Pan Ku's prose style, though drier and less flamboyant than Ssu-ma Ch'ien's, has also been greatly admired.

The writing of histories in the *Shih-chi* and *Han-shu* format continued in the post-Han years among private scholars, often working under imperial patronage as Pan Ku did. Then the T'ang dynasty set up an official historiographic commission to compile the history of the preceding dynasty, Sui. The commission also compiled new, official histories for some dynasties in the era of division to replace private works that were considered inadequate, and it began compiling detailed court chronicles for each T'ang reign, called *Shih-lu* (True Records), which were intended to preserve in orderly fashion the source materials for an eventual history of T'ang.

The T'ang dynasty's initiative established a precedent for subsequent dynasties, which regularly accepted the responsibility of subsidizing historians to compile objective histories of their predecessors and "True Records" for their successors. It was probably a unique Chinese conception that such responsibilities should be borne by the government, and there is no better testimonial to the strong history-consciousness that prevailed among China's ruling classes. History was considered an indispensable supplement to the classics; rulers and officials were expected to be guided equally by the precepts of the classics and the precedents of history. And more than one ruler was dissuaded from rash acts by admonitions about how they would be judged in later histories.

The compilation of histories in the format of *Shih-chi* and *Han-shu* was by no means the only important activity of historians in the early imperial age. Buddhist and Taoist hagiography flourished, as was noted in Chapter 8; and collected biographies of eminent women, distinguished scholars, and notably filial sons were compiled. The Later Han scholar Hsün Yüeh (148-209), under imperial orders, rewrote the *Han-shu* data into a continuous narrative chronicle called *Han-chi*; and similar narrative histories, dynasty after dynasty, came to be common companion works to every dynastic history in composite form. The classical *Chou-li* was a model for collections of administrative regulations, the earliest of the imperial age being the *T'ang liu-tien* (Six Canons of T'ang), mentioned in Chapter 6.

A tradition of particularized institutional histories was begun by the T'ang scholar Li Chao with a short history of the Hanlin Academy, *Han-lin chih*; and a more impressive tradition of encyclopedic institutional histories was inaugurated by Tu Yu (735-812) with a massive 200-chapter work, *T'ung-tien* (Comprehensive Canons), which took 36 years to complete. *T'ung-tien* provides detailed, sourcebook-like histories, from highest antiquity to A.D. 755, of China's fiscal administration, policies on recruitment for office and personnel management, rituals, music, military organization, law, administrative geography, and foreign relations.

There were also the beginnings of what eventually became a great Chinese corpus of local and regional gazetteers, or historical geographies. In the middle of the sixth century Yang Hsüan-chih wrote *Loyang chia-lan chi* (Memoir on the Monasteries of Loyang), and in the ninth century Li Chi-fu produced a gazetteer of the whole empire, *Yüan-ho chün-hsien chih* (Treatise on Prefectures and Counties in the Yüan-ho Era [806-20]). By the end of T'ang a foundation had been well laid for the voluminous, variegated historical scholarship that became one of the outstanding characteristics of Chinese civilization in the later imperial age.

Fiction. From earliest times historical and philosophical writings in China regularly lapsed into fictional or semifictional narrations, and in the Han period the writing of wholly fictional anecdotes and fables seems to have become a popular pastime among the educated. That such writings were not greatly esteemed is indicated by their being called "small talk" (*hsiao-shuo*), a label subsequently applied to all forms of Chinese fiction. Fifteen anthologies of "small talk" are listed in the bibliographic treatise of Pan Ku's *Han-shu*. By his reckoning, they included 1,380 separate stories; not one has survived.

The oldest extant materials of this sort date from the post-Han centuries. Among them are gossipy "inside stories" about scandalous goings-on at the court of Han Wu-ti such as *Hsi-ching tsa-chi* (Miscellaneous Notes on the Western Capital), of unknown authorship; Taoist-inspired tales of marvels and the supernatural such as *Sou-shen chi* (A Record of Searching for Spirits), a collection by Kan Pao (fl. 290-320); and an especially famous anthology of wit and humor reflecting the "pure conversation" escapist frivolities of the immediate post-Han years, *Shih-shuo hsin-yü* (New Specimens of Social Talk) by Liu I-ch'ing (403-44). The simple structures and the typical subject matter of these early tales are illustrated in the following famous examples, which became part of the standard repertoire of all Chinese storytellers, though often greatly embellished:

From *Lieh-i chuan* (Tales of Marvels), an anthology probably dating from the third century:

Master Tsung and the Ghost

When Tsung Ting-po of Nan-yang was young, he went walking one night and met a ghost.

"Who's there?" he demanded.

"A ghost," the ghost said. "And who might you be, sir?"

Tsung lied, "I'm a ghost, too."

"Where are you going?"

"I'm going to the Wan market."

"I'm also going to the Wan market," the ghost said.

So they walked along together for several leagues. Then the ghost said, "Walking is very strenuous. Let's take turns carrying each other."

"Very well," Tsung said. So the ghost went first, carrying Tsung for a few leagues.

"How heavy you are!" said the ghost. "Aren't you a ghost after all?"

"It's just that I'm newly dead," Tsung said. "That's why I'm heavy."

Then Tsung took his turn carrying the ghost, and it wasn't the least bit heavy. After they had changed places several times, Tsung said, "Being so newly dead, I don't know if ghosts are afraid of anything."

"We just don't like for people to spit on us," said the ghost.

Soon they came to a ford across a stream. Tsung suggested that the ghost cross first, and there wasn't a sound to be heard. But when Tsung crossed there were splashing sounds.

"Why are you making such a noise?" said the ghost.

"It's just that I'm newly dead and unaccustomed to fording streams," said Tsung. "Don't be alarmed!"

As they were about to arrive at Wan market Tsung snatched up the ghost, clapped it to his head, and held it tight. The ghost screamed, making a frightful noise, and demanded to be put down. Paying no heed, Tsung went straight into the Wan market. But when he put the ghost on the ground, it changed into a sheep. So Tsung put it up for sale, after spitting on it for fear it might change back. He got fifteen hundred coins for it and left. Hence the jingle:

> Tsung Ting-po sold a ghost as a sheep
> And got fifteen hundred in cash to keep.

From *Yu-ming lu* (Records of Death and Life), a post-Han anthology of uncertain date:

The Temple Attendant of Chiao-hu

There was a temple attendant in Chiao-hu who had a cedarwood pillow that after some 30 years had developed a small crack in its back. A traveling merchant of the county, one T'ang Lin, passed by the temple and offered a prayer for good fortune.

"If you're not married," the attendant said, "you might try the crack in my pillow."

He had T'ang crawl into the crack, and there T'ang saw vermilion gates, marble palaces, and jade terraces surpassing anything in the real world. He met a Grand Marshal Chao, who gave T'ang his daughter in marriage. He reared six children: four sons and two daughters. T'ang was appointed Court Gentleman in the Imperial Secretariat, and then was quickly promoted to Court Gentleman at the Imperial Gate.

While T'ang was in the pillow he never thought of returning, but then the unforeseen happened—the temple attendant ordered him to come out. And when he looked back at the pillow he realized that all the years he had passed inside it had actually occupied only a few seconds.

Probably the single most famous tale dating from the post-Han era was written by T'ao Ch'ien (365-427; also known as T'ao Yüan-ming), who was one of the most gifted writers of all Chinese history and an especially noted poet. Like "The Temple Attendant of Chiao-hu," his tale "The Peach Blossom Spring" belongs to a category of Shangri-la stories that enjoyed great popularity; but it has an air of much more believability than most:

The Peach Blossom Spring

During the T'ai-yüan era [376-96] of Chin a fisherman who lived in the town of Wu-ling was boating along a stream, paying no attention to how far he went, when suddenly he came to a grove of blossoming peach trees stretching several hundred paces along both banks. There were no other trees mixed in with them; their fragrance was delicate, and their falling blossoms swirled about in abundance. Amazed, the fisherman went farther on to find the end of the grove. There he found a spring and a cliff pierced by a small cave. From this there seemed to come a faint light.

Leaving his boat, he went into the cave. At first it was so cramped that a person could barely get through, but when he had gone on some tens of paces the passageway opened up into daylight; and there he saw a flat, broad territory with substantial houses, well-kept fields, beautiful ponds, and stands of mulberry trees and bamboo, all connected by a network of paths and so compact that chickens and dogs could hear one another from one household to the next. Bustling to and fro, going about their work amid all this, were men and women dressed exactly like people outside; from pale-haired oldsters to braided-hair youngsters, all were cheerful and happy.

When those nearby saw the fisherman, they became greatly agitated and asked where he had come from. He answered them fully. Then they invited him to their home, served him wine, killed a chicken, and made dinner for him. As the news of his presence spread through the village, everyone else came to interrogate him. Of themselves they said that their forebears had fled from the disorders of the Ch'in era with their wives, children, and fellow villagers and after reaching this isolated area had never gone out again. The subsequent residents had been separated from the outside world, and they inquired what era it was now. They were unaware there had been Han, not to mention Wei and Chin!

Bit by bit the visitor brought them up to date, and at everything they heard they sighed and murmured. All in turn invited him to their homes, and set out food and drink. Only after lingering thus for several days did he excuse himself and leave. The insiders reminded him, "We aren't worth telling outsiders about!"

On departing the fisherman found his boat, retraced his route, and left guidemarkers all along the way. When he reached the commandery capital, he went straightaway to see the governor and reported all this. The governor promptly dispatched men to accompany him back. Looking for his guidemarkers, they finally got lost and could never find the right route.

When Liu Tzu-chi of Nan-yang, a scholar of esteem, learned of this episode, he personally went off to investigate with great enthusiasm, but he had no luck. He took ill and died, and since then there have been no more seekers after the pass.

From such simple beginnings evolved formal short stories, or novellas, called *ch'uan-ch'i* (tales of the marvelous), which flourished especially in the last T'ang centuries and were collected in many anthologies. Though still retaining some elements of magic and the supernatural, they were predominantly tales involving realistic, well-delineated characters of both sexes and all social classes in realistic, well-plotted encounters with problems of everyday life, especially in the capital city. Love stories were particularly common. T'ang ch'uan-ch'i are much too long to be reproduced here, but their flavor and variety can perhaps be captured in summaries of a few of the most famous ones.

"Miss Jen," by Shen Chi-chi (fl. 750-800). A handsome but poor

young man of Ch'ang-an named Cheng fell deliriously in love with a
beautiful maiden he encountered on the street, and she enticed him to
her palatial residence, where he was banqueted and seduced. Later,
trying vainly to locate her house, he learned she was a fox fairy who
practiced magic and toyed with many young men. Encountering her
again unexpectedly in a shop, he persuaded her to become his mistress
in normal human fashion. They lived together happily for more than
a year, supported in part by Cheng's brother-in-law, who was also
enamored of her, and in part by sorcery, by which she enabled Cheng
to turn some good business profits. Then Cheng was summoned to
military duty outside the city. Reluctantly, she yielded to his pleas that
she accompany him. En route to his post they met a group of imperial
huntsmen, whereupon Miss Jen fled wildly in her true vixen form and
was pursued, caught, and torn to pieces by the hunters' dogs. Cheng
bought the mangled remains and gave them decent burial; and he and
his brother-in-law mourned Miss Jen, marveling at how human she had
seemed.

"Curly Beard," by Tu Kuang-t'ing (850-933). In the troubled late
years of the Sui dynasty a frustrated young patriot, fleeing toward his
home in Shansi with the beautiful slave girl of an incompetent minister,
fell in with Curly Beard, a gigantic, fierce, red-bearded rogue. Curly
Beard persuaded the young man to introduce him and a decrepit Taoist
hermit friend to the boy Li Shih-min, the future T'ang emperor T'ai-
tsung. The magnetic young Li so dazzled Curly Beard and his friend
that they there and then pronounced him China's man of destiny. Curly
Beard then told the young lovers he had fought for fame and glory all
his life but now realized his future lay in some far corner of the world.
He abandoned to them his property, which turned out to be a magnificent mansion staffed with dozens of servants and entertainers and
stocked with hoards of treasures. The newly enriched young man provided the funds that soon enabled Li Shih-min to win the empire, and
the couple lived happily on as a T'ang duke and duchess. Years later,
on hearing that a red-bearded giant had captured an island in the south
seas, they realized that Curly Beard had found his future.

"Miss Li," by Po Hsing-chien (750-826). A young provincial aristocrat, having distinguished himself in preliminary examinations, set out
for Ch'ang-an to prepare for the doctoral examination and an official
career, with a lavish two-year allowance provided by his proud father.
In Ch'ang-an he became besotted with a harlot, Miss Li, who lived with

him until he had used up all his funds, and then disappeared. Grieving and starving, the young man was finally pitied and nursed back to health by a funeral director, who trained him to join his troupe of professional mourners. The young man soon became renowned as Ch'ang-an's champion mourner, whose agonized wailing and dirges could set the whole town to weeping. A former servant recognized him and took him to his father, who had long before concluded that his son had been killed by robbers en route to Ch'ang-an. The father now felt dishonored by his son and had the young man dragged out into the countryside, flogged hundreds of times, and left for dead. Friends from the funeral home, coming to bury him, found a dim spark of life and tried to help him again. But he was so disconsolate and his wounds were so festering and ugly that even they soon abandoned him, and he became a wandering beggar, nearer dead than alive. In this state he was discovered by Miss Li. Taking full responsibility for his deterioration, she sheltered, nursed, and supported him for three years, encouraging him to renew his studies. Thanks to her, he won highest honors in the examinations and was reconciled with his father; they were married and thenceforth had successful, happy lives.

All of the anecdotes and tales so far discussed were written by scholars for scholars, in the formal prose style called *wen-yen*. Though in many cases rooted in folklore, these works only rarely lapse into the colloquial forms of Chinese that were actually used in speech, and so cannot be classed as "popular literature." But a popular literature in colloquial language existed, at least in oral tradition, from early times; storytellers are known to have been favorite entertainers, both at court and in the marketplaces. Their medium was exploited imaginatively by Buddhist missionaries and native monks, who found that Chinese audiences would listen to sermons and canonical recitations most appreciatively if they were interspersed with more entertaining fare, such as Jataka tales about the adventures of the Buddha in his many incarnations. By the seventh century both Buddhist and secular storytellers had developed a special genre of colloquial literature called *pien-wen* (popularizations). These were dramatic tales on religious and other themes, mixing songs in doggerel verse with prose, no doubt recited with great animation and illustrated with appropriate paintings held up before the audience at intervals by the preacher or storyteller. The educated elite naturally took no notice of pien-wen, but some of the pien-wen texts got written down, and a few manuscript fragments have been discovered in the twentieth century in a cave outside Tun-huang, on traditional China's northwestern frontier. They reveal that the T'ang pien-wen, though no literary masterpieces, abound in wit, imagination, suspense, and general narrative excitement. They were clearly ancestral to the great colloquial novels that are among the notable literary products of the later imperial age.

One particularly impressive pien-wen tale, known in several fragmentary versions, is "Mu-lien Rescues His Mother." It tells, in alternating prose and verse, of a young Buddhist monk's search for the soul of his mother, whose greediness in life had condemned her to an eternity of torment in one of the lowest, most dismal chambers of Hell, pinioned to a sheet of hot iron by 49 long nails. As Mu-lien makes his way through layer after layer of subterranean purgatories tended by bestial demons, he encounters lost souls at every turn who plead with him to tell their descendants that lavish funerals, elaborate mourning, and sacrificial rituals serve only to please the living—that the living can help the dead only by leading pious lives and doing good deeds. Mu-lien also encounters frustrating bureaucratic incompetence and arrogance, in both Heaven and Hell. His mother is rescued from her torments only by the personal intercession of the Buddha; but even the Buddha can do no better for her than transform her into a dog, from which state she is eventually released because of her sincere repentance and Mu-lien's extraordinary piety.

"Parallel prose" and the reform movement. The Chinese prose of antiquity and of such Han stylists as Ssu-ma Ch'ien and Pan Ku is spare and lean, with a vigorous conciseness and no unnecessary words. Relations between phrases and transitions from clause to clause normally are implicit in the rhetorical structure and are not clarified with expressions equivalent to our "but," "moreover," "so that," "thereupon," and the like. In the late Han and immediate post-Han years, prose writing tended to become more relaxed and sprawling—easier to make sense of, on the whole, but with less force and impact. Writers of prose began also to exploit the rhythmic cadences that monosyllabic Chinese easily and naturally lends itself to, and that all prose writers have used on occasion for special emphasis.

The enchantment with such flourishes grew, and in the era of division all prose writing that was intended to be accepted as literature became elegantly, artificially rhythmic and adorned with all kinds of refinements, including rhymes. The litterateurs of the Southern Dynasties courts particularly cultivated this ornate and weak style, which was called parallel prose (*p'ien-t'i wen*, or sometimes *p'ien-wen*, matching style). Even when it includes rhymes, parallel prose is distinguishable from poetry because its rhythms constantly vary; its best-known unit is the "four-six line," in which four-word and six-word phrases alternate. Beyond simple metrical parallelism, the style required the use of parallel phrases, in which adjectives, nouns, verbs, and other parts of speech were carefully matched in the lines of a couplet. A representative passage appears in Hsü Ling's (507-83) preface to a poetry anthology, *Yü-t'ai hsin-yung* (New Songs from the Tower of Jade), as rendered into English by J. R. Hightower:

> Atop the jade pavilion of the Chou king
> Inside the golden chamber of the Han emperor
> Jade trees with branches of coral
> Pearl curtains with hangers of shell—

The style was effective and beautiful in the hands of a few gifted writers, but for the most part its effete artificiality made it suitable only for displays of erudition and virtuosity, a poor medium for serious exposition or effective narration. Nevertheless, because litterateurs persuaded themselves that no other style had any literary merit, the parallel prose style was dominant in all writings even through the T'ang period, and it persisted in certain kinds of formal documents thereafter.

A reaction against the artificiality of parallel prose came in the late T'ang years, led by the litterateur-official Han Yü, who was discussed in Chapter 8 as an early spokesman of anti-Buddhist thought. Han Yü urged a revival of the simple, uncluttered, forceful prose of the ancient *Tso-chuan*, and he himself wrote in an "old-style prose" (*ku-wen*) with such grace and effectiveness that his peers could not long hold it in contempt. A strong ku-wen movement got under way; and though it did not wholly displace parallel prose, it is credited with making possible the flourishing of ch'uan-ch'i fiction (for which parallel prose was hopelessly ill-suited) in the late T'ang and with preparing the way for the revival of serious philosophical writing in the later imperial age. In general, the ku-wen movement restored to all Chinese prose some of the terseness, flexibility, and forcefulness that characterized its early masterpieces. It is noteworthy that this was not a movement toward writing in the vernacular; it was just the reverse. Whether in parallel prose or in ku-wen, Chinese as written by the educated elite remained far different from Chinese as it was spoken.

The poetic arts. From antiquity, as was noted in Chapter 4, the Chinese inherited two principal poetic forms. One was the shih, a song form in four-line stanzas, each line normally consisting of four mono-syllabic, equally stressed words (DA-DA-DA-DA). The other was a longer, looser, less rigid form found in the *Ch'u-tz'u*; its lines commonly include six or seven words, some of which are unstressed and often mean-ingless (DA-DA-DA-da-DA-DA-DA). The style used in the *Ch'u-tz'u* came to be categorized as the *sao* form, after the title of the most famous elegy in the collection, "Li-sao" (Encountering Sorrow). In the early imperial age, as education spread and the dominant social classes be-came ever more dedicated to literary pursuits, writing poetry became a skill required of every gentleman, and poetic forms proliferated, stim-ulated in part by a flow of new musical instruments and melodies from Central Asia and beyond. Especially in the post-Han Southern Dynas-ties, court gentlemen and ladies amused themselves with complicated poetry games and contests. By T'ang times gentlemen composed poems in prodigious quantities as a matter of daily routine—to record their fleeting moods, to commemorate commonplace events such as seeing off a traveling friend, or to send greetings and messages to their ac-quaintances. An eighteenth-century anthology of poetry from the T'ang, *Ch'uan T'ang shih* (Complete T'ang Poetry), reproduced 48,900 poems by almost 2,300 poets. All educated men, who almost by definition were officials or candidates for officialdom, were working poets as well as essayists, classical commentators, and historians. Literature was the way of life of the intelligentsia, and great poets were the most glorious stars in the literary firmament.

Chinese poets wrote on every conceivable theme. They described landscapes, animals, birds, beautiful women, handsome boys, spirits, demons, strange foreigners, and other interesting people and things of every sort. They wrote narrative poems long and short about love affairs, military campaigns, humorous and poignant happenings. They also expressed a wide range of emotions—love, anger, homesickness, frustration, loneliness, compassion, contentment, patriotism, joy, and sorrow. Although the Chinese tradition does not lack long poems, poets mostly preferred brevity; there are no Chinese poems of epic length and grandeur in the style of Homer or Milton. Also, although some poets indulged in florid and ornate effusions, the most durable poetry is simple to the point of understatement. Even the most lyrical Chinese poet seldom expressed his emotions directly, wailing and beating his breast in a wild poetic frenzy; rather, he used indirection and suggestive imagery. "The autumn wind chills the yellowing leaves" was preferable to "Darling, I am growing old." Browsing comparatively in anthologies of English and Chinese poetry is likely to give readers some other striking impressions: the disproportionate emphasis on romantic love in English poetry and on nature appreciation in Chinese poetry, the relative absence of Chinese poems expressing religious emotions or glorifying war, and the abundance of Chinese poems that treat of simple events and ordinary everyday life.

The great exception to most such generalizations about Chinese poetry is a form called the *fu*, an outgrowth of the *Ch'u-tz'u* tradition. The fu is an almost indefinable mixture of verse and prose, very flexible in such considerations as length and meter. It is normally rather long, normally descriptive of places or scenes, and normally ornately verbose. The lines of any one fu may vary from four to nine or more words, and they abound in parallelisms of the sort that characterize parallel prose. The writers of fu generally shared the parallel prose artist's verbal virtuosity, and like parallel prose, the fu easily degenerated into lexicographical exercises. Fu were among the most admired poems in Han times, and the effete courtiers of the Southern Dynasties wrote fu gushing elaborate conceits. By T'ang times the fu had been harnessed in formalistic prescriptions, and candidates in civil service examinations were often called on to write fu on assigned topics and in assigned metrical and rhyme patterns, to demonstrate their command of language and of traditional literary clichés. Thereafter fu continued to be written as showpiece exercises, but the type had ceased to be living poetry long before T'ang.

Poems of more genuinely poetic spirit continued to be written in the shih form. But in Han and later times the shih attained greater flexibility and suppleness than its ancient counterparts. Its lines began to be extended more and more often to five words and even seven, until by T'ang times the four-word line had been replaced as the standard form. From the fu, the shih form borrowed the caesura, which helped to break the metronomic monotony of the ancient four-word cadence. In normal usage, the caesura comes after the second word of a five-word shih line (DA-DA, DA-DA-DA) and after the fourth word of a seven-word line (DA-DA-DA-DA, DA-DA-DA). From another Han verse form, called *yüeh-fu*, the shih adopted run-on lines, which also helped to loosen up the ancient form, in which each line was a complete statement. Through the whole early imperial age the shih was the most popular and adaptable verse form.

The yüeh-fu form is considered a free-form shih. It is named for a music bureau that was established about 120 B.C. by Han Wu-ti to provide music for court entertainments. In the tradition ascribed to the early Chou kings, the bureau was also expected to collect folksongs from all corners of the empire in order that the court might gauge the mood of the common people. About 100 such yüeh-fu folksongs have been preserved from the Han dynasty. All have a very distinct folk spirit and irregular metrical patterns that make for more melodious versification than is usually possible even in the five-word and seven-word shih. Later poets often wrote in yüeh-fu rhythms when shih patterns did not serve their purposes.

Nothing illustrates the extreme preciosity of the Southern Dynasties litterateurs more clearly than their development of another variation on the shih form—the "regulated" shih (lü-shih). Not that the standard shih was unregulated. It was in fact structurally rigid, prescribing stanzas of four lines of consistent five-word or seven-word length and end-rhyme in the second and fourth lines of every stanza. Each couplet tended also to fall into marked verbal parallelisms—noun corresponding to noun, verb to verb, and so on. What was new about the regulated shih was the careful attention to the tonal variations in the Chinese language, the sing-song tonal inflections that differentiate homophones, as was described in the Introduction. Although earlier poets had not been wholly unaware of tones—they had unconsciously or semiconsciously avoided awkward-sounding sequences of many words pronounced in the same tone, for example—the post-Han poets became self-consciously concerned with tonality.

This heightened awareness of tonal quality may have been a consequence of China's learning about India from Buddhist missionaries, for the Indians early developed very sophisticated grammatical and linguistic analyses. At all events, Southern Dynasties poets began imposing many kinds of tonal restrictions on shih. One of the early formulators of tonal rules was Shen Yüeh (441-513; also called Shen Yo), who wrote a short tract on poetic defects that should be avoided, four relating to rhymes and four to tones. He seems to have merely laid down a set of rules already widely practiced. Later, in the early T'ang period, the rules became more elaborate and put poets into a straightjacket of technicalities. Not only did poets now have to observe all the accepted conventions about meter, rhyme, and verbal parallelism; they also had to choose words belonging to arbitrarily defined tonal categories and fit them into lines with arbitrarily prescribed tonal sequences.

Tones were divided into two categories: level (*p'ing*: generally, the first and second tones of modern Mandarin) and deflected (*tse*: the third and fourth tones of modern Mandarin). Seeming rhyme-words that fall in different tone categories (for example, *chang*[1] and *tang*[3]; on the conventional system of marking the tones of Mandarin words, see Appendix B) were no longed considered rhymes at all; a word's rhyme-word had to be in the same tone category. In addition, all words in deflected tones were ruled inappropriate for rhyming (so that, for example, *li*[3] and *ti*[3] could not properly be used as rhymes). It was further ruled that no more than three words in the same tone category could occur in sequence in a line, and that three could occur only when broken by a caesura. Moreover, the second line of each couplet was ideally to be a tonal mirror-image of the first line. Sets of stanzaic tone patterns were established as approved, with only the most minor of variations being permitted, and poems were limited to a maximum of two four-line stanzas. One common tone pattern is perfectly illustrated in the poem on the next page, a famous regulated shih on Ch'ang-an's desolation after the An Lu-shan rebellion, by the T'ang master Tu Fu.

These strict rules of prosody obtained throughout the T'ang dynasty, subjecting poets to far more technical complexities than occur in the most complex verse forms in English, such as sonnets or triolets. It must be added, however, that many great poets did not slavishly adhere to the rules; and the freer "old-style" shih (*ku-shih*) and yüeh-fu forms also remained in common use.

T'ang poets are especially noted for their mastery of a truncated, single-stanza form of regulated shih called the *chüeh-chü* (stop-short), which is illustrated a few pages below. Its finest representatives are highly impressionistic, subtly understated, suggestive vignettes, which in 20 or at most 28 words masterfully set a scene, establish a mood, or start a train of thought that the reader is expected to follow through on in his own imagination.

In the eighth century another major verse form developed to fit the popular new melodies that were being introduced from Central Asia. This is the *tz'u* (song). It varies in length, has uneven lines running from a single word to ten or more words, and follows prescribed tone and rhyme sequences in more than 600 patterns, each named after the tune for which the verse was written. Through T'ang times tz'u seem to have actually been sung to the tunes whose names they bore; and many dif-

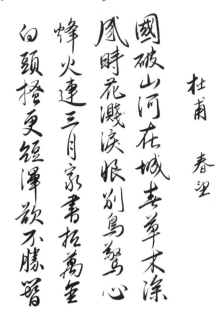

Tu Fu: *Ch'un-wang**

Kuo⁺ p'o⁺ shan⁻ ho⁻ tsai⁺
   ch'eng⁻ ch'un⁻ ts'ao⁺ mu⁺ shen⁻
Kan⁻ shih⁻ hua⁻ chien⁺ lei⁺
   hen⁺ pieh⁺ niao⁺ ching⁻ hsin⁻
Feng⁺ huo⁺ lien⁻ san⁻ yüeh⁺
   chia⁻ shu⁻ ti⁺ wan⁺ chin⁻
Po⁻ t'ou⁻ sao⁻ keng⁺ tuan⁺
   hun⁺ yü⁺ pu⁺ sheng⁻ tsan⁻

Tu Fu: *Spring Prospect*

The capital is taken. The hills and streams are left,
And with spring in the city the grass and trees grow dense.
Mourning the times, the flowers trickle their tears;
Saddened with parting, the birds make my heart flutter.
The army beacons have flamed for three months;
A letter from home would be worth ten thousand in gold.
My white hairs I have anxiously scratched ever shorter;
But such disarray! Even hairpins will do no good!

ferent tz'u share the same title, since they shared the same tune, though they might differ greatly in subject matter and in mood. It was as if modern songwriters were endlessly to churn out lyrics for love songs, martial songs, and religious songs to be sung to the music of "Auld Lang Syne," and all bearing that title. Chinese poets of the later imperial era still wrote tz'u in the prescribed patterns long after the tunes themselves were forgotten.

Didacticism was not the constraint in the writing of poetry that it was

* The superscript ⁻ represents *p'ing* or level tone, the superscript ⁺ *tse* or deflected tone. The pronunciations in the romanizations are modern Mandarin and differ somewhat from T'ang pronunciations. Characters are read from top to bottom and from the right column to the left. (It will be noticed that each two lines of romanization correspond to one line of characters.) The characters here are written in "cursive script" (see p. 263).

in the writing of Chinese prose, but poetry was not wholly exempted from the traditional expectation that all literature would reinforce the established value system. In the first century A.D. Wei Hung, a commentator on the *Shih-ching*, formulated the enduring doctrine that poetry is an expression of sentiments and thus a reflection of the transforming influence of government: good government evokes joyous poetry, and unhappy poetry is symptomatic of bad government. Even in late T'ang times it was not unknown for a poet to express the hope that his poems might help people to live proper moral lives.

Several monumental works of the era of division brought literary criticism and theory to a new level of sophistication. Among them are *Wen-fu* (Fu on Literature) by Lu Chi (261-303), which categorized and set standards for ten literary genres in a brilliant tour de force; *Wen-hsin tiao-lung* (The Literary Mind and the Carving of Dragons) by Liu Hsieh (465-531?), a comprehensive analysis in parallel prose of literary theories and critiques up to the author's time; *Wen-hsüan* (Anthology of Literature), a selective and critical compendium by Hsiao T'ung (501-31), a prince and eventual emperor of the Liang dynasty; and *Shih-p'in* (Classes of Poets) by Chung Hung (late fifth-early sixth centuries), which graded and evaluated hundreds of poets. In most cases, there was a tendency to pay lip service to the principle of didacticism and then move quickly on to accept as literature anything that gives elegant expression to genuine emotions, and to dissect and analyze literary works in a search for qualities of form, content, and intention that aspiring writers should strive either to cultivate or to avoid.

The great age of literary theory and criticism faded with the expiration of the Southern Dynasties. In T'ang times, though anthologies of many sorts were compiled, critics did not develop any significantly new principles about the practice and value of poetry.

Some master poets. The greatest Han writer of the ornate prose-poetry form called fu was Ssu-ma Hsiang-ju (179-117 B.C.). A native of Szechwan, Ssu-ma was a roguish drifter who is best remembered for a scandalous escapade with the widowed daughter of a rich family of Chengtu. By opening a tavern where he cooked and washed dishes while his bride waited on the customers, Ssu-ma forced his humiliated father-in-law to give him a princely dowry. Ssu-ma's fame as a poet prompted Han Wu-ti to summon him to the capital, where he produced a series of flattering court poems. His most famous and influential work is the "Shang-lin fu," an extravagant description of the Shang-lin Park outside

Ch'ang-an, where the emperor hunted. Its qualities—and the characteristics of fu generally—are evidenced in this brief extract from the English rendering of Burton Watson:

> The waters are loud with fish and turtles,
> A multitude of living things.
> Here moon-bright pearls
> Gleam on the river slopes,
> While quartz, chrysoberyl
> And clear crystal in jumbled heaps
> Glitter and sparkle,
> Catching and throwing back a hundred colors
> Where they lie tumbled on the river bottom.
> Wild geese and swans, graylags, bustards,
> Cranes and mallards,
> Loons and spoonbills,
> Teals and gadwalls,
> Grebes, night herons, and cormorants
> Flock and settle upon the waters,
> Drifting lightly over the surface,
> Buffeted by the wind,
> Bobbing and dipping with the waves,
> Sporting among the weedy banks,
> Gobbling the reeds and duckweed,
> Pecking at water chestnuts and lotuses.

The following anonymous work is representative of the folksongs that remain from Han times. Many of its kind express abhorrence of war. This one pursues another common theme that poets of the early imperial age delighted in—sympathy for the neglected wife.

Old Song

> Green, green, is the grass on the riverbank;
> Sad, sad, the willow in the courtyard.
> Lovely, lovely, is the girl in the tower,
> Radiant, radiant, as she stands at the window.
> Comely, comely, is her pink-powder makeup;
> Delicate, delicate, is the white hand extended.
> Once she belonged in a singing-girl troupe;
> Now she's the bride of a roistering rake.
> The roisterer does not come home from his revels.
> An empty bed is hard to face alone.

The pessimism and melancholy of the last Han years were reflected in the writings, mainly in yüeh-fu forms, of a group of poets known as the Seven Masters of the Chien-an Era (196-219). Literary historians commonly add to the group the military dictator Ts'ao Ts'ao, who was not a bad poet, and his third son, Ts'ao Chih (192-232), who was the most talented poet of his time. In the following shih, Ts'ao Chih described the destruction wrought by civil wars in the last Han years:

Poem for Master Ying

I climb to the top of Pei-mang slope
And gaze across the hills of Loyang.
Loyang—how desolate!
The palace has completely burned down.

The fences and walls are all smashed,
And thorny weeds stretch up toward the sky.
I see no familiar old-timers
And only encounter youths I don't know.

Wherever I step there are no paths;
Deserted fields are no longer tilled.
For a long time the traveler hasn't been home,
And he doesn't recognize any streets or lanes.

The central plain—how barren!
For a thousand leagues, no one's fires!
Thinking of my former home,
I choke and cannot speak.

T'ao Ch'ien (or T'ao Yüan-ming, 365-427) has already been mentioned as the outstanding litterateur of the long interval between the Han and T'ang dynasties. The scion of a family that had produced many officials, T'ao dutifully accepted a magistracy but after only 83 days of service decided he would not "bow and scrape for five pecks of rice a day" and went home. For the rest of his life he lived as a recluse in the countryside, cultivating chrysanthemums, playing the zither, gamboling with children, and writing simple poems about rustic pleasures. He was one of China's first great "landscape poets."

T'ao Ch'ien's disinclination to be entangled in public affairs is emphasized in this celebration of his return home after serving in office:

Returning to Live on the Farm

When young I had no taste for worldly pleasure;
By nature, I was fond of hills and peaks.
Then by error I fell into the trap of worldliness
And all at once I am thirty!

Birds on leashes yearn for their forest haunts;
Fishes in tanks remember their old deeps.

Opening the wilds on the southernmost border,
And cherishing simple ways, I settle on the farm.

My fields amount to some ten acres;
My thatched house, some eight or nine rooms.
Elms and willows shade the rear eaves,
And peach and plum trees are scattered before the porch.

Dim and far are other people's hamlets;
Thick is the mist over intervening wastes.
A dog barks distantly down the lane,
And a cock crows atop a mulberry tree.

In my household—no worldly infringements;
In my solitude—an abundance of leisure.
For too long cooped up in a cage,
I've now found my way back to nature.

In another famous poem, given here in William Acker's English rendering, T'ao blamed his fondness for wine on his sons:

Blaming One's Sons

White hair covers my temples—
My flesh is no longer firm,
And though I have five sons
Not one cares for brush and paper.
Ah-shu is sixteen years of age;
For laziness he surely has no equal.
Ah-hsüan tries his best to learn
But does not really love the arts.
Yung and Tuan at thirteen years
Can hardly distinguish six from seven;
T'ung-tzu with nine years behind him
Does nothing but hunt for pears and chestnuts.
If such was Heaven's decree
In spite of all that I could do,
Bring on, bring on
"the thing within the cup."

During the post-Han era of division, love poetry of an erotic nature that was not characteristic of any other period was regularly written by court aesthetes. One member of this circle was Shen Yüeh (or Shen Yo, 441-513), the prolific historian mentioned previously as an early formulator of rules for regulated shih. The following four poems seem to be all that remain of a six-poem set by Shen called "Six Rememberings":

I

I remember the times she came—
Glowing, glowing, up into the courtyard.
Earnestly, earnestly, we spoke of our partings;
Happily, happily, we expressed our longings.
We never got enough of looking at one another,
And, lost in each other's eyes, we forgot to get hungry.

II

I remember the times she sat—
Dainty, dainty, before the gauze curtain.
Now singing four or five songs,
Now plucking two or three tunes.
When she laughed she was beyond compare;
When she sulked she was still more appealing.

III

I remember the times she ate—
Such an easy manner handling the tableware!
Wanting to sit, but too shy to sit;
Wanting to eat, but too shy to eat.
Nibbling her food as if she weren't hungry,
Lifting her cup as if she hadn't the strength.

IV

I remember the times she slept—
When others slept, trying not to doze.
Loosening her gown, she needed no encouragement;
On the pillows, she embraced ever more insistently.
But afraid that her partner might be watching,
She delicately blushed in the candlelight.

In the traditional Chinese view, the great age of poetry was the eighth century, when the glory of T'ang reached its pinnacle in the reign of Hsüan-tsung (r. 712-56) only to be shattered by the devastating An Lu-shan rebellion. Of the many great poets of the century three are outstanding: Wang Wei (699-759) and especially Li Po (701-62) and Tu Fu (712-70), who are universally recognized as the two greatest poetic geniuses of all Chinese history. All served as officials at Hsüan-tsung's court, knew and respected one another, and experienced hardships during the great rebellion; but each was a distinctly different personality and poet.

Wang Wei, a devout Buddhist and a sometime physician, won equal fame as a painter and a poet. Indeed, it quickly became commonplace to say that his paintings were like poems and his poems like paintings. In both art forms he focused his attention on the natural landscape. He was certainly China's greatest "landscape poet" since T'ao Ch'ien. He is renowned also as a master of the demanding single-stanza poetic form called the chüeh-chü. Captured by An Lu-shan's rebels in 755 and imprisoned in the auxiliary capital Loyang, he was later considered a collaborator by T'ang loyalists, but he seems not to have suffered greatly in either case. Among his best-known poems are the following chüeh-chü:

Deer Fence

In the empty hills I see no one
And hear only echoes of talk,
But sunlight sifts into my thicket
And glints back and forth on the moss.

My Bamboo-Village Resort

I sit alone in a dense bamboo grove,
Plucking a zither and then crooning long.
Deep in the woods there is no one to notice,
But the bright moon comes out to take heed of my song.

One of Wang Wei's less descriptive, more expressive poems is the following, in Cyril Birch's English rendering:

To the Assistant Prefect Chang

In evening years given to quietude,
The world's worries no concern of mine,
For my own needs making no other plan
Than to unlearn, return to long-loved woods:
I loosen my robe before the breeze from pines,
My lute celebrates moonlight on mountain pass.
You ask what laws rule "failure" or "success"—
Songs of fishermen float to the still shore.

Li Po (also called Li T'ai-po) was a much gayer spirit, unquestionably the most romantically roguish Chinese poet since Ssu-ma Hsiang-ju. Tall and powerful, a man of restless activity, he impressed his contemporaries with his boundless vitality, his sensitivity to beauty in any form, and his serene indifference to the personal disasters and humiliations he regularly experienced. A swordsman and alchemist, a carousing brawler in brothels, a heroic drinker, perennial wanderer, and

Fig. 22. Idealized portrait of Li Po
by the Sung painter Liang K'ai

roisterous poet with an arrogant disregard for anyone's rules, he considered himself "an immortal banished from heaven" and treasured the friendship of sing-song girls and Taoist hermits fully as much as Hsüan-tsung's admiring patronage. He versified with astonishing facility, sober or drunk; he is believed to have produced 20,000 poems, of which some 1,800 survive. Though the story of his death is no doubt historically untrue, there is an aesthetic appropriateness to the legend that he died when, during a party with friends, he drunkenly leaned out of a boat to clasp to his bosom the reflection of the moon on the water, toppled in the river, and drowned.

There is almost no theme or topic on which Li Po did not write, and he produced regulated shih as prolifically as the freer old-style shih and yüeh-fu. His poems sometimes evoke a wistful melancholy, but most characteristically he sang joyously of the fairyland-like wondrousness of nature and life in poems that have universal appeal, even in the poorest translations. His single most famous poem, traditionally memorized by every Chinese schoolchild and early encountered by every foreign student of Chinese, is this 20-word chüeh-chü in perfect tonal and grammatical symmetry that very simply suggests a traveler's nostalgic musings about home, under moonlight on a chill autumn night:

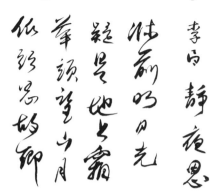

Li Po: *Ching yeh ssu**
Ch'uang⁻ ch'ien⁻ ming⁻ yüeh⁺ kuang⁺
I⁻ shih⁺ ti⁺ shang⁺ shuang⁻
Chü⁺ t'ou⁻ wang⁺ shan⁻ yüeh⁺
Ti⁻ t'ou⁻ ssu⁻ ku⁺ hsiang⁻

Li Po: *Quiet Night Thoughts*
Beside my bed the bright moonbeams bound
Almost as if there were frost on the ground.
Raising up, I gaze at the mountain moon;
Lying back, I think of my old home town.

Another famous chüeh-chü vignette reveals Li Po in a more characteristic happy mood.

The Girl of Yüeh
A girl picking lotuses beside the stream—
At the sound of my oars she turns about.
Giggling, she vanishes among the flowers,
And, all pretenses, declines to come out.

A few other samplings of Li Po's moods follow:

In the Mountains on a Summer Day
Lazily I wave a white feather fan
Over my nakedness among the green trees.
My doffed hat dangles atop a stone wall,
And on my bared head plays the piney breeze.

* Again, the ⁻ represents a *p'ing* or level tone, the ⁺ a *tse* or deflected tone. Here the characters are written in "grass script" (see p. 263). The most familiar form of this poem repeats the *ming yüeh,* "bright moon," of the first line in the third line. The form given here, with *shan yüeh,* "mountain moon" or "moon on the mountains," in the third line, is commonly found in older texts.

*Resolutions on Waking with a Hangover
on a Spring Morning*

The world is like a great empty dream.
Why should one toil away all one's life?
That is why I spend my days drinking,
Sprawled in a doze beside the front door.

Awaking, I blink at the courtyard before me.
A bird is singing among the flowers.
"May I inquire, what season is this?"
It's an oriole warbling in the springtime breeze!

I am almost moved to sighs and sobs,
But I pour for myself another drink.
Lustily singing, I await the bright moon,
And by the end of the song I've forgotten my cares.

Drinking Alone in Moonlight

Among the flowers, with a jug of wine,
I drink all alone—no one to share.
Raising my cup, I welcome the moon,
And my shadow joins us, making a threesome.

Alas! the moon won't take part in the drinking,
And my shadow just does whatever I do.
But I'm friends for a while with the moon and my shadow,
And we caper in revels well suited to spring.

As I sing the moon seems to sway back and forth;
As I dance my shadow goes flopping about.
As long as I'm sober we'll enjoy one another,
And when I get drunk, we'll go our own ways:
        Forever committed to carefree play,
        We'll all meet again in the Milky Way!

Tu Fu was a more serious poetic craftsman than Li Po. Li, in a playful
jibe, once commented in verse on Tu's sober approach to his work:

Presented in Fun to Tu Fu

On top of Mount Fan-k'o I meet with Tu Fu,
Beneath a huge coolie hat in the noon sun.
"Since last time you've grown so alarmingly thin!
Do you feel such remorse for the poetry you've done?"

Of the two, Chinese have traditionally esteemed Tu Fu the more, partly
because of the awesome erudition he displays in his work (his historical
and literary allusions make much of it untranslatable), but primarily

because of his concern about the troubles of his time and his compassion for those in distress. His poetry is less passionately lyrical than Li Po's. It often has a detached reportorial quality that evokes powerful emotions without any direct expression of them, as in the following favorite:

The Recruiting Officer at Shih-hao

At dusk I found lodging in Shih-hao village.
An officer came conscripting the men by night.
My aged host climbed over the wall and fled,
While his wife went out to see what was happening.
How angrily the officer shouted at her!
How sadly the old woman wailed and moaned!
I heard the old woman go forward and speak:
    "My three sons have served in the garrison at Yeh,
    And one of the boys has just sent me a letter—
    The other two have both died in the fighting,
    And the survivor is living on borrowed time.
    The killing has gone on so long already!
    There are no men left in this house any more—
    Only a grandson, and he is still suckling,
    And his poor mother—she hasn't yet gone
    Because she has no clothes to appear in.
    Myself, though not as strong as I once was,
    Let me follow you back tonight
    In response to the urgent summons from Ho-yang.
    I might yet get there to fix early breakfasts!"
Late in the night the sounds of talk ended.
I seemed to hear some sobbing and whimpers.
When dawn came I went again on my travels,
Bidding farewell to the old man alone.

Even in his reportorial style Tu Fu could be poignantly personal. The following poem, written on his reunion with his wife and children after a year-long separation caused by the An Lu-shan rebellion, shows a depth of feeling that the Chinese consider essentially Confucian, in contrast to the Taoist lightheartedness so often characteristic of Li Po:

Ch'iang Village

Westward beyond the high purple clouds
The sun strides down to the level earth.
My rickety gate is loud with sparrows;
The stranger comes home from a thousand leagues.

My wife and children can't believe I've survived;
Recovered from shock, they still wipe at tears.

In times of great troubles I've been buffeted about,
And returning alive is nothing but luck.

Neighbors crowd along the top of the wall,
Groaning out sighs, or sniffling and sobbing.
Late in the night we light a new candle
And confront one another as if in a dream.

In another famous poem, full of lugubrious images, Tu evokes the pangs of separation in wartime:

Thinking of My Brothers on a Moonlit Night

Frontier war drums disrupt all men's travels.
The border in autumn—a solitary goose is honking.
Beginning tonight the dew will be white with frost,
But the moon is as bright as in my old home town.

I am fortunate enough to have brothers, but all are scattered;
There's no longer a home where I might ask if they're dead or alive.
The letters I write don't ever get to where they're sent.
How terrible it is that the fighting cannot stop!

Tu Fu was forty years old before he gained recognition as a poet, and the undistinguished official career he then attained was interrupted repeatedly by the great rebellion. Both in youth and in middle age he was a wanderer across China, encountering sadness and trouble, frustration and humiliation. He no doubt became the crotchety, bitter old man he describes in some late poems, but his sympathy for all who suffered and his earnest hope that the world could again become worth living in did not diminish. The qualities that have endeared him to the Chinese—his humanness and his compassion—are reflected in the following:

Lamenting the Ruin of My Thatched Roof
by Autumn Winds

Autumn, eighth month: the wind howls loud and angry.
It strips three layers of roof thatch from my house.
The thatch flies across the river and scatters on the bank—
The highest left dangling in the trees of a long-strung copse,
The lowest tumbled to sink into riverside lagoons.
South Village boys, taking advantage of my old age and weakness,
Flaunt their ability to rob me to my face—
They openly carry my thatch into bamboo thickets!
With dry lips and throat I scream at them in vain.
Returning home, I lean on my staff sobbing.

All of a sudden the wind dies and clouds darken;
The autumn sky turns into a vast blackness.
My wadded quilt is old and cold as iron.
My beloved son restlessly kicks through the covers.
With the roof leaking, the beds have no dry spots;
The raindrops trickle in strings, without a break.
Bemoaning my troubles, I find it impossible to sleep.
How will I ever get rid of the long night's dampness?

Where might I find a great mansion with thousands of rooms
Large enough to shelter the suffering scholars of the world, every-
        one happy,
Unmoved by wind and rain, secure as a mountain?
Alas! when might I see such a mansion, rising loftily before me!
Though I alone have a ruined hovel and freeze to death, yet I'd be
        satisfied!

The best-loved poet of the later T'ang years was Po Chü-i (772-846),
a prodigy who passed the government's doctoral examination at the
age of eighteen and had a distinguished career as an official at court
and in the provinces. His literary fame rests in part on a long, fanciful,
and lugubrious ballad, "The Everlasting Sorrow," which tells of the
love affair of Hsüan-tsung and his consort Yang Kuei-fei, their flight
from Ch'ang-an during the An Lu-shan rebellion, and Lady Yang's
execution. But Po was at his best in writing short, reflective occasional
poems, characterized by reportorial restraint much like Tu Fu's and
by an appealing simplicity of language. He was reportedly never satisfied
with a poem until it could be understood by an illiterate old peasant
woman. Although often wryly humorous and even bitingly satirical,
Po shared Tu Fu's earnest Confucian concerns and commented tellingly
in his poetry on the sadness and misfortune he observed about him.
The following representative samples reflect his range of topics and
moods:

The Frivolous Rich

With their arrogant manner, they fill up the road;
The horses they ride glisten in the dust.
"May I inquire, who might that be?"
People say that's a palace eunuch.
Those with red sashes are all high ministers;
The purple tassles might signify generals.
Haughtily they go to dine with the troops,
Their prancing horses passing like clouds.
Goblets and tankards will overflow with every wine;

Water and land have yielded every delicacy.
Fresh-picked fruits, and Tung-t'ing oranges;
T'ien-ch'ih fish, all scaled and sliced.
After gorging themselves, their minds will be at ease;
Drunk on wine, their spirits will soar.
   This year drought devastated the South,
    And in Ch'ü-chou people cannibalized each other.

Comfortable Sleep

Though my family daily grows poorer,
We've not yet gone hungry or chill.
Though my body daily grows older,
It's my luck to have no painful ill.
I've seen both troubles and peace
And indulged, now and then, what I will.
I now get comfortable sleep
With no dreaming to fret me or thrill.

My New Quilted Gown

The Kueilin linen is white as snow;
The Soochow wadding is soft as a cloud.
The linen is heavy, the wadding thick,
Making a gown of surpassing warmth.
I bundle myself in it morning till eve,
And under its cover I sleep through the night.
Who would think it's the worst of the winter months?
My body's as cozy as if it were spring.
Then deep in the night—a startling thought!
Clutching my gown, I rise and stalk about.
The tailor has given me comfort for life,
But should I alone be treated so well?
How could one get such a gown so immense
As to wholly enclose every corner of earth,
That all might be as warm as me
And through the whole universe none would be cold?

Lamenting My Falling Hairs

Each morning I lamented the hairs that had fallen;
Each evening I lamented the hairs that had fallen.
When all had fallen—that was truly lamentable!
But now that they're gone, it isn't so bad.

Now I'm no longer troubled with washes and rinses,
Or even bothered with combing and grooming.
Best of all, on hot muggy days
My head feels so light without its old plaits!

Gone are the dirty wraps and caps!
I'm freed from dusty fringes and tassels!
I fill up a silver jar from a cool spring
And trickle it over my pate all night long.

It's like being doused with some buttery ointment;
I just sit and enjoy the pure cool pleasure.
Now I know why attaining monkhood
Depends so much on shaving one's head!

Golden Bells' First Birthday

When my fortieth birthday was almost upon me
Along came a daughter, Golden Bells.
Now she's survived her first full year
And is learning to sit but can't yet talk.

I'm somewhat shamed of my unsaintly sentiments,
But I can't help having normal feelings.
From now on I'm trapped by outside attachments,
And must simply find solace in my daily delights.

If only she is spared from premature death,
Soon I'm entangled in marriage arrangements!
This means that my plans to retire to the hills
Will just have to wait for some fifteen years more!

The Old Charcoal Seller

An old charcoal seller—
He cuts his wood and fires his charcoal in the southern hills.
The ashes that cover his face have given him a dark and smoky
　　look.
Both his temples have turned to white, while all his fingers are
　　black.
With the money he gets from selling his charcoal, what does he
　　plan to do?
He needs shirts and gowns to cover his body and food to fill his
　　mouth!
Alas! the clothes he is wearing now are single-thickness thin;
Yet, grieved by the falling price of charcoal, he has yearned for
　　colder weather.
And during the night, outside the city—suddenly a foot of snow!
At break of day he drives a cartload of charcoal through icy ruts.
The ox is weary, the old man is famished, the sun is already high,
When outside the southern gate of the city they come to a halt in
　　the mud.
And now two horsemen, elegantly clean, approach him—who are
　　they?

One is a yellow-uniformed officer, the other a white-shirted boy.
They hold in their hands a written edict, from their mouths tumble
	orders;
Turning the cart aside, shooing away the ox, they drag the cart to
	the north—
A whole cartload of charcoal that now is worth thousands of copper
	coins!
And what palace officers commandeer no one can dare begrudge.
Half a bolt of red silk and one short yard of damask
Have been left entwined round the ox's head as a token price for
	the fuel.

The Red Parrot

Distant Annam sends to court a red parrot,
As gaudy as peach blooms, as loquacious as we.
But learning and eloquence all meet the same treatment—
The imprisoning cage! Does one ever get free?

Although Po Chü-i has always been a favorite of Chinese and foreigners alike, his simple style was not characteristic of his time. Beginning with the latest poems of Tu Fu, T'ang poets displayed an almost sensuous fascination with ambiguous phrases and elusive images. Much ninth-century poetry has an overripe complexity of language and often an eerie, hallucinatory multiplicity of meanings that make it next to impossible to understand, much less translate. Shadowy eroticism and obscure metaphors give poems a lush tone and texture of richer quality than the explicit ornateness of traditional fu; but it is as if the poets had begun to concentrate solely on expression of quintessentially private visions and moods and had no wish to communicate. The most admired word-painter in this style was Li Shang-yin (813-58), a career official, whose style is suggested in the following poem:

[Untitled]

Hard to be together; also hard to be apart.
The east wind has no force; the blossoms are all withered.
Spring silkworms have died; the silk threads are spun out.
The candles have guttered in smoke; their waxen teardrops now
	harden.
The sunrise mirrors only sadness; tousled hair has greyed.
Nighttime mumblings—we ought to have slept; the moonlight was
	cold.
From here there aren't many routes to the isles of the magic hills,
But I'll keep alert on watch for their messenger-bird.

THE ARTS

Whereas in pre-Han antiquity the predominant art form was cast bronze vessels, in the early imperial age the work of potters, sculptors, and painters became the primary focuses of artistic interest; and whereas in antiquity art styles were predominantly decorative and nonrepresentational, the style of the early empire was mainly representational and on the whole naturalistic. It is also worth noting that, in consonance with the Buddhist impact on all aspects of Chinese life, Buddhist themes were a paramount concern of post-Han craftsmen, especially in sculpture and to a lesser extent painting. By the end of Han, too, the arts were being divided into two clearly differentiated spheres: painting became increasingly associated with the learned classes and was finally elevated to the status of true art, while pottery, sculpture, metalwork, and other crafts came to be considered unworthy pursuits for intellectuals to engage in and were forever after relegated to the domain of anonymous, professional, and often hereditary artisans. Painting did not become exclusively an occupation of the intelligentsia, but it came to have close affiliations with literature, especially poetry; and the styles of painting done and admired by the literati were the only ones considered serious art.

All arts of the early imperial age are poorly represented in present-day remains. The ravages of time alone have been sufficient to ruin most of the ceramics, the wood sculptures, and the paintings on silk and paper that were produced even as late as the T'ang dynasty; and time was abetted by the invasions and civil wars that ravaged all the imperial capitals and palaces of the early age, and by successive proscriptions of Buddhism that caused much metalwork to be melted down and stone carvings and murals to be destroyed. In A.D. 190, when the general Tung Cho sacked the Later Han capital, Loyang, his troops thoroughly looted the imperial palaces of their treasure. What was rescued—70 cartloads—was evacuated to Ch'ang-an, but half was lost en route because of bad roads and weather, and no doubt pilferage. For these reasons, what is known about early imperial art is based on limited and largely unrepresentative materials: written descriptions by contemporaries, copies of decaying early paintings made in the later imperial age, pottery and engraved or painted tiles unearthed in some early tombs, and statuary and murals remaining in some famous cliff grottoes. The art historian gets some help from early works that were preserved or imitated outside China, especially in the early Japanese capitals, Nara and Kyoto. From the glimpses into the early imperial world of art that are thus obtainable, at least some of that world's artistic glories are imaginable.

Ceramics. Samples of the potter's art that have survived from the early imperial age are for the most part funerary objects unearthed from tombs. They reveal a steady development of technology toward the fine porcelain wares that were to rank among the artistic triumphs of the later dynasties. As early as Han times there was a common stoneware that was high-fired and glazed, approaching the fineness and hardness of true porcelain; and genuine translucent porcelain appeared in T'ang times. There was also a steady development in styles, so that by T'ang times the potter had finally mastered his medium and ceased to be bound by the stylistic canons of the ancient bronzesmiths, whose masterpieces earlier potters had tried to recreate in clay. The most elegant T'ang pieces are fine white earthenware bowls and vases in polychrome glazes and beautifully dignified forms.

The best known and most popular ceramic pieces of the early age are clay miniatures of people, animals, and objects, which were buried in tombs as symbolic attendants, entertainers, and conveniences for the spirits of the dead. Han tombs regularly included replicas of houses, farm animals and implements, musicians, and women attendants— usually in rough clay that may have been painted and sometimes even crudely glazed (see Fig. 18, p. 182). Many such miniatures seem to have been mass-produced from molds. They are consistently naturalistic, though the human figurines in particular often have a sweeping stylized grace that gives them a remarkably modern flavor and great charm. To the continuing Han tradition T'ang added magnificently lifelike replicas of prancing chargers and figurines of the exotic foreigners who so fascinated the T'ang cosmopolites, usually with exaggerated representations of their un-Chinese characteristics, such as large noses and thick beards. The spirited T'ang horses, in particular, have become prized collectors' items throughout the world.

Sculpture. Sculpture was not an important element in the Chinese art of antiquity. The native tradition was carried over into the early empire primarily in the form of carved lions and other animals, real or imaginary, which were commonly stationed along the "spirit roads" leading to great tombs and at the entrances to tombs and palaces. What remains of them suggests that the Han style was bulkily monolithic—

Fig. 23. T'ang horse figurine in pottery with polychrome glaze

animal figures that conformed to the shapes of whatever boulders were at hand, not attaining full free-standing independence from the original stone and often not fully rounded. Around Nanking are some remains of Southern Dynasties sculptures that are much freer and more imaginative, with a stylized elegance of form and a softer textural quality. Winged lions and horned tigers were popular. The T'ang period was characterized by a revived naturalism, in which realism and design are finely balanced.

    Another traditional form of carving was the engraved tile, which was used to line the walls of tombs. The pictorial elements are on a flat surface from which the background has been cut away so as to leave a low-relief engraving; thus in many respects these tiles were much like the wood blocks later used in printing. The portrayals are markedly naturalistic and are predominantly of everyday human and animal figures. Horsemen and chariots were especially popular in the Han dynasty. Some later engraved tomb tiles are in sets that present elaborate, crowded scenes of historic or legendary events, of processions and celebrations, and of multiscenic constructs linking earthly activities with the heavenly doings of Taoist divinities. In their technical aspects, the tomb tiles seem to be two-dimensional copies of equally two-dimensional drawings—silhouettes, in short, that have little perspective but often a feeling of great animation (see Fig. 13, p. 166).

Chinese sculpture in the early imperial age was most of all a Buddhist art; and Buddhist statuary of the era of division and the Sui-T'ang epoch is the greatest sculpture of all Chinese history. It is preserved and best represented in great cliff grottoes that were inaugurated by the T'o-pa Northern Wei dynasty, first in 460 at Yün-kang, near the dynasty's original capital in northern Shansi, then at Lung-men near Loyang, which was made the dynastic capital in 495. Later dynasties continued to subsidize work on both these great Buddhist monuments. The Yün-kang statuary is most famous for its monumental scale; one great Buddha image there is 45 feet high (see Fig. 20, p. 209), and another is 26 feet. Roughhewn in the coarse sandstone of the site, some images are in high relief in niches on the face of the cliffs; others are nearly freestanding in the round in caves dug into the cliffs. The earliest images reflect the mixture of Hellenistic naturalism and Indian sensuousness characteristic of the early Buddhist art that came to China across Central Asia, but the native tradition of more linear, formal stylization gradually predominated as Chinese artisans became more assured and less imitative. The overall effect of the Yün-kang monuments is one of a colossal symbolic awesomeness. At Lung-men, where fine dense limestone permitted a less monolithic style, the statuary is on a smaller scale, more detailed, and more intimately spiritual in feeling. Figures of the Buddha and associated deities retain some of the formal blandness of the Yün-kang statues, but the many representations of devout emperors, empresses, and court attendants, prostrated in adoration, are dynamically, naturalistically human and individualized.

Sixth-century remains from these cave sites and elsewhere show a new sensuousness in the Buddhist statuary, no doubt reflecting more direct contact with Indian art styles; but even so naturalism is overshadowed by the traditional Chinese formalism of design and pattern. Gradually, with the rise to dominance of Mahayana doctrines, figures of the Buddha himself were less emphasized, and carvers produced more tenderly humanlike representations of the Buddhist bodhisattvas and realistic scenes of gatherings in their paradises; and more and more freestanding figures in the round appeared. Finally in T'ang times, as in the case of secular sculpture, Buddhist statuary achieved its mature Chinese balance between realism and design, and true statuary in the round reached its finest Chinese expression.

Painting. Literary references indicate that from Han through T'ang times large buildings such as palaces and monasteries were commonly decorated with frescoes. In traditional Chinese architecture, wood or stone columns support the roof beams, and walls are non-bearing surfaces. From Han times on, painters were kept busy covering these plaster-coated walls with their work. Palaces were ordinarily decorated with portraits of emperors, empresses, and famous officials and generals; religious buildings, naturally, were filled with portraits of the Buddha, bodhisattvas, and eminent lay donors, with scenes of Buddhist paradises and purgatories, and with illustrations of episodes from popular canonical and hagiographic writings—or Taoist counterparts.

All such murals were lost with the destruction or deterioration of the buildings they decorated, but their appearance is suggested by what must have been less skilled imitations—the secular murals found on the plastered walls of some early tombs, and the Buddhist murals found on the walls and ceilings of the Tun-huang grottoes. These grottoes, 486 caves and niches carved out of the cliffs at the convergence of Central Asian caravan routes, were favorite resting places for inbound missionaries and outbound pilgrims from the fourth century through the T'ang era. They contain some statuary, but the conglomerate of the cliffs is not suitable for sculpture of the type found at Yün-kang and Lung-men; the Tun-huang statues are clay modeled over a core of wood or straw, a form found in complexes of grottoes built in the same period at P'ing-ling-ssu and Mai-chi-shan in Kansu, which were rediscovered only in the 1950's. The great fame of Tun-huang rests on its numerous and elaborate murals, which must reflect at least faintly the quality of murals done in the metropolitan centers.

The Han painting style was greatly stimulated by the fanciful illustrations found on pre-Han lacquerwares associated with the Yangtze valley region, the ancient state of Ch'u. But the Han painters adapted the liveliness of the Ch'u style to their favorite subject matter, the people and activities of the real world. Literary references, the decor of Han lacquerware, and painted tomb walls (see Fig. 12, p. 158) clearly suggest that Han painters concentrated on realistic portraiture and the type of naturalistic scene that also appears on the engraved tomb tiles of the period. The art was linear, with emphasis on form rather than inner detail, and it had grace, animation, and a strong sense of movement. Little background was provided; already Chinese painters were showing a strong preference for leaving blank space and emphasizing only the essentials of their subjects.

During the era of division painting flourished far more in the southern courts than in the northern ones. (It seems probable that the finest sculpture of the period was also produced in the south, but it has not survived in any quantity.) The names of many southern painters are known, and their work is described and evaluated in contemporary writings comparable to the classics of literary theory and criticism discussed above. Unfortunately, however, their works do not remain. The man all early critics considered to be China's first great genius in painting was a Taoist eccentric who adorned the Eastern Chin court at Nanking, Ku K'ai-chih (344-406?). He was particularly praised as a portraitist and as a master of the brushstroke line, which had already become the quintessential technical element in Chinese painting.

The counterpart in art of the great literary critics of the era of division was Hsieh Ho (fl. in the early sixth century), who compiled an evaluation of 43 painters in six categories, *Ku-hua p'in-lu* (Classified Record of Ancient Painters). In the preface to this work, Hsieh laid down six principles for painting that were the foundation stones for all later art criticism, which the Chinese traditionally produced far more prolifically than literary criticism. His principles are stated very cryptically and have been variously interpreted, but he seems to have intended the artist to observe these rules:

1. The painter must strive to bring alive the spiritual essence (*ch'i*) of his subject.

2. He should emphasize structural elements with his brushwork.

3. In representing forms he should be faithful to reality.

4. He should apply colors corresponding properly to the categories of things.

5. His compositions should be carefully planned.

6. He should develop his skills by imitating prior masters.

Painting, like poetry, had a climactic development in the T'ang dynasty. Many of the Tun-huang murals date from T'ang times, and T'ang scroll paintings on both silk and paper have been found stored at Tunhuang. The subject matter is Mahayanist—for example, great unified panoramas of dignitaries residing in the Western Paradise presided over by the bodhisattva Amitabha. A few original works or early copies of some of the great T'ang court painters also survive. Among these is a scroll called "Portraits of the Emperors" by the most celebrated seventh-century painter, Yen Li-pen, who attained high office in the central government. His portraits are in the presumed Han style, which became the standard style of official court portraiture. They present rather bulky and formidable figures, unlike Ku K'ai-chih's lightly outlined figures, and there is still virtually no background. Yen Li-pen reportedly painted great scholars, strange-looking foreigners, animals and birds, and popular Buddhist subjects in the same style. Of the eighth-century genius Wu Tao-yüan (c. 700-760; better known as Wu Tao-tzu), who was subsequently rated the greatest T'ang master and perhaps the greatest painter of all Chinese history, nothing has survived into modern times. His career was largely devoted to painting murals for the great temples and monasteries of Ch'ang-an and Loyang, and his fame was so great that thousands of admirers reportedly gathered to watch him work. His painting was renowned for its dynamism, and for a spirit of free personal expression akin to that of Li Po in poetry. China's most famous painter of horses (horses seem almost symbolic of the strong and energetic T'ang spirit as a whole) also lived in Hsüan-tsung's reign. This was Han Kan, whom later critics acclaimed for capturing the essential horseness of horses—the ch'i of horses—to a degree unapproached by anyone else (see Fig. 24).

Alongside the predominant portraiture of the tradition (even the vast Buddhist panoramas were assemblages of portraits with minimal scenic contexts), there developed in T'ang times the genre that was subsequently to be considered China's greatest contribution to the world's painting heritage—landscape. Two fashions emerged. One, exemplified notably in the works of Li Ssu-hsün (651-716) and his son Li Chao-tao (d. about 735), adapted the traditional polychrome style of portraiture to landscape painting and strove for the nice balance of realism with design that had been achieved in sculpture. This colorful and somewhat elegant style, which ultimately became the specialty of official court painters and professionals, was well suited to Buddhist and Taoist fantasies and decorative scenes of imperial parks and palaces. It came to be called the northern school style. A contrasting southern school of "amateur" painters of the scholar-official class was most notably rep-

Fig. 24. Two horses with groom: painting by Han Kan (T'ang), probably as copied in Sung times

resented by the famed nature poet Wang Wei. Their landscapes were monochrome ink sketches, more impressionistic than representational and full of open space—almost abstractionist strivings to catch the ch'i of nature rather than any of its detailed particulars. The southern school style became the most famous painting style of the later imperial age.

Fine calligraphy, which the Chinese traditionally esteemed as a branch of painting, also reached full maturity in the early imperial age. The style of "clerical script" (*li-shu*) that had been established by the Ch'in dynasty remained the standard throughout all the successive dynasties into our own time. But it was early supplemented by a looser, freer style of "cursive script" (*hsing-shu*; see p. 240 for a sample), which relates to clerical script in somewhat the way our longhand forms of writing relate to print. Then at the end of Han there developed a still freer, more highly personalized, sweeping and swirling form called "grass script" (*ts'ao-shu*; see p. 248), which at its best is a strikingly lively and abstractionist art form. The greatest early master of grass script, recognized by the Chinese as one of the geniuses of their art history, was Wang Hsi-chih (321-79), a contemporary of the great painter Ku K'ai-chih at the Eastern Chin court at Nanking; and his son, Wang Hsien-chih, is reputed to have been a master second only to his father.

PART THREE

The Later Empire

960-1850

10. General History

THE FRAGMENTATION of China in the tenth century, after the long decline and final collapse of T'ang, was resolved after half a century by a new North China state called Sung, inaugurated in 960 by an army mutiny. Under the Sung dynasty, which lasted until 1279, scholar-officials finally replaced the old semifeudal aristocracy as the dominant class in Chinese society, and Chinese culture flourished as in the best of Han and T'ang times. But Sung China was hemmed in on the north and west by hostile nomadic empires and had to struggle constantly for survival. In 1126-27 the whole of North China was lost to the alien state of Chin, ruled by proto-Manchu Jurchen peoples.

The Southern Sung domain, limited to the Yangtze valley and the far south, enjoyed economic prosperity and cultural elegance for another century and a half, only to be overrun in the 1270's by the Mongols proper, who had already conquered all of inner Eurasia and probed into central Europe. Kubilai Khan, setting up a Chinese-style hereditary dynasty called Yüan with its capital at Peking, became the first alien ruler of all the Chinese. After a century of Mongol rule, which Chinese have considered the bleakest era of their history, popular uprisings terminated the Yüan dynasty in 1368 and established a new, expansive native dynasty, Ming. Under its stable rule, the Chinese again dominated East Asia as in Han and T'ang times, and conservative, autocratic institutions developed that were to characterize Chinese life into modern times.

In 1644, in one of the least disruptive major dynastic transitions of history, the Ming dynasty gave way to invading Manchus from the northeast, whose Ch'ing dynasty was the last of the imperial age. In the seventeenth and eighteenth centuries strong Manchu emperors expanded China to its greatest territorial extent; the Chinese enjoyed a high level of prosperity and culture and experienced an explosive population growth. But unresolved domestic inequities accumulated, along with new kinds of external pressures from the imperialistic powers of Europe, and in the middle of the nineteenth century China was shaken by the most destructive civil war of world history, the Taiping Rebellion. Although the Ch'ing dynasty survived until 1912, the Taiping uprising in 1850 effectively marks the point at which China's traditional history ended and its modern history began.

Establishment of the Sung dynasty in 960 was not merely an event by which the two thousand years of China's imperial history may be conveniently divided at mid-point. It set the stage for the fulfillment of changes in the patterns of Chinese life that had been germinating since the An Lu-shan rebellion in the eighth century, and others as well—changes that gave life in the later imperial age a notably different quality from that of either the Han or the T'ang dynasty. One major change has been suggested above: that as individual merit became the criterion for office, the old hereditary aristocracy disappeared, to leave civil servants the unchallenged elite in Chinese society and government. The style of governance became more autocratic, society more mobile and urbanized, the economy more commercialized. In thought, a revitalized Confucianism swept Buddhism and Taoism into the status of popular religions, only to turn increasingly introspective itself and lose much of its original emphasis on social reform. In literature and art changes of equal significance came about, creating great new traditions in drama, fiction, and impressionistic painting. The rapid spread of printing and a consequent increase in literacy, along with various other technological developments, were essential elements in many of these changes.

On a bolder level of generalization it can even be suggested that the Chinese spirit, having passed through a heroic, brash adolescence in the early imperial age, now experienced a chastened, sober, often grim and drab maturity. So, at least, it seemed to many thoughtful Chinese in the later empire, for whom the China of Han and T'ang times had powerful nostalgic appeal.

SUNG (960-1279)

The founder of the Sung dynasty was Chao K'uang-yin, known posthumously as Sung T'ai-tsu (r. 960-76). A capable young general in the service of the Later Chou dynasty, Chao was catapulted into prominence in 959 by his appointment as commander-in-chief of the palace army, the core of Later Chou military strength. Almost immediately a boy emperor succeeded to the throne, but at the beginning of 960 the army acclaimed Chao emperor instead; he took the throne at the age of thirty-two. It was not the first time in the Five Dynasties era that an army had engineered such a coup, and it seems likely that Chao was the instigator as well as the beneficiary of the mutiny. The times called for vigorous leadership.

The Sung dynasty inherited from its predecessors the dream of a restored T'ang empire, but it confronted serious external and internal problems. The increasingly powerful Ch'i-tan (Khitan) state of Liao loomed threateningly in the north and northeast. It had repeatedly interfered in North China politics since the end of T'ang, had taken control of 16 prefectures in traditional Chinese territory south of the Great Wall, and in 951 had helped establish a Chinese puppet regime, the Northern Han state, in Shansi province. In the northwest a federation of Tibetan tribes called Tanguts, who had gained certain privileges in return for helping the T'ang court put down the Huang Ch'ao rebellion late in the ninth century, had steadily expanded their territories during the tenth century and were soon to formalize their hostile independence by establishing an imperial state known as Hsi Hsia. South China remained fragmented among independent regional kingdoms. Though they did not threaten the north, they were obstacles to any northern ruler who hoped to consolidate manpower and other resources for a national effort to prevail over the nomadic raiders of the north and northwest. Moreover, in North China itself no government had yet consolidated power sufficiently to eliminate all separatist-minded warlords. The creation of Northern Han in 951 and the army mutiny that brought Sung T'ai-tsu to the throne in 960 were proof enough of North China's continuing instability.

Sung T'ai-tsu was a prudent and clever statesman who saw the folly of trying prematurely to regain territories lost to the Ch'i-tan and the Tanguts. His first priority was to centralize and stabilize North China. To this end, he persuaded his own chief military supporters to yield their commands in return for generous retirement pensions, thus forestalling the possibility of a successful mutiny against him. Gradually and tactfully, he also replaced militaristic regional governors with civil officials delegated from his court. Further, he transferred to the palace army, of which he retained personal command, the best units of the regional armies. In this way he created a military establishment in which

Fig. 25. Sung emperor T'ai-tsu: portrait by unidentified Sung dynasty court painter

the main fighting force was a large, mobile professional army garrisoned around the capital, while local forces consisted largely of substandard recruits.

T'ai-tsu also helped ensure his supremacy by expanding the examination-recruited civil service and entrusting the administration of government at all levels to its scholar-officials, who characteristically had no substantial power bases of their own but owed their status entirely to imperial favor, and by giving his central government the power to control the collection of all revenues and the appointment of all officials down to the county level. In these ways he created an institutional framework for an autocratic concentration of power in the throne beyond anything attained by earlier dynasties in a regular, institutionalized form; but T'ai-tsu did not abuse his powers. He honored civil servants, encouraged them to be imaginative and bold, and in general set an admirable precedent by seeking and heeding their advice. He built a modest palace at Kaifeng, which was located in the center of the productive North China plain and had been the capital of most of the Five Dynasties, and instituted practices that kept the whole Sung era freer of abuses by palace women and eunuchs than any other major era of Chinese history.

While establishing these fundamental dynastic policies, T'ai-tsu moved carefully and systematically to incorporate the South China kingdoms. In campaigns in 963, 964-65, 971, and 975 he subjugated one southern regime after another except the aboriginal state of Nan Chao in the far southwest, which retained its independence throughout the Sung dynasty, and the kingdom of Wu-Yüeh in Chekiang. T'ai-tsu died at the comparatively young age of forty-eight, his imperial ambitions only partially realized, but his younger brother, T'ai-tsung (r. 976-97), carried his plans forward; he accepted the peaceable surrender of Wu-Yüeh in 978 and then destroyed Northern Han, the Ch'i-tan protectorate in Shansi, in 979. Thus the traditional Chinese homeland was reunited except for the far northwest and the tier of 16 northern prefectures that Liao had seized.

The Tanguts in the northwest were sufficiently impressed by the new Sung dynasty to offer tribute and become nominal vassals. T'ai-tsung was satisfied with that because there was much greater popular resentment about the Ch'i-tan encroachment south of the Great Wall. In 979, immediately after subjugating Northern Han, T'ai-tsung personally led a campaign to recover the Peking area. Beaten off by the Ch'i-tan, he organized a second campaign only to be beaten off again, with heavy losses. T'ai-tsung then concentrated on building defenses, and defense was to be the Sung military posture through the remainder of the dynasty. The frontier situation stabilized in 1004, when a Liao probe in the direction of Kaifeng was checked. The opposing rulers then made a peace agreement that left the northern prefectures under Liao control and guaranteed "brotherly gifts" to Liao from the Sung court amounting to 100,000 taels (ounces) of silver and 200,000 bolts of silk each year. After several decades Liao demanded and got an increase of 100,000 units in each category; but the Ch'i-tan rulers kept the peace with China for more than a century. Meantime, the volatile Tangutan Hsi Hsia state provoked an inconclusive four-year war with Sung in the northwest in 1040-44. Hsi Hsia then promised to be peaceable in return for similar annual "gifts" of 200,000 taels of silver and 200,000 bolts of silk; but it continued to harass the Chinese, who launched ineffective punitive campaigns against the Tanguts in 1069 and again in 1081-82.

As always in times of prolonged domestic stability, China enjoyed great prosperity through the eleventh century. By mid-century the population regained its T'ang peak of sixty million, and by 1100 it apparently approached one hundred million. The forces of change that were rooted in the breakdown of the old T'ang order in the ninth and tenth centuries now accelerated, and distinctively new patterns of Chinese life began to take shape. The socioeconomic realm was transformed partly by government initiatives and partly by private entrepreneurship of a more flamboyant type than China had seen since early Han times. New seeds and crops were introduced, there were successive advances in the organization and technology of both agriculture and industry, production boomed, and government revenues swelled in multiples of the T'ang totals. Kaifeng and other cities became large urban complexes, serving as the centers of regional and in some cases national marketing systems. Commerce flourished to an unprecedented degree, and for the first time in Chinese history a genuinely national urban class was emerging. New kinds of careers and life-styles developed in the commercial centers. Moreover, printing, which had developed rapidly in the Five Dynasties era, promoted literacy and education—to the point where, for the first time in Chinese history, common people had realistic hopes that their sons might achieve status in the elite official class.

The intellectual life of the eleventh century was probably more exciting than the Chinese had ever known. Scholarship, literature, and art all flourished in the hands of the greatly expanded, urban-oriented literate class. Most especially, foundations were laid for the Neo-Confucian philosophical system that would soon topple Buddhism from its long preeminence among Chinese intellectuals to become China's ideological orthodoxy into the twentieth century.

Eleventh-century China was the most populous, prosperous, and cultured nation on earth. It should also have been the most powerful, for the largest share of the increasing state income was spent on maintaining a huge standing army, well equipped with mass-produced iron and steel gear, and with various incendiary weapons supplementing the traditional bows and crossbows. Considering both the forces the dynasty had at its disposal, numbering some 1,250,000 at mid-century, and Chinese military successes against northerners in earlier periods of unity and prosperity, one might suppose Sung China should never have become the intimidated vassal of such neighbors as Liao and Hsi Hsia.

Among the many explanations that can be offered for Sung's failure to achieve military predominance over the northern nomads in the pattern of the Han and T'ang dynasties, the simplest is that the Chinese were losing the will to fight. Sinicization was steadily weakening the warlike spirit of both the Ch'i-tan and the Tanguts, and the Chinese gradually realized that neither was going to engage in serious new aggressions against China. Keeping them appeased with silver and silk (the value of which never exceeded 2 per cent of Sung's state revenues) seemed a reasonable enough price to pay for peace, and Chinese of the eleventh century had more appealing and challenging things to do than struggle for the recovery of marginal territories. Such attitudes resulted in large part from the decay of the old military-minded aristocracy, a process that was hastened by the personnel policies of T'ai-tsu and T'ai-tsung. The military was subordinated to civil service control, careers in military service were disesteemed, the interests of scholar-officials became paramount in government, and the civilian values of the intellectual elite began permeating the whole society. The eleventh century produced no eminent military leaders, but it produced a galaxy of Chinese history's most distinguished and dedicated scholar-officials; and at no time in history were there more earnest efforts to achieve a golden age of benevolent government and popular welfare.

Because the Confucian tradition was just then being reformulated, because the inherited state ideology tolerated a spectrum of policies ranging from laissez-faire conservatism to dynamic reformism, and because the great scholar-officials of the age were strong, independent-minded, and determined men, the newly dominant bureaucracy became embroiled in one factional controversy after another. No one group could long monopolize all influential posts, and factionalism intensified as reformists and anti-reformists successively came to power.

Real problems were at issue in these eleventh-century controversies, generated in part by the threats from Liao and Hsi Hsia and in part by the rapid domestic changes China was experiencing. The massive professional army was costly, difficult to control, and less effective than many wished. The innovative pioneers of Neo-Confucian thought were not always tolerant of, or tolerated by, devotees of the narrowly scholastic Confucianism inherited from the early empire, not to mention the adherents of Buddhism and Taoism. Traditional rural, agrarian attitudes, especially strong in the north, clashed with the urban, mercantile entrepreneurship that flourished increasingly, especially in the south. Despite the fading away of the old hereditary aristocracy, semifeudal socioeconomic inequities persisted in the countryside, where large numbers of peasants remained in depressed, dependent status as retainers on large estates. Independent farmers, always destined to a precarious existence, were threatened from all sides—by aggressively expansive large landlords, usurious moneylenders, and avaricious tax collectors. State revenues increased, but expenditures increased faster and deficit budgets became common. Reforms of many sorts were called for, and there was room for bitter disagreements about fundamentals among even the most dedicated, public-spirited statesmen.

One of the first great reformers was the moralist Fan Chung-yen (989-1052), whose pronouncement that "the true scholar should be the first to become anxious about the world's troubles and the last to enjoy its happiness" became the credo of all subsequent Confucian activists. His ten-point reform program of 1043-44, focusing mainly on personnel recruitment and local administration, was quickly voided by conservatives. A generation later came the most controversial reform effort of China's premodern history, a 15-point program of New Laws instigated by the chief councilor Wang An-shih (1021-86).

A one-time protégé of Fan Chung-yen, Wang An-shih was a famous poet, prose stylist, and commentator on the classics. He was also an earnest, stubborn activist whose insistence that the state should take the lead in reshaping society caused many contemporaries and later historians to label him a Legalist in Confucian guise. He gave to Sung government a continuing tradition of strong leadership of the bureaucracy by the chief councilor. His New Laws, promulgated between 1069 and 1073, dealt with economics, fiscal administration, the military, education, and personnel recruitment; they called for a sweeping state manipulation of society on a scale undreamed of since the ill-fated attempts of the notorious Han usurper, Wang Mang.

Antagonized by Wang An-shih's tactless methods as much as by his policies, conservatives at court ultimately prevailed against him. These included a multitalented intellectual giant named Ou-yang Hsiu (1007-

72), who had earlier supported Fan Chung-yen and recommended Wang; the most innovative historian since Han times, Ssu-ma Kuang (1019-86); and a gifted poet and painter who was probably the greatest all-around genius of the later imperial age, Su Shih (or Su Tung-p'o, 1037-1101). Supporters of the Wang program returned to power in 1102 under the emperor Hui-tsung (r. 1100-1125), ousted anti-Wang leaders, blacklisted 209 opponents as a treasonable clique (called the Yüan-yu Party after the name of the era, 1086-93, during which they came to power), and even ordered the destruction of some of their writings.

Although Wang An-shih's principal purpose had been to strengthen the state and its officialdom, the antagonisms he provoked had the opposite effect. His partisans inherited a bankrupt state and a thoroughly demoralized bureaucracy. Hui-tsung had his good points—he was a talented painter and a great patron of the arts—but effective political leadership was not among them. And his long-term chief councilor, Ts'ai Ching, was hardly better. Unfortunately for China, it was just at this time that a powerful new alien chieftain appeared in the far northeast beyond Liao. This was Wan-yen A-ku-ta (1068-1123), of the proto-Manchu Jurchen tribes long settled in eastern Manchuria. In 1114 he raided the Liao frontier and then defeated a Liao punitive expedition sent against him. Emboldened, he then proclaimed himself emperor of a new Chin empire in 1115.

Since the Jurchen had long sent tributary missions by sea routes to Kaifeng, the Sung court assumed that the Chinese could safely take advantage of the situation to get revenge on the Ch'i-tan, and in 1118 the Sung armies began attacking Liao's southern frontier. At the same time the Jurchen continued their advance from the northeast, and in 1122 Sung and Chin concluded a treaty providing for a concerted assault on Liao to its final destruction and a sharing of the spoils. But the Sung forces were not very successful in the fighting. Jurchen took Peking and after several more years of mopping-up operations captured the last Liao emperor in 1125. Meantime, honoring the terms of the treaty of 1122, Chin turned over to Sung the 16 northern prefectures so long coveted by the Chinese, with the understanding that the tax revenues collected there would be remitted to Chin.

In 1125 the Sung-Chin alliance collapsed, partly because Sung arrogantly disregarded its treaty obligations and partly because the Jurchen came to realize there was no real deterrent to a march southward. Chin armies quickly penetrated to the Yellow River and brought Kaifeng under siege. Hui-tsung abdicated in favor of his heir, and provincial authorities were called on to send relief forces. Though the capital was defended with surprising vigor, the Jurchen were unrelenting, and when the city ran out of supplies and its citizens were reduced to cannibalism, the Sung government capitulated. The Jurchen then withdrew, leaving a Chinese puppet administrator in charge with orders to raise an impossibly large indemnity in gold, silver, silk, horses, and cattle. When the Chinese gave up trying to make the required payments, the Jurchen returned and sacked the city in 1127. Hui-tsung, his heir, and some 3,000 members of the Sung court were carried off into captivity. Chin moved its imperial capital to Peking, while the Jurchen armies marched farther and farther south.

Chinese patriots now established a younger son of Hui-tsung as successor emperor at Nanking. Known by his posthumous title Kao-tsung (r. 1127-62), he rallied miscellaneous irregular resistance forces; and for more than a decade Jurchen and Chinese struggled for control of the Yangtze valley. Kao-tsung retreated to Hangchow and finally fled the mainland when Jurchen armies captured Hangchow and even the coastal port Ningpo. But in 1130 some Chinese generals began to defeat Jurchen in the field for the first time, and by 1138 Kao-tsung was securely established at Hangchow and negotiations were under way that led to a lasting peace treaty in 1142. Sung ceded everything north of the Tsinling mountains and the Huai River—that is, the whole Yellow River drainage area—accepted formal status as a vassal of Chin, and undertook to pay annual tribute totaling 200,000 taels of silver and 200,000 bolts of silk. Historians use the year 1127 to divide the Sung dynasty into two epochs, Northern Sung and Southern Sung.

Throughout the Southern Sung period, which was generally characterized by weak emperors and strong chief councilors, there were factional controversies between advocates of peace and agitators for the recovery of the north; demonstrations by National University students were frequent, as in Later Han times. The controversies stemmed from the transition period preceding the peace of 1142, when General Yüeh Fei (or Yo Fei, 1103-41) and Chief Councilor Ch'in Kuei (1090-1155) earned their places in history as China's most lamented patriot and most vilified appeaser, respectively. In 1140, while the Hangchow court was negotiating peace, Yüeh's semiautonomous irregulars fought their way northward to the Yellow River in the Loyang region. There was

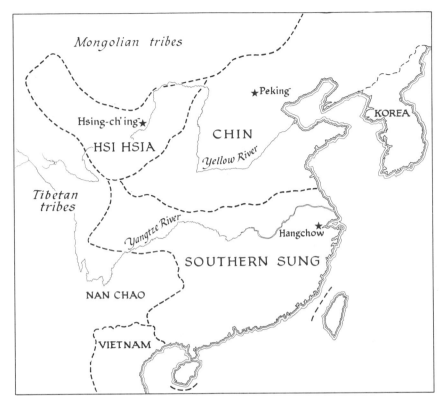

Map 6. The Chinese world, c. 1150

widespread sentiment in favor of continuing the war, but Ch'in Kuei
and other peace advocates prevailed, in some part because Kao-tsung
shared his predecessors' distrust of the military. Yüeh was soon murdered in prison—perhaps in compliance with a secret peace condition
imposed by Chin, as tradition has it.

Continuing bureaucratic factionalism at court did not impede the
flourishing of the Chinese economy and culture in the Southern Sung
era. Though the peasantry was increasingly reduced to serflike status
on the estates of large landlords, agricultural technology and productivity continued to advance; fertilizer in the form of human wastes carted
out of the populous cities contributed importantly. The bourgeoisie
became a substantial segment of the population as the pace of commercialization and urbanization quickened—perhaps a more substantial
segment than at any other time in Chinese history prior to the twentieth

century. The economy became very largely monetized, and heavy reliance on paper money bred inflation. Resurgent Confucianism was shaped into an orthodox, eclectic Neo-Confucianism by a famed synthesizer, Chu Hsi (1130-1200). Affluent scholar-officials devoted themselves ever more prodigiously to scholarship, elegant literature, and the arts, and colloquial literary forms were developed for the urban clientele. The south coastal regions were at last fully assimilated and populated by Chinese, and merchant ships from Southeast Asia and the Indian Ocean filled the coastal harbors. The Southern Sung capital at Hangchow became a metropolis not matched in the Western world until the nineteenth century, with residents numbering in the millions pursuing a kaleidoscopic variety of occupations, honorable and dishonorable, legal and illegal. The famed Venetian traveler Marco Polo, who visited Hangchow shortly after its prime, was overawed by the enormity of its population and its bustling commerce. As for Sung's principal coastal port, Ch'üan-chou in Fukien, he estimated that more ships lay at anchor in its harbor on any one day than docked at Venice or Genoa in a whole year.

Inconclusive border fighting between Chinese and Jurchen flared up anew in 1161, 1165, and 1206, and the peace treaty of 1142 was twice renegotiated, first reducing Sung's tributary payments to 150,000 taels of silver and 150,000 bolts of silk and later increasing the amounts of each to 250,000. The continuing heavy costs of war and defense, coupled with domestic extravagances, led to increasing inflation and increasing inequities between rich and poor in the Sung domain. In the 1260's the chief councilor Chia Ssu-tao (1213-75), a dilettantish careerist typical of the times, whose private passion was sponsoring cricket fights, vigorously enforced a series of agrarian and economic reforms that fanned partisan controversies anew and alienated large numbers of well-to-do families.

In Chia Ssu-tao's lifetime the situation in North China was transformed by the dramatic rise of the Mongols under Chingis (Genghis) Khan. The Mongols first attacked the far northern frontier of Chin in 1210, then captured Peking in 1215 and destroyed Tangutan Hsi Hsia in 1227. In 1232, following the same foreign policy that had been adopted against Liao more than a century earlier, Sung allied itself with the Mongols to crush Chin between them. By 1234 Chin had been destroyed and Sung was reoccupying Kaifeng and Loyang. However, instead of recovering North China as they had hoped, the Sung Chinese found themselves desperately defending themselves against Mongol onslaughts from 1235 on. The Mongols had already swept across Central Asia and subjugated Korea, and while warring on Sung they expanded their conquests in Europe and the Near East and launched the first of two famous naval expeditions against Japan. Even so, their attack on Sung was by no means desultory, and Sung resisted more strongly than is commonly recognized.

The Mongols found it especially hard to penetrate the densely populated areas north of the Yangtze River, where Sung had developed strong fortifications along the old frontier with Chin. In the west, however, the Mongols broke into the Szechwan basin from the north and then overran the old aboriginal kingdom of Nan Chao in Yunnan, so that by 1259 Sung was hard pressed from the west as well as from the north. Two walled cities in modern Hupei province north of the central Yangtze valley, Hsiang-yang and Fan-ch'eng, were the critical points in Sung's defenses, and the fighting around them was heroic and ingenious on both sides. True explosive weapons were used in the fighting, probably for the first time in world history, first by the defenders and then by the besiegers. The Mongols made good use of siege specialists imported from the Near East. When both cities finally fell in 1273 after more than four years of almost continuous siege, the Sung cause was doomed. The Mongols swarmed through the south, and Hangchow was surrendered without a fight in 1276. Sung loyalists kept resistance alive in the far south until 1279, when the last imperial heir drowned off Canton as all that remained of the Sung fleet was about to be overwhelmed. By then Chingis Khan's grandson Kubilai Khan was comfortably established at Peking as emperor of a new, Chinese-style dynasty called Yüan.

THE NORTHERN CONQUEST DYNASTIES

The successive alien invaders who, after the T'ang collapse, encroached on China's northernmost prefectures, then occupied North China, and finally conquered the whole of China were not essentially different from their predecessors in China's early imperial age. The organization and tactics of the Mongols do not seem to have evolved very notably beyond those of the Hsiung-nu who harassed the Chinese in Ch'in and Han times. The success of the new northerners can be attributed in considerable measure to a decline in China's military spirit in Sung times, as has been noted above. But the Ch'i-tan, Jurchen, and

Mongol invaders had strong leadership; indeed, the two greatest Mongol khans, Chingis and Kubilai, must be ranked among the most awesome personalities of all history. Moreover, the northern invaders zealously adopted and mastered every new Sung development in military technology. In the end, despite many creative innovations, they failed to build durable systems by which alien warriors could govern vast and populous China. On balance, they made few constructive contributions to the still-evolving Chinese civilization. Nevertheless, though the Chinese have remembered them all as savage oppressors, traditional Chinese political philosophy has required that Liao, Chin, and especially Yüan be accorded legitimate status in the long succession of China's imperial dynasties.

Liao (916-1125). More effectively than almost any other invaders of China, the Ch'i-tan resisted Sinicization and retained their original tribal, nomadic way of life. Although they patronized Buddhism and at times paid lip-service to Confucianism in government functions, the Ch'i-tan fundamentally remained shamanists. Their addiction to human sacrifice and to brutish punishments was particularly offensive to the Chinese. They showed minimal interest in the highly developed literary and scholarly traditions of the Chinese and produced no national literature of their own.

The Ch'i-tan welcomed and recruited renegade Chinese to serve in their administration and to develop an agricultural supplement to their pastoral economy. However, intermarriage was discouraged and often prohibited. The Chinese were treated as a separate, inferior caste. The Liao state was accordingly organized in a strange dualistic form, with a "north-facing" government to rule the Ch'i-tan by tribal customs and a "south-facing" government to rule subject Chinese in patterns adapted from the T'ang tradition. Educated Chinese were even brought into government service through T'ang-style examinations. Chinese peasants were drafted to provide infantry support for the Ch'i-tan cavalry.

After the dynastic founder, Yeh-lü A-pao-chi (872-926), there were no distinguished Liao rulers. The last Liao emperor, known as T'ien-tsu (r. 1101-25), cared for little but the hunt. When Liao was overthrown and T'ien-tsu captured by the Jurchen, a clansman named Yeh-lü Ta-shih (1087-1143) fled westward with some supporters, found sanctuary among the Uighurs, and then established a Western Liao state in far Inner Asia, which its Moslem Turkic subjects called Kara Khitai (Black Ch'i-tan). It endured, with some Chinese administrative and cultural characteristics, only until the Mongol conquests of the early 1200's.

Chin (1115-1234).* The Jurchen conquerors of Liao originated as forest hunters in the mountains of eastern Manchuria but became tough cavalrymen whom both the Ch'i-tan and the Koreans tried to contain by building frontier walls and palisades. From an early time they were great admirers of Chinese civilization, and after their overthrow of Liao and conquest of the Yellow River plain they rapidly lost much of their warlike character by processes of Sinicization. In 1134 their Chin dynastic government, after passing through a phase of rule by tribal councils and then one of dual administrations similar to Liao's, attained maturity as a fully Chinese-style administration dominated by a Department of State Affairs. Chinese officials were recruited in examinations, and many Jurchen nobles became serious students of Chinese classical literature. Jurchen tribesmen were settled as soldier-farmer colonists throughout North China. Although Chin emperors regularly fulminated against the neglect of the tribal heritage and sometimes issued terrible threats against any adoption of Chinese names, dress, and customs, Sinicization was not reversible in a state with a population of forty to sixty million subjects who were overwhelmingly Chinese. The North Chinese were discriminated against in many ways by their Jurchen overlords, but on the whole Jurchen-Chinese relations in the Chin state were not unpleasant. The majority of Jurchen who survived the ultimate Mongol conquest seem to have been easily assimilated into the general North China population.

The political history of Chin was dominated by early hostilities with Sung China to the south and later by defensive efforts against the rising Mongols to the north. The ablest successor to the Chin founder, Wanyen A-ku-ta, was Shih-tsung (r. 1161-89), whose reign was generally peaceful and prosperous. Shih-tsung tried to revive the militant Jurchen heritage, but in the end Chin's defenses in the north were heavily de-

---

* The names of traditional Chinese dynasties generally had geographic derivations, reviving honored names of Chou dynasty feudal fiefs. The Ch'i-tan Liao dynasty took its name from the Liao River in Manchuria, or a place associated with it. But when the Jurchen established their Chin dynasty they introduced a new pattern of dynastic names having symbolic significance. The Chinese word *liao* has iron as one of its meanings. The word *chin* chosen by the Jurchen means gold. It was chosen deliberately because gold is more precious and enduring than iron. Such symbolism was continued by later dynasties: Yüan (a beginning; a creation; primacy), Ming (bright), and Ch'ing (pure). It might be noted that the Jurchen dynastic name is not the same as the name of the post-Han Chin dynasty, which derived from the Chin state of Chou times, in Shansi province. Some historians try to avoid confusion between the Chin dynasties with the arbitrarily differentiated spellings Tsin and Kin.

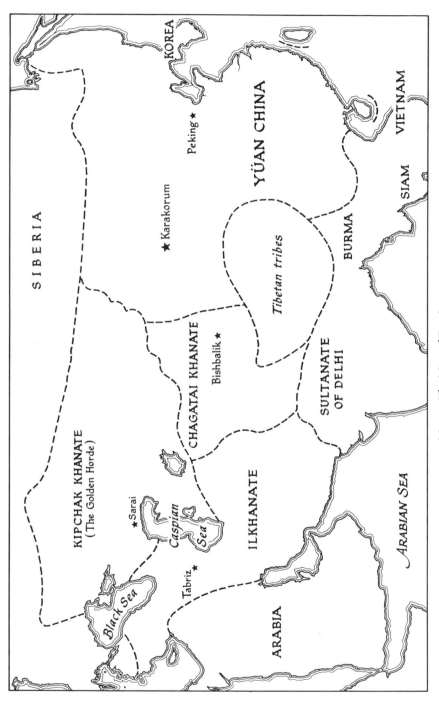

Map 7. The Mongol Empire, c. 1300

SIBERIA

KOREA

★ Karakorum

Peking ★

YÜAN CHINA

VIETNAM

SIAM

BURMA

Tibetan tribes

CHAGATAI KHANATE

Bishbalik ★

SULTANATE
OF DELHI

KIPCHAK KHANATE
(The Golden Horde)

★ Sarai

*Caspian
Sea*

ILKHANATE

Tabriz ★

Black Sea

ARABIA

ARABIAN SEA

pendent on subject Ch'i-tan tribesmen, who proved less than reliable when the Mongol challenge came.

Yüan (1264-1368). The Mongols, who arose explosively in the thirteenth century to create the vastest land empire of world history, were apparently related to the Juan-juan tribes that dominated Mongolia in the fifth century, though they claimed descent from the Hsiung-nu. During the T'ang dynasty they were forest hunters in the mountainous borderland between Mongolia and Manchuria, south of Lake Baikal. At about the end of T'ang they began migrating into the Siberian plain around the Onon River. There they spawned a variety of tribes or nations, some remaining forest hunters and fishermen while others became pastoral nomads. Among the latter tribes were the Mongols proper and the Tatars. Both names were eventually generalized to encompass all the Mongolian speakers and other northerners as well, including the non-Mongol Manchus.

The various Mongol tribes became effectively consolidated at the beginning of the thirteenth century under a princeling named Temuchin (1155-1227), who was acclaimed "universal chief" (Chingis Khan) by his followers in 1203 and was elected grand khan at a convocation of all the tribes in 1206. Already fifty-one years old, he then ignited one of world history's most astonishing uprisings. Before his death at the age of seventy-two he conquered Mongolia and Manchuria, awed Korea into vassalage, drove the Chin Jurchen in terrified retreat into the environs of Kaifeng, almost literally laid waste everything north of the Yellow River from Shantung to Shansi, destroyed Hsi Hsia in northwestern China, overran both Chinese and Russian Turkestan, and plundered the Grand Duchy of Kiev in southern Russia, so that he was unchallenged from the Sea of Japan in the east to the Caspian Sea and the Don River in the west. He proudly proclaimed there was no greater joy than massacring one's enemies, taking their horses and cattle, and ravishing their women. He especially hated cities and city-dwellers. His sons and grandsons extended his trail of slaughter southwestward through the Near East, northwestward to Moscow and on into Poland and Prussia, across Hungary and Austria to the Adriatic, and finally throughout the whole of China. To Christendom Chingis Khan was the long expected anti-Christ, the Scourge of God; and to Chinese he was the most savage destroyer of any they had known. In his first sweep across the North China plain in 1212-13, he left 90-odd towns in rubble, and when he sacked Peking in 1215 the city burned for more than a month.

Fig. 26. Kubilai Khan hunting: painting by Liu Kuan-tao (Yüan)

The first Mongol ruler of all China, Chingis's grandson Kubilai Khan (r. 1260-94), was the fifth grand khan and the first not elected in a convocation of tribal chiefs. At the death of his predecessor in 1259, Kubilai interrupted his campaigning against Sung in southwestern China, rushed to the Mongol headquarters at Karakorum in Outer Mongolia, proclaimed himself the successor, and began a four-year war against a brother who challenged him. In 1264 he moved his capital to Peking, and there in 1271, though South China was not yet under his control, he adopted the dynastic name Yüan. He is known in Chinese history by his posthumous temple designation, Shih-tsu.

Under the early grand khans it was possible to travel from Europe and the Mediterranean to China unmolested for the first time in history. The Mongols were under strict discipline and offered generous hospitality to peaceful strangers. Their "Tatar peace" (Pax Tatarica) was disrupted by Kubilai's seizure of power in violation of customary electoral procedures. Throughout his reign he fought intermittently with a coalition of resentful kinsmen in Central Asia, and neither he nor his successors in China ever enjoyed widespread recognition as grand khans. But they did directly rule an empire combining all of China Proper with most of Mongolia and Manchuria; and such neighbors as Korea, Tibet, Burma, Siam, Annam in north Vietnam, and Champa in south Vietnam accepted status as tributary vassals. Punitive campaigns against Burma and Annam in the 1280's, though not always militarily successful, brought reaffirmations of vassalage.

Unlike any of his predecessors on the Chinese throne, Kubilai aggressively extended his authority overseas, illustrating how quickly the Mongols were able to adapt their military operations to conditions altogether different from those in their steppe homeland. Kubilai sent envoys proclaiming his overlordship as far as Sumatra, Ceylon, and southern India, and in 1292 he dispatched a fleet to punish a recalcitrant potentate in Java. Twice, in 1274 and 1281, he tried to subjugate Japan with naval expeditions. The second effort combined fleets from Korea and the Yangtze delta into a huge armada of 4,500 ships and 150,000 men. Like the first, it ended in disaster for Kubilai's forces when they met fanatical Japanese resistance and their ships were severely battered by a typhoon. The Japanese persuaded themselves that their islands were sacred and protected by "divine winds" (*kamikaze*) sent by their gods.

Mongol rule in China was a thorough military occupation in which the Chinese were oppressed and exploited not only by the Mongols, but by foreign adventurers who were welcomed into the khans' service —Jurchen, Ch'i-tan, Uighurs and other Central Asians, Persians, Arabs, Russians, and even a few West Europeans. Among these was the Venetian merchant Marco Polo, who traveled extensively throughout China from 1275 to 1292 as one of Kubilai's aides. Polo's subsequent, remarkably accurate description of China amused generations of early modern Europeans, who considered him a wildly extravagant liar. They simply would not believe that "black rocks" dug out of hillsides could be burned for fuel or that money could be made of paper, much less Polo's assertions about the enormous imperial revenues, the great number and size of China's cities, and the bustling commercial life of the urban centers and crowded harbors.

Like the Ch'i-tan, the Mongols successfully resisted assimilation. The rulers conducted their court business in the Mongolian language and regularly spent their summers in Mongolia. Originally inclined to transform all China into pastureland, they yielded to the persuasions of such advisers as the Ch'i-tan Yeh-lü Ch'u-ts'ai (1189-1243) and a Chinese Taoist turned Ch'an monk, Liu Ping-chung (1216-74). Letting the Chinese pursue their traditional ways, the Mongols farmed out tax-collecting privileges to mercantile companies of Central Asians and contentedly raked in the profits. They gradually allowed Chinese to build up a facade of T'ang- and Sung-style governmental institutions masking, to Chinese satisfaction, the Mongol military structure that actually controlled the state. After much hesitation they reinstituted civil service recruitment examinations in 1315, but with quotas ensuring that Mongols and their non-Chinese collaborators, however unqualified, would get half of the few doctoral degrees awarded. Chinese seldom attained eminence in government service; principal posts in all offices down to the county level were restricted by law to Mongols, regardless of their contempt for Chinese bureaucratic procedures. Not surprisingly, the centralizing, authoritarian trends that had developed in Sung government were accelerated, and government authority was now exercised in far more violent, even brutal ways.

Although the Mongols freely expropriated land for their garrisons and even turned large tracts of rice paddies in the rich southeast into pasture-like resorts, their interest in maximizing their revenues caused them to encourage both agriculture and commerce. The Grand Canal, inoperative since Northern Sung times, was rebuilt and extended anew to Peking. Cotton production was increased over its Sung beginnings. Sorghum was introduced and quickly became an important supplemental food crop in North China. There was superficial prosperity, but the economy suffered from corrupt, inept government and especially from runaway inflation brought on by monetary manipulations. Landlordism was more rampant than ever, and more Chinese were reduced to outright slave status than at any other time in their history.

Chinese intellectual life, which the Mongols had no strong wish either to foster or to suppress, was stimulated by the still-new Neo-Confucian doctrines that had been systematized by Chu Hsi late in the twelfth century. Traditional education was maintained, particularly in the private academies that had been established by Sung scholars. Some notable Chinese painters refined the impressionistic trends popularized by Sung scholar-officials. Colloquial fiction continued its development toward the novel form, and operatic drama emerged as a new popular entertainment, with masterpieces that were considered China's theatrical classics into the twentieth century.

Cumulative ineptitude in government, murderous palace intrigues, bureaucratic factionalism, military deterioration, neglect of the water-control programs on which China's agriculture depended, and a succession of natural disasters at last combined to reduce the Yüan government to impotence in the 1340's. Chinese peasants rose in desperate, uncoordinated revolts, and in the 1350's the Mongols lost control of the Yangtze valley to fragmented rebel groups that struggled among themselves for supremacy. In the 1360's, while Mongol factions fought each other in the north, a Chinese commoner named Chu Yüan-chang gradually consolidated the Yangtze drainage area. In 1368 he inaugurated a new Nanking-based dynasty called Ming, and as his armies invaded the north the last Yüan emperor fled with his fellow Mongols back into the steppes of Mongolia.

MING (1368-1644)

Chu Yüan-chang (1328-98) was the first commoner to become emperor since the Han founder and is an equally major figure in Chinese history. More than any other single person, he was responsible for the style and tone of life that characterized China into modern times. The dynasty he founded restored Chinese prestige and predominance in East Asia to its T'ang level and gave the Chinese a long era of domestic peace and prosperity. In comparison with the aristocratic verve of the

Han-T'ang epoch or the cultural grandeur of the Sung dynasty, the Ming spirit was less heroic, less colorful, more ordinary. But this was the era in which traditional Chinese society and culture attained full modern maturity.

One thing that contributed to the somewhat lackluster character of Ming China was the dramatic social leveling attempted by the founding emperor. In nationalistic revulsion against the humiliation of Chinese commoners in Yüan times by Mongols, other aliens, and those Chinese who were patronized by the Mongols, the new regime deliberately catered to the poor and humbled the rich. Slavery was abolished, and large estates were confiscated by the government. State-claimed lands were then rented out to the landless, who were also offered seeds, tools, farm animals, and tax incentives to resettle the long-depressed and underpopulated regions of the north. Inordinately high tax rates were imposed on the rich and cultured southeastern area around Soochow, which had been the stronghold of the rising Ming regime's most threatening challenger; and thousands of wealthy southeastern families were forcibly resettled elsewhere, especially in the Ming capital at Nanking. Furthermore, though an examination-recruited civil service was restored to its Sung-style dominance in state administration, the scholar-official class was not allowed to work its way back into the high esteem that it enjoyed under the Sung. In consequence of all these policies, though the gap between rich and poor was by no means closed, the trend of early Ming life was toward a somewhat populist mediocrity, and this was accentuated by the national need to reestablish a stable normalcy —to restore and rebuild rather than to innovate.

Ming T'ai-tsu (or Hung-wu, r. 1368-98), as Chu Yüan-chang was called posthumously,* was an orphan child of itinerant peasants of An-

* Beginning in the Han dynasty, Chinese emperors irregularly announced that as of the next New Year's Day an era with such-and-such a name would commence. Era-names (*nien-hao*) were chosen as auspices of what emperors hoped the future would bring, and new era-names were adopted whenever a change of fortune seemed desirable. Chinese tabulated years accordingly, as the third year of the Yüan-yu era, and so on. Emperors commonly changed era-names several times during their reigns. Ming T'ai-tsu began his reign in traditional fashion with the era-name Hung-wu (swelling military power) and never changed it. His successors in both the Ming and Ch'ing dynasties followed his precedent, so that their era-names roughly correspond to their reign periods. For this reason, Western writers commonly use the era-names of the Ming and Ch'ing emperors as if they were personal names. However common this practice (Hung-wu said . . .), it is technically incorrect, though "the Hung-wu emperor" is a technically correct alternative way of referring to Ming T'ai-tsu. For further information on Chinese rulers' names, see Appendix B.

hwei province. Accepted as a novice in a small Buddhist monastery, he was sent out to make his way as a mendicant monk when hard times came. After several years of wandering through east-central China in that ungratifying role, he attached himself to a minor regional chief of a semireligious, seminationalistic rebel movement. In its cause he became a highly successful general, capturing Nanking in 1356. There he established a rudimentary government, eventually became an independent regional warlord, and directed subordinates in campaigns that wiped out rivals in the Yangtze valley by the end of 1367. Vigorous campaigning in 1368 drove the disorganized Mongols out of North China and simultaneously extended the authority of the new Ming dynasty to the south coast. By 1370 Ming armies had gained complete control of Inner Mongolia, and in continuing campaigns against the Mongols thereafter they pushed northeast to the Sungari River in Manchuria (1387), north into Outer Mongolia beyond Karakorum almost to Lake Baikal (1387-88), and northwest to Hami, in modern Sinkiang province, which controlled access to Central Asia (1388). Meantime Ming forces also subjugated Szechwan, Kweichow, and Yunnan. Thus by the end of T'ai-tsu's 30-year reign, his government controlled the whole of modern China Proper and dominated the northern frontier regions from Hami through Inner Mongolia into northern Manchuria. In addition, vassalage had been accepted by Korea, the oasis states of nearer Central Asia, and the various countries of Southeast Asia.

Mixing T'ang-Sung with Mongol governmental traditions, T'ai-tsu created a highly centralized administration in which he alone had significant authority. He also created a large standing army of hereditary soldiers who were self-supporting at least in theory, but he fragmented its command structure so that no one general could control a personal following. He forbade interference in government by eunuchs. To prevent abuses by local administrators, he entrusted the assessment, collection, and transport of land taxes to the rural communities themselves, and he required villages to organize themselves for various kinds of local self-government. More than any previous Chinese ruler, he fostered elementary schooling throughout the empire.

Because of Ming T'ai-tsu's success in restoring China's international preeminence, and particularly because of his commoner origin and his interest in the welfare of the peasantry, modern Chinese historians have wanted, and tried hard, to make a glorious culture hero of him. It is impossible, however, to gloss over the many serious blemishes on his record as a ruler. After his first few years in power he became a suspi-

Fig. 27. Ming emperor T'ai-tsu: caricature by unidentified 14th-century painter; official portrait by unidentified Ming court painter

cious, cruel emperor with a paranoid fear of being ridiculed because of his inglorious beginnings and his personal ugliness. He also saw himself as under constant threat by conspirators, and in a series of purges that cost tens of thousands of lives he exterminated the very subordinates who had helped establish his empire. On top of all this, he was profoundly anti-intellectual and left a heritage of despotic capriciousness that kept the Ming officialdom intimidated and awed in its relations with the throne.

The same vigorous and autocratic manner characterized the third Ming emperor, T'ai-tsu's son Ch'eng-tsu (or Yung-lo, r. 1402-24), who came to power by overthrowing the milder designated successor, his nephew, in a three-year civil war. Ch'eng-tsu rebuilt Peking, reconstructed the silted-up Grand Canal to supply the city and the northern frontier forces with grain and textiles from the rich southeast, and made it the permanent Ming capital in 1421. He began the development of an inner court-related Grand Secretariat, which soon became the prestigious but often embattled intermediary between the emperors and the regular officialdom. Ch'eng-tsu kept the Ming armies vigilantly active in the north to prevent any effective Mongol reorganization, and personally led five campaigns into Mongolia. When Annam to the south was troubled by succession problems, he intervened and incorporated it as a directly administered province of the Ming empire. Angered by Japanese coastal raiders who had harassed both Korea and China throughout the fourteenth century, he bullied Japan into accepting nominal vassalage for the first time in history. Ch'eng-tsu also sent out large armadas to collect tribute from rulers as far away as Africa. His most famous admiral, a Moslem eunuch named Cheng Ho (1371-1433), led seven expeditions into the Indian Ocean between 1405 and 1433, making China for the only time in history the unchallenged naval power in Asian waters.

This early Ming expansionism was coupled with a xenophobic isolationism. Chinese were forbidden to have contacts with foreigners except on official business or under close official supervision, as if Chinese civilization had to be protected from contamination by outsiders. The Ming mood thus contrasted sharply with the cosmopolitan openness of the T'ang era. Tributary missions from neighboring peoples were subjected to limitations and restraints, and the international trade that had been growing for centuries, especially in the southern ports, was severely curtailed.

In time the Chinese seem to have wearied of the early Ming militancy, persisting so long after their traumatic subjection under the Mongols. Ch'eng-tsu's successors, though no less autocratic, became more relaxed in their foreign relations. The great overseas naval expeditions were terminated. The court abandoned its efforts to keep the troublesome Vietnamese subdued and acquiesced in the restoration of Annam's independence in 1428. Trade relations more satisfactory to the Japanese were negotiated. Ming garrisons were withdrawn from Inner Mongolia, and the Great Wall was rebuilt into the impressive monument it remains today, more formidable than ever before. Even the pretense of Chinese military domination of Central Asia lapsed.

Although China by no means cowered within its frontiers, its attitude toward outsiders became decidedly defensive rather than aggressively expansionist. The military establishment stagnated. Under the influence of a vainglorious eunuch favorite, the emperor Ying-tsung (r. 1435-49 with the era-name Cheng-t'ung, restored 1457-64 with the era-name T'ien-shun) foolishly allowed himself to be taken captive and many of his courtiers to be slaughtered in 1449 while making a show of force against the Mongol raider Esen. A century later another Mongol chief,

Altan Khan, pillaged the settlements of the frontier zones for more than two decades until pacified with special trading privileges in 1571; and simultaneously Japan-based coastal raiders, often led by Chinese renegades, repeatedly looted the southeastern ports. The Chinese learned to cope with such annoyances by artful diplomacy as much as by arms. Occasional aboriginal uprisings in the still-unassimilated southwest were kept in check, and in the 1590's the Chinese sent large armies that helped Korea survive invasions launched by the Japanese military dictator Toyotomi Hideyoshi; but by 1600 Ming military power had waned.

During this long decline of the military spirit, however, there was substantial institutional, socioeconomic, and cultural growth. Civil servants trained in the Neo-Confucianism of Chu Hsi adapted themselves to the autocratic character of Ming governance and became a stable, competent managerial class committed to rather conservative policies. The central government at Peking was capably run by the new Grand Secretariat, which cooperated with palace eunuchs to manipulate weak emperors. Modern China's pattern of provincial-level governments came into being, carefully structured to avoid recurrences of regional separatism. The whole governmental establishment was monitored by an enlarged, active censorial service. Historians on the whole have rated the Ming governmental record highly.

North China slowly recovered from its long political and economic depression, though it did not regain either demographic or economic parity with the south until the twentieth century. The Chinese population as a whole, from a Yüan-early Ming level of less than sixty million, swelled beyond one hundred million and possibly close to two hundred million by 1600. After the initial agrarian-oriented retrenchment, which lasted through most of the fifteenth century, urban and commercial growth resumed. This combined with ever-spreading education in both government and private schools to produce a lively, affluent bourgeois atmosphere in the sixteenth century. By 1600, acknowledging the existence of a money economy, the state had converted almost all its revenues to money in the form of silver. However, perhaps because of bureaucratic conservatism among the officials, who with their relatives and hangers-on now dominated commerce, technological progress did not keep pace with population growth and urbanization. Moreover, the exploitation of tax and other advantages by officials gradually undermined the free peasantry of early Ming times, so that tenancy became increasingly widespread. The late Ming affluence was consequently neither self-perpetuating nor equitably distributed.

Ming intellectuals produced monuments of scholarship. At the same time, Yüan theatrical traditions were refined, and the centuries-long development of colloquial-language fiction for the masses culminated in a series of novels that are now recognized, but only in retrospect, as literary classics. As for philosophy, many men eventually wearied of Chu Hsi's austere rationalism and found new inspiration in the antiauthoritarian, individualistic doctrines of one of the greatest Ming scholar-officials, Wang Yang-ming (or Wang Shou-jen, 1472-1529); in the sixteenth century such men generated iconoclastic excitement in thought, art, and criticism.

The later Ming emperors remained capricious and became increasingly remote. Shih-tsung (or Chia-ching, r. 1521-67) and Shen-tsung (or Wan-li, r. 1572-1620) both isolated themselves for decades from direct contact with their ministers. The corrupt grand secretary Yen Sung (1480-1565), his disciplinarian successor, Chang Chü-cheng (1525-82), and powerful palace eunuchs provoked endless partisan wrangling in the officialdom, which made the government increasingly unresponsive to social problems and encouraged emperors to become increasingly truculent. Declining governmental effectiveness came to a climax in the reign of Hsi-tsung (or T'ien-ch'i, r. 1620-27), a young and indecisive emperor who finally gave almost dictatorial power to Wei Chung-hsien (1568-1627), the most notorious palace eunuch of all Chinese history. Wei brutally purged hundreds of officials associated with a conservative reformist group called the Tung-lin Party, and staffed the government with sycophants.

Unfortunately for the Ming, deterioration in governmental morale and effectiveness coincided with two serious threats to national stability —peasant rebellions in the economically depressed northwest and the consolidation of an antagonistic Manchu regime in the northeast. One such threat might have been contained, but the government could not cope with both at once. The domestic rebel Li Tzu-ch'eng (1605?-45) captured Peking in 1644, whereupon the last Ming emperor hanged himself in the palace grounds. A frontier general invited the Manchus to join him in putting down the rebels, and the Manchus seized the opportunity to take the throne for themselves.

While Ming China had been basking in its inward-oriented self-satisfaction and remained supremely confident of its cultural superiority over all "barbarian" peoples, the states of Western Europe were embarking on their great age of exploration, colonization, and imperialism. In 1498 Vasco da Gama rounded South Africa and reached India.

In 1511 the Portuguese conquered Malacca, which controlled access from the Indian Ocean to the South China Sea; and in 1514 a Portuguese squadron appeared at Canton seeking diplomatic and trading relations. Although discouraged by the Ming court, the Portuguese persevered and by 1557 had a permanent settlement on China's coast at Macao. From there Jesuit missionaries penetrated inland, and in 1601 Matteo Ricci was permitted to establish a Catholic missionary headquarters at Peking under imperial patronage. By the end of Ming other Europeans had also begun to make contact with China. The Chinese attitude toward them all was one of patronizing tolerance at best.

CH'ING (1644-1912)

The alien Manchus who in 1644 inaugurated the last imperial dynasty in China, called Ch'ing, were related to the Jurchen whose Chin dynasty had ruled North China from 1127 to 1234. The national name Manchu, of unclear derivation and significance, was adopted late, in 1636. Through most of the Ming dynasty these northern tribes had been forest-dwelling tributary vassals of the Chinese in far eastern Manchuria. They were troublesome enough at times to cause Ming authorities to build defensive palisades against them around the Chinese settlements in the Liao River basin. But they eventually became avid admirers and students of Chinese civilization, and when they took control of China it was their contention that they came, not as enemies, but as preservers of the Ming heritage. And as a matter of fact, their rule over their Chinese subjects was by far the least burdensome of any imposed on the Chinese by alien rulers.

The Manchus owed their nationhood to two organizing geniuses, Nurhachi (1559-1626) and his son Abahai (1592-1643). Nurhachi began life as a petty tribal chief who sold medicinal herbs to Chinese settlers in Manchuria and led tributary missions to Peking. Abahai died as emperor of a strong, effective Ch'ing dynasty headquartered at Mukden that dominated Mongolia and Korea as well as all of Manchuria and confronted Ming China's finest army at Shan-hai-kuan, where the Great Wall meets the sea. When Li Tzu-ch'eng's rebels, after capturing Peking, moved northeast toward Shan-hai-kuan in 1644 the Ming commander there, Wu San-kuei (1612-78), and the Manchu prince regent, Dorgon (1612-50), collaborated against them as friendly enemies. Li's forces, badly routed, fell back to Peking, looted the city, and then fled westward. Wu San-kuei's army and mixed Chinese-Manchu forces scattered to destroy Li and restore order in China. Promising Wu princely status and a large fief, Dorgon then enthroned his nephew at Peking as the Shun-chih emperor (Shih-tsu, r. 1644-61).

The transition from Ming to Ch'ing rule was far less traumatic for the Chinese than the thirteenth-century Mongol conquest had been; indeed, it was the least disruptive transition from one major dynasty to another in the whole of Chinese history. This was so despite the fact that, having won the Chinese throne easily, almost as if by default, the new Ch'ing dynasty took nearly half a century to secure its control of the empire. Two things eased the transition. First, the Manchus honored and perpetuated the Ming ideology, governmental patterns, and social organization; and second—in one of the remarkable ironies of Chinese history—Ming loyalists were overwhelmed as much by Chinese fighting in the Manchu cause as by the Manchus themselves, even with their Mongol allies.

In the earliest years of the Manchu uprising in the northeast, many Chinese settlers in Manchuria and defectors from defeated Ming puni- tive expeditions willingly accepted Manchu leadership because of their aversion to the partisan squabbling at the Ming court and their disgust with the ineptitude of the Ming military effort. A particularly sore point was the poor Ming record in providing adequate training and logistical support for the troops sent to repel the Manchus. In contrast, the Man- chus were well organized and disciplined. Moreover, the Manchus were not anti-Chinese; they gladly incorporated Chinese defectors into their socio-military groups, called banners, and gave competent Chinese po- sitions of responsibility. Later, when the Manchus occupied North Chi- na with the help of Wu San-kuei and other former Ming commanders, they introduced themselves as liberators from chaos rather than oppres- sive conquerors, and many Chinese welcomed them as such after the instability of the last Ming decades.

Once the rebels of the north were suppressed, Chinese armies under Wu San-kuei and other Chinese generals were instrumental in destroy- ing Ming loyalist regimes in the south. Without such Chinese support, the Manchus would undoubtedly have been content to divide the coun- try with a Southern Ming regime, as their forebears, the Jurchen, had divided it with Southern Sung. There was some prospect that such a division would come about in any event, for the southern loyalists re- sisted vigorously despite a continuation of the partisan wrangling that had paralyzed the court at Peking. Four undistinguished princes were successively installed by Ming generals in the south, and it was not until 1662 that the last of them, having taken refuge in Burma, was handed over by the king of Burma to an invading Ch'ing force under Wu San-kuei, who executed him.

Even then resistance was maintained on the offshore islands of the southeast coast by the family of a famous loyalist freebooter named Cheng Ch'eng-kung (1624-62; known to Europeans as Koxinga), who had established himself on Taiwan. At one point the Ch'ing government went so far as to order the whole southeastern coastline evacuated to deprive the Cheng raiders of looting possibilities. Moreover, Wu San-kuei and some other Ming defectors, after having been rewarded with large and almost autonomous fiefs in the south, turned against the Manchus in 1673 in what is known as the Rebellion of the Three Feudatories. For a time the rebels dominated almost the whole of South China. But in 1681, after an eight-year struggle, resistance on the mainland was crushed—ironically again, in large part by a new generation of Chinese generals serving the Ch'ing dynasty. Then in 1683 the government mounted an invasion of Taiwan that finally quelled the Cheng family's coastal harassments. Thereafter nationalistic anti-Manchu sentiments were kept alive by secret societies, which now began to thrive in the fashion of the underworld gangs of the modern West, and by members of some of the large overseas Chinese communities that had developed in Southeast Asian countries in the last Ming century. But these rumblings of discontent were more irritants than threats, and in the 1680's the Manchus stabilized their control of the Chinese empire.

The prolonged Ming-loyalist resistance served to reinforce the Manchus' original inclination to deal prudently with the Chinese. They publicly honored the many men and women who had become martyrs in the Ming cause; they refrained from punishing eminent intellectuals who refused to enter their service; they tolerated a minor cult of Southern Ming historiography; they sought Chinese cooperation in many flattering ways. Into the eighteenth century there was what some historians have called a Manchu-Chinese honeymoon.

For the first century and a half of their rule the Manchus gave China good government and strong leadership, so that Chinese life flourished in every regard. In the eighteenth century China attained the last golden age of the imperial tradition and very likely was the most awe-inspiring state in the world. It enjoyed a long domestic peace while steadily strengthening its preeminence over neighboring peoples; it grew in population and wealth and was elegantly sophisticated. Its principles of governance and social organization were so extolled by Voltaire and other Western intellectuals that Confucius became virtually the patron saint of Europe's Age of Enlightenment. A popular passion for Chinese things and themes (chinoiserie) had lasting influence on European art, literature, architecture, gardens, and decor. Much of the credit for such Chinese prospering belongs to the remarkably able early Manchu rulers, especially two dynastic giants called K'ang-hsi (Sheng-tsu, r. 1661-1722) and Ch'ien-lung (Kao-tsung, r. 1735-96).

The K'ang-hsi emperor, enthroned at the age of seven, reigned over China longer than any emperor before him and was probably the most admirable ruler of the entire later imperial age. Conscientious, inquisitive, and indefatigable, he had awesome physical and mental powers. He was thoroughly Chinese by culture, wrote literary prose and poetry of good quality, and encouraged literature, art, fine printing, and porcelain manufacture. Under Jesuit tutelage he studied Latin, higher mathematics, science, and the new Western technology; he was especially enamored of clocks and collected them with a connoisseur's relish. He corresponded with European kings and popes, but late in life he became irritated by the sectarian bickerings of Catholic missionaries and what he considered the outrageous presumption that a pope in Rome should determine what Chinese Christians could and could not believe.

A careful, frugal, and efficient administrator, the K'ang-hsi emperor made strenuous efforts to ensure honesty in government and to foster Chinese-Manchu harmony. He made six grand tours of inspection around the country to see for himself what conditions were like. He honored Chinese scholars and employed them in the production of dictionaries, encyclopedias, histories, and other monuments of scholarship, as well as in routine civil service administration. He also watched carefully over the economy and fostered water-control projects that kept agriculture flourishing.

No less than in the domestic realm, the K'ang-hsi emperor was a determined and masterly leader in military affairs. While still a youth he boldly challenged the autonomy of Wu San-kuei and other powerful Chinese generals who had been enfeoffed in the south in the earliest Ch'ing years. In the resulting Rebellion of the Three Feudatories, he personally planned the campaigns that suppressed the rebels and subjugated Taiwan. In the midst of these exertions the eastern Mongols (known as Tatars and Khalkas) revolted in the north, in 1675. The em-

Fig. 28. Court portrait of the K'ang-hsi emperor

peror reacted unhesitatingly, subdued them, and declared himself khan of all the Mongols. Subsequently the western Mongol chief Galdan (1632?-97) invaded Mongolia from Central Asia. The emperor personally led three campaigns northward in the 1690's, forced Galdan to commit suicide in 1697, and established military colonies at the Central Asian oases of Hami and Turfan. Further, by diplomatic intrigues he got an anti-Mongol Dalai Lama installed as ruler of Tibet. When Galdan's successors conquered Tibet in 1717, the emperor mounted expeditions that by 1720 had driven the Mongols out and made Tibet a submissive political appendage of China.

In the 1600's the Russians had completed the early stage of their eastward expansion across Siberia to the Pacific, and during the K'ang-hsi era they established outposts along the Amur River. Considering this Manchu territory, the emperor sent a Ch'ing army to attack the Russians' stronghold, Fort Albazin, in 1685-86. The Russians withdrew. In 1689 the Chinese and Russians negotiated China's first treaty with a European nation, the Treaty of Nerchinsk. The Russians gave up claims to the Amur River valley. Border trade was authorized, and a long era of Sino-Russian peace ensued.

The K'ang-hsi emperor was succeeded by his fourth son, the Yung-cheng emperor (Shih-tsung, r. 1722-35), a man of forty-five. Because he came to the throne by intriguing successfully against his brothers, he was a wary ruler, harsher than his father; and he increased the autocratic quality of Ch'ing governance. But he was an able emperor who reinforced bureaucratic discipline and vigorously suppressed budding corruption.

His successor, the Ch'ien-lung emperor, retired in 1796 after a sixty-year reign so as not to exceed his grandfather's record but continued to dominate the government in retirement until his death in 1799 at the age of eighty-nine. He was a more flamboyant man than his predecessors, a Grand Monarch in the style of his contemporary, Louis XIV of France. But he was also a serious man, and like the K'ang-hsi emperor, was probably the most capable ruler of his time. Domestically, he generally continued in his grandfather's footsteps, and was an especially notable patron of monumental collaborative scholarly undertakings. In his time all forms of literature and art flourished, and China's prosperity seemed boundless. As the population grew and agriculture was intensified, new market towns sprang up in the countryside by the hundreds. Regional and national marketing complexes grew, generating new urban-oriented occupations and attitudes. The well-to-do began abandoning rural life to settle in the cities and concentrate on mercantile activity; and the peasantry, now a complicated mixture of part owners, part tenants, part small landlords, became increasingly sensitive to the fluctuating market needs in the towns and cities. China exuded self-confidence and self-satisfaction.

The Ch'ien-lung emperor was proudest of his military achievements, for which he had a great flair. He pursued an aggressive policy of dominating troublesome border peoples. The western Mongols (called Eleuthes, Kalmuks, or Dzungars) were still the most troublesome neighbors. After rebelling repeatedly in the 1720's and 1730's, they ceded the eastern end of Turkestan to Ch'ing in 1735. But they continued to make trouble until the 1750's, when in a series of campaigns the Ch'ien-lung emperor completely destroyed Mongol power in Central Asia. The whole of Chinese Turkestan was then incorporated directly into the Ch'ing empire in 1759, with its modern name Sinkiang (New Dominion). A few years earlier, in 1751, an expedition had established Ch'ing control of Tibet more tightly than before, in reaction to renewed unrest. Later, in 1792, a Ch'ing army in Tibet marched southward into Nepal to punish Gurka tribesmen who had long encroached on and pillaged parts of Tibet, and Nepal was forced to recognize Ch'ing suzerainty. Ch'ing armies also campaigned extensively in southwestern China, whose aboriginal tribes did not finally succumb to Ch'ing authority until 1776. Burma and Annam suffered from Ch'ing punitive expeditions in 1765-69 and 1788, respectively, but retained their independence, as tributary vassals.

The glory of the Ch'ien-lung emperor's reign is blemished seriously by two things. One is an extensive literary inquisition that was begun in the 1770's, aimed at suppressing subversive sentiments. The other is the personal deterioration of the emperor himself in his later years. He gradually became extravagant and luxury-loving, began to surround himself with docile sycophants, and finally, from about 1775 to his death, was the dupe of a clever, unscrupulous Manchu guardsman named Ho-shen (1750-99). Handsome and amusing, Ho-shen swiftly rose from an obscure post in the imperial bodyguard into the highest ministerships, attained lavish honors, and systematically exploited every possibility of bribery and other forms of corruption. The cumulative result of the literary inquisition and Ho-shen's pernicious influence was that in the final Ch'ien-lung years the Ch'ing government began a rapid decline in morale and effectiveness.

Two major types of pressures hastened the deterioration of the imperial tradition in the nineteenth century. One was the increasing power and ambition of the West. By 1800 the English, Dutch, Spanish, French, and Portuguese had developed colonial empires in Asia, and the newly independent Americans were brandishing free-trade doctrines around the world. Yet for almost three centuries China—the most populous, wealthiest, and by Western reckoning most powerful country on earth —had resisted and carefully limited its contacts with the West. Insignificant overland trade with Russia was tolerated, but seafaring Westerners were permitted to trade only at Canton, only in trading seasons defined by the Chinese, only with a licensed monopoly of Chinese wholesalers (called by Westerners the *co-hong*), and only under close state supervision. Moreover, whereas the West clamored for such Chinese products as tea, silk, and porcelains, the Chinese had little use for any Western products, so that Western silver poured endlessly into Chinese coffers. But by about 1800 the Westerners found they could sell opium to the Chinese in abundance, even if illegally; and gradually the trade imbalance was righted in this way. By the 1830's the Canton trading situation had reversed itself: opium was pouring in and silver was pouring out. The Ch'ing government, alarmed both by the silver drain and by the spread of opium-smoking, tried to regain control of the situation and finally provoked the leading trading country, England, into war. The so-called Opium War of 1839-42, though not fought very vigorously by either side and limited for the most part to coastal skirmishes, went badly for China. To avoid more serious humiliation the Ch'ing court made peace with England, and soon negotiated treaties with other trading nations, on such terms that China became exposed to still more contacts with the rude, importunate "foreign devils." A total of five ports, from Canton to Shanghai, were opened to regular foreign residence as well as trade. Foreign influences of many sorts began making themselves felt in the interior, to the great dismay of the Ch'ing authorities.

Growing domestic discontent was a more ominous problem for nineteenth-century China. The population had grown steadily since mid-Ming times—to more than three hundred million by 1750 and four hundred million by 1850. Increasing food production—partly due to the spread of new subsidiary crops introduced from the Americas, including maize, potatoes, and peanuts—made such growth possible; but land utilization had reached its peak in the eighteenth century, even with China's very high level of premodern agricultural technology. Population growth inevitably surpassed increased food production, and the standard of living began to decline. Spreading corruption and indolence in government made conditions worse. For the first time in history there appeared a permanently dispossessed class of impoverished people for whom there were neither lands nor jobs, and their numbers could only multiply. The rumblings of anti-Manchu secret societies became more threatening every year. The centuries-old White Lotus Society ignited a rebellion in 1793 that disrupted North China until 1804. Then in the 1820's and 1830's popular uprisings became endemic. The government's humiliation in the Opium War weakened its prestige, its confidence, and its general ability to cope with its mushrooming domestic problems. Finally in 1850 South China erupted in what is called the Taiping Rebellion, which for the next 15 years shook the Ch'ing dynasty almost but not quite to its destruction. More than 15 provinces were affected, hundreds of towns and cities were damaged or destroyed, and an estimated thirty million lives were lost. The very foundations of the traditional imperial system—its basic political principles and patterns of social organization—were challenged as never before.

Contemporaries both in and outside China were slow to recognize the fact, but in retrospect it is clear that with the outbreak of the Taiping Rebellion, following close upon the changes wrought by the Opium War, traditional Chinese civilization in all its aspects was plunging into a transition unlike any experienced before. The old order, already repeatedly transformed since its origins in the unification of Ch'in and the consolidation of Han, had finally run its course. Struggling to find a new kind of nationhood consonant with the new internal and external relations in which it was enmeshed, China began its agonizing modern history, the main stages and themes of which are summarized in the Epilogue.

11. Government

IN THE later imperial age the old hereditary aristocracy was finally displaced from predominance in government, as in society, by scholar-officials chosen for state service in open, competitive, written examinations on the basis of their mastery of the Confucian classics, history, and literary skills, and promoted to high office very largely on the basis of bureaucratic competence demonstrated in service. Such a generalization must be qualified, of course, in consideration of the areas and periods in which the alien conquest dynasties ruled the Chinese, but even they paid sufficient lip-service to the bureaucratic ideal—and, in the Manchu case at least, implemented it zealously enough—to make "the age of bureaucracy" as good a label as any other for the era from 960 to 1850.

The rise of bureaucratic governance had some significant corollaries. Rulers became more autocratic than before, administrative structures more centralized, the military more professionalized and less esteemed, and dynasties more durable.

ABSOLUTISM

The general acceptance of the doctrine of the Mandate of Heaven from the earliest days of Chinese history ensured that Chinese rulers would always be absolutist in theory. During the long Chou dynasty, however, the theoretical powers of kings were curtailed in practice by the prestige and military strength of regional feudal lords; and in the early imperial age emperors were restrained by the powers of influential relatives, semiautonomous aristocratic families, and uncontrollable regional generals. To be sure, some emperors dominated their times by force of personality; Han Wu-ti and T'ang T'ai-tsung are especially notable examples. But the system of governance that then prevailed was such that emperors were normally surrounded by men who differed little from them in life-style and prestige, peers and sometimes competitors who had to be treated with respect and with caution. Regicides, palace coups, and usurpations were not uncommon.

The situation of emperors in the later imperial era was in general markedly different, especially under the native dynasties, Sung and Ming. Significant changes in the structure of the government combined both to isolate and to aggrandize the emperor to such a degree that he was no longer just a *primus inter pares*, the chief of a group of powerful men. The Ch'i-tan, Jurchen, Mongol, and early Manchu rulers in varying degrees were chieftains supported by and dependent on tribal or clan leaders who had independent power bases and who were thus not to be taken lightly. But the Chinese emperors of Sung and Ming times, and most of the Manchu emperors as well, were complete autocrats who were separated from all other men by an unbridgeable social gap and whose authority no man could challenge—in theory, in law, and generally in practice.

The clearest symbol of this change was the rigid protocol that developed around appearances before the throne. In T'ang times, it will be recalled, grand councilors customarily sat together with their emperor to discuss governmental problems. But at the Sung court, officials stood at attention in the imperial presence, and by Ming times officials were required to kneel before an emperor who grandly looked down on them from a throne on an elevated dais. The Ming emperors, continuing a barbarous Mongol custom, even had offending officials flogged in open court—a despotic exercise in which the victim, whatever his rank or prestige, was held prostrate on the palace floor with all court officials in attendance while eunuchs flayed his bared buttocks with wooden rods. Ming emperors also employed their imperial bodyguard, a totalitarian secret police almost unfettered by legal restraints, to spy on, arrest, imprison, and torture officials or anyone else who antagonized them. The atmosphere at Ming T'ai-tsu's court was so oppressive that, according to the testimony of a contemporary, capital officials bade their families farewell on going to duty every morning and on returning home in the evening congratulated themselves for having survived one more day.

The disappearance from Chinese society of the early imperial age's

Fig. 29. Ming imperial procession: detail from 16th-century handscroll

entrenched hereditary aristocracy accounts in large part for the new absolutism. The disposition of military forces in the later dynasties gave military leaders no power bases from which they might threaten the throne. Members of imperial families and imperial relatives by marriage, who in former times could have counted on being appointed to the highest civil and military offices, were now systematically excluded from any governmental positions of importance and were normally even kept at a distance from the capital. By entrusting governmental administration increasingly to nonhereditary bureaucrats who were subject to promotion, demotion, and dismissal at the imperial pleasure, emperors protected themselves from the rise of any new entrenched power group that might threaten them.

The newly dominant civil service bureaucracy of the later imperial age was thus no threat to the throne; rather, it gave the later dynasties greater efficiency and durability than had been known previously. But it should not be thought of as the acquiescent tool of despots, either. It was an organized hierarchy of proud, educated men whose prestige as intellectuals was in some measure independent of their imperially sanctioned status; and in the normal routine it was largely a self-perpetuating, self-regulating body on which an emperor depended fully as much as it depended on him. Although an emperor could dictate policies as he pleased, only the officialdom at large could put those policies into practice; and the traditional Chinese civil service learned to resist unwanted changes very stubbornly, as bureaucratic civil services everywhere are prone to do. Moreover, in reaction to despotic aberrations on the part of emperors, the Chinese officialdom regularly spawned courageous remonstrators eager to court martyrdom. Thus in the long run emperors could thrive only by cooperating with, or at least not alienating, their officials.

The Sung dynasty is generally esteemed as the high point of all Chinese history in this regard—a time of good government when theoretically despotic rulers devoted themselves to respectful cooperation with scholar-officials who were, in general, of extraordinarily high quality. The Ming dynasty, in contrast, produced several emperors who were inordinately cruel and oppressive and others who were strangely reclusive and inattentive; but it also produced a series of strong, patient, conscientious officials who kept government functioning stably. The period gave rise to some of China's most famous remonstrators as well; the most famous of all, perhaps, is Hai Jui (1514-87). On one celebrated occasion in the reign of Shih-tsung (Chia-ching, r. 1521-67), Hai presented himself at the palace gate to submit a memorial denouncing some of the emperor's notorious idiosyncrasies. The emperor flew into a rage and ordered that Hai not be permitted to escape. "Never fear, sire," the eunuch go-between told the emperor. "He has said goodbye to his family, has brought his coffin with him, and waits at the gate!" Shih-tsung was so taken aback by this news that he forgave Hai for his impertinence.

Of the alien emperors of the later imperial age, only the Manchus strove to achieve good relations with Chinese scholar-officials as a class. The great K'ang-hsi emperor was particularly conciliatory. Although a number of famous scholars resisted his lures, he was on the whole successful in bringing the educated Chinese into his service, and late in his reign such men began pursuing governmental careers as zealously as in Ming times. The Manchu emperors generally were more conscientious and reasonable than their Ming predecessors, and Chinese officials were less openly abused in Ch'ing than in Ming times. But no one forgot where power lay, and for the most part the Ch'ing officialdom was cowed, cautious, and submissive.

ORGANIZATIONAL STRUCTURE

The strong centralization of authority in the throne was the most notable development in administrative organization under the later dynasties. It was achieved by structural changes both in the central government itself and in the relations between the central government and regional governments.

In the central government, the traditional tripartite division of responsibility persisted, and until the fourteenth century the dynasties perpetuated much of the nomenclature of the T'ang alignment of top-echelon agencies: a general staff of military officers, an independent Censorate, and a Council of State consisting of the heads of three great general-administration organs (a Secretariat, a Chancellery, and a Department of State Affairs, the latter incorporating six ministries). The most noteworthy trend was a gradual consolidation of general-administration responsibilities under one agency.

Sung began this consolidation in a trend toward what is often called a "strong prime ministership" reminiscent of the powerful grand counselors of Ch'in and early Han times. The first major step, taken in the 1080's in the era of the efficiency-minded reformer Wang An-shih, was to make the two heads of the Department of State Affairs concurrently heads of the Secretariat and the Chancellery. In Southern Sung times the chief councilors even gained direct control of the formerly independent Bureau of Military Affairs (*shu-mi yüan*), which had developed out of the loosely coordinated T'ang general staff. The Sung Censorate retained its traditional independence, but its power was weakened; its staff was greatly reduced, and it was forbidden to send touring censorial inspectors throughout the country as in the T'ang system. On the other hand, remonstrating officials were moved out of their traditional subordinate status in the Secretariat and Chancellery and were given Censorate-like autonomy in a Bureau of Remonstrance, which became highly prestigious and influential.

Some specialists see in these Sung institutional changes a complicated scheme by which chief councilors gained ever more extensive control over the whole officialdom without significant interference from the

Censorate, while remonstrators (who in the early empire had been considered checks on the emperor) became checks on the chief councilors. In this interpretation, the emperor now stood clearly preeminent, the only important check on his authority having been removed. But however true this was in theory, in reality the Southern Sung emperors were rather consistently men of weak personality, and allowed themselves to be manipulated by chief councilors who were probably the most powerful bureaucratic executives of all Chinese history.

Meanwhile, the Jurchen Chin dynasty in North China was streamlining its central government by doing away with the Secretariat and Chancellery entirely. The Mongol Yüan dynasty followed the Chin precedent, but changed the name of the remaining, unified general-administration agency from the Department of State Affairs to the Secretariat. Thus the T'ang concept of a Council of State had gradually disappeared; the two senior Secretariat officials were now de facto grand counselors of the Han sort, presiding over the T'ang-style six ministries that carried out routine administrative business. Not surprisingly in an alien conquest situation, a strong and independent Bureau of Military Affairs reemerged. The Censorate (largely staffed now with Mongols) was expanded even beyond its T'ang dimensions and resumed its pre-Sung empire-wide surveillance functions, and the specialized remonstrating officials were entirely abolished. Paying lipservice to the remonstrance tradition, the Mongols called on censorial officials to take on that duty. Kubilai Khan clearly indicated the separation of functions in the Yüan government, and as clearly revealed its essential autocratic quality, by saying, "The Secretariat is my left hand, the Bureau of Military Affairs is my right hand, and the Censorate is the means for my keeping both hands healthy." (The order of precedence is worth noting as another indication of the Yüan's military emphasis: among the Mongols the right side took precedence over the left side, contrary to Chinese custom.)

The founder of the Ming dynasty originally copied the Yüan central government, making only trivial name changes; the Bureau of Military Affairs, for example, became the Chief Military Commission (*tu-tu fu*), and the Censorate's traditional name, Tribunal of Censors, was changed to Chief Surveillance Office (*tu ch'a-yüan*). But in 1380 he made the most substantial change in the structure of the central government of the later imperial age. Suspecting a chief councilor of treason, he abolished the Secretariat's executive posts, leaving general administration fragmented among the six ministries and making himself their sole coordinator—in effect, making himself his own prime minister. He also fragmented the Chief Military Commission into five agencies, all of the same name, and divided among them control over the empire's military garrisons in confusing geographic jurisdictions—thus making himself, in effect, his own military chief of staff.

Since few emperors could hope to supervise so many top-echelon agencies effectively, a new, informal coordinating agency developed early in the fifteenth century. Called a Grand Secretariat (*nei-ko*), this was a group of administrative aides, fluctuating in number from two to six, who were drawn from the venerable pool of writers and editors called the Hanlin Academy. For prestige purposes they were soon given concurrent status as ministers or vice-ministers in the general-administration hierarchy, but their lack of experience in actual administration put the successive grand secretaries at a disadvantage in dealing with veteran administrators of the outer-court officialdom. The close collaboration between grand secretaries and palace eunuchs, which was necessary for accomplishing essential paperwork in the reigns of the more reclusive and inattentive Ming emperors, made the grand secretaries especially vulnerable to suspicion and criticism on the part of the outer court. With a few notable exceptions, grand secretaries never managed to become chief councilor-like leaders of and spokesmen for the officialdom at large. Indeed, most of them became focal points of recurrent factional controversies, often ignored by dilatory emperors on one hand and vilified by antagonistic officials on the other. Many specialists consider the consequent lack of stable coordination in the central government to have been a major factor in the decline of the Ming dynasty.

The Manchu Ch'ing dynasty maintained the Ming central government structure, and the Grand Secretariat's role became regularized and stable under the strong, conscientious leadership of the early Manchu emperors. But the grand secretaries became bogged down in routine administrative paperwork; they shifted, in effect, from inner-court to outer-court status. In 1729 the Yung-cheng emperor consequently set up a new inner-court agency, the Grand Council (*chün-chi ch'u*), as a more flexible and informal advisory body. Thereafter, the Grand Council changed only to the extent that some grand secretaries were allowed to sit as members on what was now the top-level policy-recommending agency of the administration. Thus something like the

T'ang-Sung Council of State was restored. The Manchus made no other significant changes in central government structure until late in the nineteenth century.*

Structural changes in regional administration were more numerous and significant from Sung into Ch'ing times than these modifications in the central government. Counties (hsien or chou) remained the base of the formal governmental pyramid, and the T'ang pattern of supervisory prefectures (chou or fu) persisted. Below this formal structure of local government, as in earlier times, administrative responsibilities were borne by the people themselves. Especially after the reforms of Wang An-shih in the eleventh century, and even under the Mongols, rural villages were required to organize themselves so that local leaders could be designated to keep order, adjudicate disputes between families, maintain irrigation systems, organize small-scale construction projects, provide local militiamen when needed, and assess, collect, and deliver taxes. Such village leaders, whether a council of elders or a single important family head, received no remuneration from the state. In the Ming dynasty's so-called *li-chia* system, families were grouped into tens and hundreds for local self-governance on an unprecedentedly broad scale; tax collections were the responsibility of a different, overlapping network of unremunerated tax captains, each responsible for an area owing a standard, large sum. The Ch'ing dynasty imposed tax-collecting responsibilities directly on the li-chia structure inherited from Ming, and additionally superimposed on it militia functions called *pao-chia*, inherited from Sung; the system had the characteristics of police-like mutual surveillance.

The Ming and Ch'ing li-chia systems of sub-county organization were especially notable as devices for informing the peasantry about the laws and indoctrinating it with the Confucian value system espoused by the state. Members of each village community had regular monthly assemblies during which they were lectured to, usually by retired officials or low-ranking degree-holders, about Confucian values illustrated in historical anecdotes or listened to the recitation of imperial decrees exhorting them to be filial and obedient to parents, to be respectful to superiors, to be harmonious with neighbors, to educate sons and brothers, to be content each in his lot, and not to do evil.

---

* Ch'ing specialists commonly use the terminology "the six boards" in preference to "the six ministries" used for earlier periods, but only because each of these agencies now had two heads of equal status, one Manchu and one Chinese, and therefore presumably functioned in a more collegial fashion than previously.

The system was effective enough that early modern European visitors to Ming and Ch'ing China commented in astonishment at the orderliness of life among the countless masses despite the scarcity of policemen and other official representatives of state authority.

As the population increased, the formal local-government organization did not grow commensurately. Counties numbered 1,230 about the year 1000 and 1,500 about the year 1800; the number of prefectures actually declined, from about 300 to about 250, in the same period. Thus, whereas a Northern Sung county magistrate may have been responsible for some 80,000 people on average, his mid-Ch'ing counterpart governed more than 250,000 people on average; and average populations under the supervisory jurisdictions of prefects grew from perhaps 300,000 to more than 1,500,000. Contacts between the populace and the officialdom naturally grew more remote, and the officials relied more and more on appointed agents and surrogates to maintain effective relations between the counties and the grass-roots organizations of informal government.

The intermediary zone between prefectures and the central government—the trouble zone from which regional governors and warlords had repeatedly gained autonomy during the early imperial age—was kept under firm control by the later dynasties. The founder of the Sung dynasty, keenly aware of the danger of separatism, temporarily eliminated all intermediary-level agencies and established direct lines of responsibility between prefectures and the central government. Direct communication between prefectures and the six ministries in the central government remained the principal conduit of routine administration throughout the later empire. When intermediary-level officials reappeared they were coordinators, expediters, and supervisors but not governors serving as semiautonomous surrogates of the emperor—with apparent exceptions only under the alien Liao, Chin, and Yüan dynasties.

The need for intermediary-level coordination still existed, of course; its total elimination by the Sung founder could not be tolerated very long. Circuit intendants were soon dispatched as short-term regional representatives of the central government. However, the Sung intendants were limited to carefully defined duties in overlapping geographical jurisdictions. There were fiscal intendants, judicial intendants, military intendants, and intendants of transportation and monopolies, each assigned to a somewhat different group of contiguous prefectures. Thus no circuit intendant or combination of intendants had an opportunity

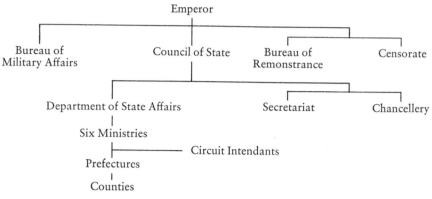

Basic governmental organization in Sung times

to monopolize power as T'ang regional governors had done at the expense of the authority of the central government.

While Sung was fragmenting authority in outlying areas by establishing these overlapping, functionally differentiated intendancies, Liao was dividing its northeastern empire into five regions, each supervised by a "capital" in direct contact with all its prefectures. (Auxiliary capitals had been designated in Han, T'ang, and other earlier times but had seldom been entrusted with significant governmental roles.) Chin, in Liao fashion, established six capitals in its northern empire and further imposed 19 supervisory circuits on its array of prefectures. Then the Mongols created the most complex system of intermediary-level agencies in Chinese history. Yüan prefectures were divided among 185 supervisory circuits (*lu*), which in turn were grouped into 60 higher supervisory regions (*tao*), each subject to a Pacification Commission (*hsüan-wei ssu*). These were further grouped into a variable but final total of 12 protoprovinces. The region around Peking constituted one such area, directly administered by the metropolitan Secretariat. The other 11 regions were administered by Branch Secretariats, which though formally its equal in rank, in practice were clearly subordinate to the metropolitan Secretariat at Peking.* In addition, the metropolitan Censorate established two Branch Censorates, one in the west and

---

* The modern Chinese word that Westerners render as province, *sheng*, derives from the name of the Secretariat, chung-shu sheng. The Yüan protoprovinces came into being one by one as Mongol control expanded. With each new conquest, the Secretariat sent out a "mobile Secretariat," *hsing* chung-shu sheng, or briefly *hsing-sheng*, for the control of, say, Kiangsi. These "mobile Secretariats" then settled into place permanently, and their territorial jurisdictions came to be called sheng.

one in the south, which divided censorial surveillance over the Branch Secretariats with the metropolitan Censorate; and 24 Regional Surveillance Offices (*an-ch'a ssu* or *lien-fang ssu*) were created to keep watch over lower-level agencies—Pacification Commissions, circuits, and prefectures. Yet another hierarchy of agencies supervised the empire's military garrisons, grouped into six geographic jurisdictions under the Bureau of Military Affairs and its five branches. In other words, Yüan China was subdivided into three different kinds of "provinces," overlapping one another—twelve for general administration, three for censorial surveillance, and six for military control.

Provinces became more clearly defined under the Ming dynasty. In the mature Ming system after 1421 the regions around Peking and the auxiliary capital at Nanking, which had a skeletal central government similar to Peking's, were both directly administered metropolitan areas. The rest of the empire was divided into 13 provinces. Supervisory responsibility over each province was divided by functions among three agencies: a Provincial Administration Office (*pu-cheng ssu*) with general-administration responsibilities, a Provincial Surveillance Office (*an-ch'a ssu*) with Censorate-like functions, and a Regional Military Commission (*tu chih-hui ssu*). (There were three additional military

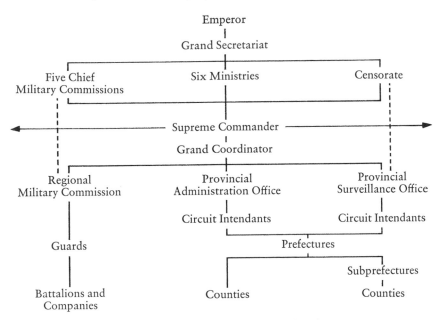

Basic governmental organization in Ming times

commissions in strategic zones along the northern frontier.) Both Provincial Administration Offices and Provincial Surveillance Offices supervised prefectures more closely by assigning officials to serve as various kinds of circuit intendants (*tao-t'ai*). The early Ming division of authority among these provincial agencies led to the emergence during the fifteenth century of two levels of higher supervisory offices. Thus every province—and in addition each of several strategic areas superimposed on the provincial grid—came to have a grand coordinator (*hsün-fu*); and large regions comprising two or more provinces came to have still more prestigious coordinators known as supreme commanders (*tsung-tu*) who, though civil officials, had principal responsibility for regional military concerns.

This Ming system of provincial-level government endured into modern times with few modifications.* The southern metropolitan area dominated by Nanking was transformed into two regular provinces, Kiangsu and Anhwei; and Mukden in central Manchuria became the Ch'ing auxiliary capital. The large Ming province in the central Yangtze region, Hukuang, was split into two provinces, Hupei and Hunan; and the farther parts of Shensi in the northwest became Kansu province.

Considered solely as an organizational structure, the mid-Ch'ing government was a stable, well-articulated, strongly centralized administrative mechanism. Its autocratic nature was reinforced by the central government's lack of any post from which one powerful bureaucratic leader could dominate the whole officialdom against the imperial interests; by the K'ang-hsi emperor's seventeenth-century practice of placing his personal bondservants in some key posts in the provinces; by the same emperor's initiation of a system of palace memorials by which both court and provincial officials could communicate directly, confidentially, and quickly with the throne, bypassing routine channels of communication in the administrative hierarchy; and not least by the repeated imperial progresses, or personal tours of inspection, that both the K'ang-hsi and the Ch'ien-lung emperors made from Peking into the densely populated south. Conducted with much pomp,

---

* Because of gradual shifts in functions that were evident by the late Ming years, specialists on the Ch'ing period prefer the terms provincial treasurer and provincial judge to the terms Provincial Administration Office and Provincial Surveillance Office, respectively; and Ch'ing grand coordinators and supreme commanders are commonly called provincial governors and governors-general, respectively. In all these cases, the Chinese terminology remained the same from Ming into Ch'ing times.

these imperial processions gave the Chinese masses a keen awareness of the presence, the majesty, and the awesome powers of those extraordinarily vigorous emperors.

PERSONNEL

Under the Sung dynasty and its successors, earlier experiments in building a civil service based on merit culminated in regularized, highly systematized, and prestigious personnel-recruitment procedures that persisted to the end of the imperial age. The Liao, Chin, and Yüan conquest dynasties naturally saw to it that their own ethnic groups dominated government despite the examination-recruitment tradition; the long-established practices of granting men official status on the basis of recommendations, inheritance privileges, and graduation from the national university continued; and in times of fiscal crises dynasties still permitted the limited purchase of official status and even of functional offices. Nevertheless, the Sung, the Ming, and even the alien Ch'ing dynasty, except in their early transitional years when irregular procedures could not be avoided, made those who had earned examination degrees the most honored members of officialdom, and officials with other backgrounds could seldom expect to attain high office.

Personnel administration generally developed in the patterns established in T'ang times. Sung made the system more open and egalitarian by fostering state-supported schools at the prefectural level, by terminating the near-monopoly on entrance to the national university that sons of officials had enjoyed in T'ang times, and above all, by making open, competitive preliminary examinations at the prefectural level prerequisite to examinations at the capital for a doctoral degree. The T'ang requirement of sponsorship by a prefect, which inevitably favored the scions of influential families, was abolished. Other efforts were made in Sung times to assure genuinely open, objective recruitment procedures. In the national, or metropolitan, examination the candidate's name on an examination paper was pasted over to prevent favoritism. Each paper was read and graded independently by three examiners. Later, when complaints of favoritism persisted in spite of these precautions, professional copyists were hired to copy out all papers before they were graded, so that an examiner could not identify the work of a protégé by his calligraphy. Finally, a third-level palace examination, in theory presided over by the emperor, was instituted to confirm the results of the metropolitan examination.

Some eleventh-century thinkers objected to this emphasis on egalitarianism in the recruitment system, which indeed served Legalist more than Confucian principles. The mid-century reformer Fan Chung-yen and others, in Confucian fashion, argued that knowledge of a candidate's family background and prior conduct was essential for predicting his success in government service. They protested the concealment of candidates' names from the examiners and urged that character references as well as examination performance be considered in rating prospective office-holders. Their arguments did not prevail and were not revived in subsequent centuries. Until the end of the imperial age the principles of anonymity and objectivity were honored, with varying effectiveness.

Sung at first relied on the great variety of doctoral examinations offered in the T'ang system, but after a reorganization of the system in 1071, instigated by the controversial reform minister Wang An-shih, the broad-ranging chin-shih examination was the only one of significance. After 1145, however, the scope of the chin-shih examination was narrowed, and candidates were thereafter allowed to choose between an examination emphasizing literary composition and one emphasizing the interpretation of the classics. Sung also followed the T'ang schedule of annual examinations for a time, but in 1067 the examinations were put on a triennial schedule, which remained standard into the twentieth century.

In Sung times the doctoral graduates seem to have provided about half of the regular officials required for service—a level that was never approached under the other dynasties of the later imperial age—and low-ranking offices were increasingly filled with prefectural graduates who could not take or pass the doctoral examinations, as well as with national university graduates, persons specially recommended by local officials, and sons of high-ranking officials entitled to inheritance privileges. It became commonplace for men who were entitled to official status by inheritance to seek the chin-shih degree through the regular examinations because of its greater prestige. The examination system produced an average of more than 200 new chin-shih a year through the Sung period. This was more than double the normal number produced annually in the late T'ang period and contrasted even more dramatically with the figures for the earliest T'ang years, when the number of doctoral degrees granted annually did not exceed 25.

The rapid rise of examination-recruited civil officials to dominance in Sung government was made possible by the spread of printing, under both government and private auspices, in the Five Dynasties era and the early Sung years. Education flourished, particularly in private academies and family schools, and candidates swarmed to the examinations in thousands.

As has been noted, the alien Liao, Chin, and Yüan dynasties tolerated recruitment examinations as a conciliatory gesture toward their Chinese subjects; but examination recruits were few and had only limited career opportunities in such times. Even the founder of the Ming dynasty, who exhibited a peasant anti-intellectualism in many ways, was hesitant about reestablishing the examinations after ousting the Mongols. He finally did so, at both the prefectural and the national level, in 1370-71. Ming T'ai-tsu was disappointed, however, with the 120 chin-shih who were produced. "We sincerely sought worthies," he said, "but the empire responded with empty phrase-makers." He suspended the examinations and did not allow them to be resumed until 1384-85. Thereafter they continued on triennial schedule through the Ming and Ch'ing dynasties.

Since Ming T'ai-tsu did not inherit from the Yüan dynasty a pool of experienced and reputable officials, he relied primarily on recommendations to staff his government in its earliest years. He also established premodern China's most extensive system of public education to produce men worthy of official appointment. Far more successfully than his Sung predecessors, he ordered the establishment of a state-supported school in every prefectural city and every county, and he authorized a quota of state-supported students for each school. From these schools a certain number of honor students were summoned to the capital as so-called tribute students (kung-sheng). There, as national university students (chien-sheng), they continued their studies and worked as apprentice officials. Upon completion of their studies, they were available for direct appointment as regular officials.

During the first half century or more of the Ming period, many graduates of the government school system had distinguished official careers. In the 1400's the degree-holders produced in the renewed examination-recruitment system once again became the bureaucratic elite, as in Sung times; even national university students preferred to win an examination degree before entering service because of its high prestige. But the state school system of the Ming period, supplemented by private academies that flourished especially in the sixteenth century, greatly expanded the supply of educated men who could be culled for service in the examinations and promoted widespread literacy. By Ch'ing times education had become so entrenched in general Chinese life that it was carried on primarily in small family and community schools. The state schools and even the private academies of the Ming tradition declined into little more than centers where certification examinations were given. The national university withered to an enrollment of about 300, in contrast to the normal Ming enrollment of 10,000.

In the examination system of Ming and Ch'ing times, the prospective degree-holder passed through three main stages on the way to a final, Sung-style palace examination. The first stage was a basic certification examination conducted at regular intervals by provincial education intendants. Candidates certified by the intendants as competent students (*sheng-yüan*, popularly called "cultivated talents," *hsiu ts'ai*) were entitled to wear distinctive caps and sashes, were exempted from state labor service, normally found themselves in demand to serve as tutors in well-to-do families, and were generally looked to for community leadership and intellectual skills. They were subject to periodic reexamination and could be deprived of their status, privileges, and prestige if they failed to maintain their scholastic competence or conducted themselves improperly.

All hsiu-ts'ai were eligible to participate in provincial examinations, which were offered every third year at each provincial capital in three day-long sessions spread over a week. By this time, only one kind of examination was given. It required a general knowledge of the classics and history, the ability to relate classical precepts and historical precedents to general philosophical principles or particular political issues, and competence in literary composition. Those who passed the provincial examination became *chü-jen* (elevated men, or licentiates), entitled to more honors and privileges. This status was permanent. A man who attained it could receive a direct appointment into some lower-level official post or could go on to take the metropolitan examination at the national capital, which was given a few months after the provincial examinations. The metropolitan examination was in the pattern of the provincial examination, on similar subject matter. Successful candidates became chin-shih (presented scholars, or doctors). The subsequent palace examination served merely to rank the new chin-shih in order of excellence. The highest-ranking chin-shih were appointed to posts in the Hanlin Academy in the expectation that the

Fig. 30. The imperial palace grounds, or Forbidden City, at Peking

most capable would eventually rise into the Grand Secretariat. They were celebrated as national heroes, publicly acclaimed as none but the greatest sports or war heroes are acclaimed in the modern West. Other new chin-shih became candidates for middle-echelon positions and were appointed to county magistracies and junior posts of other sorts as vacancies occurred.

Under both the Ming and the Ch'ing dynasties the examination competition was as intense as in Sung times, and perhaps grew more so. The number of provincial chü-jen degrees awarded each examination year rose from about 1,200 in the early Ming decades to about 1,800 in mid-Ch'ing times, and chin-shih degrees averaged 288 and 238 per examination in the Ming and Ch'ing dynasties, respectively—in other terms, only 89 and 100 a year, respectively, in contrast to the high Sung average of more than 200. Considerably less than 10 per cent of hsiu-ts'ai became chü-jen, though more than 10 per cent of all chü-jen may have become chin-shih.

The Sung examination system operated without any prescribed geographical quotas, and was criticized for creating a less representative civil service than the recommendation system had produced in Han and T'ang times. When the Yüan dynasty got around to instituting examinations in 1315, regional balance was restored to the extent that limits were set on the number of candidates from each province who could be presented for the metropolitan examination in any year. The Ming and Ch'ing dynasties carried the principle of representation further, limiting the number of chü-jen degrees that could be awarded in each province at any one time. Even so, southerners and especially southeasterners were disproportionately successful in the metropolitan examinations of the early Ming decades. In 1397 southerners took all the chin-shih degrees. Ming T'ai-tsu, himself a northerner, was infuriated; he put the chief examiner to death for favoritism, voided all the new degrees, and chose an all-northerner slate of graduates. Thereafter examiners were more prudent, but objective grading standards still placed northerners at a disadvantage. In the 1420's, consequently, strict objectivity was abandoned in favor of a regional quota system. Thenceforth candidates from the southern provinces were allowed only 55 per cent of chin-shih degrees in each examination; 10 per cent were reserved for westerners (primarily Szechwanese), and 35 per cent for northerners. In the Ch'ing dynasty the quota system was further refined to fix the number of chin-shih degrees allowed for each province. The quota systems of both the Ming and the Ch'ing dynasties generally reflected population distribution.

Ethnic considerations, as might be expected, affected the examination system under the alien dynasties. The Yüan dynasty established equal quotas for four categories of examination candidates: Mongols, Central Asians, North Chinese (that is, former subjects of the Jurchen Chin dynasty, including Jurchen and Ch'i-tan as well as Chinese), and South Chinese (who constituted perhaps 75 per cent of the total population in Yüan times). The Manchus were not so harshly discriminatory. Ethnic quotas were not established for the regular chü-jen and chin-shih examinations in Ch'ing times; Sinicized Manchus competed directly with Chinese if they wished, and some did so successfully. But a separate set of easier chin-shih examinations was provided for Manchus, Mongols, and Chinese who had early become hereditary members of the Manchu military units called banners. The number of degrees so granted was small, and Chinese scholar-officials were naturally contemptuous of them.

Several other factors reduced the intellectual quality of examination graduates in late Ming and especially Ch'ing times. For one thing, free thought was inhibited by a requirement initiated in Yüan times that candidates must utilize only classical interpretations approved by the Chu Hsi school of Neo-Confucianism; deviant interpretations of the classics were considered heretical. In addition, from mid-Ming times there developed a standard rhetorical form in which examination essays were to be written—an eight-part structure of presentation popularly called the "eight-legged essay" (pa-ku wen). Form (something that is plainly easier to grade objectively than content) became an increasingly important consideration, until by the mid-Ch'ing, examiners—and consequently students throughout the country—were more interested in the rhetorical structure of an essay than in any ideas it contained. Handbooks on the writing of eight-legged essays were produced, and by the nineteenth century the range of likely examination questions was so predictable that mass-produced answer books were available for prospective candidates to memorize. The quality of the examinations even degenerated to the point where examiners graded answers primarily on the basis of calligraphy, ignoring not only intellectual content, but even rhetorical form.

Except in the matter of recruitment procedures, the Sung, Ming, and Ch'ing dynasties generally continued the personnel-administration practices that had been standardized in T'ang times. Three years became the normal term of office in lower- and middle-echelon posts, though in Ming times appointments were made in the expectation that competent performance would result in two extensions, to a maximum nine-year term in any one post. Merit ratings by superiors and by touring censorial inspectors were regularly considered when an official was due for reappointment. Reappointment examinations of the T'ang sort gradually fell out of use in Sung times, and the principle of seniority, modified by merit ratings, gradually came to determine one's progress up the career ladder. In the first Sung century a new system of sponsorship or guaranteed recommendations was tried out. This required senior officials to recommend a specified number of capable junior officials at regular intervals. When vacancies occurred, candidates were selected on the basis of the number and the quality of the recommendations in their dossiers, and sponsors were given credit or were punished for their protégés' performance in office. Though the Sung sponsorship system was abandoned after the eleventh century as a regular procedure, later dynasties sometimes fell back on guaranteed recommendations to fill important posts.

Some of the irregularities that had troubled earlier dynasties were successfully curbed in the later imperial age. Usurpations by imperial relatives were far less common. Except in their earliest years, the Sung, Ming, and Ch'ing governments all gave stipends but very little political influence to members of the imperial family, and the relatives of empresses and imperial concubines were banned by law or at least by firm policy from important offices. The Yüan court, in contrast, was kept in turmoil by feuds, purges, and assassinations stemming from the powerful status accorded princes and empresses by the Mongols. The Sung, Yüan, and Ch'ing dynasties were all notably successful in preventing eunuch excesses—Sung apparently because of close, respectful relations between emperors and officials that gave ambitious eunuchs few opportunities to dominate emperors, Yüan and Ch'ing apparently because of ethnic solidarity in the ruling group. Ming experienced eunuch troubles as severe as any in Han or T'ang times, despite laws that harshly forbade eunuch interference in administration. The laws were largely ignored, apparently because the social gap that yawned between emperors and officials in the Ming system left emperors isolated, with no group other than eunuchs to turn to for informal discussions and relaxed personal relationships. The Ming emperors could not resist giving responsibilities and honors to these trusted friends and confidants. Partisan factionalism within the officialdom was the one major form of disruption that no dynasty successfully suppressed.

Under the Ch'ing dynasty the prestige and morale of the civil service at large declined. Whereas in Sung and Ming times scholar-officials enjoyed unchallenged supremacy as the natural leaders of society, in the Ch'ing dynasty they could never entirely escape the stigma of being collaborators with alien rulers, however Sinicized. The esteem of Chinese officials suffered further because, though they rose into high office far more freely and numerously than in earlier alien dynasties, Manchus and even Mongols of lesser scholastic qualifications entered the service more easily and rose to high rank more rapidly; in general, every senior Chinese official in the central government had to share his post and authority with a Manchu partner. Government service was demeaned by the large-scale sale of kung-sheng and chien-sheng status and privileges to anyone who could pay in the seventeenth century and again in the nineteenth, when functional posts too were sold to increase government income.

The prestige and morale of the officialdom also suffered because offi-

cial stipends were kept at their low Ming levels despite rising costs. The
Ch'ing government, recognizing this problem, authorized special salary
supplements. However, costs rose astronomically, particularly in local
governments, because population growth and ever more complex administrative responsibilities required a constantly expanding staff of
aides, clerks, and flunkeys of all sorts whose wages were not provided
for in the government budget and had to be paid by the magistrates
themselves. Even the most upright magistrate could manage only by
imposing irregular fees on the populace at every opportunity. Although
these exactions came to be sanctioned by local custom, they were cor-
rupting. Opportunities for self-enrichment by the exploitation of such
regularized corruption multiplied at every level of administration and
became irresistible. The systematic corruption of the whole governmental mechanism by the court favorite Ho-shen in the last decades
of the eighteenth century especially undermined discipline and morale;
and in the nineteenth century the trend toward apathetic, self-serving
acquiescence in corruption and deterioration seemed irreversible. By
the middle of the nineteenth century the officialdom's prestige and
morale were in a sorry state.

THE MILITARY

Military development in the later imperial age had several noteworthy characteristics. First, regional warlordism of the sort that had
recurringly disrupted earlier dynasties was successfully suppressed by
the centralization of control over the military, which prior history had
shown was essential for national unity and stability. Second, military
professionalism increased. The scholar-officials who dominated the
native dynasties generally wanted to control but not to participate
personally in military affairs, and the rulers of the alien dynasties naturally wanted to maintain preponderant military power in their own
ethnic groups. Military service thus became a separate way of life.
Hereditary soldiering became common, and China's ancient ideal of
a citizen-soldiery declined. Third, since the value system of scholar-
officials did not esteem military service, and since alien conquests led
to a xenophobic fear and hatred of soldiers among the general populace, the prestige of military careers declined. The ancient view that
military competence was integral to social leadership now gave way—
not wholly by any means, but markedly—to the view that civilian and
military competences were distinctly different things. Whereas an aris-

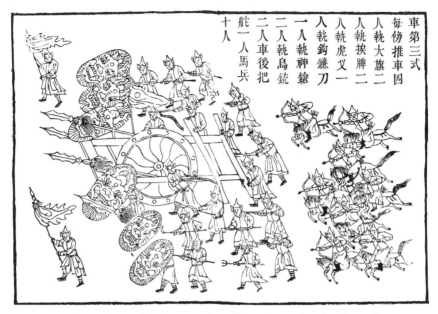

Fig. 31. Traditional woodblock print of a military formation showing a large spear-cart, flag bearers, bearers of fiercely decorated shields, pikemen, musketmen (the last row of foot soldiers), and a squad of mounted archers. From the late Ming military encyclopedia *Wu-pei chih*.

tocrat of Han and T'ang times could serve with equal distinction as a general or a magistrate, the increasingly widespread attitude in the later imperial age was expressed in a famous maxim: "The best iron is not to be used for nails, and the best men are not to be used for soldiers." Finally, firearms now became a standard part of the military arsenal, though the Chinese were quickly surpassed in this realm by the early modern Europeans.

The Sung military establishment consisted primarily of recruited professionals, the best and most numerous being stationed around the capital under generals who were directly responsible to the emperor. From the palace guard garrisons, contingents were rotated out to frontier defense units for three-year tours. Frontier generals thus had no opportunities to build personal followings among their troops. Moreover, the combined frontier forces were always outnumbered by the concentrations left around the capital. Less capable recruits were assigned to small peace-keeping garrisons scattered throughout the country under the control of military intendants. In times of need, these regional units were supplemented by conscripted militiamen. The total number of

men in service exceeded one million in the eleventh century and remained at that high level in Southern Sung times. The cost of maintaining such a force was enormous, and the career soldiers were often
arrogant and undisciplined. But they were well equipped with armor
and weapons by the iron and steel industry, which particularly flourished in Sung times, and they sometimes fought very well against the
onslaughts of Ch'i-tan, Jurchen, and Mongol invaders. In the twelfth
century the Sung armies effectively used fire bombs and tank-like carts
sheathed in iron armor against Jurchen cavalrymen, and in the thirteenth century they defended walled cities against the Mongols with a
variety of explosives shot from catapults and bazooka-like bamboo
tubes.

The eleventh-century reformer Wang An-shih tried to strengthen
Sung's defenses and reduce their costs by reinstituting the universal
militia obligations of the Ch'in-Han era. This was one of the main purposes of his pao-chia registration system, which was designed to make
the various household groups responsible for providing and provision-
ing conscripts. But the pao-chia draftees proved reluctant to serve in
more than a home-guard capacity, and the professionals resisted efforts
to introduce draftees into the palace guards and the frontier garrisons.
This aspect of Wang's reform program was therefore abandoned.

Tribal organization was characteristic of the Ch'i-tan and Jurchen
military systems, but the Mongols broke up tribal groupings into a
more centralized hierarchy of units called hundreds, thousands, and
myriads (literally, ten thousands) commanded by Mongol nobles. These
units were garrisoned throughout China and were supported primarily
from the produce of large tracts of confiscated land worked by enslaved
peasants. As in Sung times, the largest and most reliable armies were
clustered around the capital as palace guards. The elite force was a
large imperial bodyguard, the *kesig*, comprising four units that served
in daily rotation as palace attendants. The kesig, consisting largely of
sons of Mongol nobles, was a notoriously arrogant corps virtually
above the law; it played a disruptive governmental role similar to that
of palace eunuchs in some other dynasties.

The most privileged Yüan armies were those made up of Mongol
tribesmen; but there were auxiliary units, in descending order of prestige and privilege, of Central Asians, North Chinese (including Ch'i-
tan and Jurchen), and South Chinese (largely surrendered professionals
of the Sung army). Service in all the regular Yüan dynasty armies was

Fig. 32. The Great Wall near Peking as rebuilt in the Ming dynasty

hereditary. The civilian population was called on to provide militia-men for limited local police duty but otherwise was harshly forbidden to possess weapons of any sort or engage in military drills. Under the Yüan dynasty the iron and steel industry declined from its high Sung level of development, and military technology fell back to the bow-and-arrow stage where the Mongols felt most comfortable.

The founder of the native Ming dynasty built a strong military estab-lishment by incorporating some elements of the Yüan system with others traceable to the fu-ping militia of the T'ang tradition. Many of the rebel soldiers who helped him oust the Mongols joined later re-cruits, some conscripts, and certain categories of convicts in becoming hereditary members of his million-man standing army. In the traditional pattern, he clustered most of his garrisons around the capital and along the northern frontier, but he also took care to locate garrisons at stra-tegic places throughout the empire. Each garrison was allotted a tract of government-owned land (a *t'un-t'ien*, or military colony), which the soldiers themselves were required to work in shifts to provide for their own maintenance; Ming T'ai-tsu boasted that his army was not a fiscal burden on the civilian population. The basic garrison unit was a *wei* (a guard) with a normative strength of about 5,000 men; wei were subdivided into *so* (battalions or companies), often detached from the *wei* headquarters. Soldiers and officers of wei and *so* throughout the country were summoned periodically into special training divisions at the capital. Men of the garrisons along the northern frontier manned the Great Wall fortifications, and those garrisoned elsewhere manned coastal forts or filled other sorts of active duty posts—all on rotational deployment from their garrisons, under the command of tactical officers directed by provincial-level regional commanders. For large-scale campaigns, men were gathered from wei and *so* throughout the country into ad hoc tactical units commanded by officers who were specially delegated from the five Chief Military Commissions at the capital and took their orders from the civil service Ministry of War. This division of authority between garrison commanders and tactical commanders was an important factor in the successful prevention of warlordism in Ming times.

The wei-so system was not as effective as it was designed to be. Desertion early became a serious problem, and the bureaucratic mechanisms for replacing deserters and the dead according to prescribed hereditary principles were cumbersome and inefficient. Moreover, few garrisons proved genuinely self-sufficient, especially in the poor agrarian districts along the frontiers where large forces were needed. From the middle of the fifteenth century on, the central government had to provide annual cash subsidies, and these steadily increased. Even with this support, the wei-so standing army declined in strength and fighting ability. It was supplemented by local militiamen, then by conscripts from the general population, and finally in the last Ming century by recruited mercenaries in awesome numbers. In the last Ming decades the military rolls swelled to a reported total of four million men. But they were poorly equipped, ill trained, and irregularly fed and clothed; only a small fraction of the total can have been effective soldiers.

In both the Ming and the Ch'ing dynasties, the development of firearms lagged. The early Ming emperors fostered the production of some new weapons, and cannons became standard equipment in defense fortifications. In the sixteenth century the Chinese produced imitations of Portuguese cannons and handguns, and in the 1600's Portuguese at

Macao contributed both guns and gunners for Ming campaigns against the Manchus. In the Ch'ing dynasty the Manchus continued the Ming practice of imitating and borrowing Western weapons but used them as the Ming Chinese did, almost exclusively in static defense. Though in the eighteenth century Ch'ing armies employed field artillery effectively in the Ch'ien-lung emperor's campaigns against the western Mongols, the imperial forces were still unaccustomed to the regular use of firearms a century later, and the firearms that were in use were of notably poor quality compared with Western weaponry.

The military establishment with which the Manchus controlled China was founded on a grouping of Manchu tribespeople into all-purpose governmental units called banners (from their identifying insignia). The adult males of each banner constituted an army. An early set of four banners evolved into a final total of eight Manchu banners—four primary-color banners and four "bordered" banners. From among their early allies and captives the Manchus also organized eight Mongol banners and eight Chinese banners. The bannermen were garrisoned throughout the country in wei-so style, similarly provided with state lands for their own support. Like their Ming counterparts, the Ch'ing hereditary bannermen gradually degenerated in peacetime into state pensioners unfit for service. By the beginning of the nineteenth century the dynasty's military power rested in fact on recruits from the general Chinese population, organized into what were called "green standards," and the dynasty survived the mid-century Taiping Rebellion largely because of the service of these and other Chinese units specially recruited by Chinese officials. In the process of such changes a foundation was laid for a resurgence of regional warlordism, which flourished after the fall of the dynasty in 1912.

12. Society and the Economy

THE SOCIAL and economic history of China during the later imperial age is complex and controversial—not least because the development of bureaucratic centralism described in Chapter 11 favored institutional standardization, while at the same time the growth of the population and the economy necessitated many local variations in organizational patterns. The general trends of socioeconomic development from Sung into Ch'ing times are nevertheless clear. A nonhereditary, literate managerial class became the new mainstay of the social order— basically a class of landowners, but one that eventually derived as much income from commercial investments and salaried services as from land rents. The Sung era was a time of dramatic growth in population, urbanism, commercialization, monetization, and technology. These trends were arrested by the Mongol conquest and the retrenchment policies of the early Ming. Then in the sixteenth century much of the lost momentum was regained; the population grew to enormous size and became densely distributed throughout the whole of China Proper. The countryside was increasingly filled with market towns of intermediate size. Commercial pursuits became more attractive than agriculture to many families, rich and poor alike. The legal and social discrimination against artisans and merchants that had characterized the earlier age gradually disappeared. Society generally became more leveled and egalitarian. But population growth outran other kinds of growth, resulting in severe socioeconomic disequilibrium by the beginning of the nineteenth century. Technology in particular stagnated; the native tradition did not produce an industrial revolution. For the first time in history China found itself at a technological disadvantage relative to the outside world. On the domestic scene the gap between rich and poor widened, and the utterly impoverished became ominously numerous.

POPULATION

Since taxes were now based primarily on land rather than on persons, and since regular military forces were no longer conscripted systematically from the population at large, governments of the later imperial age were not particularly interested in precise head counts. Census records of the Sung and later dynasties are therefore particularly unreliable. In combination with other kinds of evidence, however, they make possible some reasonable generalizations about population. Domestic peace, new crops, and technological advances fostered a dramatic population growth in the eleventh century, from a Five Dynasties-era level of perhaps fifty or sixty million to about one hundred million. The Jurchen and Mongol invasions seem to have reduced the population of China Proper to the old T'ang level of about sixty million by the beginning of the Ming dynasty. The long Ming peace brought the level back up to one hundred million, probably in the early 1500's, and well beyond that level—perhaps even approaching two hundred million—by 1600. Despite the devastations of the late Ming rebellions, the Chinese population swelled to more than three hundred million by 1750 and beyond four hundred million by 1850.* Some of the reasons for this growth will be discussed later in this chapter.

In the Northern Sung period population was about equally divided between north and south. The Jurchen conquest of the north in the twelfth century tilted the balance southward for the first time in history: Southern Sung had a population of some sixty million compared with a total of forty million or so in the Jurchen Chin state in North China. The Mongol assaults of the thirteenth century were more devastating in Chin territory than in Southern Sung territory, so that in the Yüan period the north had no more than 25 per cent and perhaps as little as 10 per cent of the total population. The early Ming emperors took vigorous steps to repopulate the north, and by 1600 the area reportedly claimed 40 per cent of the total population once again, though it is doubtful that the recovery was as complete as all that. In addition

---

* For contrast, consider that in 1800 there were only about four million residents of the United States, fewer than in the smallest Chinese province; that the populations of the United Kingdom and France were around six million; and that the number of people in the whole of Russia approached perhaps only thirty million.

to the northward movements of people in Ming times, there were large migrations from the congested southeast to the west and southwest. It was only during this period that the substantial Chinese occupation of the age-old aboriginal lands in Kweichow and Yunnan got under way. As population pressures continued to build, the Ch'ing government encouraged migration to the only remaining significant area of low population density in China Proper, Szechwan province, where the late Ming rebellions had taken a particularly heavy toll. Otherwise, there was no place for surplus people to go except into the unproductive hilly areas that separate the Yangtze valley from the southern coastal valleys (including the hilly southwest) and the equally infertile highlands of west central China between the provinces of Szechwan, Shensi, and Hupei. Such terrain could not absorb large populations. The newly arrived farmers who worked it stripped away the last forests of China Proper, causing erosion and drainage problems. Manchuria, which had great agricultural potentiality, was closed to immigrants and kept as a special Manchu preserve.

By 1850, when the total population was about 412,000,000, the south had well over half the population and the north well under a third. The population distribution in the major regions can be tabulated as follows:

Area	Per cent	Total
Yangtze delta (Chekiang, Kiangsu, Anhwei)	27%	111,000,000
Central Yangtze valley (Kiangsi, Hunan, Hupei)	17+	77,000,000
Szechwan basin	11	44,000,000
South coast (Fukien, Kwangtung)	10	40,000,000
Inland southwest (Kwangsi, Kweichow, Yunnan)	5	19,000,000
North China lowland (Shantung, Hopei, Honan)	19+	79,000,000
Highland northwest (Shansi, Shensi, Kansu)	10	42,000,000

URBANISM

The urbanizing of Chinese life accelerated during the Sung dynasty. In the eleventh century at least ten cities were the centers of densely populated metropolitan areas of a million or more per prefecture: Kaifeng and Loyang in Honan, Taiyuan in Shansi, and Ta-ming in Hopei, all in the north; and in the south Changsha in Hunan, Chi-an in Kiangsi, Hangchow and Shao-hsing in Chekiang, and Foochow and Ch'üanchou in Fukien. The flight from the north before the Jurchen invaders in the twelfth century intensified urbanization in the south, especially in the Yangtze delta area. The Southern Sung capital, Hangchow, is estimated by some specialists to have had a resident population of two

Fig. 33. "Dragon-boat Regatta at Kaifeng": detail from scroll painting by Wang Chen-p'eng (Yüan)

million within the city walls, surrounded by another two million suburbanites. This was "the great city Quinsai" Marco Polo described to an enthralled and disbelieving Europe, whose greatest cities at that time had at most 50,000 residents. Another European visitor of the Yüan era reported that the residents of the congested market quarters at any one of the 13 gates in Hangchow's city wall exceeded the total population of Venice.

In Yüan and Ming times the pace of urbanization slackened somewhat, and the number of prefectures with populations in excess of a million probably declined. But such great Yangtze delta metropolises as Hangchow and Soochow continued to flourish. Their magnificence and beauty became legendary even among the Chinese, who circulated a ditty that boasted: "Above are the Halls of Heaven; here below, Soochow and Hangchow." Into Ch'ing times Soochow, Hangchow, and Nanking were the preeminent cities of the empire. Their only near counterpart in the north was Peking, and that city flourished only as the national capital. Shanghai, the largest city of modern China, did not become an important center until the mid-nineteenth century, when it was opened to Westerners for residence and trade.

The metropolises of Sung and later times were much more complex social structures than the important cities of the early imperial age, which had developed predominantly as administrative centers. The Northern Sung capital, Kaifeng, for example, though by no means a renowned pleasure resort, is said to have had more than 50 theaters where audiences, in some houses numbering several thousand, were regularly entertained by professional acrobats, dancers, clowns, musicians, and troupes of actors. Hangchow in its heyday as the Southern Sung capital claimed 17 amusement districts, whose theaters often had multiple tiers of balconies. The greatest Ming metropolis, Soochow, was actually more important as a pleasure resort for the wealthy than as an administrative center; but it was also a great manufacturing, trading, and publishing center and a gathering place for scholars, artists, and poets.

Through the Ming and Ch'ing dynasties the urbanizing trend had a different character than in the Sung period, in which these great metropolises had emerged and developed very rapidly. Now the great cities by and large ceased to grow. But intermediate-sized market towns mushroomed in what had been open countryside—not administrative centers at all in origin, but basically commercial centers rising in response to the spreading out and burgeoning of the population everywhere. By 1800 there was virtually no peasant village that did not have ready access to such a town, and no villager who was not well enough acquainted with city ways to be something of a suburbanite in outlook.

THE LEVELING OF SOCIETY

The growth of population, commerce, and towns in the later imperial age was accompanied by an egalitarian trend in society akin to that of the ancient Warring States epoch. Except for the ethnic inequities imposed by the alien dynasties, one's pedigree was less and less an indicator of social success. Wealth became increasingly the major determinant of social status, and people moved both up and down the social scale very rapidly. The practice of dividing properties equally among all male heirs made it difficult for any family to maintain high status for more than three generations.

The classical stratification scheme that ranked shih (office-holders, now genuinely scholar-officials), farmers, artisans, and merchants in descending order of social value persisted in theory, but in reality society was stratified in much more complex ways. The Mongol Yüan dynasty reflected this complexity in its attempts to freeze and stabilize society in a rigid hereditary system as practiced in some of the pre-T'ang Northern Dynasties. Yüan classified everyone hereditarily into minutely subdivided categories—ordinary commoners, scholars, physicians, Yang-Yin astrologers, soldiers, military agricultural workers, artisans, salt producers, miners, and so on. The more specialized occupational groups were required to provide services needed by the state according to rotational quotas.

The same system was continued in the Ming period, most notably in the cases of military families, salt-producing families, and various families of carpenters, masons, and other artisans whose services were regularly commandeered by the state. There were two types of artisan families, those permanently resident in the capital and more or less permanently employed by the state, and those living in the provinces who carried on their occupations privately but by turns traveled to the capital for prescribed periods of service. In both Yüan and Ming times it was relatively easy for artisan families to buy exemptions from state service, and by 1562 commutation to money payments was generally compulsory.

In the Ch'ing period hereditary service was required only of banner military families, salt-producing families, and a new small group of state-licensed salt-marketing families whose status was made hereditary in late Ming times. With the obvious exception of military families, the hereditary-service families never amounted to a significant proportion of the total population. Moreover, their hereditary status was solely a device for assuring the state of service; it carried no discriminatory implications.

The early dynasties' discriminatory laws against nonfarming families, which at least in theory excluded artisans and merchants from eligibility for government office, gradually became inoperative in late T'ang and Sung times. In the Ming and Ch'ing dynasties such legal discrimination was applicable only to persons of "mean status." These included the most menial servants in government establishments, slaves, prostitutes, entertainers, and various local outcast groups such as the boat people of the Canton area. "Mean status" people were notably segregated from the respectable citizenry in many ways, and their descendants were excluded from the civil service for at least three generations. But in Ming and Ch'ing times no other groups were formally discriminated against; not only members of artisan and merchant families, but even members of hereditary military families were eligible for the civil service. Finally the Yung-cheng emperor (r. 1722-35) legally "emancipated" even those of "mean status," though they continued to be discriminated against in practice.

Egalitarianism was especially facilitated by the spread of education, which is one of the most noteworthy characteristics of the later imperial age. It now became a realistic goal for vast numbers of Chinese families to release at least one son from immediately productive work to take advantage of the new opportunities for education. From the early Ming years villagers were encouraged, and sometimes forced, to establish and support village schools. There the bright sons of poor families were able to get an elementary training that might bring them to the attention of magistrates and education intendants, under whose patronage they could make a start on the road to officialdom as state-subsidized students. Private academies (shu-yüan) had flourished from Sung times, established cooperatively by the scholars of cities and towns. They accumulated libraries, sponsored lectures and discussions on philosophical subjects, and fostered the preparation of local boys for the examinations. In Ming times private academies were sometimes suppressed as centers of unorthodox or even subversive thought, but they were more often given government encouragement and subsidies in the same spirit with which earlier governments had showered gifts and exemptions on religious establishments. Well-to-do families and well-organized clans hired private tutors or established small private schools in the fashion of the earlier aristocracy, and in greatly increasing numbers in the Ch'ing period.

The role of printing in the social leveling process can hardly be overemphasized. Printing had developed steadily through T'ang and Five Dynasties times. The technique, which no doubt evolved from the early Chinese use of seals and rubbings (paper reproductions taken from stone inscriptions), was to print from carved woodblocks, giving exact reproductions of manuscript pages. The oldest datable printed materials were produced in 770—one million copies of a Buddhist charm that were run off in China on commission from a Japanese empress. Buddhists, recognizing the value of printing for the spread of religious propaganda, were among the most diligent early promoters of printing. The oldest extant printed book, dated May 11, 868, is a copy of a Buddhist sutra consisting of six sheets of text and one sheet of illustration pasted together to form a 16-foot-long scroll. The preface states it was printed "for Wang Chieh, for free general distribution, in order with deep reverence to perpetuate the memory of his parents" (an example of the ways in which Confucian social values were fostered by Buddhist practitioners). By the end of T'ang the government was regularly issuing an official gazette—a printed newspaper announcing new regulations and appointments and other matters of interest to its official clientele. In 953, in the Five Dynasties era, a complete 130-volume set of the Confucian classics with commentaries was printed under government sponsorship.

From this promising start, printing became a flourishing industry in the Sung dynasty, when government and private printers alike produced some of the most admired specimens of the art. Movable type was quickly developed—made of pottery, tin, wood, and finally, in the Yüan dynasty, lead. However, because of the formidable task of handling the huge quantity of movable type needed for even the most commonly used Chinese characters, woodblock printing remained the standard Chinese technique into the twentieth century. In the Ming dynasty multicolor block printing was perfected. Probably the most monumental printing job of the whole imperial age, and one of the greatest of all world history, was completed in the earliest years of the Sung dynasty, between 972 and 983, with the publication of the entire Buddhist canon, the Tripitaka—1,521 works totaling some 130,000 pages, each printed from a separate woodblock. The set was reprinted 20 times during the Sung and Yüan dynasties from the original woodblocks.

Besides religious and classical works, printing made possible the wide dissemination of agricultural and technological treatises that contributed to rapid increases in productivity in Sung times and of general how-to-do-it encyclopedias and works of colloquial literature in Yüan, Ming, and Ch'ing times. Not later than the sixteenth century a remarkably large proportion of the Chinese population must have been literate on at least an elementary level.

The leveling of society was also facilitated by the flourishing of clan organizations from early Sung times on. This in some part reflected the new emphasis given to Confucian values by the governments of the later dynasties. The old Ch'in-Han aversion to extended families had vanished; it was now official dogma that the more generations were kept together in one household, the stabler society would be. The noted eleventh-century scholar-official Fan Chung-yen, among others, promoted the organizing of related families of a region into a corporate clan for the common welfare—to maintain clan schools and temples, to support clan widows and orphans, to provide loans to needy clan members, and in general to foster clan interests of every sort. Fan and others arranged for parcels of land to be entailed as clan properties in perpetuity, the rental income from which was to be used for such clan enterprises. They also wrote out and published "clan instructions" setting forth standards for personal conduct and principles for the management of clan affairs. In some measure clans replaced the old aristocratic great families as locally powerful groups that could protect individuals and nuclear families against the abuses of local officials and their agents. Clan leaders were looked to by government authorities for guarantees of local stability and for leadership in establishing and maintaining desirable community projects. Clan organization became particularly prevalent in South China, and especially in Fukien province. Most of today's great southern families trace their genealogies back into the Sung period.

The secret society was another type of organization that intervened between individuals and the government. These societies had a long history in China, dating back at least to the Han period. There were societies of religious motivation (generally called *chiao*), and others of solely political motivation (*hui*). Most advocated the ideals of fraternalism, chivalry, traditional morality, and—especially in the Ch'ing dynasty—xenophobic patriotism; and each characteristically had a complicated apparatus of secret passwords, hand signs, oaths, and sacred numbers, and even a special language and script. In the pre-Ch'ing era the most active society was the White Lotus Society, originally a militant, messianic Buddhist order. It endured into Ch'ing times and often joined forces with other patriotic groups that advocated restoration of the Ming dynasty. But the dominant Ch'ing societies stemmed more directly from Ming loyalist groups of the earliest Ch'ing years. Their common base was the Hung Society, which had two main branches—one known as the Triad Society or the Heaven and Earth Society, the other as the Society of Elders. These spawned a wide range of transitory local branches with bizarre names. Although the societies had something of a gangland quality and indulged in protection and other extortion rackets, they had broad popular support, provided a framework for popular communication and organization, and were a potential threat to the stability of the Manchu empire. Their uprisings intensified in the late 1700's and early 1800's, culminating in the massive Taiping Rebellion of 1850-65.

THE NEW MANAGERIAL CLASS

Following the disappearance of the early imperial aristocracy in the rampant warlordism of the late T'ang years and the Five Dynasties era, Chinese society at large was dominated by a class that is very difficult to define with precision. It was certainly not legitimated by birth, and though military leaders emerged from or joined it, it was by no means characteristically a military class. The Chinese commonly refer to it as a class of degree-holders, which Westerners like to call the literati. Many modern Westerners refer to the class as a whole as the gentry, a term that unfortunately evokes a misleading image of the English country squire of Victorian fiction. Some innocuous term such as the social elite is perhaps best applied to the group.

The new elite, like the old aristocracy, dominated government service and managed society. It did not engage in manual labor. In Sung times, when commerce was still tainted with some social disapprobation, the elite families were typically large landowners. But as time passed and commercial pursuits became more esteemed and more profitable, they increasingly rented out their lands and supplemented their agricultural incomes with investments in mercantile, industrial, and moneylending enterprises in the cities and towns. Their life-styles consequently became increasingly urban, intellectual, and cultured. Whether as landowners or as entrepreneurs, this was the group that had greatest access to education. Adopting the Great Tradition of the long past, it steeped itself in the classics and histories and became the pillars of conservative Confucianism, while at the same time seeking profit and pleasure in the commercial bustle, the often bawdy entertainments, and the general bourgeois comforts and attractions of the towns.

In its lower echelons the elite included a broad range of shopkeepers, small-scale manufacturers and wholesalers, property managers, publishers of mass-audience literature, hack writers and painters, and government clerks. In its upper strata were millionaire businessmen; the most famous by far were the Ch'ing dynasty salt monopolists of the Huai River area, who lived on a lavish scale and were liberal in their patronage of promising scholars and litterateurs.

The social elite provided the vast majority of the candidates for the government's recruitment examinations, and was thus the single most important source from which the dynastic governments drew their officials. Since wealth gave access to officialdom, and since official status protected and generated wealth (because of tax exemptions, other legal privileges, and abuses of power), much modern scholarship has been devoted to clarifying whether wealth begot status or status wealth. But status and wealth were so intertwined and mutually supportive that the question seems unanswerable.

Another intriguing question is whether or not the new social order was more "democratic" than the old—that is, whether or not the new elite was self-perpetuating and effectively excluded "new blood." Since examination candidates had to name and identify the class status of their fathers and paternal grandfathers and great-grandfathers, it has been relatively easy to determine that men whose paternal forebears for three generations had not produced degree-holders consistently won more than half of all chin-shih degrees in Sung and Ming times but steadily lost ground in Ch'ing times, falling to a level about 30 per cent in the nineteenth century. Nonstatistical evidence supports the conclusion that men of genuinely poor backgrounds sometimes won chin-shih degrees and had distinguished official careers in the Sung dynasty, that they did so only slightly less often in the Ming dynasty, and

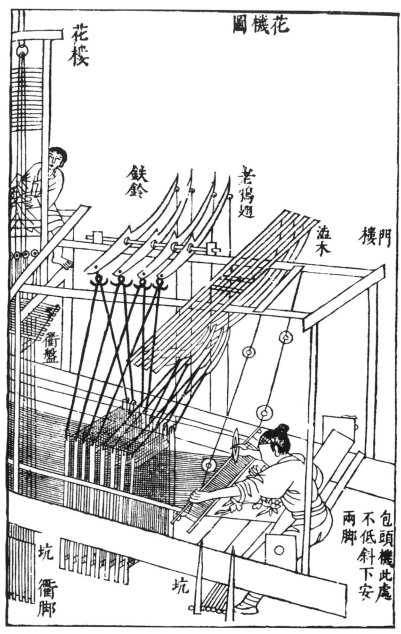

Fig. 34. Section of a drawing of a 16-foot-long drawloom for the weaving of silks, including gauzes, damasks, pongees, and even such small items as kerchiefs. From the illustrated encyclopedia of applied technology *T'ien-kung k'ai-wu* (1637).

that they seldom if ever did so in the Ch'ing dynasty. If evidence about the collateral relatives (brothers, uncles, maternal relations of all sorts) and about the economic status of candidates could be taken into account systematically, it would undoubtedly show that well-to-do families with political connections were always overwhelmingly successful in placing sons on the chin-shih lists, and that in Ch'ing times especially the Chinese equivalent of the American "log cabin to White House" ideal faded almost totally. Measuring the average number of annual chin-shih degrees against the total population, the ratio changed from about 1 : 500,000 in Sung, to 1 : 1,000,000 in mid-Ming times, and to about 1 : 4,000,000 in 1800. The odds against success were therefore always astronomical, and by the nineteenth century a young man's prospects had become crushingly disheartening to say the least.

Another aspect of the situation, however, is that lower-level scholastic degrees proliferated in Ming and especially Ch'ing times, when it became possible for almost any man of more than modest means to purchase a degree, and so acquire some government-sanctioned privileges and feel himself a person of substance. Although the lower degrees did not entitle one to bureaucratic office, they did open doors to employment as aides to officials, as tutors, secretaries, or business managers for the wealthy, and as managers of locally organized public enterprises such as water-control projects. Thus the popular saying, "Heaven is high, and the emperor is far away," was indeed true in Ch'ing times; the whole officialdom had become so elevated and remote that to see even so lowly an official as a county magistrate in person was a rare event. The average commoner could have had no realistic hope of having a son become a chin-shih. At the same time, he had every reason to expect that one of his sons, with hard work and luck, could improve the family fortunes and status substantially by rising into the lower level of the managerial elite, so that the family could escape from the drudgery of hard manual labor at least for a generation or two. For the average man, that was undoubtedly hope enough.

Even so, because of mounting overpopulation, by mid-Ch'ing times the countryside teemed with millions who lacked even this hope. Permanently disenfranchised, so to speak, they had no stake in the traditional political system and social order and no concern for the traditional cultural values of Chinese civilization. When this mass of malcontents was ignited by the Taiping Rebellion, China's imperial tradition was doomed, and the transformation began that would lead a century later to the firmly antitraditional People's Republic.

GENERAL ECONOMIC DEVELOPMENTS

Chinese of the later imperial age benefited from the long-accumulated agrarian, technological, industrial, and commercial expertise of their predecessors, and especially in the Sung dynasty they continued to be ingeniously creative in all these regards. In the eleventh and twelfth centuries China was not only the most populous and urbanized country in the world; it was also the most advanced and sophisticated country in the world in its agriculture, industry, marketing, and trade. In retrospect, Sung China seems to have been on the verge of developing a genuine "modern" economy—commercialized, industrialized, monetized, and to some extent even mechanized. In most respects, eleventh-century China was at a level of economic development not achieved by any European state until the eighteenth century at the earliest. These achievements set the stage for the later empire's explosive population growth. But the pace of economic development then slowed. The complexities of the economic system seem eventually to have outgrown China's managerial competence. And a combination of circumstances—a xenophobic withdrawal from outside contacts after the traumatic Jurchen and Mongol conquests, the introspective intellectualism bred by Neo-Confucianism, the domination of state and society by doctrinaire scholar-officials, the increasing centralization of authority, and centuries of sustained affluence—led to self-satisfied conservatism. Agriculture reached the productivity limits of available land and known technology soon after 1750, but the population kept on growing. The standard of living consequently declined, and market demand fell below manufacturing capacity. China was not prepared to cope with such problems of the domestic economy in the nineteenth century, much less those created by Westerners clamoring ever more disruptively at its ports.

Agriculture. Increases in the productive capacity of Chinese agriculture during the later imperial age were nothing short of revolutionary. There were two main phases of development: the perfection of wet-rice agriculture beginning in Northern Sung; and the introduction of new dry-field and marginal-land crops in the late Ming and early Ch'ing periods.

Through mid-T'ang times, as has been observed repeatedly in foregoing chapters, the Chinese population was concentrated in the north, and the food products of the dry north—primarily millets—were the staple foodstuffs. In late T'ang and early Sung times, as the south became more densely populated, the wet-field rice that flourishes there became an increasingly important element in total agricultural production and in the national diet. The Chinese quickly saw the advantages of cultivating rice because of its high yield of food per acre but there were problems in increasing its production. The rice crops then being grown in South China involved an enormous amount of labor per acre and required as many as 150 days to ripen after transplantation from seedbeds. In the absence of water-control systems to ensure an abundant and regular water supply, they were easily damaged by drought. And they were often ruined by the typhoons that ravage the coastal areas late every summer.

To increase rice production the early Sung emperors sent traveling agricultural experts to the south and widely disseminated pamphlets among the peasantry to introduce new farm tools such as improved plows and harrows, to foster the development of dams, dikes, sluice-gates, treadle water pumps, and other water-control devices, and especially to spread new seed strains that were originally introduced from Champa (southern Vietnam) and then further developed by selective breeding in China. The government also promoted the planting of northern wheat as a winter crop in the south and the use of fertilizers. As population growth and urbanization proceeded in the south, organic manure became easily available, and by the end of the Sung period the distribution of human wastes from cities and towns to the farming countryside for use as fertilizer had become a large, well-organized industry—the "honey-bucket" business that all Western visitors to modern East Asia quickly become aware of. During Southern Sung, also, the terracing of South China's well-watered hillsides began.

The most revolutionary and far-reaching of the Sung advances was the introduction of the so-called Champa rices. These new strains were more drought-resistant than China's earlier rices, and above all they were fast-ripening. The growing season for rice was rapidly reduced to 120 days, then to 100 days, and by the end of Sung, thanks to continuing experimentation with seed breeding, to 60 days. In post-Sung times further progress was made: 50-day, 40-day, and by Ch'ing times even 30-day rices were developed. As a result, even as early as Sung times, double-cropping of many sorts was possible, depending on local variations in soil and climate. It became standard in the south for two rice crops to be harvested from the same field each year, followed by a winter wheat crop. In some areas three rice crops a year were possible. It became especially common for quick-ripening and slower-ripening rice strains to be interplanted, so that something could be harvested every year no matter how the weather might vary.

These improvements brought unprecedented prosperity to Sung China and facilitated China's economic recovery after the disruptions of the Mongol conquest and occupation. The introduction of sorghums in Yüan as popular supplements to the wheat and millet staples of the dry areas aided the Ming efforts to repopulate the devastated north.

The great spurt of population growth from 1600 on resulted from the cumulative effects of these agrarian innovations, but also in part from the introduction in the sixteenth century of maize, sweet potatoes, and peanuts, which spread from the Americas in the wake of European exploration and colonization. Maize and sweet potatoes were especially advantageous because they could be grown in traditionally uncultivable lands—sandy soils everywhere, and the dry hills of the north and the central inland provinces. Chinese dietary preferences for millets and rice retarded the spread of the new crops, but the government encouraged their production vigorously in the early Ch'ing centuries. As a result, by 1800 maize and sweet potatoes accounted for a substantial proportion of China's total food production and were staple foods of the poor. Meanwhile, as the hillsides were turned into marginal farmlands the deforestation of China Proper was almost completed, and large tracts of lowland farms were ruined by runoff. The proportion of rice in the total food production declined, and its price rose steadily. In the end rice became more a luxury than a staple for poorer Chinese.

Food production in the later centuries of the imperial age was affected adversely when numbers of Chinese farmers began growing cash crops, especially cotton and, to a much lesser extent, tobacco. Cotton was introduced in China in Sung times and was encouraged by both the Yüan and Ming governments against stout peasant resistance, but in the fifteenth century it became a major crop. Tobacco was known in China by 1600 and rapidly became popular despite government efforts to restrain its production. As population multiplied the growing need for food products restricted and probably reduced the production of these and other cash crops.

The later imperial age experienced a transformation of agricultural organization as well as production. The confiscation of vast estates owned by Buddhist monasteries and the dissolution of the old aristocracy in the rebellions and warlordism of the late T'ang era seem to have recreated a rural population of free peasants. But, as always before, free peasants found it difficult to maintain themselves against the encroachments of the wealthy and privileged. In the Sung dynasty, though freehold peasants existed in large numbers and together with independent tenant farmers must have constituted a majority of the rural population, large landowners were again a prominent and probably dominant rural group. Their tenants, though not actually enslaved, were far from free; they were bound to the land and to service, and the Sung government enforced laws that guaranteed their serfdom and penalized the harboring of fugitives from that status. It has been argued, somewhat controversially, that the notable advances achieved in Sung times in agricultural technology and production could only have come about because of the capital resources and the large-scale operations of the large landowners.

Two of the noted Sung reformers tried to keep landlordism within reasonable bounds. Wang An-shih in the 1070's established a system of "green sprout" loans that enabled marginal farmers to escape foreclosure by landlord moneylenders. Under this program the state gave a farmer what funds he needed at planting time, and he repaid the money at harvest time (plus 40 per cent interest, which was considerably below the current private rate). And at the end of the Sung period, in the 1260's, Chief Councilor Chia Ssu-tao set a maximum limit on the acreage a landowner could hold and vigorously enforced it; expropriated excess holdings were rented out by the government. In general, however, the Sung government did not concern itself with land-tenure problems, and landlordism flourished throughout the dynasty. Still, in Sung China large landowners played no special military role of the sort associated with the great aristocratic estate-owners of earlier times or with the feudal lords of medieval Europe. Indeed, quite the contrary. They held important positions in the civil service and fostered its nonmilitary value system.

The Mongol conquest imposed a new serfdom and often outright slavery on many rural Chinese. Some large landlords of the Sung era, so recently antagonized by Chia Ssu-tao's reforms, seem to have collaborated with the new alien regime and survived with their estates and privileges intact. But the rural scene was substantially altered by the

Yüan government's confiscations of land for the support of its armies and for gifts to the Mongol nobility. Religious institutions likewise were granted great tracts of land, together with their peasant workers. Free farmers were apparently fewer and more hard-pressed than ever before.

The founder of the Ming dynasty abolished Yüan-style slavery and subsidized the resettlement of the depopulated north by freehold farmers. But large tracts of land, in Yüan fashion, were reserved as state lands for the use of hereditary soldiers in the Ming wei-so system; and many of the great estates confiscated from the Yüan elite were retained as state-owned lands and rented to tenant farmers at rates substantially higher than the prevailing land taxes. This was especially the case in the congested southeast, the Hangchow-Soochow region. Otherwise, the Ming government followed a laissez-faire policy of noninterference in land-tenure arrangements. Sung-style landlordism inevitably flourished anew, though the tenants were no longer legally bound to the land as they had been in Sung. Through Ming and into Ch'ing times freehold peasants struggled as best they could against unfettered landlordism, and tenant farmers made contractual arrangements as best they could with landlords.

Meantime, as commerce and trade increased in the sixteenth century, and especially since legal discriminations against merchants had ceased, well-to-do rural families seem to have begun diversifying their investments on an unprecedented scale and moved their residences into the cities and towns. The countryside was gradually transformed, abandoned to freehold farmers and the tenants of absentee landlords. Tenant uprisings against the abusive agents of absentee landlords in the seventeenth century hastened the movement of the well-to-do into the cities and towns and gave rise to a general system of low land rents and virtually unchallengeable tenant rights to indefinite tenure. By mid-Ch'ing times the Chinese countryside was a confusing hodgepodge of small freehold farmers, almost indistinguishable tenant farmers, and farmers who worked some fields that they owned, worked others as tenants, and owned still others that they rented out. It was difficult to categorize people as owners or tenants. Well-to-do families in the cities, whether of agrarian or mercantile origins, still invested in farmland because of its traditional prestige and long-term security, but got greater returns from investments in commercial and moneylending enterprises.

A particularly abusive practice of the Ming period was the government's creation of large estates to provide special income for the imperial treasury, for princes and princesses, for empresses and their relatives, and for court favorites including eunuchs. The practice accelerated late in the 1400's, and by 1600 much of the farmland of the metropolitan area around Peking and perhaps as much as half of Honan province had been incorporated into such estates. These estates existed only "on paper," so to speak; they were lands from which normal tax revenues were diverted to favored individuals. The tax agents assigned to the estates proved so rapacious that tax-collecting responsibilities were eventually turned back to the regular local authorities, who undertook to transfer what was collected to the privileged "owners." Since the creation of estates was seldom accompanied by reductions in the tax quotas of the affected provinces, additional tax burdens were shifted increasingly onto the remaining freehold farmers. But in the long run the practice seems not to have disadvantaged the peasantry as much as it did the state, for the creation of each new estate plainly deprived the government of part of its normal tax revenues.

Throughout the later dynasties rural taxes were managed in the pattern established by the T'ang dynasty's "two-tax" reform of 780. Taxes continued to be based primarily on land, divided into a land tax proper and a service levy. One of Wang An-shih's reforms was to graduate the land tax according to land quality or productivity, and this principle predominated thereafter. In consequence, revenues from the rich, intensively cultivated Yangtze delta area became an increasingly dominant proportion of the empire's land-tax revenues. By Ming times it was commonly said that the south contributed 90 per cent of the imperial revenues, that the southeast accounted for 90 per cent of the south's contribution, and that the richest five prefectures accounted for 90 per cent of the southeast's contribution. Soochow prefecture, which had a high proportion of state-owned land on which high "rent" was paid rather than taxes, and which suffered discriminatory assessments because it had been the capital of the Ming founder's most serious rival for control of the tottering Yüan empire, was popularly said to pay one-tenth of all state revenues from only one-eighty-eighth of the empire's taxable land.

In general, all of the later dynasties tended to lump service levies into a consolidated tax on land and commute them to some form of payment, in produce or in money. The traditional term for a service-owing adult male, *ting*, gradually became an arbitrary fiscal unit having no relation to persons. The simplification of taxes collected from land-owners was accelerated by a series of fiscal measures developed by local authorities during the sixteenth century, collectively called the "single-whip" laws, and coordinated empire-wide in the 1580's by one of the strongest Ming grand secretaries, Chang Chü-cheng. The reforms pro-vided each taxpayer with a single tax bill consolidating all sorts of mis-cellaneous levies that had been accumulating for centuries.

Rural taxes were generally collected by unremunerated community leaders of the sort described in Chapter 11, who often shared this re-sponsibility in a rotational pattern. Each local collector delivered his receipts to prescribed depots or vaults maintained by the county ad-ministration. The receipts of each county were then distributed, in highly complicated apportionments, to garrisons or other agencies throughout the empire. Only a small proportion of the total tax col-lections was actually handled by the central government.

Commerce. The restrictive measures against mercantile exploitation that Chinese governments had devised in the early imperial age were for the most part perpetuated routinely by the later dynasties. State work-shops continued to fill many of the state's own commodity needs, and in increasing volume; and other products the state required continued to be met by semiconfiscatory "harmonious purchases" from merchant and artisan guilds. The state continued to dominate the large-scale construction industry; the architectural, engineering, and managerial achievements of the late dynastic governments—in shipbuilding, water-ways maintenance, palace and tomb construction, and wall building in the new heavy masonry style necessitated by the development of explo-sive weapons—were often colossal; state projects employed tens or hundreds of thousands of craftsmen and laborers. The state continued to license and control the production and distribution of such "monop-oly" commodities as salt, and foreign trade generally remained closely supervised. The Han ever-normal granary system in one form or another had also become a standard feature of the state-managed econ-omy, to stabilize grain supplies and prices. Nevertheless, in those eco-nomic realms where private enterprise dominated, laissez-faire policies became more prevalent than ever, and private mercantile activity flour-ished as never before. Officials, eunuchs, and members of the imperial families as well as rural landlords commonly became at least part-time mercantile entrepreneurs and investors. Urban China became increas-

Fig. 35. Street scene in Sung dynasty capital, Kaifeng: detail from the long handscroll "Spring Festival on the River" by Chang Tse-tuan (12th century)

ingly a nation of small shopkeepers, and cities and towns teemed with street peddlers, wage-earning craftsmen, and day laborers of every sort.

Domestic trade slowly broke free from tight state control during the last T'ang century as the constraints against retailing activities outside of the designated market areas in cities were relaxed. By early Sung times merchant and craft shops sprawled throughout every city and town, lining the streets, intermixed with residences, and especially clustered around the gates of walled cities. Merchants dealing in a given commodity began to cluster together, and eventually a city of the later empire characteristically had one whole street of shops selling the same product or service. The old Chinese word for street or road, *hang*, was consequently applied to the guild-like associations into which merchants and artisans organized themselves to regulate conditions of trade and to apportion government requisitions equally. Governments often relied on such guilds to implement state fiscal policies at the lowest levels, much as clan elders and community chiefs were relied on to preserve order in the countryside.

In the last centuries of the empire, most notably beginning in the eighteenth century, merchant and artisan guilds greatly expanded in numbers and functions. Like well-organized modern labor unions, they provided many kinds of services for their members, social as well as commercial. They maintained social security funds, sponsored entertainment programs, and offered insurance plans to cover goods in transit. Cooperation among guilds produced the equivalents of modern chambers of commerce, which in effect governed the empire's multiplying market towns; and the guilds of every province commonly collaborated in establishing hostels and headquarters in the national capital and other major centers for their members to use on business trips. Thus a merchant of Kiangsi province, for example, could travel to Peking in confidence that he would be welcomed there by the staff of a guild hall ready to befriend and assist him.

In the small towns of the later imperial age, business was normally conducted at commercial fairs, served by itinerant merchants who regularly appeared to spread their wares in streets and other open places on a rotational schedule worked out by a group of nearby towns. Religious establishments also commonly sponsored fairs on festival days, when merchants and traveling entertainers clustered on and around temple grounds to serve the celebrants.

The dispersal of mercantile activities out of the confined market areas of the early empire gave rise to a complex of new, variable taxes on trade. Throughout the later imperial age in general, all shopkeepers had to pay inventory taxes of some sort, and in the case of the periodic fairs someone of substance always had to accept responsibility for collecting a type of sales tax. Taxes were also regularly collected on mercantile goods in transit; to this end governments established inland customs stations at appropriate points along roadways and waterways.

Among the notable developments in the state-managed sector of the economy was an unprecedented but short-lived expansion of state monopolies in Northern Sung times. By then the state had relinquished its control of iron, but Sung monopolized salt, tea, liquor, alum, and certain imported spices and luxury goods. State income from monopolies rose from eleven million strings of *cash* in 997 to more than fifty million strings in 1076. The reformer Wang An-shih—who, as has already been noted, tried to undercut private moneylenders with his "green sprouts" loans for farmers—tried more ambitiously to capture mercantile profits for the state (though not actually by monopolization). In what was called the "market and exchange program," the state set up a network of depots for the wholesale buying and retail selling of commodities of all sorts in competition with private traders. But so large a bureaucratic enterprise soon proved to be costly rather than profitable and was abandoned after 13 years.

Salt was the only significant state monopoly in Ming and Ch'ing times. For many years the Ming government tried to keep its frontier garrisons adequately supplied by requiring salt merchants to pay for state-monopolized salt with deliveries of grain to the frontiers. Ingenious merchants then established privately subsidized agricultural colonies in barren frontier areas to produce grain where it was needed and thus reduce their transportation costs, and in this way they contributed in some measure to the repopulation and economic recovery of the north. However, the grain-for-salt system did not prove advantageous to the government in the long run. It reduced the direct cash income from the salt monopoly without substantially reducing the chronic shortages of grain on the frontiers. The system was therefore finally abandoned in favor of direct government payments in cash to the frontier soldiers, who bought their food in whatever markets were accessible to them. In the late Ming years the government reduced its direct role in the salt industry by farming out salt distribution to a small group of merchants who served as super-wholesalers. These salt merchants became China's most famous and richest mercantile group in the Ch'ing dynasty.

Overseas trade, though discouraged in almost all other periods, was actively encouraged by the Sung government, which even sent special commissioners abroad seeking new trade opportunities. Newly designed Chinese ships regularly plied the South China Sea in competition with Arab merchantmen, which had long dominated the East-West sea trade. The Chinese traded silks and porcelains for spices and other luxury goods, 30 per cent of which normally went to the government as customs duties. Chinese ships traded as far as the Malabar coast of India, using the first magnetic compasses known in world history and accumulating excellent navigational charts. Superintendencies of Trading Ships were established by the state at Canton, Ch'üan-chou, Ningpo, and Hangchow to supervise the trade and collect the tariffs, which in Southern Sung times became a substantial proportion of state revenues.

Sung's aggressive overseas trading policies were reversed by the Ming emperors; the great Indian Ocean expeditions of the early fifteenth century were diplomatic undertakings, not trading enterprises. The Ming government preferred tightly controlled tribute arrangements to open trade. It forbade Chinese to deal privately with foreigners, and overseas merchants were gradually confined to Canton. In the Ch'ing dynasty, as has been noted in Chapter 10, trade with foreigners was restricted to a small group of licensed Canton brokers known to Europeans as the co-hong, and the government made strenuous efforts to restrict the economic and other influences of Westerners. From mid-Ming times on, however, silks and other Chinese manufactures flowed out through Canton to the West, and silver flowed in. An especially noteworthy aspect of the trade was the transport of silk by Fukienese traders to the Spanish colony at Manila, where it was exchanged for Peruvian or Mexican silver. Eventually silver coins specially minted in Mexico for the China trade became standard currency on the China coast, known as Mexican dollars. China's favorable balance in the overseas trade changed in the early 1800's as Westerners began flooding China with opium; silver then drained out of China in such quantities as to create serious monetary problems for the Ch'ing government.

In the private sector, one of the noteworthy developments of the later imperial age was a great flourishing of the iron and steel industry in Northern Sung times. Spectacular growth was made possible particularly by the close proximity of good iron and coal deposits to the greatest domestic market, the capital at Kaifeng, where the government was zealously manufacturing iron or steel armor and weapons for its armies. Independent entrepreneurs who operated large-scale coal and iron complexes in the Kaifeng region, commonly employing hundreds of workmen, accounted for about half of China's total iron production in the late eleventh century. One huge complex at Ch'i-ts'un in Hopei employed more than 700 coal miners, 1,000 ore miners, and 1,000 furnace workers, and annually consumed some 35,000 tons of ore and 42,000 tons of coal to produce over 14,000 tons of pig iron. National iron production soared to a total of 125,000 tons a year—a sixfold per capita increase since the ninth century. In addition to military armor, sword blades, arrowheads, bows and crossbows, manufacturers turned out such nonmilitary products as nails, plowshares, harrows, hoes, and

Fig. 36. Traditional household tailoring activity: detail from an old painting by un-identified artist

spades. After the Northern Sung period China's iron and steel industry declined, in part because there was never again a preeminent market located so advantageously near concentrated iron and coal deposits.

Textile manufacturing was a major industry through the whole imperial age, and from an early time cloth was an important Chinese export, as is evidenced in such English terms as shantung (from the Chinese province), nankeen (from Nanking), and satin (from Zayton, the name by which Marco Polo and other early Westerners knew the Fukien port Ch'üan-chou). But important as textiles were as an export item, they were sold in far greater quantity in the domestic market, and with grain constituted the bulk of interregional trade. During the later dynasties textiles became manufacturing specialties of the great south-eastern metropolises, especially Soochow and Hangchow. The development of cotton in Yüan and Ming times naturally altered conditions in the textile market; silk goods were increasingly restricted to luxury uses, though they were still produced in substantial quantities.

Copper coins remained in common use in the later dynasties, but after the eighth century China suffered an endemic shortage of coins. In part, this was due to the burgeoning of commercial activity and the growth of interregional and national markets in T'ang and Sung times, which required a constant increase in the amount of money in circulation. But the situation was exacerbated because many neighboring countries—especially Vietnam, Korea, and Japan—adopted Chinese coins as their own common currency. From T'ang times on, therefore, governments regularly forbade the private use of copper. (It was for this reason that porcelain became a major industry in the later imperial age: bowls, plates, and many other ordinary household items of porcelain were mass-produced to replace the copper or bronze ware of former times.) Sometimes iron coins, lead coins, or even pottery coins were circulated because of copper shortages.

The shortage of coins was more than an index of commercial growth; it was an index of the extent to which a genuine money economy was developing at all levels of society. Sometimes governments tried to stem the process—for example, by ordering that silk or other commodities had to be accepted in the payment of private debts. But monetization steadily accelerated in the Sung period. In 1065 government revenues in cash surpassed commodity revenues for the first time in Chinese history: cash receipts amounted to 51.6 per cent of all government revenues in that year, having grown from a mere 3.1 per cent in 749. Fluctuations in the money supply caused disruptive rises and declines in commodity prices, and the Sung government became quite sophisticated in its deliberations about inflation and monetary policy. By 1073 the government was minting six million strings of *cash* annually (of 1,000 coins each), some 20 times the maximum annual production in T'ang times; and there was still not enough money in circulation.

Paper money was invented in China to alleviate this chronic shortage of coins—and also to ease the handling of money in large amounts. As large-scale interregional trade began developing in the late T'ang years merchants could not be troubled to haul cartloads of money with them across the country. They began keeping their cash on deposit in widely respected business offices (from which a banking system grew) or even in government offices. The receipts they were given were passed around in business transactions in the fashion of convertible certificates of deposit. Finally, in the early Sung years, the government began issuing its own printed promissory notes (valued in terms of strings of coins), and by the beginning of the eleventh century paper money in circulation had reached a total of one million strings. Foreseeing inflation, the government tried to limit paper money to that amount. But the demands for more and more money to meet military costs during the Jurchen invasions caused runaway inflation in the twelfth century, and it could not be reversed. It became routine in the Southern Sung period for billions of paper notes to circulate that were unbacked by hard currency. Commodity prices naturally skyrocketed.

The Mongols continued the use of paper money—at first warily, but finally even less responsibly than Southern Sung. The Ming dynasty tried anew, but by Ming times the Chinese people had learned not to trust paper money. The Ming government kept its paper money circulating only by requiring that it be used to pay certain kinds of taxes. But the populace at large had reverted to a modified barter economy. Bulk silver became the favored unit of exchange, one tael (ounce) of silver being theoretically equivalent to one string of copper *cash* and also to one picul of rice. Although in practice such values did not hold firm in any marketplace, bulk silver gradually won acceptance as the standard monetary medium. The greatest significance of the "single whip" tax reforms of the sixteenth century stems from their transforming almost all tax payments from commodities into silver. The silver tael remained the standard monetary medium and accounting unit through the Ch'ing period. Chinese governments did not experiment further with paper money until the 1900's.

Since China from Sung times on became so notably commercialized and industrialized in comparison with other areas, and since abundant investment capital was available from both government and private sources, the question naturally arises: Why did traditional China not generate its own industrial revolution? The question has bedeviled specialists for generations. It is increasingly clear that as early as Sung times Chinese science and technology were already at a level that should have made full industrialization an easy next step, at least in certain manufacturing realms. Was there something inherent in China's national psychology or its patterns of political and social organization that made that step impossible? Difficult, perhaps; impossible, probably not. Even the availability of a large, cheap supply of human labor should not have been a deterrent; at least, it did not deter the Chinese from developing many sorts of labor-saving devices that utilized animal, wind, and water power. It can be argued persuasively that smothering governmental control of large-scale business stifled private investment in innovations that might have significantly altered the economic order, or that technology and manufacturing capacity in the later dynasties were so much more than adequate for the existing market that there was no incentive for such innovations. However, since there seems to be no natural law of progression that propels societies inevitably from preindustrial to industrial status, it will probably always be easier to analyze the peculiar combination of circumstances that caused or allowed Europe to generate an industrial revolution than to explain why China did not.

That Chinese technological development essentially stabilized or stagnated in Ming and Ch'ing times while Europe was catching up and gathering momentum for its explosive industrialization in the nineteenth century is nevertheless, all things considered, the most important fact of China's later imperial history. Certainly in Sung times, and probably as late as the sixteenth century if not later, the Chinese economy was sophisticated and productive beyond comparison with any other region and gave the Chinese a higher standard of living than any other people in the world. But by 1800, beneath a facade of prosperity and self-satisfied conservatism, domestic economic problems were turning China into a powder keg waiting to be exploded, and the consequent political deterioration exposed China to exploitation by a militantly expansionist West and, most humiliatingly, by a rapidly Westernizing Japan.

13. Thought

AFTER A millennium of Buddhist dominance, Chinese intellectual life developed a markedly new tone in the later dynasties. Buddhism and its imitative rival, Neo-Taoism, continued to exist as popular religions. But their intellectual attractions dimmed, and they ceased to absorb China's more speculative minds as they had through most of the T'ang age. In Sung times Confucianism, which for centuries had languished as a vague code of ethics and governance and a tradition of rather antiquarian classical scholarship, suddenly surged into prominence as the dynamic creed of the newly dominant scholar-official class. Assimilating metaphysical elements from Buddhism and Taoism just as Tung Chung-shu's eclecticism had accommodated cosmological and numerological speculations more than a millennium earlier, Sung Confucianism generated a new intellectual excitement about the nature of man and his relation to the cosmos, spreading to Korea and Japan as well as throughout China.

Many modern specialists consider this Neo-Confucianism, as Westerners label the new philosophical currents, China's greatest achievement in the later imperial age. In Yüan, Ming, and Ch'ing times Neo-Confucianism was the state-espoused orthodoxy on which civil service recruitment examinations were based and which consequently became the standard subject matter of almost all education. In the process it lost some of its original dynamism. However, since it seeks truth primarily by reinterpreting the Confucian writings and other classics of antiquity, Neo-Confucianism gave fresh impetus to China's tradition of classical scholarship. Printing and the spread of literacy encouraged a scholarship of unprecedented scope, diversity, and abundance, which reached very high levels of philological sophistication in Ming and

Ch'ing times. Meanwhile, intellectual contacts between China and the West were making contributions to Europe's Age of Enlightenment. But China's commitment to Neo-Confucianism, even as it declined into conservative scholasticism, remained strong enough to resist significant Western philosophical influences until late in the nineteenth century, and Neo-Confucianism had by no means lost its intellectual force in the twentieth century.

LATER TAOISM AND BUDDHISM

Intellectually, the importance of Taoism and Buddhism in Sung and later times lies principally in their contributions to Neo-Confucianism. Neither doctrine independently produced a major new thinker or work. Both emulated Confucian scholarship in some degree and developed their own traditions of canonical research. The original edition of the Buddhist Tripitaka, printed between 972 and 983, was reprinted regularly. Taoist canonical writings, commonly called the Taoist Tripitaka (*Tao-tsang*), were first printed under the auspices of the Sung state in 1019 and were also reprinted, though not as often as the Buddhist canon. Learned monks participated in the philosophical disputations that enlivened Chinese intellectual life from Sung times on, and many scholar-officials who were considered staunch Confucians studied Buddhist and Taoist writings with respect. Considered as independent philosophical traditions, however, neither Taoism nor Buddhism was a significant vital element in the intellectualism of the later imperial age.

Of the many Buddhist sects that persisted, the populist Ching-t'u (Pure Land) and meditative Ch'an sects predominated, but both were disunited. Ching-t'u monasteries and associated lay societies spread their doctrines of salvation by faith without any hierarchical coordination; each large monastery was the headquarters of an autonomous subsect. Ch'an devotees also had large monasteries but were as often found living unobtrusively among the general populace, each with a small following of disciples. In Sung times Ch'an developed a doctrinal cleavage between northern and southern schools; the northerners were the more gradualist in their approach to enlightenment. But doctrinal differences among Buddhists seldom provoked animosities. Pan-Buddhist unifying movements began in the Sung period and grew stronger thereafter. One of the most notable Pan-Buddhist activists was the Ming monk Chu-hung (1532-1612), who stimulated the development of lay Buddhist organizations and was one of Chinese Buddhism's early writers of tracts denouncing Christianity.

Fig. 37. "The Sixth Ch'an Patriarch Cutting Bamboo" by Liang K'ai (detail)

Taoism was even less coordinated than Buddhism. The most characteristic practitioner was an isolated village or neighborhood priest, akin to a local shaman. Taoism never lent itself to unifying efforts comparable to the Pan-Buddhist movements, though the Chang family of Kiangsi province remained the generally acknowledged popes of religious Taoism throughout the later imperial age.

The main trend in popular religion in this era was a broad eclecticism, an incorporation of Buddhist, Taoist, and Confucian religious elements into one hodgepodge system called *san-chiao* (the Three Doctrines). San-chiao practices were widespread among Sung Chinese, and in the Ming dynasty san-chiao eclecticism was championed even in philosophical circles, especially in the sixteenth century. Although san-chiao was officially condemned as heresy, its practices dominated popular religion into the twentieth century. Chinese families did not consider it contradictory or inappropriate to observe state-sponsored Confucian rituals and practice ancestor worship at home according to Confucian teachings while also revering Taoist and Buddhist divinities and engaging in Taoist and Buddhist religious exercises at local temples and shrines. San-chiao shrines have remained part of the Chinese religious scene into our own time outside the communist People's Republic. They normally contain images of Confucius, Lao-tzu, and the Buddha, and are tended, largely on a hereditary basis, by often illiterate mendicants who seem predominantly of Taoist persuasion but would probably be hard pressed to state their religious beliefs with any precision. Such shrines are intermixed among others that are identifiably Taoist or Buddhist, and all enjoy general community support, official as well as private. At this local religious level, Taoism and Buddhism have not been notably antagonistic, and Confucian-indoctrinated state officials have tolerated them and san-chiao alike. Both Buddhists and Taoists have published and preached from treatises advocating hygiene, neighborly cooperation, personal morality, and other behavior patterns that the traditional state also espoused; and Buddhist and Taoist organizations have equally sought to provide useful public services of secular sorts.

Taoism and Buddhism were subject to more consistent state control under the later dynasties than earlier. There were no large-scale persecutions such as Buddhism suffered in the 840's, but Sung and later dynasties, alien as well as Chinese, monopolized the ordination of all monks as a state function and tried to limit the wealth and power of religious organizations. In the eleventh century the Northern Sung government, in need of new revenues, began the large-scale public sale of ordination certificates, and all later governments followed this precedent. The practice was one of the reasons for the subsequent steady decline in monastic morale, discipline, and prestige down to our own time. The Yüan, Ming, and Ch'ing governments placed all monks under the disciplinary control of governmental agencies called Taoist Registries and Buddhist Registries, established at national, prefectural, and county levels and staffed by religious dignitaries who were held accountable for their fellow monks. Restrictions seem never to have been implemented severely, however; church organizations were no longer threats to the state, and token control was sufficient.

The most generous imperial patrons of religion in the later imperial age were the Mongols. Chingis Khan particularly esteemed the Taoist Ch'ang-ch'un (Ch'iu Ch'u-chi, 1148-1227) and made him patriarch of all religious orders in the far-reaching Mongol empire. Chingis's grandson Kubilai Khan was greatly influenced in his governance of China by the Buddhist Liu Ping-chung (1216-74), who gave up his ordination to serve in the central government. But most of all Kubilai Khan showered favors on the shamanistic Tibetan version of Buddhism called Lamaism, partly for diplomatic reasons. In 1260 the lama 'Phags-pa (1238-80), best remembered for devising an alphabetic script for the Mongolian language, was named Kubilai's imperial mentor and given viceregal authority in Tibet. 'Phags-pa was Kubilai's intimate adviser and inducted fellow lamas into government service in China. Kubilai and later Yüan emperors gave lamas greater prestige and privilege than any other religious order, alien or native, had enjoyed in Chinese history, and one of the reasons for the subsequent Chinese vilification of the Yüan rulers is that they allowed lamas to abuse their privileges and immunities outrageously. The Ming and Ch'ing emperors treated high-ranking Tibetan lamas respectfully in diplomatic relations but gave them no special privileges in China.

While Lamaism was gaining favor with the Mongols, Taoist and Buddhist groups struggled openly in a final series of great religious debates at court of the sort that had not been uncommon in the early imperial age. Under Ch'ang-ch'un's successor as Taoist patriarch, Taoists took advantage of wartime chaos to appropriate Buddhist monasteries and properties and began to circulate anew the old tracts arguing that Lao-tzu in his old age had "civilized" and converted the Buddha himself. Buddhists protested. Mangu Khan (r. 1251-59) convened court conferences to consider Taoist-Buddhist charges and counter-charges in 1255, 1256, and 1258. The last conference, presided over by the future Kubilai Khan, was a huge affair, bringing together 300 Buddhists, 200 Taoists, and 200 Confucian scholars. The Taoist claims were judged false in all instances; disputed properties were given to the Buddhist claimants, "slanderous" Taoist books about the Buddha were ordered burned, and a few leading Taoists were forced to recant and take Buddhist vows. In 1280-81, when it became evident that many Taoists were unrepentant, Kubilai ordered more effective suppressions; and gradually the millennium-old feud over the chronological priority of Lao-tzu and the Buddha died out. Taoism lost prestige and the wealth and strength of its organizations declined steadily, but it was not generally persecuted. Neither Taoism nor Chinese Buddhism was denied continuing imperial patronage despite the favoritism shown Tibetan lamas by the Mongol khans. As Yüan emperors, the Mongols tolerated all religions and dealt generously even with representatives of

Islam, Nestorianism, and European Christianity. Central Asia had been converted to Islam during the T'ang dynasty, and from Yüan times on there were large minority populations of Moslems in the western parts of China Proper.

In sum, Taoism and Buddhism remained important aspects of Chinese life throughout the later imperial age. Their monastic communities survived, even if with diminished prestige; and individual monks often enjoyed great social esteem and occasionally political influence. The Chinese masses continued to seek from religious practitioners the charms, amulets, medicines, prognostications, and consolations they required in their everyday lives. Many Chinese, as earnestly as ever, hoped for Taoist prolongation of life or Buddhist salvation in the afterlife, if not both. Beyond that, Taoist and Buddhist themes continued to shape Chinese architecture, art, and literature despite the loss of philosophical vitality and creativity suffered by both religions as a revived, revised Confucianism moved decisively to the forefront of Chinese intellectual life.

NEO-CONFUCIANISM

The revival of Confucianism in Sung times was in part a xenophobic reaction to centuries of alien influences on Chinese politics and thought. In part it was also a natural outgrowth of the scholastic training and interests of the increasingly dominant examination-recruited civil servants, who in the Sung dynasty had unprecedented opportunities to try applying the principles they learned from ancient Chinese writings to the realm of practical governance. Most of all, however, it was a cumulative intellectual excitement generated by a succession of discoveries that the dazzling metaphysical problems with which Buddhism and Taoism had so long preoccupied Chinese minds—What is the real me, and how does it relate to the cosmos?—could be answered by reinterpretations of the classical Confucian literature, and answered in ways more consonant with traditional Chinese notions about the proper organization of state and society and about proper individual life-styles. It is not inappropriate to consider Neo-Confucianism a reassertion of ancient Confucian political and moral values buttressed by cosmological and metaphysical conceptions adapted from Buddhism and Taoism, but Neo-Confucianism is much more. It is a fermenting of new truths out of old rhetoric—"Confucian" truths that philosophically undercut otherworldly Buddhism and unworldly Taoism and gave vibrant life to the positivist, optimistic doctrines that human fulfillment is found in life as mankind knows it, and that everyone has the potentiality of realizing such fulfillment. Like the revival of classical learning centuries later in Europe, Sung Neo-Confucianism gave off sparks that revitalized almost all facets of life. It was bound up integrally with all the changes that made China of the later imperial age so different from the China of the preceding epochs.

Sung Neo-Confucianism, often given the general designation *Tao-hsüeh* (study of the Way), was a highly intellectual and academic movement. It grew in state schools and especially in private academies. Its principal philosophical doctrines are found in annotations that successive scholars appended to the traditional classics, which focus on philosophical interpretation rather than on dry philological explication in the style of pre-Sung annotations. In addition, since the Neo-Confucians were usually fervent teachers and debaters, they made important use of a form of writing favored by Ch'an Buddhists—extensive, sometimes disjointed reports by disciples of their masters' talks, teachings, and debates, called records of conversations (*yü-lu*). Neo-Confucians also commonly corresponded with one another voluminously, and some of their points of view are most clearly stated in their preserved letters.

Of the ancient writings, Neo-Confucians had little use for the no-nonsense practicality of Hsün-tzu but found special inspiration in the *Meng-tzu*, which they, like Han Yü of the late T'ang era, considered the last transmission of the genuine Way of the ancient sage-kings and of Confucius. They were also intrigued by several works that were peripheral to original Confucianism: the *Chou-li* (Chou Rituals) as a source of utopian political thought, the *I-ching* (Classic of Changes) and its Han appendixes with their cosmological and numerological emphases, and two short formulaic chapters long buried in the *Li-chi* (Ritual Records), namely, the *Ta-hsüeh* (The Great Learning) and the *Chung-yung* (The Doctrine of the Mean). It was Sung Neo-Confucians who exalted the *Ta-hsüeh* and the *Chung-yung*, together with Confucius's *Lun-yü* (Analects) and the *Meng-tzu*, into special status as the Four Books, the core of Neo-Confucian education and philosophical scholarship; and the chain syllogisms of the *Ta-hsüeh* cited in Chapter 4, with their vague exhortations about "cultivating the person," "rectifying the mind," "making intentions sincere," "extending knowledge," and "investigating things," became the interpretive ground over which the greatest Neo-Confucian disputations raged.

Neo-Confucians succeeded in persuading Chinese intellectuals that the world perceptible to the senses is real, not illusory as Buddhists maintain; and that mankind attains fulfillment by earnest participation in society, not by standing aloof from it as Taoists are inclined to do. They disdained Buddhism's promises of spiritual salvation and Taoism's promises of physical immortality. They accepted the human cycle from birth to death as normal and good, and they concentrated on social and political reform in this world and on individual self-cultivation in this life. As Neo-Confucianism evolved through time, however, it passed through several phases with changing emphases. Its early Sung reformist zeal came to be subordinated in Ming times to an intense emphasis on individualistic self-cultivation, and in Ch'ing times, in reaction to what were considered Ming excesses, it tended to become a conservative scholasticism devoid of philosophical vitality.

Political and social reformism. One of the ways in which Neo-Confucianism undercut Buddhism was by reviving in the family, the secular community, and the state a strong sense of social-welfare activism. The early Sung reformer Fan Chung-yen's dictum that "the true scholar should be the first to become anxious about the world's troubles and the last to enjoy its happiness" proved to be an effective Neo-Confucian counterpart of the charitable, compassionate appeal of Mahayana Buddhism's bodhisattva ideal. Fan himself pioneered in developing patterns of mutual responsibility and mutual help within the extended family or clan. The entailment of clan-held lands for charitable purposes, the sponsorship of clan schools, and the promulgation of clan rules that reiterated and reinforced the old Confucian ethos became widespread. Successive Sung intellectuals, such as the statesman-historian Ssu-ma Kuang (1019-86) and the great philosophical synthesizer Chu Hsi (1130-1200), compiled much-imitated regulations for family living.

Cooperation and mutual help came to be promoted systematically in community compacts (*hsiang-yüeh*) among village families, which provided for a measure of local self-government by outlining goals and procedures for settling interfamily disputes, establishing community schools, fostering economic development projects such as irrigation systems, and maintaining local order. One of the earliest community compacts of this sort was prepared in Northern Sung times by a Lü family of Honan province. It was widely emulated and was later revised by Chu Hsi. The Ming statesman-philosopher Wang Yang-ming (1472-1529) was a notably active promoter of community compacts and community schools, and one of his followers, Ho Hsin-yin (1517-79), organized a utopian, egalitarian local community, almost a commune, aggressively dedicated to educational, cultural, and socioeconomic self-development and self-regulation. The Ming and Ch'ing imperial governments also fostered community compacts as useful instruments of social control and indoctrination.

In government, the reformist impulse was most notably evidenced in early Sung times in the controversial policies and programs of Fan Chung-yen and Wang An-shih (1021-86) discussed in the preceding chapters. From this time on, to an extent not rivaled even by the Han activists Wu-ti and Wang Mang, central governments assumed responsibility for the total well-being of all Chinese and asserted regulatory authority over all aspects of Chinese life. "To enrich the state and strengthen the army" was the utilitarian goal of many political activists, especially Wang An-shih and the Ming grand secretary Chang Chü-cheng (1525-82). Their somewhat Legalistic inclinations naturally aroused opposition among officials more devoted to popular welfare than to administrative efficiency, and political reforms of any sort often seemed threatening to conservative bureaucratic careerists who were comfortable with the status quo. All political reforms consequently stimulated bureaucratic controversies, and factionalism so weakened the morale and effectiveness of the officialdom that imperial autocracy thrived and reform efforts became steadily more difficult. Yet the determination to serve in government and to achieve a governmental system that realistically addressed the needs of the people and society remained a persisting aspect of Neo-Confucianism.

After the early Sung governmental reform movements, the Neo-Confucian emphasis on practical effort (*kung-li*) and effective government (*ching-shih*) yielded markedly to Neo-Confucianism's corollary emphasis on cultivation of the self. The speculative aspects of Neo-Confucianism, originally less prominent than reformist activism, developed slowly during the Northern Sung period and then became the most prominent element of the Neo-Confucian movement in the twelfth century. At that time two philosophical currents emerged as the irreconcilable Neo-Confucian mainstreams. One, often characterized as dualistic and rationalistic, is known to the Chinese as *li-hsüeh* (study of principles) or as the Ch'eng-Chu school. The other, often characterized as monistic and idealistic, is known to the Chinese as *hsin-hsüeh* (study of the mind) or as the Lu-Wang school.

The Ch'eng-Chu school. All Neo-Confucian philosophical speculation rests on a common base of cosmology shaped by a series of eleventh-century thinkers. Their cosmology was derived from long, highly developed traditions of Buddhist and Neo-Taoist metaphysics and was adapted to concepts found in the ancient *I-ching* and its Han appendixes. Much of its terminology was borrowed from the analysis of the third-century Neo-Taoist Wang Pi. Nearer at hand, the cosmology derives from esoteric cosmic diagrams prepared by a tenth-century Taoist recluse, Ch'en T'uan. The principal early shapers of the Neo-Confucian cosmology, all students of the *I-ching*, were Chou Tun-i (1017-73) of Hunan province, who held several minor official posts in the south; Shao Yung (1011-77) of the modern Peking area, who spent most of his career as a private teacher in Loyang; and Chang Tsai (1020-77) of Shensi province, who was ousted from government for opposing Wang An-shih's reform program and devoted himself thereafter to private teaching. Their influences came to a focus in two brothers of Hopei province who spent most of their lives in Kaifeng and Loyang; and with these brothers, Ch'eng Hao (1032-85) and Ch'eng I (1033-1108), Neo-Confucianism began coalescing into a full-scale philosophical system. They actively studied both Buddhist and Taoist traditions, but as students of Chou Tun-i, friends of Shao Yung, and nephews of Chang Tsai they began coordinating *I-ching* cosmology with ancient Confucian ethical teachings.

Although the Ch'eng brothers themselves seem not to have been aware of any significant philosophical differences between them, the teachings of Ch'eng I were transmitted through a chain of teacher-disciple relationships to Chu Hsi, who synthesized and expanded them into the doctrine called li-hsüeh, whereas the teachings of Ch'eng Hao evolved into the rival doctrine called hsin-hsüeh, championed by Chu Hsi's contemporary Lu Chiu-yüan (1139-93) and developed more fully in the sixteenth century by Wang Yang-ming. Hence the labels of the two schools: Ch'eng-Chu and Lu-Wang.

The Neo-Confucian cosmology, presented by Chou Tun-i in a complex of linked circles called the Diagram of the Supreme Ultimate and most fully explained by Chu Hsi, focuses attention principally on an impersonal, immaterial Supreme Ultimate (*t'ai-chi*), usually equated with the old Confucian concept of Tao (the Way). In contrast to the Supreme Ultimate is primordial ether, stuff, or matter (*ch'i*). The Supreme Ultimate is an aggregation of perfect abstract forms or prin-

Fig. 38. "P'an-ku Holding the Egg of Chaos": 19th-century lithograph of the mythological founder of the universe holding the symbol of the Yang and Yin forces that motivate all things

ciples (*li*, not the same word as the *li* meaning ritual and courtesy). Particular things of the material world come into being by a process akin to coagulation of matter and then, in due time, dissolve away into the formless basic stuff out of which they appeared. The motive power in this process is provided by the interaction of the inseparable cosmic forces Yang and Yin, of the Five Elements (fire, water, earth, wood, and metal conceived of as elemental forces), and to some extent of Heaven and Earth (also conceived of as forces). Things are what they are (men, women, dogs, cats, rocks, and the like) because of the abstract form, or li, that combines with and shapes the matter, or ch'i, that embodies them, and things of any one category have their individual particularities because of the particular complexities of cosmic forces that happened to govern the combining of form and matter in their particular instances.

The ethical system that Neo-Confucians of the Ch'eng-Chu school built on this Taoist-influenced cosmology is dominated by the realization that one's essential identity, or li, is inseparably linked with the Supreme Ultimate. The original perfection of one's li is marred by the embodiment of li in matter, or ch'i, as the reflections of a mirror are dulled by coatings of dust. Although one shares with all other things and especially with all other human beings the physical, material qualities of ch'i, so that "all men are brothers" and owe each other bodhisattva-like compassion and help, the individual can fulfill himself only by trying to rid his li of the imperfections of his ch'i in order that his essential identity might manifest itself with a clarity approaching its original perfection. Neo-Confucians thus often spoke of "dusting off one's mirror" in the same sense that Mencius had earlier spoken of restoring one's "lost child's mind." Becoming a sage, which is the fulfillment sought by Neo-Confucians generally, lies precisely in attaining the realization of one's essential identity and resisting the selfish desires and other unworthy impulses that arise from one's ch'i. The sage does not become immortal, spiritually or physically. When he dies he goes to a well-earned rest.

In the pursuit of sageliness, most Neo-Confucians engage in Ch'an-like meditative "quiet-sitting" during temporary withdrawals from the hustle and bustle of everyday life, and great emphasis is placed on cultivating an attitude called *ching*, meaning seriousness or earnestness or sincerity. Some advocates experience sudden enlightenment in the Buddhist fashion. But the practice of Neo-Confucianism is primarily rooted in the methods of self-cultivation (and, by extension, of improving society) prescribed in the ancient *Ta-hsüeh*, namely, rectifying the mind by making one's intentions sincere, making one's intentions sincere by extending one's knowledge, and extending one's knowledge by investigating things. For the Ch'eng-Chu school in particular, the investigation of things meant rational, objective consideration of the li, or principles, of worldly phenomena, leading to a gradually expanding acquaintance with the aggregation of all li, the Supreme Ultimate.

In the Ch'eng-Chu attitude there are seeds of modern scientific methodology; finding the Supreme Ultimate by considering the characteristics of the many material forms in which it is manifested is a method not unlike hypothesizing general laws through analysis of particular phenomena. And Neo-Confucianism did undoubtedly stimulate many of the encyclopedic compendiums of all sorts that appeared in China's later imperial age. However, Neo-Confucians were not interested in the same things as modern scientists. They were interested in morality, and the Ch'eng-Chu school was particularly interested in the principles, or li, of humankindness, righteousness, filial piety, and the other moral values that suffused the ancient Confucian teachings. Self-cultivation in the Ch'eng-Chu style therefore became an effort to absorb such values by intense study of the precepts of ancient thinkers and the conduct of historical exemplars.

The twelfth-century synthesizer of these Ch'eng-Chu doctrines, Chu

Hsi, whose role in the development of Neo-Confucianism is often compared to that of Saint Thomas Aquinas in European Christianity, was a brilliant thinker, a prolific scholar, an exciting teacher and debater, and a somewhat reluctant official. The son of an official, he was born in Fukien province, part of the affluent southeastern heartland of Southern Sung China, and at the early age of eighteen, in 1148, won the coveted chin-shih degree. After 1153 he spent his life in a succession of government offices—often sinecures as temple custodian that gave him abundant leisure for studying, writing, and teaching. He repeatedly submitted memorials denouncing the cliques of do-nothing opportunists that dominated the Southern Sung government, generally siding with the "war party" that advocated firm resistance against pressures from the Jurchen masters of North China. He was offered several central government posts but declined them with moralistic haughtiness. Finally in 1194, when in his sixties, he accepted an appointment as adviser to a new emperor, Ning-tsung (r. 1194-1224); but he was driven into retirement by partisan enemies after less than two months' service. He was purged from the civil service entirely, along with many other intellectuals, when the whole Neo-Confucian movement (Tao-hsüeh) was proscribed as false and seditious learning that diverted men from the original teachings of Confucius and Mencius. Then in 1199 he was restored to honorable status as a retired official, but he died the next year without having taken office again.

Like many other Neo-Confucians, Chu Hsi was fascinated by Buddhism and Taoism in youth; it was not until he was about thirty that he was thoroughly won over to the doctrines of the Ch'eng brothers. Among the voluminous writings that he produced thereafter, in which philosophical attacks on Buddhism and Taoism are freely interspersed, were commentaries on the Four Books, interpretations of the writings of Chou Tun-i and Chang Tsai, an edition of the works of the Ch'eng brothers, an explication of the I-ching, and an abridgment of a general history of China in which he evaluated historical events in accordance with his philosophical principles. He taught large numbers of disciples, many of them at the White Deer Grotto Academy he founded in Kiangsi province; and by the time he was fifty he had won fame and prestige as a scholar.

Neo-Confucianism in Chu Hsi's or any other version was not universally accepted in his lifetime. It was resisted by many conservative intellectuals, and Chu Hsi himself was sometimes violently denounced

Fig. 39. Traditional portrait of Chu Hsi by unidentified artist

as a traitor and heretic; some enemies even demanded that he be put to death. But his reputation continued to grow after his death, and before the end of Southern Sung his classical interpretations were commonly used in civil service examinations. Under the Yüan, Ming, and Ch'ing dynasties the Chu Hsi interpretations were prescribed by the state as the only correct interpretations and the standards to be used in education and the examination system. In consequence, his influence on the thinking of all later Chinese has been enormous.

The best known distillation of Chu Hsi's ideas is a compact work called *Chin-ssu lu* (Reflections on Things at Hand), which he compiled in 1175-76 with the help of a friend. It is an anthology-like guidebook to the principal li-hsüeh doctrines, intended specifically to serve beginning students as a stepping-stone into the Four Books; and it is unquestionably the most influential single work of philosophy produced in all East Asia during China's later imperial age. The following excerpt, which characteristically includes allusive references to passages in the *Analects* of Confucius, the *Chung-yung*, and the *I-ching*, may suggest what earnest efforts at self-cultivation Chu Hsi's form of Neo-Confucianism demanded of its followers:

The urgency about seeking what is to be desired is that if we try to establish our minds in a state free of doubts, then our progress will be facilitated as by the breaking forth of a great river. . . . Even Confucius, magnificent as his talents were, was nevertheless diligent in his efforts. For anyone of lesser endowments to let things develop of themselves, willy-nilly, is unheard of.

Understanding the good is fundamental, and if we hold this firm we shall have begun. If we enlarge it, we can become great; but if we regard it lightly, we shall shrivel. The potentiality of its flourishing rests with man and no other.

So let us now set our minds on honoring our virtuous natures and pursuing our studies. Let us every day seek to find in ourselves whether or not we have been remiss about anything in our studies and whether or not we have been lax about anything in our virtuous natures. This spirit also makes us broadened by literature and disciplined by propriety, able to penetrate higher things by studying lower things. If we urge ourselves on in this way for a year, how can we not develop? Every day we must seek some amount of improvement, learning what we do not yet know and changing for the better whatever is not good; thus we shall improve our virtuous natures. In reading books we must seek for righteous principles, and in making compilations we must assemble in order things that are relevant, not merely copying along, always becoming more widely acquainted with former precepts and past examples; thus we shall improve our studies. We must never relax for a moment. If we pass our days in this fashion, then in three years we might have made a bit of progress.

The Lu-Wang school. In the lively intellectualism of Southern Sung times, which thrived despite the dominance of anti-intellectualism in the central government, Chu Hsi encountered many philosophical opponents, with whom he often debated publicly at his White Deer Grotto Academy and elsewhere. Among these was a Chekiang pragmatist, Ch'en Liang (1143-94), who argued for practical activism in government service despite having a disastrous political career himself (he was imprisoned three times) and despite not winning his chin-shih degree until the year before his death. Ch'en believed that material reality is the only reality, and that metaphysical speculation about the Supreme Ultimate was impractical and wasteful. Another opponent—of greater subsequent philosophical significance—was Lu Chiu-yüan, who wrote little and consequently had little impact on the intellectual currents of his own time but was later considered the founder of the hsin-hsüeh school of Neo-Confucianism.

Lu Chiu-yüan (or Lu Hsiang-shan), the youngest of six sons in a wealthy Kiangsi family, became a chin-shih in 1172 and held a series of official posts but always preferred studying and teaching to active political life. He believed Chu Hsi quibbled too much about metaphysical subtleties. For example, Chu argued that one's li is seated securely in one's nature, and that one's nature differs from one's mind, the center of cognitive and emotive activity, where he believed li was mixed up with ch'i and contaminated by it. Lu rejected this duality, arguing that one's nature and one's mind (hsin) are in fact the same thing and, moreover, that one's mind and one's li are the same thing. Indeed, he went so far as to suggest that the individual mind encompasses all li, so that "the universe is my mind and my mind is the universe." Therefore, he insisted, investigating li in other things is fruitless; one finds fulfillment only by cultivating—or discovering by intuitive enlightenment—the moral values that are embedded in one's own mind.

While Chu Hsi's li-hsüeh and Lu Chiu-yüan's hsin-hsüeh, among other variants of Neo-Confucianism, were contending in Southern Sung, Chinese bureaucrats serving the Jurchen Chin state in the north perpetuated traditional Confucianism, characterized by earnest personal morality and a sober sense of public duty. Conservative northern Confucians came under Mongol control long before Southern Sung collapsed and were the only Confucians who enjoyed any respect, little as it was, in the early years of Mongol control of all China. To many of them, the whole Neo-Confucian movement must have seemed an unfortunate aberration among unstable, overly effete southerners; and the taint of Buddhist and Taoist metaphysics was on it, clearly. However, Chu Hsi's thought infiltrated the north early, and his voluminous writings were a scholarly challenge that could not be ignored. Li-hsüeh soon became the rage in Yüan dynasty private academies.

From the point of view of the Yüan, the Ming, and finally the Ch'ing rulers, li-hsüeh was an appealing and comfortable version of Confucianism. It did not advocate extreme political activism. It recognized external standards of value and authority, and it urged zealous self-cultivation through sober study of the precepts and precedents of the past. On balance, it seemed moderate if not conservative, and authoritarian enough to serve as an ideological support for autocratic emperors. In contrast, the assertive individualism inherent in Lu Chiu-yüan's hsin-hsüeh doctrines—like the otherworldliness of Buddhism and the unworldly, antiestablishment traditions of Taoism—must have seemed to the Yüan and early Ming rulers an unattractive and even dangerous alternative, to the extent they were known at all. Thus rulers and intellectuals combined to let Lu Chiu-yüan's doctrines lie dormant for centuries, while Ch'eng-Chu doctrines won universal esteem and official state endorsement.

The conditions of intellectual life in the first Ming century were not conducive to unorthodox philosophizing. After the long era of alien invasions followed by the civil wars of the late Yüan years there had to be an enormous expenditure of energy in military, administrative, and general social reconstruction; disciplined practicality was in order. Moreover, the mode of government established by the autocratic early Ming emperors encouraged conservative conformism. Such conservatism was expressed by the scholar Hsüeh Hsüan (1392-1464): "Since the time of Chu Hsi the Way has been clearly known. There is no more need for writing; what is left for us is to practice."

The prevalent practicality of the time, however, diverted the interests of early Ming scholars away from the cosmological metaphysics of the Ch'eng-Chu school, and the conditions of government service caused many sensitive men to live simple, rustic lives at home, devoted to self-evaluation and self-cultivation. The most esteemed philosopher of the first half of the Ming dynasty, Ch'en Hsien-chang (1428-1500), though attaining fame as a living sage, declined proffered honors and chose to spend his life studying and teaching in the remoteness of his home province, Kwangtung. Ch'en unostentatiously challenged Chu Hsi on many points. He conceived of the universe in wholly naturalistic terms, taught the importance of naturalness and quiescence, and engaged in "quiet-sitting" meditation. Although he did not openly endorse the views of Lu Chiu-yüan, his teachings led directly to the full development of hsin-hsüeh doctrines by Wang Yang-ming, the greatest of the later Neo-Confucian thinkers.

A man of Chekiang province, Wang Yang-ming (Wang Shou-jen) was the son of an official and from boyhood became thoroughly versed in governmental realms of the utmost practicality, such as military defense. He won his chin-shih degree in 1499 and became one of the most eminent statesmen of his era, especially noted for his effective suppression of banditry and fostering of socioeconomic stability. At one time he was supreme commander with military and logistical supervision over five provinces in the south. His career was interrupted briefly in 1506, when he was exiled in disgrace to spend three years among the aboriginal tribespeople of Kweichow province in the southwest. But far from blemishing his reputation, this punishment actually increased his prestige; it was a mark of honor to have opposed and offended a notoriously tyrannical eunuch clique that then dominated the emperor Wu-tsung (r. 1505-21). Besides being a successful and admired official, Wang was also an elegant litterateur. But his place in Chinese history is best secured by his creative philosophy, which systematized the long-neglected views of Lu Chiu-yüan and expanded them into a confident individualism that directly challenged the authoritarianism inherent in the orthodox Ch'eng-Chu doctrines. Wang's teachings were a major catalyst in the dynamic diversity that characterized sixteenth-century life in China.

From childhood Wang Yang-ming, like Chu Hsi, was determined to become a sage. He studied the Ch'eng-Chu doctrines assiduously but later reported, no doubt hyperbolically, that his efforts to practice them by the concentrated observation of a bamboo stalk for seven days not only gave him no insight into the li of bamboo but actually made him ill. He studied Buddhism and Taoism as well but concluded they were as wrong as Chu Hsi. Encounters with disciples of Ch'en Hsien-chang led him in different philosophical directions, including serious consideration of Lu Chiu-yüan. Finally, while in his southwestern exile, he experienced a Ch'an-style sudden enlightenment, realizing that mind and universe are a unity and that all li, far from being external, are complete within oneself. This led him eventually to expound the doctrine that moral virtues such as righteousness and humankindness are part of the individual mind's intuitive knowledge (liang-chih), and that being a sage—that is, fulfillment or perfection—lies merely in naturally and spontaneously practicing in one's everyday conduct what one knows intuitively to be right. Wang insisted on "the unity of knowledge and action"—that knowledge is the source and guide of proper conduct, and that proper conduct is the realization or fulfillment of knowledge.

Wang Yang-ming was a moderate, restrained individualist. One's intuitive knowledge reveals what ought to be, he believed; but carrying out such a revelation in action with true naturalness and spontaneity can be accomplished only through hard study and stern discipline. During the second half of the sixteenth century, however, some second-generation followers of Wang widely proclaimed that every man was his own judge of right and wrong, that every impulse should be translated unthinkingly into action, and that "the streets are full of sages." They preached egalitarian, libertarian doctrines to large, excited crowds in the towns and cities. Iconoclastic nonconformity was especially flaunted by Li Chih (1527-1602), a Fukienese Confucian official turned Ch'an Buddhist. A freethinker who completely renounced Confucius and the classics as standards of right and wrong, Li believed in the ready-made perfection of the individual's "child-mind" and considered selfishness and profit to be worthwhile motivations. He denounced traditional Confucians as slavish job-seekers; ardently championed and studied the popular colloquial-style literature that orthodox Confucians publicly disdained; advocated marriage by free choice; and gave philosophical sanction to the syncretistic san-chiao doctrine that Confucianism, Buddhism, and Taoism are of equal truth and value. While holding public office he sometimes conducted official business in Buddhist temples and garb.

As Li Chih's writings became popular, traditional Confucians grew increasingly alarmed about Wang Yang-ming's "left-wing" disciples, or what was commonly called the "mad Ch'an" movement. Li Chih was eventually arrested as a heretic, and in 1602 he committed suicide in prison pending trial. In 1604 a group of moderate Ch'eng-Chu traditionalists established the Tung-lin Academy at Wusih, inland from Shanghai, as a rallying point from which to fight against the moral decay and political corruption that sprang, they felt, from the philosophical distortions of the Wang Yang-ming school. Although the Tung-lin Party met disaster in court politics in the 1620's, Wang Yang-ming extremism was effectively discredited and died out when Ming China was taken over by the Manchus. Wang's own writings were not suppressed, but Ch'eng-Chu orthodoxy remained the mainstream of Chinese philosophy into the twentieth century. Wang Yang-ming was better appreciated in Japan (as Ōyōmei, the Japanese rendering of his name), where his doctrines had great influence on the nineteenth-century zealots who began the transformation of Japan into a Westernized state.

The Manchu takeover of China in 1644 did not put a complete stop to unorthodox thought. It was inevitable that the Ming debacle should arouse serious soul-searching among some Chinese intellectuals, and their inclination was to turn away from Ch'eng-Chu rationalism as well as from Lu-Wang intuitionism, rejecting both schools as Buddhist and Taoist subversions of original Confucianism. The ideas of four men in particular are worthy of note. Yen Yüan (1635-1704), a realist and pragmatist, opposed speculative intellectualism in general and urged practical training in everyday occupations as the only route back to the golden age of Yao and Shun, the legendary sage-kings revered by Confucians of all schools. Tai Chen (1724-77), the most brilliant abstract thinker of the Ch'ing dynasty, shared Yen Yüan's conviction that matter, or ch'i, is all that exists, li being merely the form or structure in which ch'i appears. He advocated the rational, empirical observation of objective reality and the development of Confucian virtues out of instinctive tendencies in human nature. In the narrower realm of political thought, Huang Tsung-hsi (1610-95) bitterly blamed autocracy for most of China's troubles and denounced officials as a class for being self-satisfied and impractical and for thinking of themselves as servants of the rulers rather than of the people. He urged a broadening of civil service recruitment qualifications to include practical, professional expertise, and as a corollary, stricter evaluation of officials on the basis of their demonstrated competence in service. Wang Fu-chih (1619-92), who like Huang fought against the Manchus and remained a Ming loyalist all his life, exuded xenophobic disdain of everything un-Chinese and exalted those dynasties—Han, T'ang, and Ming—that in their heydays had strongly asserted the superiority of Chinese culture. Wang also disdained the Confucian tendency to idealize the past; he believed that China's distant ancestors had been bestial barbarians, that culture advanced in evolutionary fashion, and that institutions must be changed to accommodate changing situations.

Significant as their views appear in retrospect, all these early Ch'ing theorists had little influence on their contemporaries. Ch'ing intellectuals in general did not engage in speculative philosophizing but devoted themselves to politically safe scholarship in many realms.

CLASSICAL SCHOLARSHIP

Reinterpretation of the classical literature was the means used by almost all of the great Neo-Confucian thinkers to present their philosophical innovations. From Sung through Ming times a large propor-

tion of China's intellectual energies was spent in re-editing and anno-
tating the classics over and over, by philologists as well as philosophers.
The endeavor absorbed Chinese minds more fully than Biblical exegesis
ever monopolized the attention of intellectuals in Christendom; it was
every Chinese intellectual's avocation, and much of it was subsidized
by successive dynastic governments. The tradition was encouraged by
the Manchu emperors, who saw in the patronage of classical scholarship an important way of legitimating themselves in Chinese eyes, and
it has continued into our own century.

The most impressive scholarly movement of Ch'ing times was an
effort to circumvent the philosophical biases of the li-hsüeh and hsin-
hsüeh interpreters and rediscover what the classical writings really said
and meant in their own time. There was a turning back to pre-Sung
philological methodology and especially to the Han annotaters, who
had their own doctrinal biases but at least had the advantage of being
free of Buddhist influence and, in comparison with the Sung-Ming interpreters, were closer in time to the classical age by a thousand years
and more. The movement was consequently called the School of Han
Learning, and it produced remarkable philological refinements in both
internal, or textual, criticism and external, or historical, criticism. The
movement had been anticipated by some Ming scholars. The sixteenth-
century scholar Mei Tsu had questioned the authenticity of sections
of the *Shu-ching* (Classic of Writings), and Ch'en Ti (1541-1617) had
made a pioneering phonological analysis of the *Shih-ching* (Classic of
Songs); but the masterpieces of the new inductive, objective scholarship
appeared in Ch'ing times.

The early giant of the Han Learning movement was Ku Yen-wu (or
Ku T'ing-lin, 1613-82), a member of a prosperous Kiangsu clan who
gained some stature as a scholar and minor official in the late Ming
years, took part in the Ming resistance to the Manchus in the south,
and resisted all subsequent enticements to join the Ch'ing officialdom.
He traveled widely in China, read voraciously, and produced a number
of monumental works in several fields of learning. His greatest contribution to classical studies was perfecting Ch'en Ti's phonological research methods so as to reconstruct the ancient pronunciations of
Chinese words and contrast them with T'ang-era pronunciations.

A series of subsequent scholars, including the philosopher Tai Chen,
used Ku Yen-wu's techniques to produce a large corpus of studies on
phonetics and etymology marked by a sophistication not matched in
the West until the nineteenth century. Especially noteworthy among

them was Yen Jo-chü (1636-1704), a Kiangsu neighbor and friend of Ku, who worked on the textual histories of the *Ta-hsüeh* and the *Meng-tzu*, compiled a guide to place-names in the Four Books that had enduring value, and conclusively disproved the authenticity of the "old text" *Shu-ching*, which had been the accepted version for more than a thousand years. The Han Learning movement was monumentally commemorated by the completion in 1829 of a 366-volume compendium of Ch'ing classical scholarship, *Huang Ch'ing ching-chieh*, which included more than 180 separate works. This was sponsored by one of the great late-empire patrons of learning, Juan Yüan (1764-1849), another Kiangsu native, who was one of the most eminent officials of his age.

In retrospect, the most impressive classical scholar of the Ch'ing dynasty was a poor small-town teacher of Hopei province who was little known to his contemporaries but was rediscovered and greatly admired in the twentieth century. This was Ts'ui Shu (or Ts'ui Tung-pi, 1740-1816), who has been called one of the most perceptive textual scholars of world history. He distrusted the Han dynasty classical annotations as much as later ones and concentrated on the texts of the classics themselves. Unaware of Yen Jo-chü's work, he came to similar conclusions about the authenticity of the *Shu-ching*. He questioned traditional claims about the authorship of the *Ta-hsüeh*, the *Chung-yung*, and many other early writings, and most importantly about the life and teachings of Confucius. His most admired production is a long scholarly biography of Confucius, in which he skillfully used both internal and external evidence to strip away exaggerated legends and reconstruct a believable image of the ancient sage as a human being.

SINO-WESTERN INTELLECTUAL CONTACTS

After the introduction of Buddhism from India, China received no further major intellectual stimuli directly from the outside world until its encounter with the West beginning in the sixteenth century. In the long interval between, Chinese of T'ang times had become acquainted with Manichaeism, Islam, and the Nestorian variant of Christianity through contact with Near Easterners, and small Jewish communities appeared in China, most notably in Kaifeng. But none of these foreign doctrines seems to have entered into the general intellectual life of Sung China at all. During the Mongol occupation of China, Moslem astronomers modified the calendrical calculations that were essential to the imperial ideology, and other Moslem and Nestorian groups mixed with the Chinese. The Roman Catholic church made direct contact with China for the first time in this period, sending the Franciscan John of Montecorvino (1246?-1328) to be archbishop at Peking. A few other Franciscan friars were dispatched later to establish a bishopric at the southeastern port city of Ch'üan-chou (Zayton to medieval Europeans) in Fukien province. But the mainstream of China's intellectual life was not affected by these developments, though in the Ming dynasty Moslem Uighurs continued in court service as astronomers, large numbers of Islamicized Chinese (or Sinicized Central Asian Moslems) inhabited western frontier areas, and a Jewish community persisted in Kaifeng.

When the Portuguese opened a sea route around Africa to India at the end of the fifteenth century, they made it possible for European Christendom to undertake sustained missionary work in South and East Asia. In 1552 Saint Francis Xavier, founder of the militant Jesuit order, died off the South China coast awaiting an opening into Ming China, having already established a promising missionary enterprise in Japan. In the mid-1550's Portuguese traders were granted a foothold on the coast at Macao, and from there Jesuits finally began evangelical work inland in 1583, in the garb of Buddhist monks. The pioneer, Matteo Ricci (1552-1610), soon saw the wisdom of adopting the dress and manners of Confucian literati and cultivating the friendship of scholar-officials. His perseverance, learning, and tact won him the privilege of living in Peking from 1601 to his death in 1610. By the time of his death there was well under way one of the strangest episodes in world religious history—a tireless but largely frustrated effort of European Christians to convert the Chinese, the most numerous nation and therefore the most challenging of all unbelievers.

The Christian effort in China during late Ming and early Ch'ing times was almost exclusively a Jesuit effort, and it benefited from the astute leadership of three great men: the Italian Ricci, the German Adam Schall von Bell (1591-1666), and the Belgian Ferdinand Verbiest (1623-88). They perceived that Christianity could make headway in China only by accommodating itself to the traditional Chinese state system and the Confucian ideology on which it rested. Accordingly, they used the rapidly advancing Western astronomical methodology to win favor at China's court and official posts in the imperial bureau of astronomy, and they chose to regard ancestor worship and other Confucian practices as "civil rites"—that is, nonreligious exercises that were no bar to conversion. They were vulnerable to criticism on both counts, for "playing court astrologers for Oriental potentates" and for tolerating heathen practices by church members. Rival sectarians, the Dominicans and Franciscans, denounced their policies and provoked a prolonged Rites Controversy that handicapped the Jesuits throughout the seventeenth century and terminated only gradually in the eighteenth century. A succession of papal decrees were issued, culminating in the ruling in 1742 that no Chinese could become a Christian without giving up ancestor worship and related rituals. Meanwhile, Manchu emperors were enraged by foreign attempts to define what was proper and improper for the Chinese, and imposed ever more severe restrictions on missionary activity. By the middle of the eighteenth century the Jesuit effort in China effectively ended, though Jesuits and other foreign Christians were still permitted to reside in Peking.

At the beginning of the nineteenth century a determined Protestant effort was begun, primarily by English and American churches, to succeed where the Catholics had failed. During the course of the century, as the Western nations encroached on the independence of the Ch'ing empire, the Protestant missionary effort expanded and Catholic missionary work resumed. But the Chinese were never very significantly impressed by the work of the Christian missions. It has been reliably estimated that Chinese who were converted to Christianity at no one time numbered more than one million, and few converts wholly abandoned their traditional beliefs.

All of the Western missionaries, of course, were more than preachers of a strange doctrine; they were culture-carriers on a large scale. They piqued Chinese curiosity by introducing ingenious devices manufactured in Europe, beginning in Ricci's time with clocks and telescopes. More than that, they produced Chinese writings and Chinese translations of Western writings, not only on Christian theology, but on world geography and Western science as well. The Jesuit record in this regard is especially impressive, for the Jesuits were well-educated men in all realms and were sometimes chosen for service in China because of their scholarly knowledge in fields that the Chinese esteemed, such as astronomy. The Jesuits consequently were not unwelcome among Chinese intellectuals, and they were treated with great respect by the late Ming and early Ch'ing emperors. Protestant missionaries to China in the nineteenth century were generally less broadly educated than their Jesuit predecessors and more narrowly theological and evangelical in their approach. Their nontheological publications in Chinese were few and not scholarly, consisting for the most part of elementary texts for school use. These made no favorable impression on Chinese intellectuals.

The first Jesuit publication in Chinese was a theological tract by Michel Ruggieri, issued at Canton in 1584. Ricci himself wrote more than 20 Chinese works, including treatises on mathematics and psychology as well as religious tracts; and in 1602 he printed a much-admired world map, with China tactfully placed in the center. Jesuits were especially active in publishing Chinese works in the seventeenth century, when they issued at least 369 new writings or translations. Thereafter, as the Rites Controversy increasingly handicapped and distracted them, their publishing activities declined notably. In addition to mathematics and geography, their publications introduced to China Western knowledge of mechanics and hydraulics, pharmacology and anatomy, zoology, mineralogy, meteorology, phonetics, and firearms. Information about philosophy, education, and government was not neglected; and some works of Western literature were issued in Chinese translations, beginning with *Aesop's Fables* in 1625.

To what extent all this Western knowledge penetrated and influenced Chinese intellectual life prior to the middle of the nineteenth century is not clear. Mainstream scholarship and philosophy in Ch'ing times reflects no direct interest in or influence from the West. Even in the early nineteenth century Chinese intellectuals and officials were almost totally ignorant about the West; if anything, they were probably more ignorant and unconcerned in this regard than their seventeenth-century counterparts had been.

The reverse process, by which information about China seeped into Europe, always had greater impact. Rumors and fantasies about distant China had titillated Europeans since Han times, when Chinese silk fascinated fashionable Romans, and interest increased steadily during China's later imperial age. Columbus stumbled on the Americas trying to find a westward route to China, and as late as the seventeenth century Henry Hudson was searching for a northwest passage to China via the St. Lawrence River. By his time cultured Europeans had access to extensive and remarkably accurate information about the size, populousness, government, history, and culture of China, though some Westerners nevertheless insisted until late in the nineteenth century that the Chinese must be one of the lost tribes of Israel.

The single most famous book about China ever written by a Westerner is Marco Polo's *Description of the World*, based mainly on his observations in China from early 1274 to late 1290. It was dictated to a literary hack while both men were imprisoned in Genoa in 1298, and was quickly translated from the original French into every other major European language. More than 100 manuscript versions are still known. The book describes China from the point of view of the Mongol conquerors, who were Polo's hosts and patrons, but it does so in such awed and admiring tones that for centuries most Europeans ridiculed it as a book of lies, however entertaining. According to tradition, even when Polo lay dying in 1324 close friends begged him in vain to purge himself of all his lies.

Portuguese and Spanish who were active in East Asia in the 1500's wrote letters, reports, and eventually books that rapidly dispelled this disbelief about China. The major work of the period was a general history and description of the country written in Spanish by Juan Gonzalez de Mendoza, an Augustinian friar who had not himself visited China but under papal auspices consolidated information then available in a clear and lively style. His book was published in 1585 and became a standard reference throughout Europe, in many reissues and translations. Ricci's extensive journals were edited and published in Europe in 1615 by his colleague Nicolas Trigault (1577-1628) under the title *History of the Christian Expedition to China*. Among the many influential Catholic publications that followed were two widely circulated periodical works, *Edifying and Curious Letters Written from Foreign Missions* (collected into 26 published volumes, 1780-83) and *Memoirs Concerning the Chinese by the Missionaries of Peking*, accumulating to 17 volumes (1777-1814), both of which regularly offered translations of Chinese historical, philosophical, and literary writings as well as descriptive articles. Chu Hsi's abbreviated general history of China was translated and extended into the eighteenth century by the French Jesuit J. M. de Mailla (13 published volumes, 1777-85).

While missionaries were sending home to Europe their descriptions and translations, traders were carrying to Europe an increasing quantity of Chinese goods, including tea and silk, porcelains and lacquerware, scrolls, screens, and wallpapers. By the early 1700's Europeans were producing a flood of things in Chinese styles (chinoiserie), at their best including Watteau's landscape paintings, Chippendale's furniture, and the Duke of Kent's famous garden at Kew. The *philosophe* Voltaire found in China a model of enlightened despotism; his popular play "The Orphan of China" was a tribute to the moral superiority of the

Fig. 40. Confucius as visualized by 18th-century Europeans, from J. B. du Halde, *Description . . . de la Chine* (1736)

governmental traditions of China. In Germany Leibnitz and Christian Wolff praised China's antimilitarist attitudes and its goal of social harmony. French economists of the physiocratic school, led by Madame de Pompadour's physician, François Quesnay, advocated a Chinese-style fiscal order. In consequence of all these and other Chinese influences, Confucius has often been called the patron saint of the European Enlightenment.

Two developments were of major importance in bringing the great age of Sinophilism in Europe to an end in the early nineteenth century. One was the republican revolution in France, which tolled the death of absolutism in the West. The other was the rise of a new, puritanical morality in Protestantism, which found in China a classic case of the genteel, tolerant, unmilitant, and unprogressive urbanity that it considered corrupt. Thus many of the Chinese qualities that Westerners had previously admired and often idealized now came to be scorned and reviled. The new mood is well illustrated in S. Wells Williams's *The Middle Kingdom* (1848), which was the most widely respected general description of China into the twentieth century, especially in England and America. Although Williams, an American Protestant missionary, was more objective and knowledgeable about China than most writers of his time, his book abounds in condescending, patronizing opinions about the moral depravity and general backwardness of Chinese society and government.

Unfortunately for China, the West's changing standards of judgment about China coincided with real decline and stagnation in many aspects of Chinese life between the seventeenth and nineteenth centuries. And intellectual conservatism was as important a factor as political, military, and technological deterioration in making late Ch'ing China ill-prepared to cope with the challenges generated by the dynamically expanding West in the 1900's.

14. Literature and Art

CHINA'S CULTURAL vitality in the later imperial age, so evident in the development of Neo-Confucian thought, manifested itself with equal dynamism in literature and art. The counterpart of Neo-Confucianism in literature, the neoclassical "old-style prose" movement inaugurated in the late T'ang years, reached its zenith in the eleventh century and remained dominant into the twentieth century. Historiography became steadily more varied and, like classical scholarship, more sophisticated. The new bibliomania stimulated by printing produced monumental encyclopedias of every sort. Traditional forms of poetry were written in ever greater abundance by the growing literate class, and new song forms evolved endlessly. The writing of poetry became part of the everyday activity of educated people in the new age; though few geniuses emerged to rival the T'ang giants, journeymen poets abounded. Popular entertainments, after centuries of development in obscurity, expanded explosively in the increasingly urban and literate society of the Sung dynasty and flowered in fully evolved operatic dramas in Yüan and Ming times and in short stories and novels in Ming and Ch'ing times, the drama and the novel being the two major new genres added to Chinese literature in the later imperial age.

Among the arts, that of the sculptor finally sank to the level of handicraft work, such as lacquerware and jade, but that of the potter reached its finest forms in the graceful monochrome porcelains of Sung and the decorative polychrome porcelains of Ming; and Chinese painting attained its most admired style in impressionistic landscapes and other abstractions by Sung masters and their successors in the later dynasties. State, society, and culture became so integrated in the new educated elite class that it was now commonplace for one man to earn some distinction as a statesman, a scholar and litterateur in several genres, and a painter as well as a classicist and philosopher; most officials at least hoped and strove to excel in all these realms. By the nineteenth century, however, as in the case of Neo-Confucian thought, creativity in literature and art had declined into imitative conservatism, part of the general stagnation that characterized Chinese civilization at the end of the imperial epoch.

LITERATURE

The later imperial age is so easily characterized as the age of drama and the novel that it is appropriate to emphasize here that such a judgment is a modern, retrospective one and does not accurately reflect the literary climate between Sung and mid-Ch'ing times. For centuries after their appearance, these genres were not esteemed, or even recognized as exciting new art forms, by Chinese intellectuals. Contemporary litterateurs generally considered them fare for the masses, at best harmlessly entertaining and at worst shamelessly immoral but in any case unworthy of the serious attention of high-minded, properly educated men—in the same fashion, in short, as serious dramatists and novelists of our time scorned moving pictures and television when these new media appeared. Esteemed literary men of the later dynasties, when not preoccupied with official duties and classical scholarship, devoted themselves to writing histories and traditional forms of literary prose and poetry; and it was their spirit that dominated the literary circles of their times, not that of dramatists or novelists.

Above all else, the late empire intellectuals were prolific writers, and printing made it possible for their writings to be circulated widely and preserved in abundance. During the Sung dynasty it became common for men of any distinction—even of merely regional or local reputation—to publish their collected writings, or for friends or descendants to do so. Hundreds of such collected works have been preserved from the Sung dynasty, and extant examples from the Ming and Ch'ing periods number at least 1,500 and 3,000, respectively. Any random sampling reveals the staggering productivity and versatility of traditional China's litterateurs. Ch'ien Ch'ien-i (1582-1664), a Kiangsu dilettante not untypical of the Ming-Ch'ing transition era, had a preliminary version of his collected works published in 1643 in 110 chüan, including poetry (21 chüan), prefaces and postfaces (17), biographical and genealogical sketches (10), obituaries and epitaphs (20), funeral odes and

eulogies (2), essays (6), historical annotations (5), critiques of poetry
(5), memorials (2), other official documents (13), and letters and mis-
cellany (9). To this was eventually added a supplement in 50 chüan.
Such collected works usually did not include substantial scholarly undertakings—in Ch'ien's case, an anthology of Ming poetry in 81 chüan,
a draft history of the Ming dynasty in 100 chüan, and annotated editions of several Buddhist texts. The voluminousness of all these writings
can be appreciated by noting that one chüan seldom falls short of 20
printed pages, and a chüan of poems often includes as many as 100
separate pieces.

Learned and literary prose. Despite the reform efforts of Han Yü and
a few followers in late T'ang times, the stilted and elegant form of writing called parallel prose was still the only form considered suitable for
documents and serious literary use in the early Sung decades. The
ultimate triumph of the simpler, more straightforward and supple old-
style prose (ku-wen) championed by Han Yü was brought about almost
single-handedly, and against much opposition, by one of the all-around
intellectual giants of Chinese history, Ou-yang Hsiu (1007-72). A member of an impoverished family of a rising clan of Kiangsi province, Ou-
yang was born in Szechwan in western China while his father was there
on official duty. After his father's early death, he was reared and tutored
by his devoutly Buddhist mother, who was too poor to afford brushes
and paper and made the boy learn characters by drawing them with
reeds on the ground. He had a checkered career as a civil servant, ranging from lowly local magistracies to prominent court positions; and in
his maturity he was the most respected and influential intellectual of
his age.

Supremely humanistic and rationalistic, Ou-yang was not attracted
to the *I-ching* and metaphysical speculations based on it, through which
mainstream Neo-Confucian thought was evolving; he was not a great
philosophical interpreter of the classics in general. Neither was he a
zealous political reformer; he questioned the historicity of the institutions described in the ancient *Chou-li*, from which such utopian planners as his contemporary Wang An-shih drew their inspiration. Ou-
yang was a good-humored, moderate advocate of gradual social and
political improvement through the proper molding of men and institutions. He was in this undramatic way one of the eleventh-century
shapers of the activist Neo-Confucian spirit. He avidly studied ancient
histories such as the *Ch'un-ch'iu* and the *Tso-chuan*; he decried the

influences of Buddhism and Taoism and called Chinese back to their Confucian duties in the family, in society, and in government service; and he enthusiastically sought out, encouraged, patronized, and recommended men of promise. His protégés included men of such widely divergent personalities and views as the reformers Fan Chung-yen and Wang An-shih and two of the leaders in the opposition to Wang, the brothers Su Shih (or Su Tung-p'o, 1037-1101) and Su Ch'e (1039-1112). Ou-yang's memorials and essays in old-style prose were of such unexcelled lucidity and power that Wang and the Su brothers among many others emulated the style, and by the time of Ou-yang's death it was firmly established as the standard style for belles-lettres. Parallel prose nevertheless continued in use for some very formal kinds of government documents until the end of the imperial age. All intellectuals of the later dynasties did literary exercises in it, and a complete novel was even written in parallel prose during the Ch'ing dynasty as a literary tour de force.

Ou-yang Hsiu, Wang An-shih, and the Su brothers are traditionally ranked among the greatest prose masters of the later imperial era. But almost every subsequent generation also had noted prose artists, whose works have been read with delight into modern times. In the Ming and Ch'ing dynasties writers commonly grouped themselves into rival stylistic schools, some claiming affinity with such classical works as the *Tso-chuan*, others with Han Yü and Ou-yang Hsiu, and yet others with still-later exemplars. Of all the post-Sung stylists, the one most deserving of mention here is Kuei Yu-kuang (1506-71) of Soochow, whose essays and anecdotes are often almost poetic in their gentle, understated evocations of moods and feelings. By the nineteenth century prose style was dictated by a conservative school stemming from Fang Pao (1668-1749) and Yao Nai (1732-1815) that called itself the T'ung-ch'eng school after the name of their home town in Anhwei. More scholarly intellectuals considered the works of the T'ung-ch'eng stylists to be all style and no substance.

Historiography in the later imperial era is remarkable primarily for its abundance and variety. Dynastic histories continued to be compiled by imperial commissions in the pattern set by Ssu-ma Ch'ien and Pan Ku. Detailed reign chronicles (*shih-lu*; true records) also survive for the Ming and Ch'ing dynasties, providing modern scholars with a wealth of official documentation not available for earlier periods. In all dynasties central governments published exhaustive compilations of administrative regulations (*hui-yao* or *hui-tien*), collections of imperial edicts, and many other kinds of valuable source materials that have few counterparts in other contemporary civilizations.

State-sponsored historiography was supplemented by even more varied works by private scholars. They reconstructed administrative regulations for earlier dynasties, wrote private dynastic histories, and produced specialized historical studies of institutions, epochs, and incidents. Ou-yang Hsiu was co-author of a revised T'ang history and sole author of a revised history of the Five Dynasties era. But the acknowledged greatest historian of the later empire, and the most influential innovator in the field of historiography since Ssu-ma Ch'ien, was Ssu-ma Kuang (1019-86), who happened also to be the most prominent political opponent of the reformer Wang An-shih. Rising to be chief councilor after Wang's New Laws were revoked, Ssu-ma in 1070 was forced into a 15-year retirement by the pro-Wang faction at court. He then devoted himself to one of the best-organized and most systematic historiographic enterprises of world history: the production of a compendious, integrated chronicle of Chinese history from 404 B.C. to the establishment of the Sung dynasty in 960. His work, entitled *Tzu-chih t'ung-chien* (Comprehensive Mirror for Aid in Governance) and presented to the throne in 1084, established a new genre of historical writing, set new standards for the breadth of sources used, and introduced a methodology noted for remarkable sophistication and objectivity. The main work was accompanied by a compendium of essays on disputed points, in which the merits of contradictory sources are fully discussed and justification is given for the presentation in the main text. A series of continuations appeared in later dynasties, and a famous condensation (*Tzu-chih t'ung-chien kang-mu*) was written by the Southern Sung philosopher Chu Hsi and his disciples, who gave their episodic summaries "headlines" to facilitate skimming.

Another new genre of historical writing was created by Yüan Shu (1131-1205), who rearranged all the chronological data of Ssu-ma Kuang's work into topical chapters. This type of presentation, called *chi-shih pen-mo* (recording events from beginning to end), is traditional China's closest approximation to the style of writing generally favored by modern Western historians. Yüan Shu's pioneering effort was followed by topical rearrangements of almost all the dynastic histories by later scholars.

Whereas Ou-yang Hsiu's highly intellectual approach to history produced somewhat abstract and interpretive works, Ssu-ma Kuang's interest was in assembling facts. His *Tzu-chih t'ung-chien* is therefore a well-edited chronological compendium of historical anecdotes, and into our own time Chinese have been fond of browsing in it. The following short but noted excerpts exemplify Ssu-ma Kuang's anecdotal style and also the kinds of subject matter that scholar-officials of the later empire thought best taught the lessons of history.

[One day in the year 628, when T'ang T'ai-tsung was still in his early years on the throne] the emperor said to his attendants, "I have been looking in the collected works of the Sui ruler Yang-ti. His writings are profoundly learned. I now realize that he was indeed a Yao or Shun [legendary sage-rulers], not a Chieh or Shou [the tyrannical last kings of the ancient Hsia and Shang dynasties]; yet how contrary his conduct was!"

Wei Cheng responded, "Even though a ruler may be wise as a sage, he must humble himself and yield to others. Then the intelligent will offer him their counsel and the brave will exert themselves to the fullest for him. Yang-ti trusted in his own genius and was arrogantly self-reliant. Thus while speaking like a Yao or Shun he acted like a Chieh or Shou. Not understanding his limitations, he brought on his overthrow."

The emperor exclaimed, "The past is not far off; it is our teacher!"

[In 756 the scholar-official Chang Hsün and a small T'ang-loyalist force he had recruited were besieged in the walled town of Yung-ch'iu, Honan, by an army of An Lu-shan's rebels under the command of a defected officer, Ling-hu Ch'ao, for more than 40 days.] When the city's supply of arrows was exhausted, Chang had more than 1,000 straw figures made up, dressed them in black uniforms, and in the night let them down with ropes outside the wall. Ling-hu's troops frantically shot at them, not realizing they were straw men until too late; and Chang in this way acquired more than 100,000 arrows. During a subsequent night, when he let soldiers down with ropes, the rebels joked about them and paid no attention. Thus 500 daredevils slashed their way into Ling-hu's camp. Ling-hu's forces were thrown into total confusion. Fleeing from their burning stockade, they were pursued more than ten miles. Humiliated, Ling-hu resumed the siege with a larger army.

Chang sent his general, Lei Wan-ch'un, to parley with Ling-hu from atop the wall. The rebels shot at him with crossbows. Though hit with six arrows, he did not withdraw. Ling-hu suspected it was a wooden figure, but when his spies found out the truth he became very alarmed. He called from afar to Chang, "Having seen General Lei, I know your mettle; but how can you evade Heaven's will?" Chang retorted, "Since you have no regard for proper human relationships, how can you know anything of Heaven's will!"

Before long, Chang emerged on the offensive, captured 14 rebel generals, and cut off more than 100 heads. The rebels then decamped in the night, regrouped in the walled town of Ch'en-liu, and dared not reemerge. [But after several more victories, Chang Hsün died in battle.]

The transition from Ming to Ch'ing rule stimulated an unaccustomed analytical focusing on recent history; Ming loyalists attempted both to explain why the Ming state had collapsed and to commemorate the valor of the champions of the losing Ming cause. A number of noteworthy historians appeared. Outstanding among them was Huang Tsung-hsi, the political theorist discussed in Chapter 13, whose greatest work was a monumental, pioneering intellectual history of the Ming era—*Ming-ju hsüeh-an* (Case Studies of the Ming Confucians).

Another category of major contributions to historical study by late empire scholars is the so-called scholar's notebook (*pi-chi* or *sui-pi*), a collection of random jottings about miscellaneous subjects, usually historical. Invaluable sources for social as well as political history, these include many works that were browsed in with delight by later generations of Chinese. Most admired are *Jung-chai sui-pi* (Jottings from the Leisure Studio) by Hung Mai (1123-1202) and *Jih-chih lu* (Record of Day-by-Day Knowledge) by Ku Yen-wu, the early Ch'ing founder of the School of Han Learning.

Local histories flourished greatly in the Sung and later dynasties. Two extremely valuable works in this genre describe the bustling urban life of the Sung capitals: *Tung-ching meng-hua lu* (Record of a Dream of the Eastern Capital's Delights; preface dated 1147) by Meng Yüan-lao, a nostalgic memoir on Kaifeng after the loss of North China to the Jurchen, and *Meng-liang lu* (Record of a Dream of the Hangchow Region; published 1275) by Wu Tzu-mu, a similar work on Hangchow produced as Southern Sung was about to fall to the Mongols. A more common type of local study is the gazetteer (*ti-fang chih*), which describes the history and geography of individual counties, prefectures, and eventually provinces, in an organization roughly like that of the dynastic histories. Gazetteers began to be produced regularly in Southern Sung times, when almost 200 appeared. Publication greatly accelerated in Ming times, from which about 1,000 examples are still preserved; and in the Ch'ing dynasty the compilation of gazetteers became a commonplace activity of both individual scholars and government agencies. More than 5,000 Ch'ing gazetteers still exist. The genre was especially stimulated by the Ch'ing scholar Chang Hsüeh-ch'eng (1738-1801), who brought to this project an unaccustomed seriousness of purpose and sophistication of technique. Collectively, Chinese gazetteers constitute one of the world's greatest treasure troves of basic historical data, especially valuable for socioeconomic analyses.

Encyclopedic compendiums of many sorts were also among the products of the later empire's scholars. A comprehensive history of governance by topics, the *T'ung-tien* by Tu Yu of the T'ang dynasty, was followed by the *T'ung-chih*, an ambitious attempt by Cheng Ch'iao (1104-62) to cover the whole of Chinese history in one work in the pattern of the dynastic histories; its topical treatises are especially admired summaries of institutional history in the broadest sense. Then came the *Wen-hsien t'ung-k'ao* by Ma Tuan-lin, who lived from late Sung into Yüan times; it is an institutional history even broader in scope than the *T'ung-tien*. Each of these monumental prototypes was provided with continuations by later scholars into the Ch'ing period. The complete series is known as the *Shih-t'ung* (the Ten Encyclopedic Histories of Administrative Institutions). Meantime, other kinds of encyclopedias appeared in awesome numbers. A few of the most important ones are the following:

T'ai-p'ing yü-lan (983) by an imperial commission: extracts from histories and other works about events that emperors should know about.

T'ai-p'ing kuang-chi (978) by the same commission: fictional and other "unorthodox" materials of interest but not "serious" enough to be included in *T'ai-p'ing yü-lan*.

Ts'e-fu yüan-kuei (1013) by another imperial commission: on the lives and achievements of notable rulers and officials throughout history.

Yü-hai by Wang Ying-lin (1223-96): materials that examination candidates ought to know.

Pen-ts'ao kang-mu by Li Shih-chen (1518-93): a materia medica summing up China's traditional pharmacological knowledge.

San-ts'ai t'u-hui by Wang Ch'i (chin-shih, 1565): an illustrated encyclopedia of everyday utensils and activities, flora and fauna, and technology.

Nung-ching ch'üan-shu by Hsü Kuang-ch'i (1562-1633): a history and description of agronomy and agricultural technology by the late empire's most prominent convert to Christianity.

Wu-pei chih by Mao Yüan-i of late Ming: an illustrated encyclopedia on all aspects of warfare (see Figs. 14, p. 168, and 31, p. 324).

T'ien-kung k'ai-wu by Sung Ying-hsing of late Ming: an illustrated encyclopedia on applied science, especially industrial technology (see Fig. 34, p. 340).

Huang Ming ching-shih wen-pien (1638) by an imperial commission: a compilation of documents establishing precedents for the actual practice of governmental administration.

Ku-chin t'u-shu chi-ch'eng (1725) by an imperial commission: texts, data, drawings, maps, charts, and diagrams on every important and useful subject; no doubt the most colossal encyclopedia ever printed anywhere, in 10,000 chüan.

Another example of the later imperial age's craze for compendiums was the reproduction of whole independent works in uniform-format sets known as collectanea (*ts'ung-shu*). These are reprint editions—for example, of all rare works in a particular library, or important works on a particular subject, or important works by writers of one period or region. Many works that would otherwise have been lost are preserved in the nearly 3,000 collectanea, small and large, that were printed in Ming and Ch'ing times. The most ambitious efforts of this sort were two government-sponsored projects that set thousands of scholars to work reproducing all extant literature of significance. The first effort produced the *Yung-lo ta-tien* (Great Canon of the Yung-lo Era) in 1407, which incorporated more than 22,000 chüan in an edition of almost 12,000 volumes. Even the ambitious Yung-lo emperor shrank from the prospect of printing such a compendium. It was left in manuscript form. Two additional manuscript copies were made in the 1560's, but various disasters scattered or destroyed all three sets, so that now fewer than 400 volumes are known to exist.

The second effort to collect all important writings came in the 1770's. The result was another great imperial manuscript collectanea called the *Ssu-k'u ch'uan-shu* (Complete Writings of the Four Treasuries), the four treasuries, or categories, being classics, histories, philosophical writings, and belles-lettres. Seven complete sets of roughly 36,000 volumes each were eventually made; some of these sets have been preserved to the present. An invaluable by-product of the endeavor was the compilation and publication of an annotated catalog of more than 10,000 works seen by the compilers; it remains the most useful bibliography for serious students of China's past. Yet the reputation of the Ch'ing dynasty compilation suffers from the fact that the project was undertaken for a dual purpose—not only to collect and preserve important works, but to purge traditional writings of all disparaging references to the Manchus and even to their nomadic predecessors. This was the culmination of several Manchu literary inquisitions. In the preparation of the *Ssu-k'u ch'uan-shu* some 3,000 works were tampered with editorially, and there were strenuous efforts to suppress totally almost 2,500 books, mostly by Ming authors.

Poetry. Until very recently poets of the later empire have been noted for their productivity rather than their creativity, in part because they and later critics alike have stood in awe of the T'ang poetic giants. Poets of the Sung and later dynasties often imitated their great predecessors, or at least consciously strove to apply earlier poetic devices and idioms to new subject matter. Many of their poems consequently are no more than scholastic exercises and deserve little attention. Moreover, as poetry came to be written assiduously by an ever-growing literate class, it was inevitable that many of the poems written by any generation merit the oblivion into which almost all have fallen. But a large amount of good poetry was written in every era, as modern scholarship is gradually revealing.

Among the few broad generalizations that might safely be made about later empire poetry, one is that poets wrote about a vaster range of subject matter than their predecessors, and with greater attention to the minutiae of life and of their subjects. Poetry thus became less concise and suggestive, more explicit and discursive. It served to express thought as well as feeling and included philosophical, descriptive, and narrative pieces in abundance. These trends were already apparent in some of the pre-Sung masters discussed in Chapter 9; now they became more universal, and most earlier poetry by contrast seems somewhat insubstantial. Moreover, as the Neo-Confucian movement gradually weakened the world-negating influences of Buddhism and Taoism, poetry generally became more optimistic, and the mood of despair that suffused so much of the poetry of the early imperial age was slowly dispelled.

The traditional form of poetry called shih remained the standard poetic medium throughout the later dynasties, with its regular five-word and seven-word lines stacked in quatrains. The regulated shih in all its tone-pattern complexities—both the normal two-stanza form and the single-stanza variant called the chüeh-chü—flourished together with the freer old-style shih. All types of shih gradually became intellectual more than emotional expressions; and the shih was so strongly felt to be the only "serious," respectable poetic form that other forms, to which emotional expressions were now relegated, were seldom included in the collected works of a late empire litterateur. One exception was the ornate rhyme-prose fu, in which litterateurs continued to exercise and demonstrate their virtuosity as they did in parallel prose.

The song-form tz'u that developed in late T'ang, characterized by lines and stanzas of irregular length but with prosodic prescriptions of other sorts that were as rigid as those of regulated shih, reached its zenith of popularity in the tenth and eleventh centuries, even though the tunes for which tz'u were written were already being forgotten. Tz'u continued to be written thereafter but were eventually as wholly unrelated to music as shih were. Musical styles changed, especially as new instruments and tunes were introduced from Central Asia in the period of Mongol dominance. To suit the new music, another song form emerged, called *ch'ü* or *san-ch'ü*. Freer in form than tz'u, ch'ü admitted more colloquial language and became the most popular form for emotional expression, often erotic. Its history is closely related to that of operatic drama (see the next section); shih and tz'u remained the dominant poetic forms among intellectuals to the end of the imperial epoch.

Among the noteworthy poets of the later imperial age, Li Yü (or Li Hou-chu, 937-78) is unique both as a person and as a poet. Li was ruler of the Nanking-based state of Southern T'ang, which was absorbed by emergent Sung in 975; he was taken prisoner and lived as a closely restricted "state guest" at Kaifeng until he died in 978, apparently of poisoning. He was a writer of intensely lyrical and personal tz'u. Those of his early life celebrate the dilettantish gaiety of court life at Nanking, but his best-known poems are poignantly nostalgic ones written in captivity. The following translation of a much-admired poem from that period suggests both the metrical irregularity and the rhyme pattern of the original:

> *Song to the Tune "The Beauty Yü"*
>
> Spring blossoms, autumn moon—how long does the cycle last?
> How much is remembered of what is past?
> In my little garret an east breeze was beckoning again last night,
> But I couldn't bear to turn my head toward my old domain in
>   the moonlight.
> The carved railings and marble steps must still be in place;
> It's just that the royal red has left no trace.
> I ask you, how much can one's sorrow be increased?
> As much as a Yangtze flood in springtime flowing east!

The next two selections are equally admired laments by Li Yü in the tz'u form:

Song to the Tune "Wave-Washed Sand"

Outside the curtain the rain drips and plops;
The springtime mood is all withered away.
My thin silk quilt can't withstand the chill of the fifth watch;
But in dreams I'm not aware I'm a "guest,"
And for a while I'll savor that pleasure.
Alone at evening I lean over the railing.
What a limitless landscape!
Parting, easy;
Reunion, hard.
Flowing streams, falling blossoms—spring is gone,
In nature as among men.

Song to the Tune "Clear Calm Music"

Since my departure it is halfway to another spring,
And the swelling sadness bursts my vitals.
At the foot of the steps the falling plum leaves tumble about
        like snowflakes;
No sooner brushed off than I am covered all over again.
The geese come, but their promises can't be trusted;
The way is far, and the dream of going home is impossible to
        fulfill.
Homesickness is just like spring grass—
However far away one goes, it flourishes there, too!

Ou-yang Hsiu's most famous protégé, Su Shih (or Su Tung-p'o, 1037-1101), was as versatile an intellectual as Ou-yang and had a similarly checkered official career. Su was not a supremely rational intellectual of Ou-yang's sort, but an aesthete—probably the outstanding all-around aesthete of the Chinese tradition. Not famed as a scholar or philosopher, he excelled in all forms of belles-lettres and is especially considered a poetic genius in the somewhat unorthodox spirit of T'ao Ch'ien and Li Po. He wrote both unregulated and regulated shih with equal brilliance; he is commonly rated China's greatest tz'u master; and he wrote rhyme-prose fu with a freshness and magnificence unapproached since Han times. In addition, he is admired as a painter and calligrapher of the first rank; he popularized what became a widespread Chinese practice—the writing of "landscape poems" about, and inscribed on, landscape paintings. His contemporaries also rated him an authoritative connoisseur of inks, wines, and cookery; he was an engineer who supervised water-control projects that made Hangchow and its West Lake one of the beauty spots of China; and he practiced Taoist yoga and alchemy. The following samples of his poetry may suggest why later Chinese have found his happy, humane spirit irresistible and have considered him the greatest of all post-T'ang poets.

Song to the Tune "The Immortal Watching Over the River": Returning at Night to Lin-kao

Drinking at night on East Slope, I sober up only to get drunk
      again,
And it must be nearly the third watch when I return.
The houseboy's snores are thunderous roars.
I bang on the gates, but no one waits.
So I lean on my staff and listen to the river churn.

I heave long sighs that my life is not my own.
When will I get free from these trifling troubles!
Late in the night the wind grows calm, the waves become
      bubbles.
In a small boat I could break away from here with ease
And give my remaining life to the rivers and seas!

The East Slope

A good farmer conserves the land's fertility.
I'm lucky this plot lay for ten years fallow.
The mulberry trees haven't yet matured,
But a crop of wheat can probably be expected.
I sowed my seed, and before a month had passed,
Among the clods some green already appeared.
A peasant elder gave me a sound warning:
     "You mustn't let the sprouts shoot up too fast!
     If you want the richest kinds of cakes and dumplings
     You'd better graze your cow and sheep in there."
I bowed: I appreciate the good advice,
And when I get my fill I won't forget you!

Enjoying the Peonies at the Temple of Good Fortune

When a man is old it's no disgrace to wear flowers in his hair,
Though the flowers ought to feel ashamed atop such an
      oldster's head.
People giggle as I go home drunk, supported along the road,
And for ten leagues window blinds are enticed halfway up.

Visiting Old Haunts

I must have come to Hangchow in a former life;
Wherever I go, it's always like visiting old haunts.
I wish I could live as a recluse in a misty cave,
Or linger awhile in the cloister of some small monastery.

The Pavilion Window

The eastern neighborhood has many aspens;
At night they sound like driving rain.
By my window I alone can get no sleep,
And autumn insects swarm around my lamp.

[Untitled Poem with Preface]

Preface: On New Year's Eve I was on duty at the office, which
was jammed with prisoners in chains. Even at nightfall I didn't
get to go home, so I inscribed this poem on the wall.

New Year's Eve calls for going home early,
But official business keeps me at work.
Gripping my writing brush, seeing through tears,
I grieve for these prisoners bound up in chains.
Rascals scrambling for something to eat—
Trapped by the law, they've displayed no remorse.
But me—I'm so fond of my miserable stipend,
I put up with anything not to retire.
It isn't a question of who's honored or humble.
Like everyone else, these are schemers for meals.
Does anyone dare give them holiday furloughs?
I blush at the mercy of the old-time judges.

On the Way to Hsin-ch'eng

An eastern breeze, aware of my wish to travel into the hills,
Has blown the sound of the lingering rain out from under the
    eaves.
Clouds have gathered into fleece-white caps perched atop the
    peaks,
And the rising sun hangs in a treetop like a bronze-red gong.
Wild peach trees are smiling from beyond the low bamboo
    fence,
And shoreline willows are swaying over the clear sandy stream.
Families of these western hills especially must be happy,
Cooking mallows and bamboo shoots to feed the springtime
    plowmen.

On Reading the Poetry of Meng Chiao (751-814)

At night I read the poems of Meng Chiao,
In script as minuscule as oxen hairs.
In harsh light from the lamp my vision blurs,
And striking phrases occur but now and then.
Some lonely blossoms pop up in the wastes,
But the words are harder than in the *Shih* or *Li Sao*.
The froth from boulders in the clear stream's flow

Makes it too tumultuous for poling.
At first it's just like eating tiny fish;
What you get is hardly worth the effort.
Then it's like the boiling of small crabs,
Which leaves you in the end with empty claws.
His meaning measures up to the monk Chia Tao,
But in style he's not the equal of Han Yü.
The life of man is brief as morning dew,
Or a flame consuming oil both day and night.
Isn't it sad to force my two good ears
To listen to the drone of such a miserable insect!
I'm better off to put it all aside,
And have some drinks of my jade-white wine.

Of Southern Sung poets, one is remembered as a rarity in China's cultural heritage—a patriotic poet. This was Lu Yu (1125-1209) of Chekiang. In emotional verses differing in mood from the philosophical calmness of late empire poetry in general, Lu wrote ringing challenges for his countrymen to drive away the Jurchen who occupied the north. But he was not solely a patriotic poet. Like most litterateurs of the later empire, he was an interested observer of everyday things and wrote occasional poems of every variety; and he was incredibly prolific, turning out more than 9,000 pieces of verse. His best-known work, echoing his lifelong patriotic passion, is one of his last poems:

For My Son

When dead and gone one finally knows the vanity of all things,
But I still regret that I won't see the realm reunited.
When the imperial armies recover the Central Plain to the
				north,
In the family devotions don't forget to let your father know.

Other expressions of his patriotic frustrations include the following:

Song: Taking Up Residence at Lung-hsing Temple

The Central Plain is forsaken, the long peace broken;
In flames of war barbarians have taken both our capitals.
An aged retainer, following his lord in a ten thousand-league
				retreat,
Arrived here in the winter cold and listened to the sounds of
				the Yangtze.

Song to the Tune "The Wizard of Magpie Bridge"

In my decorated stirrups I rode with reckless abandon;
From my carved saddle I shot arrows on the gallop.

But who took note of my heroics then?
Drinking companions one after another have got honors,
While I alone have been sent away
To be a fisherman on the river.
A light boat eight feet long,
With only three patches of sail!
I enjoy as I can the misty rains of my weed-covered islet.
But a lake refuge is really for a loafer;
Why must it be presented to an active official?

The following examples represent, however inadequately, the work of a few of the innumerable noteworthy poets of the later dynasties, each renowned in his time. The first is by Liu Yin (1249-93), a northern scholar who refused to serve in Kubilai Khan's government; it alludes to a dictum by Mencius that the creation of a well-ordered society first of all requires a certain kind of ruler.

Miscellaneous Poem

In my retreat in the hills I seek the exalted Way.
In youth I busied myself in worldly affairs,
But when I look back and speak of things that were,
With glowering brows I find I loathe my life.
The streams and hills now shelter thieves and bandits;
The fields are now abandoned to brambles and thorns.
Our heritage is a burden of moral obligations,
But we lack a ruler who grieves at committing murder.

The next example, translated by F. W. Mote from a sequence entitled "On Going Out Beyond the City, to the Eastern Village," is by Kao Ch'i (1336-74), a Soochow litterateur who somewhat reluctantly joined the early Ming court and was soon executed on far-fetched charges of sedition.

[Untitled]

Sitting long, my body stiff and cramped,
I close my book and stroll out the garden gate.
Reaching the brook I happen to look to the west:
Squarely in view there—Mount Ch'in-yü.
The wilds seem empty, wintry trees stand sparse.
The stream flows on. The birds of dusk return.
'Midst this, a poem takes sudden form.
My heart soars; all cares disperse.
I go along home with shepherds and woodsmen,
Singing and laughing as the evening sun goes down.

Wang Shih-chen (1526-90), represented here by the following occasional poem, was an eminent official, a historian, and for two decades the doyen of Ming literature and scholarship.

For Brother-in-Law Wei on His Departure for Home

> Your sister has been helped to her bed in tears;
> Our children cling to my knees with shrieks.
> "Safe trip!" is only a couple of words;
> We dare not think of your Yangtze crossing!

The last poem in this sampling is by Cha Shen-hsing (1650-1727), an editor of gazetteers and poetry anthologies and a literary hanger-on at the court of the K'ang-hsi emperor.

On Duty Alone at the Southern Archive During Rain

> Cloistered within the Nine-fold Gates,
> Far back on Congratulation Heights:
> With the coming of rain, the hush grows deeper;
> I can relax as if throned in Heaven.
> I muse that it's quite like having a holiday;
> With aimless footsteps I roam to and fro.
> The palace culverts are flooded anew;
> When I go home I'll listen for their gurgles.

Drama. The major form of traditional Chinese theatrical entertainment is a distinctive type of operatic drama or operetta combining speaking and singing with action expressed through pantomime, dancing, and acrobatics. The plots, which are generally taken from the traditional storyteller's repertoire, are characteristically melodramatic in the extreme and almost without exception, even after the most tragic story development, end on an uplifting note—not always with happy endings in the usual sense, but with gratifying endings in which justice triumphs over evil. They exude the value system of the late empire's scholar-official elite, consistently suggesting, for example, that passing the civil service examinations is the worthiest of all goals and the key to success and happiness.

Because Chinese theatrical troupes have usually been highly mobile, ready to travel wherever crowds might gather for trade fairs and religious festivals, they have not burdened themselves with elaborate sets or props. The manipulation of ordinary chairs and tables by stagehands working in full view of the audience during the action effectively suggests even the most sumptuous setting, and conventionalized body movements suggest mounting and dismounting from horses, boarding and riding in boats, and other activities that cannot be portrayed realistically on a crude stage. Partially in compensation for the barren stage, actors and actresses rely heavily on gaudy costumes and exaggerated facial makeup; and these too are conventionalized to help the audience identify characters by stock stereotypes, each with many subtypes. Moreover, major players customarily introduce themselves to the audience on their first appearances and, in soliloquies and asides throughout a performance, explain their private feelings and motives.

Dramatic singing, which is accompanied by a small orchestra of strings and percussion onstage or just offstage in the wings, seldom contributes anything to the plot of a Chinese drama. It only accentuates or enlarges on the emotions of the singer or singers at especially dramatic moments. But the songs have traditionally been considered the finest literary elements in drama, and the singing of female impersonators became particularly esteemed in the latter half of the Ch'ing dynasty, when public stage performances by women were banned.

Drama of these general characteristics was another of the cultural innovations of the later imperial age. It took shape about the time of the Mongol conquest of North China in the first half of the thirteenth century. Its form has changed very little since; the Yüan dynasty dramas are considered China's classics in this genre. Called *tsa-chü* (variety show), the form was a combination of elements from two predecessors. The name tsa-chü, together with nonsinging acting techniques, came from skits that were prominent among the vaudeville presentations of Northern Sung playhouses. The musical elements came from suites of ch'ü songs all in the same musical mode or key, called *chu-kung-tiao* (medleys), that became popular in North China under the Jurchen Chin dynasty. These suites traced back to an even earlier day, originating late in the eleventh century as sad, romantic narrations interspersed with erotic songs that were performed by courtesans in tea-houses and better-class brothels. Precisely where and by whom the two forms were merged is not clear, but by the mid-thirteenth century Yüan tsa-chü were thriving in Peking and other cities of the north.

Concurrently, in South China, the early Sung tsa-chü was developed into a different operatic form called *nan-hsi* (southern drama). Whereas Yüan tsa-chü have a standard four-act structure, and their ch'ü are sung in rigid medley suites and only by the leading performer in any one play, nan-hsi are irregular in length and looser in musical form. Their ch'ü do not occur in suites; they are sung in duets and choruses as well as in solos; and no distinction is made between singing and non-singing roles.

The tsa-chü and nan-hsi dramatic forms flourished side by side into Ming times, written both by professional playwrights and by literati enthusiasts of the ch'ü verse form. Nan-hsi, or ch'uan-ch'i as they came to be called (this is the same term used for literary short stories, meaning tales of the marvelous), gradually surpassed tsa-chü in popularity, and regional variations in musical styles abounded. In the early sixteenth century a particularly soft and melodious musical style was popularized by a professional musician of Soochow's K'un-shan district. Called *K'un-ch'ü* (songs of K'un-shan), this soon became the predominant style in which ch'uan-ch'i were performed everywhere, and it endured into the nineteenth century. After the Taiping Rebellion, which ravaged southeastern China, the heartland of K'un-ch'ü, regional variations flourished anew. By the end of the century, though regional forms persisted, a hybrid interregional dramatic form evolved in Peking, mixing tsa-chü and ch'uan-ch'i elements into what is now famed as Peking Opera, which the Chinese call *ching-hsi* (capital drama).

The single most famous play in China's dramatic repertoire is *Hsi-hsiang chi* (Romance of the West Chamber), a tsa-chü composed early in the thirteenth century by Wang Shih-fu of Peking, perhaps with help from the most renowned Yüan dramatist, Kuan Han-ch'ing. It is an unusual tsa-chü in that it is a cycle of five play-length units, each in four acts. The plot derives from a famous ch'uan-ch'i tale by the T'ang litterateur Yüan Chen (779-831), which had gone through many transformations in the hands of storytellers and composers. In brief, it tells of a love affair between a young student, Chang Chün-jui, who is resting up for the civil service examinations in a rural monastery, and Ts'ui Ying-ying, who stops for a time at the monastery while traveling with her domineering, ambitious, widowed mother. Thanks to the connivings of Miss Ts'ui's sly maid, the boy and girl overcome many obstacles and become lovers. But suddenly the monastery is besieged by brigands, and their chief demands the girl for himself. Panic-stricken, Mother Ts'ui promises Ying-ying in marriage to anyone who might raise the siege and deliver them. Young Chang saves the situation, not by heroics, but by writing an appeal to the regional governor, who is so impressed with Chang's literary promise that he sends government cavalry to the rescue. But Mother Ts'ui haughtily rejects Chang's claim to Ying-ying, since as yet he is nobody of social significance, and a happy ending is not achieved until Chang triumphs gloriously in the examinations, whereupon Mother Ts'ui is flattered and proud to marry her daughter to such a social lion.

Mu-tan t'ing (Peony Pavilion), written by the famed Ming litterateur T'ang Hsien-tsu (1550-1616) in 55 acts with music in the K'un-ch'ü style, is probably China's most celebrated ch'uan-ch'i; at least two women reportedly died of grief when it was first produced because of its beautiful sadness. Its heroine, Tu Li-niang, the daughter of a Southern Sung provincial official, is visited and loved by a young student in a dream. She later hides a portrait of herself in her garden for her dream lover, but she pines away yearning for him in vain and dies of lovesickness. Her father is then transferred to a frontier post, and in his absence Liu Meng-mei, a student traveling to Hangchow for the civil service examinations, is allowed to recuperate from illness in the Tu residence. Discovering Miss Tu's portrait, he falls in love. She visits him in his dreams, recognizes him as her own dream lover, and instructs him to open her grave. She is revealed to be beautifully alive in her coffin. They marry and proceed to Hangchow. Before the examination results can be announced, Miss Tu sends Liu off to find her father, reported to be endangered by Jurchen raiders. Father Tu denounces Liu as a grave-robbing impostor, and Liu suffers a cruel flogging. He is saved from a worse fate by the arrival of a delegation hailing him as first-place graduate in the examinations. Misunderstandings are then untangled, and all eventually ends joyously.

Fiction. Many of the imaginative tales written by the scholar-officials of late T'ang were collected in anthologies by Sung and Ming intellectuals, but they wrote few ch'uan-ch'i tales themselves, perhaps because the form seemed frivolous to Neo-Confucians. The tradition did not die out completely, however, and early in the Ch'ing dynasty it culminated in a masterwork by an eccentric named P'u Sung-ling (1640-1715). P'u apparently would not discipline himself in classical scholarship; he was unable to pass the civil service examinations even at the provincial level. He was fascinated by ghost stories and similar esoterica, and he devoted his adult life largely to collecting and creating them. Some of his tales circulated widely in manuscript copies, but their literary style made them unattractive to publishers of colloquial fiction, which then had a large audience, and P'u remained too poor to have them printed himself. A grandson finally published P'u's collected tales in 1740 under the title *Liao-chai chih-i* (Strange Stories from an Eccentric's Studio), and the work quickly won renown as a classic—not only equaling or surpassing T'ang chu'an-ch'i in story interest, but offering the literary prose style at its elegantly simple best. Most commonly, its tales deal with earnest young scholars who are beguiled into danger, humiliation, and destruction by fox-fairies disguised as alluring maidens.

Of more significance for historians of late empire literature is a gradual development from Sung times on of both short and long works of fiction in colloquial Chinese, or *pai-hua* (plain speech). Fully developed pai-hua fiction so self-consciously presents itself as a writing-out of oral traditions, even in wholly original works, that the presence of a narrator always intrudes, and chapters in novels commonly end on a suspenseful note with the author saying, for example, "If you want to learn how So-and-so gets out of this unhappy predicament, you must turn now to our next chapter." The reader is constantly called on to imagine himself listening to a storyteller who in such ways lures his audience back for the next day's performance or wheedles a few *cash* from the listeners as an inducement to carry on.

In Sung, Yüan, and early Ming times the only written forms of colloquial fiction were skeletal "plot books" (*hua-pen*), which were published by the storytellers' guilds of Hangchow. It was not until the latter part of the sixteenth century that the "plot book" tradition evolved into full-blown colloquial short stories written and published for the large bourgeois clientele. They included rehashes of Sung tales in Sung settings and popularizations of historical events and legends from earlier times; but they also included fresh tales about contemporary life, with realistic portrayals of a wide spectrum of sixteenth-century common people. Many of the late Ming short stories are erotic and pornographic in the extreme.

Since colloquial fiction was still considered an unsuitable genre for reputable litterateurs to work in, and especially since much of it grossly offended the state-espoused morality that educated people publicly endorsed and strove to exemplify, the authors of these short stories either remained anonymous or adopted strange pseudonyms to conceal their identity. But the movement reached its peak of creativity and artistry with an author who is known despite his use of a variety of pseudonyms —a Soochow man named Feng Meng-lung (1574-1646). Like his literary-fiction counterpart P'u Sung-ling, Feng had failed in the civil service examinations. He collected and edited existing stories and wrote new ones, and in the 1620's he published three anthologies that became best-sellers. Known collectively as San-yen (The Three Sayings), the anthologies contained 120 stories. Another unsuccessful candidate for a degree, Ling Meng-ch'u (1580-1644) of Chekiang, quickly churned out two competing anthologies, consisting almost solely of his own original stories. Then an enterprising publisher issued a collection of the 40 best stories by Feng and Ling under the title Ku-chin ch'i-kuan (Marvels Old and New). This work drove its predecessors into oblivion and became the classic anthology of colloquial short stories down to the present. Other late Ming tales, including the most pornographic ones, were effectively suppressed by the Manchu Ch'ing government and might have been lost entirely if copies had not been hoarded in Japan, where twentieth-century Chinese rediscovered this almost forgotten part of their literary heritage.

During the Ming dynasty, also, there began to appear long works of fiction in the colloquial style, creating in China the only great heritage of novels found in a premodern civilization outside Europe. Six novels in particular are prototypes and classics of the principal genres that emerged.

San-kuo chih yen-i (Romance of the Three Kingdoms or, more literally, History of the Three Kingdoms Fictionalized) is the least colloquial and least fictional of the classic novels. Written in a simple literary style with strong colloquial influence, especially in its conversational parts, it is a retelling in lively, dramatic episodes of China's political and military history in the years 184-280. It treats the late Han military dictator Ts'ao Ts'ao as a cruel, semiliterate, and rather stupid villain while glorifying Liu Pei and his supporters in the Shu state of Szechwan as heroic defenders of the civilized Han tradition that was destined to be extinguished. Liu Pei's mentor Chu-ko Liang is especially idealized as a loyal, resourceful strategist and statesman. Most major characters are drawn very realistically and became as familiar to Chinese of the late empire and the twentieth century as the greatest Shakespearian characters are to the English. The novel in its present form is normally attributed to Lo Kuan-chung (1330?-1400?), a Shansi man who migrated to Hangchow in the Yüan-Ming transition era and reportedly wrote other novels and also dramas. It was first published in 1522 and by the end of the Ming dynasty had appeared in more than 20 editions.

Shui-hu chuan (Water Margin, known in one English translation as *All Men Are Brothers*), which is fully in colloquial language, is also attributed to Lo Kuan-chung by some specialists, but is ascribed by others to a late Yüan man named Shih Nai-an, of whom virtually nothing is known. It is a rambling account of how 108 outlaws, 36 of whom must be reckoned major characters, separately get into trouble with the authorities and make their way to a mountain hideout surrounded by marshes in Shantung province; the time is early in the twelfth century, as Northern Sung approached its end. Giving a panoramic view of Chinese life at all social levels, the book abounds in coarseness and brutality, but the scalawags, bullies, and scamps who people it are presented sympathetically as enemies of a corrupt social order and of abusive officials. Under the loosely acknowledged leadership of a faintly historical bandit named Sung Chiang, they engage in escapades often as funny as they are violent. Usually, in a Robin Hood-like spirit, they aim to harass and humble the oppressors of society and to right the wrongs done to the oppressed. *Shui-hu chuan* is unquestionably traditional China's best-loved novel. Its earliest known version, published in 100 chüan in 1540, has a long denouement recounting moralistically how the outlaws finally disperse and meet violent deaths. A 70-chüan version that was first published in 1641 ends with a dream in which the dispersal and destruction of the gang are foreshadowed; this remains the current version.

Hsi-yu chi (A Record of a Pilgrimage to the West, best known in English translation as *Monkey*) is a fantastic, allegorical, satirical retelling of Hsüan-tsang's seventh-century pilgrimage to India in search of new Buddhist texts. It is attributed to Wu Ch'eng-en (1506?-82?), a well-educated man who failed the examinations and spent much of his life on the fringes of eminent social and political circles at Nanking. First published in 1592, *Hsi-yu chi* is often called the Buddhist *Pilgrim's Progress*; but its aim is pure entertainment. It takes the high-minded but easily frightened monk from China to India through a series of wholly unrealistic, often hilarious adventures. He is accompanied by a cowardly, lecherous pig and a mischievous, magical monkey. Monkey is the real hero—an irrepressible madcap prankster who has been assigned to escort Hsüan-tsang in penance for having almost laid Heaven in ruins, to the great annoyance of the Buddha and Lao-tzu as well. When, with Monkey's help, Hsüan-tsang finally reaches the Buddha's head-quarters in paradise, he finds to his dismay that he must put up with the officiousness and corruption of an elaborate hierarchy of bureau-cratic officials. He does take home a load of precious canonical texts, but only after a false start with blank scrolls given him by Buddhist officials displeased at his inability to give them bribes.

Chin P'ing Mei (known in the fullest English rendering as *Golden Lotus*) is an original work by an unknown sixteenth-century author. Legend ascribes it to the noted scholar-official Wang Shih-chen, who is said to have written the novel for the sole purpose of presenting it to a political enemy in the expectation that the enemy could not resist reading through it greedily, licking his fingers to turn the pages and thus poisoning himself with the arsenic Wang had smeared on the edges of the pages. The only plausible aspects of this legend are that the au-thor was indeed a literary genius, and that the novel is read with great relish by those who enjoy pornography, for it abounds in more explicit details about sex than the most salacious modern erotica. It is a well-plotted novel about a merchant named Hsi-men Ch'ing, his relations with his six wives, and his affairs with neighbors' wives, maids, and prostitutes. Its pornographic qualities easily obscure its literary merits, which are numerous. It is China's earliest novel about the personal lives of believable, contemporary middle-class people; the first novel to focus significantly on female characters and to evoke their individual person-alities clearly; and a cutting satire about many social groups, including irreligious Buddhist and Taoist monks and graft-hungry officials. More-over, the book concludes with a terrible indictment of immorality. Hsi-men Ch'ing's roisterous life does not lead him to a horrible retribution, as Chinese literary conventions normally required; he dies from over-indulgence. But after his death his family is destroyed, and his son takes up monastic asceticism to atone for his father's excesses.

Ju-lin wai-shih (An Unofficial History of the Confucian Literati, known in English translation simply as *The Scholars*) is the least cohe-sive of the great traditional novels, being merely a succession of episodic anecdotes without any predominant characters or continuing plot de-velopment. It derives what unity it has from a central theme—the good-humored ridicule of the scholar-official class. It was written in the early

Ch'ing period by Wu Ching-tzu (1701-54), a man of scholarly family background from the Nanking area who disliked examinations and did not strive for an official career.

Hung-lou meng (Dream of the Red Chamber) was written by the impoverished scion of a wealthy and powerful early Ch'ing family, Ts'ao Hsüeh-ch'in (1724?-64), and depicts the degenerate life of just such an upper-class household as he must have remembered from his youth. It does so on a panoramic scale and in dense detail. It is peopled with 30 well-delineated major characters and more than 400 individualized lesser characters, ranging through the whole social scale from the imperial family down to the commonest peasants. The main plot revolves around the cloistered but tempestuous adolescence of a pampered, sickly, temperamental boy, whose entire life to young manhood is spent in a female-dominated household and who is the family's hope for the future. The climax comes when the hero is tricked into marrying a cousin in the belief that she is his true love, another cousin who is actually on her deathbed. The novel has stylistic beauty and narrative power, superb characterization, and abundant descriptive detail. On balance, it is a realistic, believable, and sensitive story of young love and domestic life; yet over it hangs an ethereal aura of dreamlike mysticism and unreality. Many modern Chinese are fond of saying that *Hung-lou meng* is the key to understanding the subtle refinements of Chinese culture in the late imperial era.

The literary heritage contains many imitations and continuations of these six outstanding novels—historical fiction, picaresque fiction, fiction about the supernatural, erotic fiction, satirical fiction, and "genre" fiction about domestic life. For a brief period in the late Ming years, when unorthodox thinking in many realms sprang from Wang Yang-ming's emphasis on individualism and spontaneity, colloquial literature even had some outspoken champions. The heretical philosopher-official Li Chih published an edition of *Shui-hu chuan* at the end of the sixteenth century and proclaimed that it, together with the Yüan drama *Hsi-hsiang chi*, deserved recognition as a literary masterpiece. Another late Ming iconoclast, Yüan Hung-tao (1568-1610), also praised colloquial literature in general and *Shui-hu chuan* in particular, saying that the novel surpassed even the ancient classics in literary merit. Finally, a Soochow eccentric, Chin Sheng-t'an (1610?-61), developing a fairly systematic critical technique, argued that the Chinese literary heritage contained six works of superlative genius: the *Chuang-tzu*, the poetry of Ch'ü Yüan, the *Shih-chi* history by Ssu-ma Ch'ien, the poetry of Tu Fu, the drama *Hsi-hsiang chi*, and the novel *Shui-hu chuan*. He published heavily annotated editions of both *Hsi-hsiang chi* and *Shui-hu chuan*, in which he pointed out and savored their literary excellences. Chin actually considered *Shui-hu chuan* the greatest of China's literary masterpieces. But all these unorthodox critical views gradually died out, as creative philosophy did, under the puritanical conservatism nurtured by the Manchus. As has often been suggested, the greatest weakness of the Ch'ing emperors was their determination to preserve China's traditional Chineseness at all costs—and the prevalence of colloquial literature was one of the symptoms of what conservatives denounced as cultural deterioration in the Ming era.

THE ARTS

Ceramics. Although the great ages of bronze and statuary art had passed, anonymous craftsmen of the later imperial age maintained a declining tradition in these media and attained ever higher levels of skill and technological sophistication in such other media as architecture, jade-carving, textiles, lacquerware, and, from Yüan or early Ming times on, cloisonné. In ceramics above all they produced wares of variety and magnificence that came to be known and coveted throughout the world; the later empire porcelains must be reckoned among China's greatest cultural treasures.

By Sung times the technique of high-fired, hard-glazed porcelain was fully developed. Chronic shortages of copper caused pottery to become the standard ware for such everyday household goods as cups and bowls, and in these simple forms—elegantly, classically simple in the finest examples—porcelains were produced in abundance for use in the imperial palace and commoners' homes alike, and increasingly for export throughout Asia and across the Indian Ocean to Africa and the Mediterranean world. In keeping with the simplicity of their designs, Sung porcelains are characterized by at most a faint incised decor and often have none at all. They are also predominantly monochromes.

The Sung porcelains are normally categorized by their places of manufacture, since each issued pieces of distinctive coloration. The popular works of Northern Sung times were products of the north, especially the Kaifeng region. State kilns near Kaifeng produced two principal kinds of ware: Ju, including some very thin eggshell porcelains, predominantly white but with a faint blue-green tint; and Kuan, a glossy blue-gray ware. Other well-known porcelains of the north include Ting, a sumptuous ware with a pure white body, often incised with floral designs, which is overcoated in a cream glaze running into teardrop clusters and often also rimmed with bands of silver; Chün, a heavy and durable ware with a gray body and a thick, bubbly glaze in a wide spectrum of colors ranging from blue to blood-red; and Tz'u-chou, a gray-bodied ware with a cream glaze, sometimes with a painted design in black, brown, or red. Southern wares, which naturally predominated after the Sung court and elite families retreated from the north before the invading Jurchen in the 1120's, most notably included celadon—ware with an off-white body thickly covered with a translucent greenish glaze. The Lung-ch'üan celadons of Chekiang and Kiangsi, which often have carved or molded designs, are particularly fine examples, and at their best attain a delicately soft and subtle beauty. Celadons became particularly important export items from Sung through Ming times, and the celadon technique rapidly spread to Thailand, Korea, and Japan. Another southern ware that is especially prized in Japan (where it is known as *temmoku*) is Chien, produced in Chekiang and neighboring Fukien. This ware characteristically has a black body and is covered with a thick purplish glaze often mottled with brown; its dark colors lend themselves particularly to the appreciation of tea. Ko wares produced at Hangchow, also with very dark bodies, are especially famed for their crackled greenish or yellowish glazes. The crackles result from the thick glaze cooling faster than the body, and potters became expert at controlling the process to create the designs they esteemed. The crackles were sometimes accentuated with a red or black stain.

Although these Sung pottery styles remained popular throughout the later dynasties, they were overshadowed early in the Ming era with the development of more colorful and elaborately decorated polychrome wares. The new styles are especially associated with Ching-te-chen in northern Kiangsi province, an old pottery center that flourished as the site of the Ming and Ch'ing imperial kilns. At its peak, more than 3,000 kilns were kept busy at Ching-te-chen; but it was among the institutions that were devastated by the Taiping Rebellion in the 1850's.

All Ching-te-chen wares are noted for their delicate white bodies,

Fig. 41. Porcelains of the later imperial era. Upper left: Southern Sung greenish-gray Kuan ware vase. Upper right: Ming Blue-and-White jar of the 15th century. Lower left: Ming Blue-and-White covered jar of the 16th century. Lower right: Ch'ing polychrome bottle vase, of the 18th-century famille-rose type.

which at their finest are eggshell-thin and translucent. The earliest of the famed Ming products at Ching-te-chen are the Blue-and-White wares, examples of which are to be found in all of the world's great museums; they stimulated Europeans to produce the imitative "willow-pattern" tablewares that adorned middle-class American homes not too many decades ago. The Ming products are thin, well-formed cups, plates, bowls, and vases with charming floral or "genre" designs painted on the body in a striking cobalt blue and covered with a transparent glaze. A later Ming development was an enameling process: painting on the glaze itself with colors that could not endure cooking on the "biscuit" or uncovered body—greens and yellows and reds, in many different shades. Enameling in three colors and eventually five colors, often combined with a monochrome blue under the glaze, produced richly decorative effects that well suited, and symbolized, the burgeoning affluence of urban life in the sixteenth century.

These Ming traditions attained their greatest popularity and most ornate designs in the Ch'ing dynasty, coming to a climax in the eighteenth century. Large quantities of heavy, strong porcelains were produced specifically for European consumption—some on special order, decorated with European coats of arms or shaped into figurines with European faces and costumes. Monochromes remained popular—in reds, blacks, blues, and lavenders particularly—and Ming-style Blue-and-White wares remained standard items. In the K'ang-hsi reign (1661-1722) a style of polychrome ware known to Westerners as "famille verte"—predominantly greenish and yellowish combinations—came to be popular, soon to be succeeded by a "famille rose," in which pinkish colors predominated and designs became more delicate. The eighteenth century also introduced "lacework" pieces, with designs deeply incised as semitransparencies, and "rice-grain" pieces, with lozenge designs cut entirely through the biscuit and only partly filled with glaze. It was such examples of preciosity as famille verte and famille rose porcelains that were imported and imitated by Europeans in the eighteenth-century craze for chinoiserie.

China's thriving ceramics industry was dealt a severe blow by the Taiping rebels in the 1850's; they not only destroyed the imperial kilns at Ching-te-chen but also disrupted production in other centers. Though the industry survived the mid-century upheavals, the production of ceramics was not given a high priority in China's efforts to regain stability in the changed circumstances the nation confronted in the next 100 years, and the industry never regained its pre-nineteenth century distinction.

Painting. Chinese commonly rank calligraphy and painting alongside poetry as the three great aesthetic expressions of their traditional culture. Like poetry, calligraphy and painting became such commonplace activities among the educated men of the later imperial age, and the educated class expanded so vastly, that any attempt to enumerate even major artists of the later empire would be impossible here. Literally thousands of late empire paintings have been treasured and preserved in China and Japan and in museums and private collections the world over.

Students everywhere are accustomed to the judgment that Sung paintings are great, Yüan paintings occasionally good, and Ming and Ch'ing paintings increasingly imitative and sterile. This is a tradition derived from Japanese collectors; but it does not correspond to the judgment of the Chinese themselves, largely because outsiders do not understand the Chinese penchant for what is so easily taken for "imitative" painting. Like other artists everywhere, Chinese painters learned their techniques by "imitating" past masters, and the quality of many early masterpieces has been transmitted to the present day only in faithful, journeymen's reproductions of originals that are now lost. But the products that many later Chinese painters labeled imitations are in fact reinterpretations comparable in creative power to the improvisations of a virtuoso jazz musician on a theme from Tchaikovsky, which no one would think to dismiss as a copy or imitation. Moreover, some later paintings done "in the fashion of" early masters have no perceptible similarity to the originals at all; the artist in fact made no effort to copy anything, but rather tried to inspire in himself the original creative spirit that motivated his predecessor. When he was successful, the artist produced a work of wholly independent aesthetic validity, not derivative in any significant sense. Only in recent years have Western specialists begun to understand what the later artists were trying to do, and thus to appreciate that every dynastic age had its quota of highly creative geniuses.

Any outsider hoping to appreciate Chinese paintings fully must first of all take into account the conditions imposed on Chinese painters by the materials they worked with. Except for murals, Chinese traditionally painted on silk and paper with watercolors or sooty inks—inks that each painter prepared for himself by rubbing hard sticks of dry ink on moistened, flat, fine-textured stones. One of the many important consequences is that, unlike a worker in oils on canvas, the Chinese painter could not proceed by trial and error, scraping off what did not please him. The moment he put his brush to silk or paper he made an irretrievable commitment. Unless he had in mind from the beginning a complete vision of what he wanted to paint, he floundered. The Chinese therefore have not commonly painted from life; their art has been a studio art and a highly intellectualized one—rendering on silk or paper a mental image that has no necessary relation to any particular reality. Another consequence is that, though composition has by no means been disesteemed, the Chinese themselves base their aesthetic judgments largely on the quality of the brushstroke or the vitality of the line. Lines are classified in categories of infinite refinement—hesitant or bold, weak or strong, raw or delicate, relaxed or pulsating with vibrant power. The spirit and personality of the painter are thought to be exposed in the character of his brushwork, and the viewer of a painting is expected to commune and interact with the mind of the painter fully as much as to appreciate his subject matter and design.

One of the striking differences between Chinese paintings and those of the tradition to which most Westerners are accustomed is that Chinese have generally felt no compulsion to fill up their canvases with details. The traditional painters often provided no background at all and always concentrated on whatever might be the essential elements of their compositions, whether they happened to be handled with relative realism or in more abstract fashion. Their paintings seldom have a cluttered look, and what is essential stands forth clearly, perhaps in varying shades of light but almost never with any shadowed obscurities. In landscapes, sections are often separated by blank space or atmosphere, which itself becomes a vital element of the composition.

Similarly, the traditional Chinese painter did not handicap himself with conventions about perspective similar to those customary in the modern West. The viewer of a Chinese painting is not as if rooted to the ground in one place. In the case of landscapes, particularly, the viewer is as if suspended in air, and shifts from one point of view to another to see the different parts of the scene to best advantage and in full, unobstructed clarity. Looking at a vertical hanging scroll, one gradually moves up the picture, from things near at hand to the middle distance and finally to the far distance—but in each case seeing each section frontally. Looking at a horizontal hand scroll, one encounters each section in turn from the frontal point of view most advantageous for seeing it. The result, remarkably, is not flatness; there is usually a quality of infinite depth, which draws the viewer into the picture.

The subject matter of Chinese painters is often catalogued in three categories: calligraphy, bamboo, and other things. As was noted in Chapter 9, calligraphy was acclaimed very early as the quintessential refinement of the brushwork artist; it was a medium in which subject matter least represented anything in concrete reality—one in which brushstroke lines were most obviously the only things of significance and in which the inner spirit of the painter was exposed most revealingly, without subject-matter distractions. It matters little to the Chinese connoisseur what style of calligraphy is used; it may be sharp and precise, or sweeping and curling, or wild, crude, and jerky. What matters greatly is that it must have integrity and character. Few Westerners are ever likely to develop competent judgments about what makes Chinese calligraphy good or bad in Chinese eyes, but good calligraphy has great appeal to modern Western tastes. The painting of bamboo is a closely related art form in which, similarly, interest focuses predominantly on brushstrokes.

The later imperial age had a long succession of masters whose calligraphy and bamboo paintings have been extravagantly admired. The great early Sung poet Su Shih was famed in both realms. His contemporaries Mi Fei (or Mi Fu, 1051-1107) and Huang T'ing-chien (1045-1105) are also considered to rank among China's greatest calligraphers. In the Yüan dynasty, when a long-developing tradition of "amateur" or "literati" painting reached an early climax, calligraphy became integrally incorporated into landscape painting as a regular practice, and a number of famed calligraphers flourished; the most celebrated is Chao Meng-fu (1254-1322). The painting of bamboo flourished simultaneously, reportedly because the naturally pliant but durable bamboo symbolized the spirit cultivated by many intellectuals of the time, who though forced to accept alien overlordship did not forsake their traditional cultural pursuits. One Yüan scholar, Li K'an (1260?-1310), devoted himself exclusively to the study and painting of bamboo and wrote an influential manual on the art.

Calligraphy continued to flourish through the Ming and Ch'ing dy-

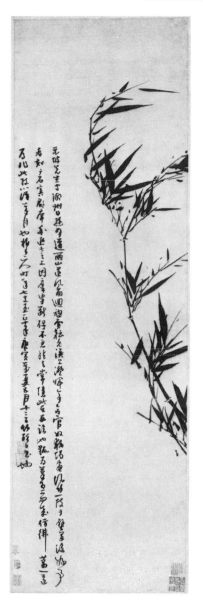

Fig. 42. "Bamboo Branch in the Wind":
painting by Wu Chen (Yüan)

nasties with constantly renewed dynamism. The extreme individualism
of the late Ming "mad Ch'an" philosophical movement had some particularly interesting repercussions in calligraphy, seen most strikingly
in the extravagantly wild brushwork of an eccentric poet and play-
wright, Hsü Wei (1521-93). The late Ming painter and critic Tung Ch'i-

Fig. 43. Calligraphy of the later imperial era. Top: poetry inscribed by Mi Fei (Sung). Center: detail of poetry inscribed by the Sung emperor Hui-tsung. Bottom: painting of bamboo with inscription, by Hsü Wei (Ming).

ch'ang (1555-1636) established a lively, cursive calligraphic style that was emulated to the end of the eighteenth century.

The "other things" that absorbed the attention of late empire painters can be subdivided into human figures, including both portraiture and "genre" paintings of everyday scenes; a category that the Chinese label "flowers and birds," which includes paintings of all types of flora and fauna; and landscapes. In the great age of chinoiserie it was the highly refined and elegantly decorative "flowers and birds" paintings that eighteenth-century Europeans most admired and imitated, but in the twentieth century Chinese landscapes have been judged by Westerners to be the finest products of Chinese culture and have had much influence on Western art, especially in the post-Impressionist movement.

In categorizing painters by technique, Chinese commonly speak of a northern school stemming from one group of T'ang masters and a southern school stemming from another. These terms have no real geographic significance; they arose by analogy with the divergent schools of Ch'an Buddhism—a northern one that was relatively disciplined and gradualist in its approach to enlightenment, and a southern one with an expectation of more sudden, spontaneous enlightenment. Applied to the realm of painting, the term northern school refers primarily to the style of professional court artists who decorated palaces with portraits, flowers, and birds in polychrome watercolors. Southern school refers primarily to the style of scholar-officials who painted as an avocation (but by no means amateurishly) and are best known for their monochrome ink landscapes. The same sort of distinction is made between academic (northern) and literati (southern) painters and painting styles. These various categorizations have some validity but are not to be used rigidly. There were professional court painters who produced landscapes in the southern style, just as there were litterateurs who made their living primarily by painting, and rendered portraits, flowers, and birds in the northern style. Painters of the Ming and Ch'ing dynasties, especially, were often deliberately eclectic, painting in whatever style suited them at any given moment.

The Northern Sung period, though producing gifted literati painters such as Su Shih, Mi Fei, and Huang T'ing-chien, was on the whole dominated by the academic watercolor style. It was an age of massive, monumentally rugged, misty landscapes, rather realistically representational attempts to capture the essential spirit of nature. Among the great masters of the age and the style was Kuo Hsi (1020-90?), who in addition to painting rugged panoramic scenery wrote a famous treatise on the theory of landscape painting that was influential throughout the later dynasties. Genre painting also flourished; one of its most famous examples, done early in the twelfth century by Chang Tse-tuan and repeatedly copied, is a long horizontal hand scroll giving a detailed view of the varied life of Kaifeng at spring festival time (see Fig. 35, p. 349). The academic emphasis of the age culminated in the reign of the last Northern Sung emperor, Hui-tsung (r. 1100-1125), who was himself a painter of great precision and merit, especially of flowers and birds, and who patronized a large group of court artists of similar tastes. One of Hui-tsung's monuments is an annotated catalog of the imperial art collection, listing 6,396 paintings by 231 artists.

In Southern Sung, court painters still predominated. But their landscapes were greatly influenced by the style of such literati as Mi Fei, who had shunned the rather ponderous and austere manner of his academic contemporaries in favor of moodily impressionistic, highly simplified and selective landscapes; they are considered to have emotional and romantic rather than intellectual qualities. The new style was popularized among academicians soon after the settlement of the Sung court at Hangchow and was perfected by two court painters who lived from the twelfth into the thirteenth century, Ma Yüan and Hsia Kuei. Both were master technicians, and their works are very similar. Like the best traditional chüeh-chü poems, their landscapes are simple and understated, the very antithesis of explicit depiction, but powerfully suggestive of moods. They especially evoke the mystic grandeur of nature. Most of their known works are small in scale, and there seems to be not a line or dot that is superfluous. In a corner in the foreground may be a clear, small headland jutting into a river or lake, with a few small, sharply drawn huts, fishing boats, and human figures; or the craggy edge of a mountainside with a thin path winding to a small pavilion, in which sits a tiny figure looking outward. But the rest of the scene is always swallowed up by thick, moist air, into which the viewer finds himself drawn. The drawings have a cartoon-like sketchiness; the brushwork is vigorous and clear; and the compositions are delicate. By any standard Ma Yüan and Hsia Kuei were superb painters, and their works have been very highly esteemed in the modern West.

Another intriguing art style that reached its climax in Southern Sung was that adopted by Ch'an Buddhist artists resident in the Hangchow monasteries. These were learned, urbane men who associated with the

Fig. 44. "Landscape in Rain": traditionally attributed to Hsia Kuei

Fig. 45. "Riverside Village on a Late Autumn Day": fan painting by Ma Yüan

great litterateurs and aesthetes of their time but practiced their own independent art, which reflects their philosophical view that truth is here
and now, to be discovered by spontaneous enlightenment. They did
highly abstract, impressionistic ink paintings of commonplace objects,
or outline sketches of Ch'an masters and other figures. Their style apparently derived in part from a ninth-century Ch'an monk who left
some marvelously grotesque caricatures of saints; and it perhaps owed
something to a late T'ang fashion of slapdash abstract paintings having
much in common with the "action paintings" of our own time. The
leader and greatest master of the Southern Sung Ch'an movement was
a monk called Mu-ch'i, who painted anything that caught his eye but
is now famed throughout the art world for a multishaded ink rendering
of six persimmons lined up irregularly in a field of blank space. Mu-

ch'i's best-known follower was Liang K'ai, who began his career as an orthodox academy painter at court but retired to Mu-ch'i's monastery and thereafter painted only in the Ch'an style. His most familiar works are two brilliantly simplified figure paintings—one of a Ch'an patriarch chopping bamboo, in which the brushstrokes almost jump with vitality (see Fig. 37, p. 359), and another of Li Po reciting a poem (see Fig. 22, p. 247).

Yüan dynasty artists made an important transition in the development of Chinese painting. Turning away from the refined prettiness that they saw in the works of the Southern Sung academicians, they sought inspiration instead in the Northern Sung masters such as Kuo Hsi. They painted nature in more sweeping views and in greater detail than Ma Yüan and Hsia Kuei did, with clarity and austerity. Their works are not suggestive and impressionistic, but rather are richly descriptive and expressionistic. The subject matter is seldom new, and at first glance viewers might be tempted to judge them monotonous, rather primitive and crude echoes of a lost Southern Sung refinement. But the specialist's eye sees in the works of such men as Huang Kung-wang (1269-1354) and Ni Tsan (1301-74) remarkable experimentations with the brush, resulting in a "cool," crisp, intellectual style of painting without any sentimentality, in which brushstroke technique is the overwhelming interest.

In Ming times, while court painters upheld the traditions of portraiture and decorative bird, flower, and genre paintings, landscapists split into two schools, one in Chekiang that revived the academic style of Ma Yüan and Hsia Kuei, and one in Soochow that worked in the new Yüan style. The Ming emperor Hsüan-tsung (r. 1425-35), the most gifted emperor-artist since Sung Hui-tsung, especially stimulated the revival of Southern Sung styles. The Soochow literati group included the most energetic and renowned Ming painter, Shen Chou (1427-1509), whose landscapes are strong but intimately expressionistic, and Shen's most talented disciple, Wen Cheng-ming (1470-1559), a highly disciplined and intellectual painter.

At the very end of the Ming period Tung Ch'i-ch'ang, already mentioned as a calligrapher but also a high-ranking official, a poet, and a famed connoisseur of all the arts, brought the literati-painting tradition to its final triumph. Tung proclaimed and established the doctrine that one paints not to impress anyone or to capture outward reality even in spirit, but to give free expression to the inner reality of one's own char-

Fig. 46. "Mountain Scenery with River Lodge": scroll painting by Ni Tsan

Fig. 47. "In the Shade of Summer Trees": scroll painting by Tung Ch'i-ch'ang

acter and one's own grasp of natural principles. In Tung's view, only the
disciplined, cultured man was prepared to express anything of value,
and he did so by expressing inner truth—not sentimentality and not
prettiness—through the integrity of his brushstrokes. Tung's own landscapes are notably simple and abstract. Under his influence, great man-
uals were produced that became the texts from which Ch'ing painters
worked; they illustrate, for example, 26 ways of painting rocks and 27
ways of painting leaves.

The eclectic, individual style prescribed by Tung Ch'i-ch'ang was
practiced successfully in early Ch'ing times by several admired masters.
It was characteristic of their style that Wang Hui's (1632-1717) work
can be described as "imitations" of Shen Chou's fifteenth-century reinterpretations of Huang Kung-wang's fourteenth-century works "in the
fashion of" one or another tenth-century Sung master. Two interesting
nonconformists of the early Ch'ing period were Chu Ta (or Pa-ta shan-
jen, 1626-1705?), a reputed madman who painted wildly distorted landscapes, flora, and fauna; and Tao Chi (or Shih-t'ao, 1630-1707), a versatile, original, intensely personal expressionist whose paintings have a
curious awkwardness and whose calligraphy is lush and splashy. Eigh-
teenth- and nineteenth-century painters have not yet been carefully
evaluated by specialists, but it will probably prove difficult to revise
very substantially the current view that they represent a genuine decline in artistic creativity. In the affluent mid-Ch'ing society, painters
abounded and demonstrated great versatility; but they generally painted
"by the book."

In art as in government, thought, and literature, China's prolonged
stability under Manchu rule bred conservative conformism. By the nineteenth century, underneath the surface appearance of competence and
self-satisfaction, the vitality of traditional Chinese civilization in all its
aspects was at a low ebb. It is for this reason that the sting of the Opium
War followed by the hammer-blows of the Taiping Rebellion precipitated an almost total collapse, not merely of the Ch'ing dynasty, but of
the whole cultural tradition. China plunged into a traumatic process of
reorientation and reidentification from which even now, after more
than a century, it has not emerged with new characteristics that are
clearly defined and clearly durable.

Epilogue

URING THE century since the Taiping Rebellion, China has suffered the most traumatic convulsions of its long history and the
most agonizing transformations experienced by any nation in modern
times. Historians conventionally divide the era into three periods, each
a fascinating study in itself: the decline of the Ch'ing dynasty and its
overthrow by republican revolutionaries in 1911-12; the shaky emergence of the Republic of China, dominated after 1928 by the Nationalist Party of Sun Yat-sen (1866-1925) under the leadership of Chiang
Kai-shek (1888-1975); and the fluctuating fortunes of the People's Republic of China since 1949 under the Chinese Communist Party led by
Mao Tse-tung (1893-   ).

A new China is being forged, but slowly, very slowly, and for good
reason. Vast, topographically diverse, with a huge population now near
800,000,000, China is a social planner's nightmare. It is probably even
more important that China has come into modern times not as a have-
not nation anxious to improve itself but as the proud heir of a high
cultural heritage, not as a grateful recipient of outsiders' instruction
but as a civilization-giver. Unlike most underdeveloped peoples in our
time, the Chinese have been slow to perceive the advantages of mod-
ernization and quick to emphasize its threat to everything of value that
remains from the past.

Americans and other non-Chinese have been inclined to take upon
themselves much of the blame for the various traumas of China's recent
history, and indeed outsiders have much to repent of in this regard:
among other things the opium trade, territorial encroachments, economic exploitation, and gross insensitivity to Chinese pride and prob-

lems. But the basic motive forces of change in modern China have been the Chinese themselves.

The most significant changes of the past century have resulted from successive reevaluations by China's leaders of the viability of traditional Chinese civilization—its institutions, its socioeconomic patterns, and its ideology—in the face of deteriorating domestic conditions. These reevaluations are perhaps best seen in terms of three overlapping waves or phases: conservative reformism, from 1850 to 1928; West-inspired, gradualist progressivism, beginning in the 1890's and still the norm today among the Nationalists on Taiwan; and anti-tradition, anti-West, genuinely revolutionary radicalism, beginning about 1919 and culminating in Maoism, the ideology of the People's Republic.

In the last half of the nineteenth century, Manchu and Chinese leaders responded to the economic and military incursions of the West with the so-called Self-Strengthening Movement, an effort to adapt Western technology to China without disturbing the traditional political and social order or the traditional ideology. The leaders of this movement set up Western-style arsenals, steamship companies, and other modernizing institutions while preserving the social system of their forebears and exalting its Confucian rationale. From the 1870's into the 1890's China appeared to be making a successful adjustment to its new international situation. Even though the appearance proved to be misleading and the reforms inadequate, the ideals of the Self-Strengthening Movement persisted beyond the fall of the imperial order in 1911-12: the warlords who dominated the Republic until 1928 were equally conservative at best. In the end reformism of this sort failed because of its indifference to domestic socioeconomic inequities.

By the end of the nineteenth century, some Chinese leaders realized that grafting modern technology onto the traditional political and social order was not enough. Blaming Manchu intransigence for most of China's troubles, they considered representative, constitutional government to be the source of the power of the Western nations and emergent Japan. They consequently urged that China adopt Western political institutions in addition to technology, though most shared the conservatives' reluctance to disrupt the ideological and social foundations of the traditional order. This was the ethos of Sun Yat-sen and his protégé, Chiang Kai-shek. It was their Nationalist Party that after 1928 sought to modernize China gradually through legislation, education, and a mixture of private and state capitalism. In their Taiwan sanctuary after 1949, the Nationalists by following these policies have achieved political stability and a standard of living second in Asia only to Japan's. On the mainland, however, any prospect of success for their gradualist approach was lost in their struggles with the warlords, the Japanese, and the Communists. Success may in any event have been beyond their reach, since, like the conservatives before them, they were not inclined to respond urgently to the increasingly critical distress of the Chinese peasantry.

More truly revolutionary radicalism, hostile to the very foundations of the Chinese tradition, flourished in the aftermath of the famous May Fourth Movement of 1919. This movement began as a patriotic outcry against the Treaty of Versailles, which confirmed Japan's territorial infringements on China during World War I; and it quickly expanded into the championing of "Mr. Democracy and Mr. Science" against traditionalism of all sorts. The example of the Soviet Union led many activists into more and more agitation for left-wing causes, so that by the 1930's Chinese intellectuals were overwhelmingly impatient with the Nationalists, if not overtly hostile; and peasant discontent was steadily growing. During the Second World War and the civil war that followed, Mao Tse-tung adroitly blended intellectual radicalism, peasant frustration, and patriotism into a unified political and military weapon that cut down the Nationalist Republic. In daring to violate orthodox Leninist-Stalinist dogma by arousing peasant-powered mass violence, from which prior Chinese reformers and revolutionaries had shrunk with revulsion, Mao unleashed a whirlwind of social turmoil. In sum, Mao Tse-tung's Communists, learning from the Nationalists' difficulties in trying to make changes gradually from the top down, undertook to transform China abruptly from the bottom up.

China's century-long turbulence has taken an incalculable toll in human lives and physical destruction. Other disruptions have been equally awesome. The traditional political structure is gone. The traditional ideal of the extended family has been wiped out, and the nuclear family has lost its primacy in the social order. Traditional folk religions have been repudiated; Confucianism has steadily lost esteem and is now denounced as a tool with which the people were traditionally kept in a state of "feudal" bondage. Individuals, though freed from many of their past constraints, are subordinated—at times arbitrarily and ruthlessly—to the demands of production brigades and communes. With the humiliation and displacement of the elite class that fostered them, traditional gentility and elegance have given way to Communist populism: drab clothing, shrill political slogans, poems about tractors.

These changes are balanced, under the People's Republic, by measurable improvements. Peasant discontent inherited from the past has been greatly reduced by imaginative organizational and technological rearrangements in the countryside. The people no longer live under the threat of mass starvation, as they did for decades prior to 1949. Class distinctions have been minimized, and women have gained an equality with men that is perhaps unmatched elsewhere in the world. Agricultural surpluses have paid for rapid industrialization, so that China now produces automobiles and trucks as well as bicycles, television sets as well as radios, airplanes as well as railroads, and sophisticated modern armaments including nuclear weapons. Moreover, the Chinese exude an unprecedented national consciousness and a national pride surpassing that of the most glorious imperial ages. They enjoy more widespread education and literacy and more egalitarian participation in the national culture and polity than ever before.

Despite all these changes, the past casts a long shadow over modern China. Traditional characteristics have persisted to a remarkable extent even in the loudly antitraditional People's Republic. Though specific institutional structures have changed, the state still glorifies its founding leader and is administered by a hierarchical bureaucracy of merit committed to an orthodox ideology in which persuasion by example is preferred to coercion by law. Commerce and industry are still closely regulated by the state, to serve state purposes and priorities. As in the late empire, nonconformist thought and behavior are tolerated only to a relatively low level, beyond which the state is quick to suppress them as threats to social stability. Maoism perpetuates China's age-old optimism about the perfectibility of man and society, and its age-old skepticism about anything beyond this world. This is by no means to suggest that the more things change, the more they are the same; but it can be argued that the Chinese found in Communism the approach to the solution of their modern problems that was least incompatible with their traditional, distinctively Chinese ways.

Maoism today deliberately perpetuates turbulence in a continuing revolution aimed at transforming human nature, with the ultimate goal of producing individuals who will selflessly serve the common good. Until that goal is reached, Maoists believe, recurrent social disorder is the only way to avoid complacent backsliding—specifically, to prevent

the technocrats who are industrializing China from entrenching themselves as an elite and thereby provoking anew the peasant discontents
that have undermined every other modern Chinese government. There
seems little reason to expect that this policy can long survive Mao Tse-
tung himself. Just as Ch'in extremism had to yield to Han moderation,
and Sui extremism to T'ang moderation, so Maoist radicalism must one
day yield to a more moderate order. So at least it would seem from the
perspective of China's imperial past. What form the post-Mao order
will ultimately take, and whether or not it will stabilize China in a
status commensurate with its great heritage, are among the most fascinating questions of contemporary world history.

Appendixes

Chronological Chart of Chinese History

The dynasties and governments given in boldface letters are the major ones in Chinese history. The italicized city names are the dynastic or national capitals. These names, like other place-names in the chart, are modern names unless otherwise indicated.

2000 Hsia dynasty (unverified), 2205?-1766?
B.C.
      Shang dynasty, 1766?-1122? (last capital at *Yin*, in Honan)

1000 **Chou** dynasty, 1122?-256
      Western Chou era, 1122?-771 (*Sian*, then called *Hao*)
      Eastern Chou era, 770-256 (*Loyang*, then called *Lo*)
500   Spring and Autumn period, 722-481
      Warring States period, 403-221

      Ch'in dynasty, 221-207 (*Sian*, then called *Hsien-yang*)

200 **Han** (or former or Western Han) dynasty, 202-A.D. 9 (*Sian*, then called *Ch'ang-an*)

A.D. Hsin dynasty, A.D. 9-23 (usurpation of Wang Mang; *Ch'ang-an*)

      Later Han (or Eastern Han) dynasty, 25-220 (*Loyang*)

200 Three Kingdoms era, 220-280

NORTH	WEST	SOUTH
Wei, 220-266 (*Loyang*)	Shu Han, 221-263 (*Chengtu*)	Wu, 222-280 (*Nanking*)

300 Chin (or Western Chin) dynasty, 266-316 (*Loyang* to 311, then *Ch'ang-an*)

Era of North-South Division, 316-589

SIXTEEN KINGDOMS, 301-439

Based in Shansi and Shensi	Based in Szechwan	Based in Kansu
Han or Chao, 304-329 (Hsiung-nu)	Ch'eng Han or Shu, 301-347 (Tibetan)	(Former) Liang, 313-376 (Chinese)
Later Chao, 319-352 (Hsiung-nu)		Southern Liang, 397-414 (Hsien-pi)
(Former) Ch'in, 352-410 (Tibetan)	Based in Hopei	Later Liang, 386-403 (Tibetan)
Later Ch'in, 384-417 (Tibetan)	(Former) Yen, 348-370 (Hsien-pi)	Western Liang, 400-421 (Chinese)
Hsia, 407-431 (Hsiung-nu)	Later Yen, 383-409 (Hsien-pi)	Northern Liang, 397-439 (Hsiung-nu)
Western Ch'in, 385-431 (Hsien-pi)	Southern Yen, 398-410 (Hsien-pi)	
	Northern Yen, 409-436 (Chinese)	

A.D.   Era of North-South Division (*cont'd*)

NORTHERN AND SOUTHERN DYNASTIES, 317-589

Northern dynasties, 386-581	Southern dynasties, 317-589
(Northern) Wei, 386-534 (T'o-pa)	Eastern Chin, 317-420 (*Nanking*)
Eastern Wei, 534-550 (T'o-pa)	(Liu) Sung, 420-479 (*Nanking*)
Western Wei, 534-557 (*Loyang*)	Southern Ch'i, 479-502 (*Nanking*)
Northern Ch'i, 550-577 (in northern Honan)	Liang, 502-557 (*Nanking*)
Northern Chou, 557-581 (*Ch'ang-an*)	Ch'en, 557-589 (*Nanking*)

400

600   **Sui** dynasty, 581-618 (*Ch'ang-an*)

T'ang dynasty, 618-907 (*Ch'ang-an*)

900   Five Dynasties era, 907-960

NORTH: Five Dynasties, 907-960	SOUTH: Ten Kingdoms, 907-979	
Later Liang, 907-923 (*Kaifeng*)	(Former) Shu, 907-925 (in Szechwan)	Southern T'ang or Ch'i, 937-975 (in Nanking area)
Later T'ang, 923-934 (*Loyang*)	Later Shu, 934-965 (in Szechwan)	Wu-Yüeh, 907-978 (in Chekiang)
Later Chin, 936-947 (*Kaifeng*)	Nan-p'ing or Ching-nan, 907-963 (in Hupei)	Min, 907-946 (in Fukien)
Later Han, 947-951 (*Kaifeng*)	Ch'u, 927-956 (in Hunan)	Southern Han or Yüeh, 907-971 (*Canton*)
Later Chou, 951-960 (*Kaifeng*)	Wu, 902-937 (in Nanking area)	Northern Han, 951-979 (actually in north, in Shansi)

1000   **Sung** (or Northern Sung) dynasty, 960-1127 (*Kaifeng*)

Northern Conquest dynasties, 916-1234

Liao dynasty, 916-1125 (Ch'i-tan; in Inner Mongolia)

1200   Chin dynasty, 1115-1234 (Jurchen; in Manchuria; *Peking* from 1127)

Southern Sung dynasty, 1127-1279 (*Hangchow*)

Yüan dynasty, 1264-1368 (Mongol; *Peking*)

1400   **Ming** dynasty, 1368-1644 (*Nanking* to 1421, then *Peking*)

Ch'ing dynasty, 1644-1912 (Manchu; *Peking*)

1900   **Republic of China**, 1912-1949 on mainland, 1949- in Taiwan (*Peking* to 1927, *Nanking* to 1949, then *Taipei*)

People's Republic of China, 1949- (*Peking*)

APPENDIX B

Notes on the Chinese Language

As is indicated in the Introduction, pp. 6-10, Chinese is written in non-alphabetic graphs, or characters. Each of the thousands of characters in use normally represents a single word, or cluster of related meanings, though some characters serve extra duty, representing more than one word. In spoken Chinese, each word is a one-syllable sound, with no variations to indicate number, tense, gender, and so forth. Mandarin, the official and most widespread form in which Chinese is spoken, makes use of only about 400 monosyllables. Although in theory each monosyllable can be pronounced in four tones, the number of word-sounds actually used is fewer than 1,600. Thus any one monosyllable can carry dozens of word-meanings, all of which are pronounced identically, as homophones, like *sail* and *sale* or *to, too*, and *two* in English. For example, fourth-tone *shih* carries the word-meanings *to be, fact, world, shape, to try, room, scholar, market*, and *persimmon* among many others; second-tone *shih* carries as many more, including *ten, time, to know, true, to eat, to collect*, and *stone*. To avoid confusion, Chinese speakers have developed a large number of conventional combinations of word-sounds, or compounds. Thus *world* is *shih-chieh* and *to try* is *shih-i-shih*, though the appropriate *shih* character alone could suffice in writing. The traditional writing style, *wen-yen*, is considerably more cryptic than spoken Chinese, *pai-hua*; *wen-yen* also commonly relies on archaic expressions and is especially difficult to understand because of the number of different words and nuances that attach to any one character and because of the substantial differences between its grammatical patterns and those of *pai-hua*. Nowadays Chinese write Chinese as it is spoken, in *pai-hua*; and only scholars read *wen-yen*.

Romanization

English speakers normally alphabetize or "romanize" Chinese words as they are pronounced in Mandarin and in what is called the Wade-Giles system, after the two Englishmen who devised it. The Wade-Giles system, with a few customary modifications, is used throughout this book, except for widely known variants of some place-names and personal names (for example, Peking rather than Wade-Giles Pei-ching, and Chiang Kai-shek rather than Wade-Giles Chiang Chieh-shih). The four tones in which Mandarin syllables are pronounced are usually not noted in romanization but can be indicated in several ways, one of the most common being the addition of superscript numerals 1, 2, 3, and 4, as in tao^4 te^2 $ching^1$.

The sounds represented in the Wade-Giles system do not always correspond to the sounds that English speakers usually associate with the alphabetic letters. The following simplified explanation of the Wade-Giles system may therefore be helpful:

VOWELS

a   *ah* as in *father*

e   *uh* as in *but*, but sometimes *eh* as in *wet*; thus *men* rhymes with English *pun*, but *yen* rhymes with English *pen*

i   *ee* as in *keep*

ih   something like the *i* in *shirt* with a hint of the following *r*; thus *ch'ih* is something like the *chu(r)* in *church*

o   *aw* as in *paw* except in *ko*, *k'o*, *ho*, and *o*, where it is *uh* as in *but* (and accordingly sometimes romanized as *e*)

u   *oo* as in *goo* except in *yu*, where it is most commonly pronounced *yo* as in *yogurt*, and in *tzu*, *tz'u*, and *ssu*, where it stands for a very unemphasized, almost unpronounced *uh* (and accordingly is sometimes romanized *ŭ*); thus *su* is pronounced *soo*, but *ssu* is essentially *ss*

ü   as French *u* or German *ü*

DIPHTHONGS

ai   rhymes with *shy*; thus *lai* sounds like English *lye*

ao   rhymes with *now*; thus *ch'ao* sounds like English *chow*

ei   rhymes with *stay*; thus *lei* sounds like English *lay*

ia   rhymes with German *ja*; thus *liang* is pronounced *lyahng* (one syllable)

ie   rhymes with *yeah*; thus *nien* is pronounced *nyen* (one syllable)

ieh   rhymes with *yeah*; thus *lieh* is pronounced *lyeh* (one syllable)

iu   varies between *yo* of *yogurt* and *you* of *youth*; thus *liu* may sound like the name *Leo* pronounced as one syllable or the name *Lew* (one-syllable *lyu*)

ou   rhymes with *know*; thus *lou* sounds like English *low*

ua   *wah* as in *suave*

ui   rhymes with *way*; thus *sui* sounds like English *sway*

uo   *waw* as in *walk*

CONSONANTS

Consonants are uniformly not voiced, but a difference is made between those that are aspirated and those that are not. The consonants *l*, *m*, *n*, *ng*, *r*, *s*, *sh*, and *w* are pronounced as in English. Others are pronounced as in

English if they are aspirated (indicated by an apostrophe in the Wade-Giles system):

ch'	as in *cheat*	t'	as in *top*
k'	as in *king*	ts'	as in *its*
p'	as in *put*	tz'	as in *its*

English speakers are not habituated to pronouncing consonants that are both unaspirated and unvoiced, and are usually content with the following voiced equivalents:

ch	as *j* in *job*	t	as *d* in *dog*
k	as *g* in *got*	ts	as *dz* in *adze*
p	as *b* in *but*	tz	as *dz* in *adze*

Chinese *h* is pronounced gutturally, like Russian *kh*. The spelling *hs* represents a hissed *s*, the spelling *ss* a long *s*. The most difficult Chinese sound of all for English speakers is represented by *j*; it is somewhere between the *j* of French *je* and the *r* of *rump*. English speakers usually settle for the *r* sound.

The Wade-Giles system is not the only conventional romanization system. The People's Republic of China has officially espoused a different one, known as Pinyin (*p'in-yin* in Wade-Giles); and Pinyin romanizations are becoming more and more common in English-language publications. Pinyin varies from Wade-Giles primarily in that (a) aspirated consonants are indicated by their common English equivalents (*ch* rather than *ch'*, etc.); (b) unaspirated consonants are indicated by their voiced English counterparts (*j* or *zh* rather than *ch*, *g* rather than *k*, etc.); (c) Wade-Giles *ts'* and *tz'* both become *c*, and *ts* and *tz* both become *z*; (d) Wade-Giles *j* becomes *r*; and (e) Wade-Giles *hs* becomes *x*.

Names

In standard Chinese practice, the surname precedes the given name, as in the case of Mao Tse-tung. Surnames are most commonly single syllables, and given names are most commonly two syllables; but opposite forms often occur. Thus one encounters such varied forms as the following (surnames italicized): *Li* Po, *Wang* Shou-jen, *Ou-yang* Hsiu, and *Ssu-ma* Hsiang-ju.

Chinese have traditionally had several kinds of personal names. Formal given names (*ming*) were not properly used in direct address. A man was known and referred to by a "style" or nickname (*tzu*), normally chosen by himself on reaching maturity. Eminent Chinese often additionally acquired appellations (*hao*) considered suitable to their achievements or status; these were either adopted by the persons themselves or conferred by friends, students, or associates. Posthumous epithets (*shih*) were commonly conferred on distinguished officials by the government. Subsequent writers might refer to a person by any one of these several kinds of names, often without use of the surname at all. For example, the influential philosopher-official of the fifteenth and sixteenth centuries whose formal name was Wang Shou-jen can be referred to by his tzu, Po-an; by his hao, Yang-ming; or by his shih, Wen-ch'eng.

It was not until modern times that married Chinese women came to be known by their husbands' family name. Traditionally, they were known by their maiden surname even after marriage. Thus a prosperous Mr. Li might have two wives, known as Madame Wang and Madame Ho.

All Chinese names have the meanings normally carried by the graphs in which they are written, and given names were deliberately chosen with great care to reflect parental hopes or ambitions for their children. Popular male names carried such meanings as "Great Talent," "National Treasure," "Follower of Righteousness," "Victorious," "Heroic," "Brave," "Attain Imperial Favor," and "Examination Success." Female names often refer to flowers, fruits, and gems, although in romanization they are of course indistinguishable from male names.

Until the Jurchen Chin dynasty (1115-1234) dynastic names generally denoted geographic areas deriving from the names of feudal fiefs in antiquity. Beginning with Chin (gold), dynastic names had auspicious symbolic senses. (See footnote on p. 281.)

Traditional Chinese rulers can be referred to in several ways. Like all other Chinese, they had personal names, but these were seldom used in historical writings. In most common use are epithets by which emperors were posthumously addressed in ancestral temple ceremonies, including the terms *tsu* (grandfather or progenitor), *tsung* (clansman or ancestor), or simply *ti* (emperor). Founding emperors of dynasties were commonly designated Kao-tsu (exalted grandfather) or T'ai-tsu (grand progenitor), and second emperors were often designated T'ai-tsung (great clansman). Thus the founder of the Han dynasty, whose name was Liu Pang, is normally referred to in historical writings as Han Kao-tsu; and the second emperor of the T'ang dynasty, Li Shih-min, is known as T'ang T'ai-tsung.

Emperors of the last two dynasties, Ming and Ch'ing, are sometimes referred to in Western writings by the era-names (*nien-hao*) that are properly applicable only to their reign periods. Thus the founding emperor of the Ming dynasty, named Chu Yüan-chang and known in most Chinese histories as Ming T'ai-tsu, can logically be called the Hung-wu emperor (that is, the emperor who reigned during the era called Hung-wu, much as Americans might refer to Lincoln as the Civil War president) but is often simply called Hung-wu, as if that were his name; and the grand monarch of eighteenth-century China, the Manchu Hung-li, whose official posthumous designation is Ch'ing Kao-tsung, is most commonly known to Westerners as Ch'ien-lung, the name of his era.

Suggested Additional Readings

REFERENCE AIDS

Charles O. Hucker, *China: A Critical Bibliography*. Tucson, Ariz., 1962. Needs updating but remains the most useful introductory reference; provides topical essays and full annotations of selected books and articles, arranged by topics covering all aspects of both traditional and modern China.

Chun-shu Chang, *Premodern China: A Bibliographical Introduction*. Ann Arbor, Mich., 1971. Can be used to update the preceding; is inconsistent about annotations and not carefully selective.

Bibliography of Asian Studies. Published annually by the Association for Asian Studies as the separate September issue of the *Journal of Asian Studies*, 1956- . Regular comprehensive lists of books and articles about China and other parts of Asia, arranged by regions and topics.

Herbert A. Giles, *A Chinese Biographical Dictionary*. 2d ed. Shanghai, 1912; reprinted New York, 1966. Still the only work of its kind identifying important Chinese of all periods.

The Cambridge History of China. Forthcoming multivolume set, expected to be detailed and authoritative.

SPECIALIZED STUDIES: THE FORMATIVE AGE

Kwang-chih Chang, *The Archaeology of Ancient China*. 2d ed. New Haven, Conn., 1971.

William Watson, *Cultural Frontiers in Ancient East Asia*. Edinburgh, 1971.

Herrlee G. Creel, *The Birth of China: A Study of the Formative Period of Chinese Civilization*. New York, 1937; reprinted New York, 1954.

T. K. Cheng, *Archaeology in China*. Vol. 1: *Prehistoric China*. Vol. 2: *Shang China*. Vol. 3: *Chou China*. Cambridge, Eng., 1959-61.

Herrlee G. Creel, *The Origins of Statecraft in China*. Vol. 1: *The Western Chou Empire*. Chicago, 1970.

C. Y. Hsü, *Ancient China in Transition: An Analysis of Social Mobility, 722-222 B.C.* Stanford, Calif., 1965.

Derk Bodde, *China's First Unifier: A Study of the Ch'in Dynasty as Seen in the Life of Li Ssu, 280?-208 B.C.* Leiden, 1938; reprinted London, 1967.

SPECIALIZED STUDIES: THE EARLY EMPIRE

Han dynasty

Burton Watson, trans., *Records of the Grand Historian of China* [from Ssu-ma Ch'ien's *Shih-chi*]. 2 vols. New York, 1961.

Michael Loewe, *Everyday Life in Early Imperial China*. New York, 1968.

Homer H. Dubs, trans., *History of the Former Han Dynasty* [from Pan Ku's *Han-shu*]. 3 vols. Baltimore, 1938-55.

C. Martin Wilbur, *Slavery in China During the Former Han Dynasty, 206 B.C.-A.D. 25*. Chicago, 1943; reprinted New York, 1967.

A. F. P. Hulsewé, *Remnants of Han Law*. Vol. 1. Leiden, 1955.

T. T. Ch'ü, *Han Social Structure*. Ed. Jack L. Dull. Seattle, 1972.

Y. S. Yü, *Trade and Expansion in Han China: A Study in the Structure of Sino-Barbarian Economic Relations*. Berkeley, Calif., 1967.

T'ang dynasty

Woodbridge Bingham, *The Founding of the T'ang Dynasty: The Fall of Sui and the Rise of T'ang*. Baltimore, 1941; reprinted New York, 1970.

Arthur F. Wright and Denis Twitchett, eds., *Perspectives on the T'ang*. New Haven, Conn., 1973.

Edwin O. Reischauer, *Ennin's Travels in T'ang China*. New York, 1955.

Edwin G. Pulleyblank, *The Background of the Rebellion of An Lu-shan*. London, 1955.

Denis C. Twitchett, *Financial Administration Under the T'ang Dynasty*. 2d ed. Cambridge, Eng., 1971.

Arthur Waley, *The Real Tripitaka* [Hsüan-tsang] *and Other Pieces*. New York, 1952.

———, *The Poetry and Career of Li Po*. New York, 1951; reprinted New York, 1958.

William Hung, *Tu Fu, China's Greatest Poet*. 2 vols. Cambridge, Mass., 1952; reprinted New York, 1969.

Arthur Waley, *The Life and Times of Po Chü-i*. New York, 1949; reprinted New York, 1951.

Edward H. Schafer, *The Golden Peaches of Samarkand: A Study of T'ang Exotics*. Berkeley, Calif., 1963.

———, *The Vermilion Bird: T'ang Images of the South*. Berkeley, Calif., 1967.

———

Gungwu Wang, *The Structure of Power in North China During the Five Dynasties*. Kuala Lumpur, 1963; reprinted Stanford, Calif., 1967.

SPECIALIZED STUDIES: THE LATER EMPIRE

Sung dynasty

James T. C. Liu and Peter J. Golas, eds., *Change in Sung China: Innovation or Renovation?* Lexington, Mass., 1969.

Jacques Gernet, *Daily Life in China on the Eve of the Mongol Invasion, 1250-1276*. Trans. from the French by H. M. Wright. New York, 1962.

James T. C. Liu, *Ou-yang Hsiu: An Eleventh-Century Neo-Confucianist.* Stanford, Calif., 1967.

John Meskill, ed., *Wang An-shih: Practical Reformer?* Boston, 1963.

Edward A. Kracke, *Civil Service in Early Sung China, 960-1067.* Cambridge, Mass., 1953.

James T. C. Liu, *Reform in Sung China: Wang An-shih (1021-1086) and His New Policies.* Cambridge, Mass., 1959.

Yüan dynasty

Réné Grousset, *Conqueror of the World: The Life of Chingis-khan.* Trans. from the French by Denis Sinor and Marian MacKeller. London, 1967.

Michael Prawdin, *The Mongol Empire: Its Rise and Legacy.* Trans. from the French by Eden and Cedar Paul. London, 1940.

E. D. Phillips, *The Mongols.* New York, 1969.

H. D. Martin, *The Rise of Chingis Khan and His Conquest of North China.* Baltimore, 1950; reprinted New York, 1971.

Marco Polo, *The Travels of Marco Polo.* Trans. R. E. Latham. New York, 1961.

John W. Dardess, *Conquerors and Confucians: Aspects of Political Change in Late Yüan China.* New York, 1973.

Ming dynasty

Charles O. Hucker, *The Traditional Chinese State in Ming Times, 1368-1644.* Tucson, Ariz., 1961.

Frederick W. Mote, *The Poet Kao Ch'i, 1336-1374.* Princeton, N.J., 1962.

Wm. T. de Bary et al., *Self and Society in Ming Thought.* New York, 1970.

J. J. L. Duyvendak, *China's Discovery of Africa.* London, 1949.

Charles O. Hucker, *The Censorial System of Ming China.* Stanford, Calif., 1966.

——, ed., *Chinese Government in Ming Times: Seven Studies.* New York, 1969.

Matteo Ricci, *China in the Sixteenth Century: The Journals of Matthew Ricci, 1583-1610.* Trans. Louis J. Gallagher. New York, 1953.

Dictionary of Ming Biography. Ed. L. C. Goodrich. Forthcoming.

James B. Parsons, *The Peasant Rebellions of the Late Ming Dynasty.* Tucson, Ariz., 1970.

Ch'ing dynasty

Arthur W. Hummel, ed., *Eminent Chinese of the Ch'ing Period.* 2 vols. Washington, D.C., 1943-44.

Franz Michael, *The Origin of Manchu Rule in China: Frontier and Bureaucracy as Interacting Forces in the Chinese Empire.* Baltimore, 1942; reprinted New York, 1965.

Jonathan D. Spence, *Emperor of China: A Self-Portrait of K'ang-hsi*. New York, 1974.

———, *Ts'ao Yin and the K'ang-hsi Emperor: Bondservant and Master*. New Haven, Conn., 1966.

Harold L. Kahn, *Monarchy in the Emperor's Eyes: Image and Reality in the Ch'ien-lung Reign*. Cambridge, Mass., 1971.

T. T. Ch'ü, *Local Government in China Under the Ch'ing*. Cambridge, Mass., 1962.

K. C. Hsiao, *Rural China: Imperial Control in the Nineteenth Century*. Seattle, 1960.

Arnold H. Rowbotham, *Missionary and Mandarin: The Jesuits at the Court of China*. Berkeley, Calif., 1942; reprinted New York, 1966.

C. L. Chang, *The Chinese Gentry: Studies on Their Role in Nineteenth-Century Chinese Society*. Seattle, 1955.

Sybille van der Sprenkel, *Legal Institutions in Manchu China: A Sociological Analysis*. New York, 1962.

David S. Nivison, *The Life and Thought of Chang Hsüeh-ch'eng (1738-1801)*. Stanford, Calif., 1966.

Arthur Waley, *Yuan Mei: Eighteenth Century Chinese Poet*. New York, 1956; reprinted Stanford, Calif., 1970.

———, *The Opium War Through Chinese Eyes*. London, 1958; reprinted Stanford, Calif., 1968.

SYMPOSIUM VOLUMES OF GENERAL HISTORICAL INTEREST

John Meskill, ed., *The Pattern of Chinese History: Cycles, Development, or Stagnation?* Boston, 1965.

E-tu Zen Sun and John de Francis, eds., *Chinese Social History: Translations of Selected Studies*. Washington, D.C., 1956; reprinted New York, 1966.

Raymond Dawson, ed., *The Legacy of China*. London, 1964.

Arthur F. Wright, ed., *Confucianism and Chinese Civilization*. New York, 1964; reprinted Stanford, Calif., 1975.

Etienne Balazs, *Chinese Civilization and Bureaucracy: Variations on a Theme*. Ed. Arthur F. Wright and trans. from the French by H. M. Wright. New Haven, Conn., 1964.

HISTORICAL STUDIES OF SPECIAL TOPICS
Relations with Neighboring Peoples

Herold J. Wiens, *Han Chinese Expansion in South China*. Hamden, Conn., 1970. (Original 1953 title: *China's March Towards the Tropics*.)

C. P. FitzGerald, *The Southern Expansion of the Chinese People*. New York, 1972.

Owen Lattimore, *Inner Asian Frontiers of China*. 2d ed. New York, 1951.

Réné Grousset, *The Empire of the Steppes: A History of Central Asia*. Trans. from the French by Naomi Walford. New Brunswick, N.J., 1970.

John K. Fairbank, ed., *The Chinese World Order: Traditional China's Foreign Relations*. Cambridge, Mass., 1968.

Society and the Economy

Johanna M. Menzel, ed., *The Chinese Civil Service—Career Open to Talent?* Boston, 1963.

P. T. Ho, *The Ladder of Success in Imperial China: Aspects of Social Mobility, 1368-1911.* New York, 1962.

————, *Studies on the Population of China, 1368-1953.* Cambridge, Mass., 1959.

Dwight H. Perkins, *Agricultural Development in China, 1368-1968.* Chicago, 1969.

L. S. Yang, *Money and Credit in China: A Short History.* Cambridge, Mass., 1952.

T. T. Ch'ü, *Law and Society in Traditional China.* New York, 1961.

Derk Bodde and Clarence Morris, *Law in Imperial China.* Cambridge, Mass., 1967.

Mark Elvin, *The Pattern of the Chinese Past: A Social and Economic Interpretation.* Stanford, Calif., 1973.

Philosophy

Herrlee G. Creel, *Chinese Thought from Confucius to Mao Tse-tung.* Chicago, 1953; reprinted New York, 1960.

Y. L. Fung, *A Short History of Chinese Philosophy.* Ed. Derk Bodde. New York, 1948; reprinted New York, 1960.

Wm. T. de Bary et al., *Sources of Chinese Tradition.* New York, 1960.

W. T. Chan, *A Source Book in Chinese Philosophy.* Princeton, N.J., 1963.

Charles E. Moore, ed., *The Chinese Mind: Essentials of Chinese Philosophy and Culture.* Honolulu, 1967.

Religion

C. K. Yang, *Religion in Chinese Society: A Study of Contemporary Social Functions of Religion and Some of Their Historical Factors.* Berkeley, Calif., 1961.

Laurence G. Thompson, *Chinese Religion: An Introduction.* Belmont, Calif., 1969.

Arthur F. Wright, *Buddhism in Chinese History.* Stanford, Calif., 1959.

Kenneth K. S. Ch'en, *Buddhism in China: A Historical Survey.* Princeton, N.J., 1964.

Literature

W. C. Liu, *An Introduction to Chinese Literature.* Bloomington, Ind., 1966.

Cyril Birch and Donald Keene, eds., *Anthology of Chinese Literature from Early Times to the Fourteenth Century.* New York, 1965.

Cyril Birch, ed., *Anthology of Chinese Literature.* Vol. 2: *From the Fourteenth Century to the Present Day.* New York, 1972.

James J. Y. Liu, *The Art of Chinese Poetry.* Chicago, 1962.

C. T. Hsia, *The Classic Chinese Novel: A Critical Introduction*. New York, 1968.

A. C. Scott, *An Introduction to the Chinese Theatre*. New York, 1959.

Art

Laurence Sickman and Alexander C. Soper, *The Art and Architecture of China*. Baltimore, 1956.

Michael Sullivan, *A Short History of Chinese Art*. Berkeley, Calif., 1967.

William Willetts, *Chinese Art*. 2 vols. Harmondsworth, Eng., 1958.

James F. Cahill, *Chinese Painting*. Cleveland, 1960.

Science and Technology

Joseph Needham et al., *Science and Civilisation in China*. 10 vols. projected. Cambridge, Eng., 1954- .

T. F. Carter, *The Invention of Printing in China and Its Spread Westward*. Rev. ed. New York, 1955.

——

Frank A. Kierman, Jr. and John K. Fairbank, eds., *Chinese Ways in Warfare*. Cambridge, Mass., 1974.

BASIC WORKS ON CHINA SINCE 1850
General

John K. Fairbank, *The United States and China*. 3d ed. Cambridge, Mass., 1971.

Lucian W. Pye, *China: An Introduction*. Boston, 1972.

Immanuel C. Y. Hsü, *The Rise of Modern China*. New York, 1970.

S. Y. Teng and John K. Fairbank, eds., *China's Response to the West: A Documentary Survey, 1839-1923*. Cambridge, Mass., 1954.

Late Ch'ing

John K. Fairbank, *Trade and Diplomacy on the China Coast: The Opening of the Treaty Ports, 1842-1854*. Cambridge, Mass., 1954.

Franz Michael, *The Taiping Rebellion*. Vol. 1: *History*. Seattle, 1972.

Mary C. Wright, *The Last Stand of Chinese Conservatism: The T'ung-chih Restoration, 1862-1874*. Stanford, Calif., 1957.

Nationalist Movement and Era

O. Edmund Clubb, *Twentieth Century China*. New York, 1964.

Mary C. Wright, ed., *China in Revolution: The First Phase, 1900-1913*. New Haven, Conn., 1968.

Howard L. Boorman and Richard C. Howard, eds., *Biographical Dictionary of Republican China*. 4 vols. New York, 1967-71.

James E. Sheridan, *Chinese Warlord: The Career of Feng Yü-hsiang*. Stanford, Calif., 1966.

Donald G. Gillin, *Warlord: Yen Hsi-shan in Shansi Province, 1911-1949.* Princeton, N.J., 1967.

T. T. Chow, *The May Fourth Movement: Intellectual Revolution in Modern China.* Cambridge, Mass., 1960.

James C. Thomson, Jr., *While China Faced West: American Reformers in Nationalist China, 1928-1937.* Cambridge, Mass., 1969.

Communist Movement and Era

Lucien Bianco, *Origins of the Chinese Revolution, 1915-1949.* Trans. from the French by Muriel Bell. Stanford, Calif., 1971.

Benjamin I. Schwartz, *Chinese Communism and the Rise of Mao.* Cambridge, Mass., 1951.

Jerome Ch'en, *Mao and the Chinese Revolution.* London, 1967.

Edgar Snow, *Red Star Over China.* Rev. ed. New York, 1968.

Theodore H. White and Annalee Jacoby, *Thunder Out of China.* New York, 1946.

Chalmers A. Johnson, *Peasant Nationalism and Communist Power: The Emergence of Revolutionary China, 1937-1945.* Stanford, Calif., 1962.

William Hinton, *Fanshen: A Documentary of Revolution in a Chinese Village.* New York, 1968.

Dick Wilson, *Anatomy of China: An Introduction to One-Quarter of Mankind.* New York, 1969.

Franz Schurmann, *Ideology and Organization in Communist China.* 2d enl. ed. Berkeley, Calif., 1968.

Acknowledgments

TRANSLATIONS

Translations from the Chinese that are included in the text are the author's own, with the following exceptions:

Pages 112-13. The *Ch'u-tz'u* selections are from David Hawkes, *Ch'u Tz'u: The Songs of the South* (London: Oxford University Press, 1959), pp. 28, 32, 106-7; by permission of the Clarendon Press, Oxford, and courtesy of Professor Hawkes.

Pages 200, 203. The selections from Ts'ui Shih and Pao Ching-yen, with slight alterations in punctuation, are from Etienne Balazs, *Chinese Civilization and Bureaucracy: Variations on a Theme*, tr. H. M. Wright, ed. Arthur F. Wright (New Haven, Conn.: Yale University Press, 1964), pp. 210-11 and 243; by permission of Yale University Press, and courtesy of Professor Arthur F. Wright.

Page 235. The Hsü Ling selection is from p. 77 of James Robert Hightower, "Some Characteristics of Parallel Prose," *Studia Serica Bernhard Karlgren Dedicata* (Copenhagen, 1959), pp. 60-91; by permission of the proprietors of *Acta Orientalia* (Copenhagen), and courtesy of Professor Hightower.

Page 242. The Ssu-ma Hsiang-ju selection in Burton Watson's translation is from Cyril Birch, ed., *Anthology of Chinese Literature from Early Times to the Fourteenth Century* (New York: Grove Press, 1965), pp. 143-44; by courtesy of Professors Watson and Birch.

Page 244. The T'ao Ch'ien poem "Blaming One's Sons" is from William Acker, *T'ao the Hermit* (London, 1952); reprinted in Cyril Birch, ed., *Anthology of Chinese Literature from Early Times to the Fourteenth Century*, p. 187; by permission of Thames and Hudson, London; and courtesy of Professor Birch and the family of the late William Acker.

Page 246. The Wang Wei poem "To the Assistant Prefect Cheng" in Cyril Birch's translation is from Cyril Birch, ed., *Anthology of Chinese Literature from Early Times to the Fourteenth Century*, p. 224; by courtesy of Professor Birch.

Page 400. The untitled Kao Ch'i poem was translated especially for use in this volume by Professor F. W. Mote of Princeton University.

ILLUSTRATIONS

Many of the illustrations in this volume are from the collections of, and are reproduced with the kind permission of, the National Palace Museum, Taipei, Taiwan,

Republic of China; they are identified with the abbreviation NPM in the full list of credits below.

1. Shang oracle bone. From T. H. Tsien, *Written on Bamboo and Silk* (Chicago, 1962), plate 2; by permission of the University of Chicago, and courtesy of Professor Tsien.

2. Rubbing from a Han tomb relief sculpture. From Edouard Chavannes, *Mission Archéologique dans la Chine Septentrionale: Planches* (Paris, 1909), plate 60; by permission of l'Ecole Francaise d'Extrême-Orient, Paris.

3. Shang tomb under excavation, and skeletons in a Shang tomb. From Academia Sinica Institute of History and Philology, *Hou-chia chuang* (Chinese Archaeological Reports, series 3), vol. 6 (Taipei, 1968), plate 3, and vol. 2, part 2 (Taipei, 1962), plate 28, item 1; by permission of the Academia Sinica Institute of History and Philology, Republic of China, Taipei.

4. Coins of the Warring States period. From T. H. Tsien, *Written on Bamboo and Silk* (Chicago, 1962), plate 7; by permission of the American Numismatic Society, New York, and the University of Chicago; and courtesy of Professor Tsien.

5. Traditional portrait of Confucius. NPM.

6. Woodblock print of Confucius visiting Lao-tzu. From *Sheng-chi t'u* (1874 ed.), p. 76.

7. Han document on wooden slats. From T. H. Tsien, *Written on Bamboo and Silk* (Chicago, 1962), plate 17; by permission of the Academia Sinica Institute of History and Philology, Republic of China, and the University of Chicago; and courtesy of Professor Tsien.

8. Bronze vessels. Shang *kuei* and early Chou *fang-i* by courtesy of the Smithsonian Institution, Freer Gallery of Art, Washington, D.C. Early Chou *li-ting* by courtesy of the Museum of Fine Arts, Boston. Shang *chia* by courtesy of the Nelson Gallery-Atkins Museum, Kansas City, Mo. (Nelson Fund).

9. The *t'ao-t'ieh* design. From William Willetts, *Chinese Art*, vol. 1 (Harmondsworth, Eng., 1958), p. 161; by permission of Penguin Books Ltd., and courtesy of William Willetts.

10. T'ang T'ai-tsung greeting a Tibetan envoy. From *China Reconstructs*, April 1960 supplement "Labour and Struggle," p. 14.

11. T'ang Hsüan-tsung's flight. NPM.

12. Han tomb-tile painting (detail of officials) by courtesy of the Museum of Fine Arts, Boston.

13. "Battle on a Bridge" by courtesy of the Nelson Gallery-Atkins Museum, Kansas City, Mo. (Laurence Sickman collection).

14. Woodblock print of two-man crossbow team. From Mao Yüan-i, *Wu-pei chih* (late Ming ed.), 85.18b.

15. Han tomb figurine of dancing drummer. From *China Reconstructs*, April 1960 supplement "Labour and Struggle," p. 19.

16. T'ang palace concert. NPM.

17. Pottery models of T'ang court ladies playing polo, by courtesy of the Nelson Gallery-Atkins Museum, Kansas City, Mo.

18. Han mortuary models in pottery by courtesy of the Asian Art Museum of San Francisco (Avery Brundage collection).

19. "Scholars Collating the Classics" (detail) by courtesy of the Museum of Fine Arts, Boston.

20. Colossal Buddha statue at Yün-kang. From Seiichi Mizuno, *Unko sekkutsu: Yün-kang—The Buddhist Cave Temples of the Fifth Century A.D. in North China*, vol.

14 (Kyoto, 1954), plate 4; by courtesy of the Kyoto University Research Institute of Humanistic Sciences, Japan.

21. The bodhisattva Kuan-yin by courtesy of the Nelson Gallery-Atkins Museum, Kansas City, Mo. (Nelson Fund).

22. Portrait of Li Po by Liang K'ai, by courtesy of the Tokyo National Museum, Japan.

23. T'ang horse figurine by courtesy of Mr. and Mrs. James W. Alsdorf, Winnetka, Ill.

24. "Two Horses with Groom" by Han Kan. NPM.

25. Sung T'ai-tsu. NPM.

26. Kubilai Khan hunting. NPM.

27. Ming T'ai-tsu in official portrait and caricature. NPM.

28. Portrait of the K'ang-hsi emperor by an unidentified nineteenth-century court painter, by courtesy of the Metropolitan Museum of Art, New York (Rogers Fund, 1942).

29. Ming imperial procession (detail). NPM.

30. The Forbidden City at Peking. From Donald Mennie, *The Pageant of Peking* (Shanghai, 1920), plate 27.

31. Woodblock print of military formation. From Mao Yüan-i, *Wu-pei chih* (late Ming ed.), 83.10b-11a.

32. The Great Wall. From Donald Mennie, *The Pageant of Peking* (Shanghai, 1920), plate 23.

33. "Dragon-boat Regatta at Kaifeng" (detail). NPM.

34. Silk drawloom. From Sung Ying-hsing, *T'ien-kung k'ai-wu* (1637 blockprint ed.; photographically reproduced in *Chung-kuo ku-tai pan-shu ts'ung-k'an*, Peking, 1959), 1.36b.

35. Street scene in Kaifeng. From portfolio *Wen-wu ching-hua* published by the Chung-kuo ku-tian i-shu ch'u-pan she (Peking, 1958).

36. Household tailoring. NPM.

37. "The Sixth Ch'an Patriarch Cutting Bamboo" by Liang K'ai (detail) by courtesy of the Tokyo National Museum, Japan.

38. "P'an-ku Holding the Egg of Chaos" by courtesy of the British Museum, London.

39. Traditional portrait of Chu Hsi. NPM.

40. Eighteenth-century European portrait of Confucius. From Jean B. du Halde, *Description géographique, historique, chronologique, politique, et physique de l'Empire de la Chine et de la Tartarie Chinoise* (The Hague, 1736), vol. 2, facing p. 343; by courtesy of the Rare Books Department, the University of Michigan Library, Ann Arbor, Mich.

41. Porcelains. Southern Sung vase courtesy of the National Palace Museum, Republic of China; Ming jar of the fifteenth century by courtesy of the Metropolitan Museum of Art, New York (gift of Robert E. Tod, 1937); sixteenth-century Ming jar and eighteenth-century Ch'ing bottle vase both by courtesy of the Asian Art Museum of San Francisco (Avery Brundage collection).

42. "Bamboo Branch in the Wind" by Wu Chen, by courtesy of the Smithsonian Institution, Freer Gallery of Art, Washington, D.C.

43. Calligraphy. Mi Fei and Sung Hui-tsung samples both by courtesy of the National Palace Museum, Republic of China; Hsü Wei sample by courtesy of the Smithsonian Institution, Freer Gallery of Art, Washington, D.C.

44. "Landscape in Rain," traditionally attributed to Hsia Kuei; formerly in a private collection in Japan.
45. "Riverside Village on a Late Autumn Day" by Ma Yüan, by courtesy of the Museum of Fine Arts, Boston.
46. "Mountain Scenery with River Lodge" by Ni Tsan. NPM.
47. "In the Shade of Summer Trees" by Tung Ch'i-ch'ang. NPM.

Index

Index

Index